1986

German Literature under National Socialism

J. M. RITCHIE

CROOM HELM
London & Canberra
BARNES & NOBLE BOOKS
Totowa, New Jersey

© 1983 J.M. Ritchie
Croom Helm Ltd, Provident House, Burrell Row,
Beckenham, Kent BR3 1AT

British Library Cataloguing in Publication Data

Ritchie, J M
    German literature under National Socialism
    1. German literature – 20th century – Political
    aspects.
    I. Title
    830.9'00912   PT405

    ISBN 0-7099-2217-5

First published in the USA 1983 by
Barnes and Noble Books
81 Adams Drive
Totowa, New Jersey, 07512

Library of Congress Cataloging in Publication Data

Ritchie, J.M. (James MacPherson), 1927-
    German literature under National Socialism.

    1. German literature – 20th century – History and
criticism. 2. National socialism and literature.
I. Title.
PT403.R54   1983   830'.9'00912   83-10557
ISBN 0-389-20418-8

Printed and bound in Great Britain

CONTENTS

GLOSSARY OF GERMAN TERMS AND ABBREVIATIONS

Anschluss: The Union of Austria with Germany in March 1938

Ausbürgerung: Depriving exiles of citizenship and nationality

Blut und Boden: Blood and Soil, the slogan of Nazi agrarian Romanticism

Bund Proletarisch-Revolutionärer Schriftsteller (BPRS): League of Proletarian-Revolutionary Writers

Bundesrepublik Deutschland (FRG): Federal Republic of Germany

Deutsche Arbeiterpartei (DAP): German Workers' Party founded in 1919 by Anton Drexler. The forerunner of the NSDAP

Deutsche Demokratische Republik (GDR): German Democratic Republic

Endlösung: The Final Solution. After other 'solutions' including exile, this meant the plan to exterminate all the Jews in areas under German control

Entartung: Departure from racial purity, degeneration

Freikorps: Free Corps. Right-wing paramilitary units which came into existence in different parts of Germany after 1918

Führer: The Leader (Adolf Hitler)

Gauleiter: The Gau (an old Germanic word) was a region. The Gauleiter was a District Leader of the Nazi Party

Gestapo (Geheime Staatspolizei): Secret State Police, later incorporated into the main security office of the Reich and headed by Heinrich Müller

Gleichschaltung: Literally switching on to the same current. In effect this meant coordination and subordination of all aspects of life to Nazi Party doctrine

Heimatkunst: Homeland art and literature

Hitlerjugend (HJ): Hitler Youth

Kampfbund für deutsche Kultur: League of Struggle for German Culture founded in 1929 by Alfred Rosenberg

Konzentrationslager (KZ): Concentration camp

KPD (Kommunistische Partei Deutschlands): German Communist Party

Lebensborn: Spring of Life. Part of the programme for breeding pure Aryans in an SS stud farm

Lebensraum: Living Space. Although taken over from Grimm's African novel, this came to be applied to expansion into central and eastern Europe.

Nationalsozialistische Deutsche Arbeiterpartei (NSDAP): Nazi for short. The National Socialist Workers Party developed out of the earlier DAP—see above

Parteiamtliche Prüfungskommission (PPK): The Nazi Party Supervisory Commission to check Nazi party publications

Rassenschande: Defilement of racial purity by marriage or sexual intercourse with a member of an 'inferior' race

Reichskanzler: Reich Chancellor, i.e. Adolf Hitler

Reichskristallnacht: The night of 9 November 1938, the great pogrom against the Jews in Germany. The crystal refers to the smashing of glass

Reichskulturkammer (RKK): Reich Chamber of Culture

Reichsschrifttumskammer (RSK): Reich Chamber of Literature

Reichstag: Parliament. The Reichstag Fire of 27 February 1933, burning down the Parliament buildings, marked the start of the Nazi reign of terror eliminating all opposition

Rotfrontkämpferbund: The Red Front Fighters' Association was the Communist equivalent of similar right-wing bodies

Schutzstaffel (SS): Literally Protection Squads. These black-shirted groups, formed in 1925, were Hitler's personal bodyguard. They grew from this to become the most powerful body in National Socialist Germany under Heinrich Himmler

Schutzverband Deutscher Schriftsteller (SDS): German Writers Defence Association

Schwarze Korps, Das: *The Black Corps*. This was the official weekly paper of the SS

Sicherheitsdienst (SD): The security service of the SS was founded in 1932 and directed by Reinhard Heydrich

Sozialdemokratische Partei Deutschlands (SPD): The Social Democratic Party, outlawed in 1933

Sozialistische Einheitspartei Deutschlands (SED): The Socialist Unity Party of the German Democratic Republic

Stahlhelm: Steel Helmet. National ex-servicemen's organisation founded in 1918 by Franz Seldte

Sturmabteilung (SA): These Storm Troopers or Brownshirts were founded in 1921 and came under the control of Ernst Röhm. He and his followers were eliminated in the infamous massacre of June 1934, the Night of the Long Knives

Völkisch: From *Volk*, hence national, racially pure, ethnic

Völkische Beobachter, Der: *The Racial Observer*. The official newspaper of the Nazi Party

Glossary

Volksgemeinschaft: Community of the People. This indicated the class-less form of national solidarity to which the regime aspired

Volksgenosse: Genosse means 'comrade'. The Nazis moved the concept away from class to race. Hence the term means racial comrade, a member of the German race

Fuller information in Robert S. Wistrich, *Who's Who in Nazi Germany* (London, 1982)

INTRODUCTION

Many commentators claim that there was no Nazi literature; others claim that Nazi literature did exist, but that it was all written *before* 1933 — that is, *before* Hitler came to power and before the restrictive and prescriptive nature of the National Socialist regime made free expression by the creative artist impossible. Of course a great deal was also written inside Germany *after* 1933, but only comparatively few historians have been prepared to take the beliefs of the time seriously, and to start from the assumption that in such literature there was some kind of idealism at work, and that many writers and intellectuals did believe in what they were doing — reacting against the supposed corruption and 'decadence' of the modern age and reasserting traditional values. This is what I have attempted to do here. Instead of dismissing all Nazi literature whether written before 1933 or after as rubbish, I have tried to understand what National Socialists thought they had to offer that was new and valuable. Very often, too, surveys of the period become obsessed either with theories of fascism or with the machinery of power and accordingly spend most time on the ideology or on the Reichsschrifttumskammer. In their fascination with the organs of censorship they ignore what was actually being written by believers inside this system, overlooking the fact that Nazi cultural organisations were also supposed to promote the new literature and art of the Third Reich. So, while not neglecting entirely the significance of the propaganda ministry and the laws and restrictions characteristic of National Socialist Germany, I have also tried to show first of all that there was in the Weimar Republic a powerful tradition on which the National Socialists could build. After this first section I consider those writers, dramatists and poets who firmly believed (at least initially) in the Führer and his mission and the novels, plays and poems they produced in the light of this belief. Despite National Socialist contempt for intellectualism and theory, such writers were by no means fanatics, blindly following national guide-lines developed by Goebbels with his 'steely Romanticism', or by others like him.

While the National Socialists rejected the 'decadence' of the Weimar Republic, republican writers forced into exile for racial as well as political and literary reasons rejected the 'barbarism' of the

National Socialists. From the point of view of literary history the result has been that what was written outside Germany between 1933 and 1945 has tended to be treated separately from National Socialist literature. It cannot be said that this 'exile literature' has benefited from such separate treatment. While Nazi literature has for long been neglected as not worthy of serious examination, exile literature has also been neglected, not because it was thought lacking in quality, but for a variety of other reasons, not the least of which was the fact that it was a painful reminder of a period many preferred to forget. The great names like Thomas Mann and Bert Brecht were taken out and dealt with separately, but the phenomenon of exile in itself and the effects of exile on literary productivity were ignored. Some scholars did start to examine the problem of exile at an early stage, but only in the last two decades has exile literature come to attract more widespread attention. At the same time the realisation has gradually dawned that exile cannot be separated from the movement which brought it about in the first place. Hence the last few years have seen the first attempts to consider cause and effect, National Socialism and exile together. This is what I too have attempted to do in this volume.

Clearly, with so much ground to cover and so many authors and books to analyse, a great deal has had to be excluded. Focusing on books and authors means that less time is spent on organisations and outright politics. It also means there is little consideration of the congresses, public rallies, manifestos, declarations, et cetera which were a feature of the time.

What may also perhaps make this book rather different from any other such survey of the literature of the period is not only a readiness to take what was written at the time seriously, but also the focus on the problem of Germany itself. The National Socialists thought *they* represented the real Germany, while writers in exile felt it was they who had to keep the memory of true German culture alive. Inside Germany those not in favour of the regime could attempt to withdraw into their own 'inner' Germany, or seek for sources of strength in Germany's democratic traditions in order to resist. It is a conviction of this book that there *was* resistance to Hitler's Germany and that this resistance found powerful literary expression not only outside Germany in the exile community, but also inside Germany itself. The most immediate example of such resistance to Hitler's Germany was the Spanish Civil War, in which many German writers fought and died. This was a war which saw Germans fighting against Germans, democrats against Nazis, although the anti-fascist forces were defeated and with

Hitler's and Mussolini's help Franco was victorious. Despite this the message was not lost on the rest of the world. It was possible to resist and there were Germans as well as others prepared to do so. Hitler's victories were staggering and embraced large areas of Europe and Russia, but the defeats when they came were also equally all-embracing and catastrophic. After it was all over Europe was devastated, Germany lay in ruins and millions were dead. When the end came the full evil of the regime began to be revealed, especially what had been done to the Jews. In view of such horrors it is not surprising that there has been a tendency to consider all German literature of the period contaminated — Nazi literature certainly does reek of blood and soil and no claim is made here that there are lost or forgotten masterpieces among its remnants. Yet it cannot be ignored: indeed it must be examined, even if only because not so long ago it constituted the reading matter enthusiastically devoured by millions of people. Exile literature too must become better known, both for its intrinsic quality and for the problems it confronted, for these problems have not gone away.

When I started work on this book I thought I was a pioneer in this country, especially in the sphere of Nazi literature. I quickly discovered that in fact several of my own colleagues had preceded me, with excellent (though regrettably unpublished) dissertations.[1] I have benefited greatly from Hugh Ridley's Cambridge thesis on National Socialism and Literature; from A.D. White on Kolbenheyer; G.P. Hutchinson on Rosenberg; Roger Wood on Jünger; and E.P. Dickins on inner emigration; my grateful thanks go to Angela Rutter, who let me read her University of Sussex project work on Inner Emigration and resistance. They will all recognise traces of their work in this book. I have also drawn on many American dissertations now more readily available as books through the University Microfilm Service and on many specialist studies, especially those by Orlowski, Brekle, Gisela Berglund, Günter Hartung, Ernst Loewy, Wolfgang Emmerich, H.A. Walter and John Spalek. I learned a great deal through personal contacts with Jan Hans and Lutz Winckler, thanks to a semester at the University of Hamburg's Research Centre for Exile Studies. I am also particularly grateful for the Fellowship from the Leverhulme Trust which made this stay in Hamburg possible. My gratitude extends equally to the staff in the Deutsche Bibliothek in Frankfurt and in the Literaturarchiv in Marbach whom I was able to consult at the same time. The longest periods were spent in the university library in Sheffield and I am grateful to Eileen Ryan and others there who found books and references for me that others had failed to find. Students from the Sheffield University School of Librarianship were extremely helpful with assistance in literature searches. Finally, however, my thanks go to my wife Sheena, who has read the manuscript more than once and improved it where necessary (which was often); and to Barbara Zeun who has typed draft after draft and version after version.

PART ONE

1914-1933—GERMANY SLEEPS

1 THE WEIMAR REPUBLIC'S SECRET GERMANY

In discussing the Third Reich it is as well to remember that the Reich was an ancient and hallowed concept which Hitler and the National Socialists appropriated and distorted.[1] It had a long history; three was a magic number combining power, culture and well-being, the people of this Third Reich would be a master race inheriting all the cultural, spiritual and temporal riches of the Reichs which had preceded it; all disharmony would be resolved by the third, permanence would be guaranteed for one thousand years, the millennium would be assured. The medieval German Reich had been a successor to the Roman Empire and like it had covered the greater part of Europe, bringing German rule and German law to a vast area. During the long period of the existence of the First Reich many political weaknesses developed, yet when it finally collapsed these tended to be forgotten and only the memory of German unity and greatness remained. The word Reich had religious as well as political reverberations. Reich was the word used in the Luther Bible in such phrases as 'Dein Reich komme' ('Thy kingdom come'). The First Reich was holy. It had been founded in 962 when Pope John XII crowned and anointed as Roman Emperor Otto I, King of Germany. This First Reich lasted until 1806, by which time, as Voltaire had said, it was neither holy, Roman, nor an Empire. Yet the collapse of the First Reich created a vacuum; there remained only a confusion of conflicting German states of different sizes and political complexion. The heart of the 'German problem' after 1806 was what the future of these states would be geographically, politically and spiritually if a Second Reich were formed. Some of these states came together in the German Confederation of 1815 and the forces for further unification continued through the nineteenth century. Metternich's Austria was far more powerful than Prussia and when the revolutions came in 1848 reaction seemed about to crumble but no democratic, united Germany emerged from the disturbances. The Second German Reich which Bismarck fashioned in 1871 was deliberately a little German solution excluding not only Austria, but many other areas as well. It collapsed in 1918. The Weimar Republic which followed satisfied no one. The official title of the federal Germany proclaimed at Versailles on 18 January 1871 was Deutsches Reich. This title was retained by the Weimar

Republic and by the National Socialist regime. Third Reich was an *unofficial* name which in fact was banned after 1939.

In addition to its political and religious associations the idea of a Third Reich also has a rich literary and philosophical tradition, which Hitler was quick to exploit. Aspirations to a future state of perfection had been fostered as early as the thirteenth century by the preacher Joachim de Floris, who had foretold the coming of a third kingdom. This prophecy lingered on and was put into more poetic form by Jakob Böhme in his allegory of the new dawn, *Aurora.* Herder developed a similar theme in his *Maran Atha or The Lord Cometh* and following the publication of this work, which roused much comment at the time, belief in chiliasm became widespread in Germany. Evidence of Herder's influence and of these chiliastic beliefs is shown by Goethe's *Märchen*, which even Carlyle interpreted as heralding the coming of the New Universal Kingdom. Lessing too developed the idea of the Third Kingdom from Herder and the whole concept was expanded philosophically by Kant, Fichte and Schiller. Following this trend the whole Romantic generation seemed to be filled with a longing for the Golden Age, satisfied in part by reviving the memory of the medieval Reich as the ideal of unity and harmony. This kind of literary regression reached its climax in works like Novalis' mystical-historical romance *Heinrich von Ofterdingen*, but Hölderlin too became a favourite of conservative-nationalist thinkers, not only for his German themes, but also for his stress on the Third Reich, that would combine Christianity and paganism into a new synthesis. Hegel and Schelling developed the same ideas, yet ironically it was the Young Germans (and in particular Heine) who were to become the apostles of the philosophy of the Third Reich. Basically, throughout the nineteenth century, all schools of literary thought, whether conservative, liberal or even Socialist, were fascinated by the concept.

> As the mystics of an earlier age had awaited the kingdom of God on earth, so now the Socialists, heralded by Jean Paul, awaited the coming of a time when a new social order would rule everywhere and all suffering and evil come to an end. Socialism is but a worldy form of Chiliasm.[2]

Hitler promised a Socialism that was also national. Whether all suffering and evil came to an end with the creation of his Third Reich is another matter.

One of the poets the National Socialists liked to look back to as one of their spiritual ancestors was Ernst Moritz Arndt, and he gave a linguistic answer to the question about the extent of the German Reich. To the question 'What is the German's Fatherland?', he replied, 'Germany is wherever the German tongue resounds.' This was extremely tempting as a cultural ideal as long as the Reich existed only in the mind. Hitler made this into a territorial demand. All of the implications of the word Reich discussed so far had been in the air for a long time before Hitler. Richard Samuel sums up all the possibilities as follows:

> The Reich constituted a supra-national idea, it could embrace — in theory — all Germans and at the same time provide historical reasons for including non-German minorities. The linguistic idea never came to grips with the fact that in many border regions of Germany people with German and non-German speech were so intermingled that no disentanglement was possible.[3]

Samuel might have continued that disentanglement was made possible through the wars and genocide which proved to be Hitler's method. The Third Reich which, according to the ancient legend, should have been an age of eternal peace and harmony, was distorted into an age of death and destruction. The notion of the Reich was linked with that of the divine mission of the German people. In the words of the 'herald of the Reich', the poet Emanuel Geibel, in 1861:

Und es mag am deutschen Wesen
Einmal noch die Welt genesen.

(What is German may one day restore the world.)

This German mission too Hitler interpreted rather differently to mean the superiority of the Aryan race, the claim to *Lebensraum*, including the right to deprive inferior races of everything, even of their lives. This was yet another corruption of what had been a high ideal. If the Reich was holy, then the German *Volk* too was holy. In Arndt's words: 'The Volk is as holy as the rabble is unholy.' Certainly there were anti-Semitic elements in German Romanticism, but the word *Volk* did not have any racial connotations, on the contrary Germany was the 'Volk der Mitte', the people which through its central geographical position had a peculiar destiny — 'the destiny to absorb in itself the spirit of West and East and to combine in itself the cultural achievements of Europe'.[4]

This was lost and *Volkstum* and *Deutschtum* came to denote a form of 'Germanhood' never envisaged by Herder and his contemporaries in the Age of Idealism. *Völkisch*, as used by later Nazi pseudo-scientists and cultural historians, came to have a purely racial meaning.

Had German history been different the concept of the Third Reich as a glorious but impossible ideal, a Utopia, a paradise, in which all contradictions would be resolved and all the secret longings of the German people satisfied, would have remained a myth to be studied by medievalists and literary historians. During the chaotic days of the 1918 revolution, when the Second Reich was collapsing and it appeared that a neo-conservative state might take its place, the myth of the Third Reich enjoyed a sudden revival. It came to the surface again, especially in Eugen Diederich's journal *Die Tat*, and was taken up seriously by national political circles. Their revolution would be a conservative one ushering in a new German Utopia. Artur Moeller van den Bruck's *The Third Reich* (1923) became one of the gospels of the new right during the Weimar years.[5] Hitler's *Mein Kampf* began to appear two years after *The Third Reich.* Six years later Hitler came to power and his Thousand Year Third Reich was a political reality.

As has been seen, the concept of the Third Reich had a considerable literary and cultural history. In the same way, before the appearance of a literature which was identified with the NSDAP, there already existed a literature which helped to prepare for it and to establish it once it became a political reality. It is, of course, fairly easy to characterise National Socialist literature simply as racist, aimed primarily at the elimination of all Jewish elements.[6] It is equally easy to divide literature and culture according to a rigid dichotomy of friend and foe, and Nazi commentators, literary historians and censors were wont to do just this. They approved of what was healthy, ethnic, heroic, instinctive and drawn from the organic folk-community and disapproved of the intellectual, sceptical, ironic, divisive culture of the big city with its suggestions of disease and decay. As early as the 1890s, Adolf Bartels divided literature into two ideological camps—a conservative folk camp and a liberal social-democratic camp, applying to the latter the term 'decadent'. This approach was also adopted by Mahrholz in the 1920s when he spoke of a 'Secret Germany' reacting against the Naturalist spirit of enlightenment in the direction of a new mysticism.[7] In his quest for a new Leader who would (like Luther) help build the 'Third Reich', he pointed to writers like Hermann Stehr and Hans Carossa. Mahrholz had absolutely no political aims in mind, but the proposition of the two Germanies looked different, when apropos the Burning of the Books Paul Fechter wrote an essay on 'The Change-over from One Literature to Another' corresponding to the change-over from one Germany to another. His view too was that there had been two literatures in Germany for the previous twenty years. One of them could be called the 'official' literature, the literature of the middle-class left in all its many manifestations from the periphery of social democracy through to Communism. This was a false literature of psychology, 'analysis' and eroticism, a literature concentrating on problems which had no real life outside of magazines with aesthetic pretensions. Alongside this false literature there was a second type, which was the real, truly German one, because it was not merely literature but art in the traditional German sense of the word. When the 'official' representatives claimed that the great German authors were called Remarque, Feuchtwanger, Heinrich Mann and Arnold Zweig, then the other Germans claimed that the people who really counted had quite different names and lived in localities which were completely inaccessible to the representatives of official writing. When pressed they spoke of Paul Ernst and Hans Grimm, Hermann Stehr and Will Vesper, Agnes Miegel and Peter Dörfler, listing writers whose names were rarely heard. This was, as it were, a literature below the surface, an art of depth, which was there but yet not there, because the 'people who mattered' did not know about it. It was known to only a few people, and was far removed from the literary cliques of the big city.

What Fechter claims here was of course not true; his truly *German* Art was not really an underground literature, nor was it widely ignored or passed over in silence; on the contrary publishers' records show that some of it enjoyed massive sales and great popularity. Nevertheless, the resentment and sense of exclusion was real. What Fechter was doing was preparing the way for a take-over bid, which would eliminate all left-wing, Jewish, democratic literature. He wanted to clear the way for a racially and biologically based literature which would serve the NS cause. What was felt to be the most appropriate form of literature for the new Germany was the literature of the peasant. It was to this that the NS histories devoted the greater parts of their surveys. Literature of the city was not only decadent and rootless: it inevitably involved a demonstration of class conflict. Such conflict was to be removed from the literary scene and its place taken by the Germanic ideal of the harmonious society in which there was no longer bourgeois, peasant or worker, only a united folk-community, not brothers or comrades in the Communist sense, but Germans in the harmony of one race. To this end the Third Reich attempted to construct a unified line of descent showing the inevitability of its own creation. Some of its roots it sought in German Romanticism, in Adam Müller, for example, or in Görres, some a little later in the national Wars of Liberation in a spokesman like E.M. Arndt. Hölderlin was admired as the poet of the 'Gesang des Deutschen' ('Hymn of the German') with the much quoted first line: 'Oh sacred heart of nations, Oh Fatherland'. He was quoted too as the poet of the greatest war poem in the German language, 'Death for the Fatherland'.[8] Grabbe was resurrected as the dramatist who saw the problematic relationship between leader and people, while Hebbel was considered Nordic enough because he did make his way towards Germanic themes like the *Nibelungen*. Wagner, of course, was proclaimed not only for his treatment of Germanic mythology, but also for his anti-Semitic essays, while Riehl was rediscovered as the first to make folk-orientated sociological surveys of the German people. There were in addition various anti-liberal philosophers and thinkers who could be harnessed to the nationalist cause, not least Nietzsche, though he could only be selectively exploited as he was a known critic of German culture, an admirer of the French and denouncer of the Blond Beast. Much more influential were lesser lights like Gobineau, Lagarde or Houston Stewart Chamberlain.[9] Moeller van den Bruck churned out his thousands of pages about *The Germans* in which he elaborated his categories of national stereotypes, but much more important was his book with the prophetic title *The Third Reich* (1923). Attempts were made to demonstrate the perfect identity between the 'German Socialism of Adolf Hitler and the Prussianism of Spengler', but despite courting by Goebbels the author of *The Decline of the West* refused to join the party.[10] As far as literature was concerned, NS ideologues also found their way back to the so-called Homeland literature of the turn of the century: the Rembrandt-German Julius Langbehn, Friedrich Lienhard and Adolf Bartels.[11]

Langbehn's *Rembrandt the Educator* (1890) was an enormously successful book which went into many editions and sold thousands of copies. The prime aim of the book was cultural criticism. The Second Reich of Bismarck had demonstrated that economic and political triumphs do not necessarily bring cultural success in their wake. It was necessary to prepare the path for the great German culture to come, one which would be truly representative of the Reich in all spheres. Bismarck and Wilhelm II had created and consolidated the Second Reich, and for that they were to be praised, but a new kind of spiritual renewal was now required, one based on the small businesses of the middle classes, on rootedness in the German region, indeed on all forces directed against the atomistic forces of capitalism and democracy. Rembrandt had been a great artist, but also a great low German, a realist and an idealist. This was the model for the future:

> Artist, peasant, king stand and fall together; they stand and fall with what man calls his homeland; and with what is for him the dearest thing in the world. Sick natures consider it a peculiarity of the ideal that it should be infinitely far away; and yet it is infinitely near: the homeland is the ideal! In this sense the German and (if you prefer) the Low German, is an especially ideal nature.

What *Rembrandt the Educator* strove for was a union of petty bourgeois, peasant and the power centres of the Reich. The Rembrandt-German attacked liberalism as the party of progress and also positivistic science, in both of which could be detected the democratic, destructive spirit of the age which reduced everything and everybody to the same level. Rampant modern capitalism was also a force for change, but attacks upon it were redirected against assimilated Jews and big-city parvenus. The crude cult of money was dismissed as something North American and Jewish, with Berlin falling more and more under its sway. The true German reader was invited to do something to purify the cesspool of the city. All in all the ideal held up was that of the corporative state, one which should be imposed upon the whole of Europe, so that Germany, once it had the power, would become the natural leader in a United States of Europe. (This latter idea was one of those ideals which the National Socialists with their incredible literal-mindedness were to prove only too eager to put into practice.[12]) As far as literature was concerned, *Rembrandt* was on firmer ground when attacking than when making concrete proposals for the future. These were far from clear. What did emerge clearly was aggressiveness against Lessing and the whole of the Enlightenment and the rejection of Zola and Naturalism. This too was to become the official line under National Socialism. As far as Naturalism was concerned, Gerhart Hauptmann, its most celebrated exponent, had been officially honoured by the Weimar Republic, especially on the occasion of his sixtieth birthday in 1922. The celebrations lasted for four months, starting with the Gerhart Hauptmann Festival in Breslau at which the President of the Republic had given the address. In 1933 Hauptmann did not leave Germany, indeed he hastened to ingratiate himself with the new regime, echoed the government's words when Germany left the League of Nations in

November 1933 and was present at the official opening of the Reichs-schrifttumskammer.[13] The *Völkischer Beobachter*, in an article of 16 November 1933, was ironic about Hauptmann's readiness to give the Nazi salute and join in the singing of the Horst Wessel Song at a National Socialist gathering. Despite this readiness he was categorised as 'undesirable' under the Third Reich, while his works were designated 'unsuitable' and frequently attacked. The Nazis knew that his *Gleichschaltung* was merely an external gesture, and they treated him and his works accordingly. Even before 1933, Hauptmann and Naturalism had been attacked. The arguments brought up against him, as against other Naturalists like Sudermann and Holz, were always the same — Naturalists were only good at being negative, or at accusing and criticising, they presented no ideals and in their creative works there were no heroes, they had nothing positive to offer, they gave no hope for the future. Besides, true German art could never be naturalistic, as that had been the 'literary manifestation of the positivistic, rationalistic age and therefore especially susceptible to Jewish intellectualism'. So, grand old men like Hauptmann could be exploited for propaganda purposes, especially towards the outside world, but they should not be allowed to enjoy any real acclaim inside National Socialist Germany.

Langbehn's influence can be observed in Adolf Bartels who carried over the same basic attitudes towards the Enlightenment and Natural-ism. One of the most influential forerunners of National Socialism, his histories of literature provided many of its basic attitudes. Hitler was personally deeply impressed by Bartels and visited him in Weimar in 1926. On the occasion of the author's eightieth birthday in 1942, he made Bartels an honorary member of the NSDAP and awarded him the Golden Badge, given as a rule only to 'old fighters'. Bartels was noted for his anti-Semitism, which he transported into the literary sphere and applied with unheard-of viciousness and unrelenting hatred. There had been anti-Semitic utterances in German literature before in some of the Romantics, while in the latter half of the nineteenth century Freytag, the successful national-liberal novelist, consistently brought comments about Jews into his works, often in a financial context. In the political sphere Ferdinand Lassalle, the organiser of the German working class, was among the first to be subjected to anti-Semitic attacks. Houston Stewart Chamberlain put these two elements of finance and Socialist politics together and associated them with one common enemy — the Jew. This was the combination which Bartels took over and applied to literature, making the Jew a liberal, a Socialist and a capitalistic exploiter at one and the same time. Like Langbehn his point of departure was criticism of the cultural situation in the Second Empire. He denounced the 1870s as a corrupt Age of Journalism, and called for a spiritual renewal against the 'decadence' of liberal corruption and democracy, which he saw all around, and attributed especially to the Jews. Bartels' approach was biological, appealing to national resentment against foreign cultural imports and seeking the seeds of cultural decline far back in the past, for example, in Jews like Heine. Capitalism according to him led to a lust for pleasure, the modern age was characterised by vulgar materialism and brought low by social democracy: hence its main characteristic was unhealthy pessimism and immorality. Wedekind was for Bartels 'the height of late German decadence'. While this was the negative aspect of his cultural survey, he had a positive message to offer, because salvation was possible and could be achieved, if the trend to decadence were halted through a return to home art, which he saw as a source of regional pride, health and optimism. All in all he saw himself as representing a return to 'ideals in a particularly Germanic sense', and put his ideals into practice in creative as well as critical works. His most popular novel, *The Dithmarshers*, sold over 200,000 copies by 1928. Nor was he by any means a lone voice crying in the wilderness. Clubs and literary journals were normally associated with the Bohemian life of the despised cities, nevertheless nationalist circles did have them and Bartels found like-minded spirits in Ferdinand Avenarius, who published the *Kunstwart*, in Heinrich Sohnrey with his journal *Das Land*, in von Grotthuss with his *Türmer* and, most important of all, in Friedrich Lienhard, who became famous not only through his regional novels, but also through his pragmatic work *The Predominance of Berlin*, in which he denounced the decadent capital city and called for a return to the land. For various reasons, but basically because he was sincere and truly idealistic, his 'back-to-the-land' slogans were taken up by the Nazis, while Lienhard himself, who had died in 1929, was left in comparative obscurity.

What all of these forerunners and predecessors of National Socialism had in common was their regressive view of art. Modernism was rejected and instead the perspective was backward-looking: back to certain aspects of German Classicism (without its essential ingredients of humanity and *Bildung*): back to a selective vision of individualism (especially if this involved the great artist or the great leader): back to the post-revolutionary years of the 1850s in which Bartels could find figures like the Poetic Realist Otto Ludwig and the north German Hebbel to admire. The basic elements of this regressive view which

were to become, through Bartels, the characteristic features of the
coming fascist literature, were a pale surface realism and a classicistic
monumentalism. Anything non-German, like anything modern, was
rejected.

In the cultural sphere the National Socialists felt fortunate in
having one giant from the nineteenth century they could claim as their
own. Wagner was Romantic enough and *völkisch* enough to satisfy all
their requirements. Houston Stewart Chamberlain had already shown
the way by marrying into the family in order to get close enough to
the master, and had started the cult of which Hitler himself was to
become a follower. Bayreuth was declared a national shrine and
Wagner exploited to educate Germans to the Nazi version of the
Volksgemeinschaft. He was the ideal combination of artist and
musician, spiritual and political leader, and of course he was an outspoken anti-Semite. Wagner developed the world of Germanic
mythology, he presented Germanic heroes, and according to Rosenberg,
he expressed the Nordic soul, the Nordic ideal of beauty, the power of
the will, the struggle for greatness and honour. Wagner offered not
only heroes but also villains in a manner which was to be followed by
the Friend-or-Foe Nazi manner of thinking.

> The authoritarian pretensions, the romantic allusion to a classless
> people's community and the clear portrayal of a timeless villain
> (made possible only by means of the myth) were combined in the
> music-dramatic offering of serious combat and malicious joy — the
> model for the Unter- and Übermensch relationship.[14]

Here as elsewhere the Nazis were appropriating Germany's cultural
heritage for their own purposes. Wagner in fact was a modernist, he
was decadent, he was certainly more of a pessimist than a happy
optimist and it was crude manipulation to take him over as a pioneer
of National Socialism; nevertheless there was enough there for the
Nazis to work on, even to the forebodings of universal destruction and
suggestions that 'the Third Reich had to be destroyed like the epic
hero Siegfried'.[15]

Yet it must not be thought that there was no support for Bartels'
view or that by eliminating so much he left too little. It is only too
easy in any time in any country to marshal popular support for
denunciations of modern art as difficult and dangerous, shapeless and
decadent, yet this was no mere political ploy for the National
Socialists, it was consistent with their basic beliefs. The National

Socialists made themselves into a mass party by competing with the Socialists, the Communists and the National and Centre parties to gain the support of blue-collar and white-collar workers and country people. To this end they were prepared to engage in tactical manoeuvres. In the same way, in the literary sphere, National Socialists saw themselves as a movement of cultural revolution and some were tempted to align themselves with the radical avant-garde. It was at this point that Expressionism nearly became the style of the party. However, it was only by turning to the traditional literature of the regions that the Nazis could hope for mass support and this is what they did. Besides, literary regression into biological and mythical zones could satisfy all that the NS ideology required of an art form. In the village and in the rural community Socialism had never really put down roots and it was there that feelings ran high about threatened possessions and the defence of what one owned. Not all regional literature of the homeland is fascist and in this genre Germany like other countries had some fine novels, of which Wilhelm von Polenz' *The Büttnerbauer* is a good example. What such works had to offer was rootedness and permanence as against the restlessness of the modern age. Capitalism broke down age-old rules governing man's relationship with his work and his place in society. This was particularly noticeable in the countryside, where certain traditions and ways of life had tended to continue unchanged for centuries. Freedom of movement and the flight from the land to the cities had meant therefore not only the sudden appearance in Germany of massive conurbations, but the dissolution of bonds which had for centuries been thought of as indissoluble. Many people, the rich as well as the poor, the feudal landlord as well as the serf, felt uneasy about such drastic changes and longed for an assurance, even if only in the illusory form of literature, of some permanence amid a world of change. Hence literature of the homeland was welcomed in many quarters for its sense of intimacy with the surroundings in which one had grown up, and for its feeling of security far removed from the social and political conflicts and contradictions of the modern world. At the same time such tales were by no means harmless, for they often included an invitation to be ready to fight for what was one's own. Moving back from the city to the land meant by no means a return to a *completely* idyllic, pastoral, harmonious age, for the peasant like the soldier had to be shown as able to defend himself and his native land—with his blood if necessary. From the start, then, this kind of regressive literature could also be extremely aggressive. Nor was literature of this kind confined to Germany, as names like Giono,

Timmermanns and Maurice Barrès indicate, though it was generally to the Nordic countries that National Socialist Germany was to look for the kind of books it could admire.[16] Trygve Gulbranssen was among the most widely read authors in the Third Reich, though he never declared his allegiance to it. The Icelandic writer Gunnar Gunnarson received rave notices in Germany, especially after 1934 when he came out publicly in favour of the new regime. In 1937 he received the Henrik Steffens Prize from the city of Hamburg and in 1940 after a tour through Germany with the Swedish authoress Clara Nordstrom and the Dutch authoress Jo van Ammers-Küller, he was received in Berlin by the Führer. Knut Hamsun was equally active in his support of the Third Reich. After 1933 his works were given an enthusiastic reception in Germany and he was always lavishly praised as the true friend of Germany. He made many public statements in favour of the Third Reich, even defended the German invasion of Norway, declared Norwegian resistance to be senseless, came out in favour of Quisling and advocated a Europe under German leadership, fighting against England. For Vesper he was 'the greatest epic writer of our time'.

The novel was not the only traditional genre honoured and revered by the National Socialists. The ballad in Germany had long clung to its mythical origins and so it too, with its laconic language, its sense of fateful inevitability and its love of death, was bound to appeal to the new nationalistic wave. Wedekind and Brecht attempted to demonstrate that the ballad form could develop in different directions, by exploiting the demotic language of the cities, but this was totally rejected as un-German in nationalistic circles and the trend backwards through the nineteenth century and beyond was preferred. The traditional ballad enjoyed a striking revival with Börries von Münchhausen, Agnes Miegel and Lulu von Strauss und Torney as its leading exponents. All figured prominently on the literary scene in the Third Reich.

But by far the greatest popularity was achieved by the work of another author from this sphere of traditional literature of the German region, namely Hermann Löns. Today he is remembered for his simple, folksy poetry, far removed from any sphere of ideological conflict, though he was also the author of the anti-British song, 'Denn wir fahren gegen Engelland', sung in both world wars. Apart from this he survives in the song-books with verses about the German countryside, hunting and the simple life of the soldier. When he moved on from poetry and song to the more extended narrative, a further ideological element was added: the marriage between ancient nobility and ancient peasantry. *The Wehrwolf* (1910) shows this most clearly. This novel, which Walter Linden rightly described as the basic book of the *Volk* movement, provided the model and the behavioural patterns for the nationalistic Freikorps groups and Feme murderers of the post-World War One period. It gave the *völkisch* youth groups their symbol and furnished Hitler Youth fighters in the final stages of the Second World War with their name. This was a novel which exercised a far-reaching impact of a kind which it would be hard to overestimate. It had sold some 565,000 copies by 1939, (375,000 of these by 1933). The theme of the novel is the action taken by peasants against marauding soldiers and looters in the Thirty Years War. Lest there be any possible mis-understandings the peasants are shown as in no way comparable with revolutionaries. This is done by portraying them as far removed from the ranks of the propertyless proletariat. Only those who own land and their followers are allowed to join the exclusive ranks of the Wehrwolves. In addition the Wehrwolves are careful to ensure the approval of both their prince and their church for their actions, thereby marking what they do as entirely legitimate and praiseworthy. The peasant (the novel demonstrates) is more than a man whose life is devoted to making the soil fruitful for his kith and kin: he must also be capable of defending his land against attack. In the same way the priest, whom the Wehrwolves acquire in the course of time, is more than a mere preacher of the gospel of peace; he too must be shown to be capable of fighting and indeed killing if necessary.

The essential elements in Blood and Soil literature have been described as, firstly, settlement, and, secondly, aggression in defence of the settlement. This is the basic pattern to this novel. The first chapter is devoted to the peasants of the heath, who in far distant times came down from the north with their pale faces and blond hair, found a place and built a house, before clearing the land and fighting with the bears and the dark brown people who lived in the swamp. Time passes until the year 1623 is reached and there is talk of war. War, hunger, fire and pestilence come upon the land, and the point is reached when the peasants have to take a decision on their own behalf. One of them puts the question of defending the homeland this way:

Any gypsies or other foreign folk that put in an appearance here will immediately be greeted with the whip, for that rabble shows the robbers (for that's all the soldiers are) where there's something to steal. In Ehlershausen last week two of these fellows who stole a horse from the field were quietly strung up. And that is absolutely right: because first of all they are not real people and besides why don't they stay where they belong?

The language is that of the vigilante who takes the law into his own hands. This in any event is the policy which is adopted, the ideology of encirclement, the policy of the white man's laager defending the kraal against all comers. All agree to stick together and Wulf uses, for the first time, the phrase, which he will repeat many times thereafter: 'before I let anybody touch a hair of my head, or that of any of my people, I'd rather wade up to my ankles in blood'. Before the end of the book he will be wading that deep in blood. Killing is continuous, and the score is kept by cutting notches on the handle of one's weapon. By now the peasants have had to withdraw into the rough country to build a defensive position, an oath is sworn and the magic number of initiates elected.

It must not be thought that such a novel is completely devoid of love interest. It soon becomes clear that the role in life of the Germanic lady is to be faithful and true to her warrior-peasant husband, to be a good housewife and good mother. A great deal of breeding goes on, though the love scenes tend to be pure and sentimental rather than erotic or stimulating. The close-knit community continues to thrive, because there are no divisions among them, they are a community of industrious people, all working for themselves and at the same time working for the whole. Only the external world is against them, but though they kill constantly, no blame attaches to them. This is confirmed by their padre, who tells them their consciences are clear, and by the Duke, who also recognises that what the peasants are doing is right and proper; indeed he even rewards them for their bravery and commends them as a model to be followed by everybody. The basic appeal of the novel is its combination of killers' lust and legitimacy. And clearly, from the way the novel is told, its message is not meant to be limited to the seventeenth century, but rather is clearly intended as a model for the problems of the modern world. The last words of the novel express pleasure at the election of a peasant to the Reichstag, but the whole thrust of the novel is not directed towards the solution of social and political problems by means of parliamentary processes: the examples given on page after page are examples of collective aggression. The effect of such a novel was considerable — through the agency of the right-wing publishers Eugen Diederichs this Peasants' Chronicle sold in hundreds of thousands. Its simple message expressed in simple language, its sentimentality and its crude frontier humour made it irresistible fare for many. Löns himself followed his own doctrine, joined up as soon as the war broke out and was killed in September 1914, but not before he had launched an appeal for a hero who would emerge from the masses to save the German nation and lead it to triumph.[17]

Paul Ernst did not have the same mass effect, yet he too was recognised by the National Socialists as one of their forerunners and admired and propagandised accordingly. He attempted the regional novel without great success and passed through a period of social concern and naturalistic endeavour before finding his true home finally in historical epics and dramas of the most formal and traditional kind, offering nobility, leadership and a tragic awareness of fate. Ernst's classicism was of the monumental kind that the National Socialists could admire. In the long article in the *Völkischer Beobachter* in which Dr Rainer Schlösser attempted to sketch the duties of a National Socialist theatre, he called for both heroic and folksy plays and he named Johst's *Schlageter* and Paul Ernst's comedy *Pantalon and his Sons* the cornerstones of an ideal NS repertoire. Paul Ernst declared himself a National Socialist just after the seizure of power and shortly before he died.[18]

The difference between Löns and Paul Ernst and the literature which followed the First World War was that now radical nationalism existed in real political terms and that literature as a whole tended to be politicised. What had emerged from the war was a republic, which could never be accepted in nationalist quarters, hence traditional anti-democratic sentiments were now aggravated by the military defeat, by the revolution, and by the upsurge of Socialist forces which apparently divided it. The front-line fighters saw themselves deprived of the fruits of victory, deprived of the honour and glory they felt was rightly theirs and confronted by an entirely different social and political situation from the one they had left behind when they set off for the trenches. It is true there was still military work for them to do in the Freikorps and home guard groups, and to some extent the Weimar government itself directed such forces against the revolutionaries, but this was still not what they had hoped for and clearly it could not last. War had been their life and it is not surprising that the 1920s saw a spate of war books glorifying the new German who (it was claimed) had emerged from the cauldron of war. On the surface many such war books by front-line soldiers seem mere documentary accounts, but it quickly becomes clear that they were more than that, for they were filled with hatred for the post-war Germany with whose complications their authors found themselves incapable of coping. The general tendency of such books was to concentrate exclusively on the war itself, reducing the world to the front line as the only place where a man could show his worth. There in the midst of death, life had been lived to the full, boredom was unknown. In these works the Germany of before the war simply did not exist or was shown as something dead and mechanical, behind the front the homeland was exploited by crooks and profiteers, politics was a dirty, corrupt game, the country was divided by competition and class warfare. How much better everything could be made to appear at the front, where, as in the brotherhood of the Wehrwolves, it was all for one and one for all. At the front there was a real basis for collective action, there it was possible to find a model of true popular spirit and comradeship. In this kind of front-line community relationships were clearly fixed by the authority of the leader over his men. All became part of a greater whole, a team which alone was capable of ensuring the survival and ultimate victory of each of its members. This kind of appeal was clearly directed at the masses who were to be won over from the counter-attractions of the Marxist models of collective action and it must be said that such works were not without their successes. National Socialism set out to be a mass movement and this was one of the methods it used to attract the masses. The war had demonstrated its own kind of Socialism, a Socialism of a national, not a political or proletarian kind, a Socialism which set out to mobilise the nation totally for the war effort. Making the worker into a soldier was the equivalent of making the peasant into a soldier — as in the *Wehrwolf.*

If, despite the later translation of the ethos and symbols of the *Wehrwolf* into the reality of National Socialist Germany, it is thought that there is too great a gap between the novel and the party, an even better example is provided by another novel, namely Hermann Burte's *Wiltfeber, the Eternal German. The Story of a Man Seeking his Home-land* (1912), which not only combined Nietzschean ideas with *völkisch* ideology and the message of the pure *Krist* (a Germanic version of Christianity of an anti-Semitic kind), but also provided the regime with one of its most important symbols. After a scene in this historical novel in which the decline of true Germanic blood is sketched in ('there are more genuine Jews around than there are genuine blond people'), in an age in which the blood-leader is replaced by an elected bureaucrat, the Germanic hero Wiltfeber makes his stand:

And Wiltfeber stood in the dusty street and with his stick he drew a cross of St John in the dust, lightly and loosely. And then he drew in the half cross more strongly and lo, there in the sand with highlights and shadows was the ancient *Hakenkreuz*. The Knight spat blood from his lips and said: 'Do you believe in it? What if it were to come to life again?'[19]

In fact it was to come to life quite soon, for in the course of the abortive Kapp Putsch in March 1920 Captain Erhard's naval Freikorps hoisted the swastika over Berlin. The hooked cross had a vast history which had been described by Guido List in 1910 in a book called *The Hieroglyphs of the Ario-Teutons*. After that this symbol of fire and sun and salvation came to be used increasingly by pan-German pagan societies and anti-Semitic groups. Three months after the abortive Putsch Hitler appropriated the swastika as the flag of his party, just as he appropriated the concept of the Third Reich. In *Mein Kampf* the three Imperial colours were reinterpreted as follows:

The red reflects the socialist, the white the nationalist ideas of the movement, the (black) Swastika symbolises the mission of the struggle for the victory of Aryan man and simultaneously the victory of the idea of creative work which itself has always been anti-semitic and will remain anti-semitic for ever more.[20]

Burte was to become one of the leading literary figures during the NS regime. His career was assured. In one of his poems on the role of the poet, he wrote the lines:

Help native blood
Home to its own soul!
Impart courage to the downhearted, courage,
What they need are words of command!

In a slightly later historical novel Artur Dinter attempted to help native blood find the way back to its own soul. His novel *The Sin against the Blood* (1922) recounts the story of Hermann, who falls passionately in love with Johanna and persuades her to marry him.[21] The resultant marriage is not a happy one, although she does everything that could be expected of the perfect wife. Johanna has a past which comes to light when she gives birth to her husband's child. To his horror it turns out to be a Jewish child with black curly hair and a

swarthy skin. She then confesses that ten years before she had been
seduced by a Jewish officer and subsequently deserted. The child she
bore then died at birth, nevertheless Hermann's child looks like her
first child. This puzzle is resolved when Hermann discovers the
breeding law that any thoroughbred mare is ruined if it has once been
mated with an inferior partner. The whole organism of the thoroughbred is poisoned. The consequences of this insight form the moral of
the book:

> Now consider the damage which year in, year out, is inflicted upon
> the German race by Jewish youths who every year seduce thousands
> upon thousands of German maidens!

Hermann immediately demands the name and regiment of the Jewish
officer from his wife, goes straight to him to demand satisfaction in a
duel and when this is refused, shoots him on the spot. No one attempts
to stop him as he leaves and when he gets home he finds his wife and
child both dead, the morphia needle still sticking in the region of her
heart. This novel was to become one of the most praised works during
the NS period, although Dinter did not enjoy the glorious literary
career he might have expected.[22]

2   THE MAKING OF A PEOPLE

Anti-Semitism was not an ever present element in the works of the forerunners of National Socialism, for there were also other 'inferior' races, as was often demonstrated by authors from the periphery of the German-speaking world. One such was more concerned about the Slavs than the Jews: Erwin Guido Kolbenheyer survived the collapse of the Nationalist Socialist regime.[1] To the end he never saw any necessity to revise his opinions or to doubt in any way the intellectual path which had led him to accept Adolf Hitler and 'the movement' as the solution to Germany's problems. Clearly he was a writer rather than a politician and he can perhaps be excused for failing to see the implications of the nationalist line he personally followed and also advocated in his novels, dramas, poetry and pamphlets. Born in Bohemia, he saw at an early age the disintegration of the Austro-Hungarian Empire and the rise of the militant Slav. The German language, the one single factor which seemed to hold the whole rambling Empire together, was forced to give way to Czech as the language of administration. For him this seemed to mark the beginning of the end of the Sudeten Germans. In fact the dissolution of the Austro-Hungarian Empire was to take another fifty years, but nevertheless his basic attitudes were formed at an early age — the desire to preserve the German language and resentment against the Slavs, combined with longing for a greater German fatherland. Little wonder that the *Anschluss* with Austria, which Hitler brought about, was welcomed by such people. When Kolbenheyer started his career as an author he was the typical apolitical German intellectual; however, he was born into an age in which the world of aesthetics was being radically politicised and he gradually moved further and further to the right, in what was to become a characteristic manner for the time. The frontiersman became more German than the Germans. Living in Germany after the war he found the republic less than satisfying and was soon denouncing the shortcomings of the parliamentary system. His position has been described as close to that of Thomas Mann's *Reflections of an Unpolitical Man.* They shared the same rejection of democracy, ostentatious conservatism, belief in a German mission for Europe, dependence on Nietzsche as a model of the precarious and paradoxical radical conservative, approval of the war mania of July

1914 in Germany, insistence on a powerful Germany as a pre-condition
for European peace, a metaphysical conception of the *Volk*, a tendency
to equate Goethe with Bismarck, a view of the leader as exponent of
the people, and an admiration of the German performance in war. Yet
although Kolbenheyer and Mann both started off expressing beliefs
of this kind, Thomas Mann was to develop into a strong defender of
the republic and an enemy of National Socialism, while Kolbenheyer
was to come more and more to denounce the one and acclaim the
other. Probably the difference between them lay in the very fact that
Kolbenheyer was a border German. As Kolbenheyer the Sudeten
German saw the Slavs as the enemy, this made him only too ready to
accept nationalistic concepts. But Kolbenheyer was a true intellectual
who had studied philosophy, psychology and natural sciences. He was
no crude racist: instead he attempted to apply *biological* concepts to
problems of social and cultural history and as a result developed a vast
historical panorama, in the manner of the time, which he called the
Bauhütte — Elements of a Metaphysic of the Present (1925). At the
core of this philosophy Kolbenheyer sees something he calls Plasma,
the fundamental stuff of life; from this, through the plant, animal
and human world, he builds up a universal picture embracing races
and people, but also families and individuals. The heart of the matter,
however, is the 'white race' and the need for the young and healthy
(Germanic) race to take over the leadership from the old and
exhausted (Romance-Mediterranean) race: what he demonstrates in
mystical pseudo-scientific terms is *Volkwerdung*, the ineluctable
progress of a race like the Aryans to leadership and maturity.
Mysticism, soul, heart, life he conceives of as characteristic elements
of the German race; civilisation, the profit-motive, quantification and
logic he rejects as un-German, and his projection of such qualities on
to an external enemy (be it Jewish, Mediterranean or Slav) was to
prove only too 'convergent' with the NS ideology. Indeed it has been
pointed out that what Kolbenheyer claimed as the first true and
correct view of history was an almost direct forerunner of
Rosenberg's *Myth of the Twentieth Century*.[2] Kolbenheyer's
political activity was mainly in the twenties and thirties when in
many essays and pamphlets he propagated the national revolution, but
his major essays, *The Biological Foundations of the Liberation Movement in the People* (1933) and *The National Revolution and the
Revival of the German Spirit* (1933) give some indication by their
titles alone of the thrust of his biological view.[3] By 1932 he had
joined the NSDAP, because it meant for him liberation from the

claims of Versailles and also the possibility of a greater Germany. Germans inside Germany itself were in his view much less aware of the biological imbalance than were the Germans outside. Hitler's political actions did justice to what for Kolbenheyer were the natural facts. Hitler came from the Austrian border, and so he could see things from the outside. His whole life was devoted to Germany as a whole. It has been argued that the difference between Hitler and all other nationalist extremists lies in the importance he placed on the German/Austrian Slav frontier and the conclusions he drew from his awareness of it. This was certainly what appealed to Kolbenheyer. It did not make him an out-and-out supporter of the party or the regime—he was too much of an individualist for that, yet he was prepared to go a long way in his polemics against the opposition, attacking Romain Rolland, defending the burning of books, and repeating his conviction that German nationalism was only the preliminary stage on the way towards the ideal of a Europe united under German leadership. In time Kolbenheyer became 'the figurehead of Nazi cultural support for the Sudeten Germans' by accepting the presidency of the Sudeten German Cultural Society. This meant that to some extent he was in a position to help some literary colleagues who fell foul of the regime. So, for example, in 1933 he was able to effect the release from Dachau of Karl Bröger, the worker-poet whose poems about the cameraderie of the First World War the Nazis exploited. But there can be no suggestion that he in any way acted against the regime or engaged in any kind of resistance. In effect he supported the Hitler regime right up to 1945, though he claimed afterwards to have been totally unaware of the horrendous crimes committed in the name of National Socialism. He himself was never anti-Semitic and said he knew nothing of the policy directed at the extermination of the Jews. Without doubt it was Kolbenheyer's Sudetenland background combined with his 'biologically' based ultra-nationalist beliefs which led him into the National Socialist camp. At the same time he was sensitive, as were so many of the nationalist writers, about what he felt was the lack of recognition afforded his works (despite all the prizes) and was prepared to engage in practically any ideological contortion in order to prove that the National Socialist ideology accorded with his own, if this meant he could gain the recognition he felt he rightly deserved. His Bauhütte philosophy had not brought enough recognition, nor had his novels and plays, though much admired, brought him the wider recognition he sought. So perhaps, when he felt his creative powers decline, he moved more into the directly political sphere. It cannot be

said to have been to his ultimate advantage. Certainly his reputation
as a writer now remains severely tarnished and few will be prepared
today to give serious consideration to the once much-acclaimed
Paracelsus trilogy which projected its hero as a genius and artist, whose
life and work, culminating in the 'Third Reich of Paracelsus', sums up
the 'German' values of depth of feeling, religiosity and strength.

Another writer equally rooted in the cultural traditions of the
Austro-Hungarian Empire, and one destined to become just as much of
a pan-German nationalist as Kolbenheyer, was Josef Weinheber. At first
sight this prophet of pure form and poetry seems the last person one
would expect to find among the uniformed ranks of the brown-shirted
barbarians; yet he claimed to have been converted to National Socialism
at an early stage and he certainly remained one of its most prominent
figureheads on the cultural stage right to the very end. Like many of
his generation he went through a Nietzschean phase with 'pride in
loneliness, delight in perverse evil and affirmation of life', yet the
working-class young man trying to make his way in the world of letters
never really had the strength, confidence or social poise to put these
ideals into practice. What he clearly wanted more than anything else
was acceptance, recognition and fame. As an Austrian he shared some
of Hitler's cultural background and certainly developed one feature
associated with Hitler's Austria, namely anti-Semitism. Like many he
also felt excluded by the 'other' literature: indeed it was only with the
national revival in 1933 that his eventual breakthrough came. By that
time Weinheber had connections with the Austrian NSDAP, though as
a party it was still illegal, because it threatened the stability of the
Austrian republic.[4] His collection of poems *Nobility and Decline*
betrays no direct references to events of the time, and yet the divisions
of the collection were remarkably consonant with Nazi tastes, especially
the grandiose classicism of his verses on classical models, his variations
on the Nazi favourite Hölderlin, his attempts at the 'pure poem', and
his 'Hymn to the German Language'.[5] Weinheber specialised in
denunciations of the decadence of the age, from which the poet
withdraws into isolation or against which he reacts with existential
heroism. In effect Weinheber shared the reactionary distaste for
democracy, disliked the republic, developed an extremely
nationalistic view of German culture, and was anti-Socialist and
ambitious. Will Vesper took up his work, and by March 1935
Weinheber was being invited to give broadcasts on the German
radio. His longing for recognition in Germany and not merely in
Austria was about to be more than satisfied. He received an

honorary doctorate, he was awarded the title of professor by the
Austrian government, he was awarded the Mozart Prize and he visited
Germany where he met Kolbenheyer, with whom he had much in
common. Not surprisingly the butcher's son from the city bought a
house in the country and attempted to show by his poetry that he too
was rooted in the soil. Yet it was not for this kind of poetry that he
became widely known or famous, but rather for *Wien wörtlich*, a
cycle of poems about the ancient city of Vienna. Weinheber set his
sights very high. Repudiating competitors like Rilke, George, Hofmannsthal and Werfel, he strove to raise himself to the level of the great
masters of the past by taking as literary models the Greek, Latin and
Italian verses of Sappho, Alcaeus, Homer, Horace, Dante and
Michelangelo, and the works of German authors who had preceded
him—Hölderlin, Mörike, Droste-Hülshoff and Goethe. Weinheber had
in other words a fixed idea of what constituted *real* poetry, and
aspired to reach it by imitation. In such an age, however, it was
impossible to withdraw into the timeless sphere of pure poetry, and
so he also wrote a hymn in praise of the *Anschluss*, various poems to
the Führer, and a 'Hymn to the Munitions Worker'.[6] His Nietzschean
love of what was great and his amoral love of grandeur for its own sake
led the 'pure' poet to commit himself totally to National Socialism,
despite or perhaps even because of the ruthlessness and brutality of it.
Here at last was the oneness of the *Volk* he looked for, uniting German
and Austrian. History was being made and he was part of it. Politics
meant something other than party political manoeuvring. The *Volk*
had spoken as one. His 'Hymn to the Home-coming' was written for
the celebrations for Hitler's birthday, held in the Burgtheater in
Vienna on 20 April 1938; it consists largely of a comparison between
Hitler's return to Austria and Odysseus' return to his beloved Ithaca
after long years of wandering. It concludes:

This in the name of the people!
This in the name of the blood!
This in the name of suffering:
Germany, eternal and great,
Germany, we greet you!
Führer, sacred and strong,
Führer, we greet you!
Homeland, happy and free.
Homeland, we greet you!

The *Volk*, the blood, the Führer, Germany, the homeland – this is Nazi language unadorned. With poems like this and his 'Austria 1934' he 'prostituted his honour in the cause of political murderers and black-mailers'.[7] He was not an unworldly idealist who could be exploited by the Nazis for propaganda purposes: he was a realist determined to demonstrate his political reliability to the new masters. Needless to say he was not completely blind, yet such criticism of the movement as he expressed from time to time tended to be after the manner of the believer rather than the doubter, admitting that foreigners were perhaps right to describe the National Socialists as barbarians, but claiming that this was because they could be aware only of the external trappings of the national upsurge, not of its essence and true nature. Similarly, the Austrian in him felt some resentment from time to time at German interference in Austrian matters, but this did not stop him from penning a panegyric when the insignia of the Empire, the supreme symbols of Austria's cultural heritage, were removed from Vienna by the new German masters and taken to Nuremberg. The declaration of war indissolubly linked Austria's fate with that of Germany, and Weinheber's literary destiny even more with victory for the regime. The war for him was not about mere conquest, but about the survival of the white race, the triumph of the German cultural mission. Throughout the course of the war, nevertheless, Weinheber avoided all jingoistic poetry and instead devoted himself to what seemed on the surface much loftier ideals. In the same way as he had previously appeared as the poet of pure form, so now he strove to cultivate the word in its purest form. The lofty, almost biblical ring of the title, *Here is the Word*, gives some idea of his intentions. In this he is in line with a powerful German tradition from the turn of the century on, marking a reaction against the abuse of language in the age of mass communications (not least in the journalistic language of newspapers) and the distortion of language by mass political parties. But Weinheber, who felt he had a special relationship with Goebbels, was clearly not one to see direct applications of his critique of language to an expose of the propagandistic distortions of National Socialism: his linguistic theories are more in line with those of a Jünger. In the volume *Leaves and Stones* (1934) Jünger's essay 'In Praise of Vowels' appeared. This was an exercise which had been attempted elsewhere (notably by Rimbaud), but in this case the outcome was rather different. Rainer Stollmann uses this example as the climax and culmination to his book on 'the aestheticisation of politics'.[8] Weinheber's exercises in the inner form of the word, or the symbolic significance of particular letters of the alphabet, are somewhat similar, and by no means stop him from finding reasons for extreme nationalism. As Ridley points out, in an earlier collection like *Nobility and Decline* it was but a small step from the 'Ode to the Letter of the Alphabet' to the 'Hymn to the German Language' and later, in the lectures on language which he gave to students at the University of Vienna, he still found reasons for the defence of Blood and Soil writing. Significantly, language was for Weinheber not a means of communication, but a mystical entity expressive of an immutable racial essence: and this mystical essence was essential for the war effort, for ultimately in 'loyalty to the German language lay the only true hope of victory'.[9] By the end Weinheber found himself more directly involved with the struggle for German victory than he had expected would be necessary for a German poet. By 1944 the war was going so badly that all belletristic publications were banned and his *Here is the Word* could not be printed. Air raids destroyed the stocks of his other works, while he himself daily expected to be called to military or munitions service. By the end of 1944 the man who in the First World War had somehow escaped military training or service at the front was in the *Volkssturm*, and when the Russian tanks reached his village the following year he took an overdose of morphia and died: it is not clear whether this was by mistake because he was an addict, whether in terror at the thought of falling into Russian hands, or in despair at the collapse of the regime, to which he had become too closely attached. A remarkable number of people are still sufficiently impressed by Weinheber's formal talents to think of him as a real poet.

A writer from an entirely different part of the German-speaking world, but one nevertheless whose extreme patriotism and love of the German soil led him into close contact with National Socialism, was Hans Grimm.[10] This author's real life took him outside Germany to the colonies and yet his literary life was to become intimately bound up with Germany itself, with the nationalist movement, with Blood and Soil and with National Socialism. After leaving Germany Hans Grimm lived for years in South Africa as trader, farmer, reporter and writer. He also lived later in German South West Africa. On his return to Germany he bought the Lippoldsberg Cloister House and made it into a national literary and cultural centre. Grimm was a prolific writer and the complete edition of his works contains dramas, stories and novels as well as collections of essays. Of particular interest is his African narrative *The Judge in the Karu* (1926), not only for its style and African background, but also for the author's fairly explicit statement of his belief in the superiority of the white race over the black. However, his most successful book was his massive novel of 1,300 pages called *People without Living Space* (1926). The title was immediately taken up and exploited as a political slogan by the National Socialists, although Adolf Hitler was more interested in *Lebensraum* in the East and had no desire at that time to become involved with England, the world power, over colonial demands. Nevertheless the whole concept appealed to the ultra-nationalist factions in Germany. As F.L. Carsten has put it:

> Of all the political slogans current in Germany in the 1920s and 1930s, none exercised a stronger influence on the youth of the country in school and university than that which proclaimed that Germany needed more space, that the nation—to be able to live—required more *Raum*. Deprived of its colonial empire by the Treaty of Versailles without any justification—thus the young were taught in the German schools—the Germans had become a *Volk ohne Raum*, a nation without living space.[11]

This message is explicitly proclaimed by the author in the very first chapter of the book, entitled 'Homeland and Constriction'. In his own rather pretentious and inflated style the author appeals to all German men and women, boys and girls of all classes and walks of life to raise their arms to God, so that together in their millions He may be made aware of the horrific nature of the German fate. This will be revealed through the story of one simple German whose fate will be representative for that of His people. To answer any superior doubter who might claim that the German people will always live, he then examines more closely what is meant by living. The sick man lives, the thief lives, the whore lives and worm eats worm—'but the German needs living space around him and sun above him and freedom inside him, in order to become good and fine. Is he to have waited centuries in vain for it?'

The hero of *Volk ohne Raum*, Cornelius Friebott, is a Low German, born (as Lulu von Strauss und Torney was to put it) in the most German part of the country and by the most German river, the Upper Weser. He shares the typical fate of the landworker of the end of the nineteenth century through being forced to tear up his roots in the soil and move into the big city. Where this leads is shown by the fact that he is no longer involved in healthy work, but instead is subject to the machine. He declines into a worker, a member of the proletariat, and even goes so far as to desert his peasant background

completely and become involved with the Socialists! As a result of
activities on behalf of the Social Democrats he is dismissed and is
sentenced to imprisonment. At this point he leaves this Germany of
class warfare and emigrates to South Africa, which proves to be a land
of opportunity for a German like himself who is prepared to work
hard. He joins the Boer Army to fight against the British, is wounded,
captured and imprisoned. This whole section of the book, needless to
say, not only provides plenty of adventure and excitement, but also
permits the author to express his resentment against the colonial,
imperialist British, who treat Germans as second-class citizens. Further
excitement comes when the hero moves to the new German colony,
fights the Hottentots, prospers on a farm and makes money in the
diamond rush. This whole wonderful world collapses on the outbreak
of the World War, when he is again exposed to rough treatment at the
hands of the British authorities. Indeed he is even sentenced to death
merely for killing an African in self-defence; but he escapes from
British territory to Portuguese Angola, is re-arrested and finally shipped
back to Germany. By this time the war is over and he finds his homeland in a depressed, defeated state and makes it his duty to tour
Germany, conveying to his countrymen the message of *Lebensraum*.
During one of his speeches calling upon Germany to awaken he is
killed by a stone thrown by a worker in the crowd. His message is
taken up, however, by the author Hans Grimm, who from the very
first page figures prominently in the novel; the book is written to
carry on the torch from the point where Cornelius Friebott was
violently forced to put it down.

There is no doubt whatsoever that this blockbuster of a book is a
'good read'. For one thing it is almost deliberately not modern or
difficult in its style, for another Grimm has a great deal of natural,
narrative drive, and he tells a good, adventurous yarn, setting it
against an exotic background. It is true there are many digressions
and the author tends to preach at his readers; but there is also no
doubt that it was as much the message as the story that made the
book sell in hundreds of thousands of copies. According to Carsten
it had reached the half million mark before 1938, and even after the
Second World War it was still selling well, though sales have now
declined and the whole ethos of the book has dated. Grimm, the outspoken exponent of colonial imperialism, was quite clear in his own
mind about the superiority of the Nordic *Herrenvolk* over other
inferior races, and it was this racism which was quickly identified and
praised by Nazi critics in the 1930s.

Hans Grimm shows the particular difficulties which ensue for the
worthy Germans as against other colonial peoples, quite simply from
the superiority of the race . . . *Volk ohne Raum* belongs among
those works in our literature which will last and in which most
distant generations will experience the true nature of the people,
the eternal power of its being and the voice of its blood, shuddering
before the weight and magnitude of its Fate.[12]

An early doctoral dissertation which examined Grimm as one who
'prepared the way for the Nordic view' came to the conclusion that
the political ideas of Adolf Hitler and Hans Grimm converged at four
main points: in the general question of race, in the particular question
of the place of the Jews, in the stress given to the significance of the
Aryan as Nordic man, and finally in the question of the German stance
vis-à-vis England.[13] Apart from the basic idea of *Lebensraum*, the
novel's militant nationalism also appealed to NS ideologues. Grimm
released emotions and struck chords which could not fail to have their
effect on a receptive public. But it must also be remembered that
though he consciously acted as a propagator of the Nordic world view,
he was more of an old-fashioned, crabbed national conservative than
an out-and-out Nazi. Indeed he never joined the party and always
avoided the formula *Heil Hitler*. While it is true he allowed himself to
be elected Senator of the Literary Academy and accepted a high
position in the Reichsschrifttumskammer he never made any secret of
his doubts about Hitler and about Goebbels' literary policies. In the
period between 1933 and 1945 he published only two speeches and
he never received any of the many cultural prizes of the Third Reich.
His relationship with Goebbels was a tense one, because the Doctor
found it impossible to make Grimm toe the party line. Grimm
remained the individualist who approved in general of what was
happening, but disapproved of any restriction on his personal freedom.
Of course, as the 'poet of the national epic', enjoying a special relationship with Goebbels, his position was a unique one, and he could get
away with more than many of his less prominent colleagues. Nevertheless,
his life under National Socialism was strange. Like many, he dried up
as far as creative writing was concerned, but his great wealth enabled
him to develop widespread activities, most notable of which were the
Lippoldsberg Literary Gatherings, to which he invited leading German
national-conservatives like Edwin Erich Dwinger, Moritz Jahn, Rudolf
Alexander Schröder and Paul Alverdes.[14] Even after 1945 meetings
still took place there at which Kolbenheyer, Schumann and Pleyer

engaged in discussions about Germany's place in the new Europe.
Grimm himself remained completely unchanged and true to himself.
Like a Christian defending the early Church and primitive Christianity
Grimm continued to defend 'original' National Socialism. It was his
opinion that there had been nothing wrong with the movement, indeed
it had attempted a great deal that was right for Germany and for
Europe. It was only through Hitler's paranoia that it had gone wrong
and crimes and excesses had crept in. Grimm remained one of the
incurables. Attempts to rediscover him and find new readers for his
works failed. As for the old readers, they had been ready to die for
their belief in *Lebensraum* and when the war came they did so:

> Their graves are to be found from the Arctic Circle to the
> Caucasus, but Hans Grimm lived to deny vociferously any
> responsibility for the events of the Third Reich. It is true that he
> was not a National Socialist and differed from them in certain
> matters. Rather he was an extreme Nationalist. In Germany
> nationalism of a violent and anti-western type has a much stronger
> tradition than national-socialism; this kind of fervent nationalism
> is much more likely to stage a come-back than Hitler's brand of
> German fascism.[15]

Another author, of an entirely different type, but nevertheless one
who, like Grimm, could claim that he was never a National Socialist,
one who, like Grimm, preached a nationalism of an extremely
violent, anti-democratic kind; and one who, like Grimm, gave thousands
of young Germans ideals to live and die for, was Ernst Jünger, who is
still writing to this day. Countless studies have been devoted to Ernst
Jünger, not least in an attempt to discover the extent to which he was
or was not associated with National Socialism, but no satisfactory
conclusion has yet been arrived at.[16] Admirers and defenders of this
brilliant stylist, philosopher, botanist, aesthete and adventurer are
almost as numerous as those who describe him as 'one of the most
dangerous of all fascist thinkers'. Ernst Jünger is constantly changing,
modifying and manipulating his writings and so any quotation from
his work can be countered by its opposite. Yet despite the
contradictory nature of his place in the conservative revolution, and
of his personal and ideological relationship with National Socialism in
general and with Hitler and Goebbels in particular, there is no doubting
the role of war in his writings. This was for him, as indeed for all his
generation, the fundamental experience, the primal vision, and to it he

constantly returns. Born in Heidelberg into a solid middle-class home, his youth seems to have been characterised by the same paralysing boredom and longing for release that was to find literary expression in a play like Wedekind's *Spring Awakening*, in novels like Musil's *Törless* and Hesse's *Under the Wheel*, or in the poets of the immediate pre-war expressionistic generation. In 1910 Georg Heym wrote in his diary: 'It is always the same, so boring, boring, boring. Nothing happens, nothing, nothing, nothing. If only something would happen, which wouldn't leave this stale taste of everyday things.' German middle-class youths of this generation seem to have been filled with disgust at the deadly poison of ennui, with hatred of the money-grubbing business mentality, and with contempt for the merchant's longing for safety and security. They were brim-full not with the spirit of adventure, but with the longing for an explosion, for some liberating action of any kind. Jünger shared these feelings and it was not surprising that in 1913 he ran away from home to join the Foreign Legion and only returned on the promise of a chance to join an expedition to Africa to climb Kilimanjaro. When the war came he delayed only long enough to take the emergency School Leaving Certificate before joining up. By the end of 1915 he had reached the rank of lieutenant and had become a shock-troop leader. He survived the war, but not without wounds. In the final chapter ('My Last Storm') of *Storm of Steel* (1920) he amuses himself in hospital counting the number of times he has been hit:

> I found that I had been hit in all fourteen times; six times by rifle-bullets, once by a shrapnel bullet, once by a shell splinter, three times by bomb splinters, and twice by splinters of rifle-bullets. Counting the ins and outs, this made precisely twenty punctures, so that I might confidently with that Roman centurion, Holkschen Reiter, take my place in every warlike circle.

Before the end of hostilities he was made a Knight of the Order 'Pour le mérite', the highest possible decoration in the German armed forces. He was a national hero. Jünger remained in the army after the war, and it was during this time in the twenties that he started to write. All his titles reveal war as the central experience: *Storm of Steel* (1920); *Struggle as Inner Experience* (1922); *Storm* (1923); *Copse 125. A Chronicle of the Trench Fighting* (1915); *Fire and Blood. One Small Segment from a Major Battle* (1925); *The Adventurous Heart* (1929); *Total Mobilisation* (1931). The last title, based on one of Jünger's own concepts, is yet another example of a literary-intellectual idea which was taken over and turned into reality by the National Socialists.

Jünger's first and perhaps his most influential work, *Storm of Steel*, reveals his literary starting-point. As the subtitle indicates, it was written as 'The Diary of a Storm-Trooper-Leader'. It was first published at the author's own expense, and indeed at first sight it does look like the amateurish effort of a typical regimental officer. Jünger signs himself a volunteer (that is not conscript), then lieutenant and company commander, he names his regiment (of which he is inordinately proud) and gives full military details of regimental casualties. The aim of the book is to be *sachlich* (objective), a term taken up later as the style of the post-war generation; yet despite such claims Jünger is far from being an exponent of the New Objectivity, and in many ways is closer to Expressionism, a movement of which he was certainly aware. His style is in fact not so much objective as visionary and apocalyptic, without the more glaring stylistic excesses of the Expressionists. What started off as a fairly technical military account, of direct interest only to a limited number of specialists, came in time to be read as one of the key books of the period. But it was not until the wave of war books started in 1928 that this came about. Then Mittler the publisher, who had re-issued *Storm of Steel* in 1922, brought out a third edition of 10,000 as a counter to the pacifism and anti-militarism of Remarque's *All Quiet on the Western Front*. It was only then that a book which had been read almost exclusively in army and Stahlhelm circles began to be read by a far wider public and that Jünger began to be characterised in the reviews as a propagator of militarism, and as a central figure in the process of mental rearmament. In this the author's self-dramatisation and the 'legend' that surrounded him, together with his personal charisma, did a great deal to further his new literary and intellectual career and he began to emerge as a German author to place alongside Lawrence and Malraux.

Gide praised *Storm and Steel* as the finest piece of writing to come out of the war. Certainly it is quite unlike anything of its time — none of the pastoral musings of Siegfried Sassoon or Edmund Blunden, no whiffs of cowardice as in Hemingway, none of the masochism of T.E. Lawrence, or the compassion of Remarque. Instead Jünger parades his belief in Man's 'elementary' instinct to kill other men — a game which, if played correctly, must conform to a chivalric set of rules.[17]

After the war Jünger withdrew from the army into the study of botany, entomology and marine biology. Here again he appears at first sight to be following the typical nationalist path towards that crude form of Darwinism the National Socialists were able to adopt because semi-scientific slogans like the 'Struggle for Existence' or the 'Survival of the Fittest' permitted them to rationalise the elimination of the gypsies and the extermination of the Jews as inferior races. But Jünger was far too much of a real scientist to be taken in by such pseudo-science and besides he leaned towards the kind of biology concerned with Linnaean classification rather than eugenics. Jünger became that contradiction in terms, the conservative intellectual, the man-of-action turned scientist, the aesthete and bibliophile. In effect the super-cool Prussian had all the hallmarks of the *dandy*, namely contempt for the masses, contempt for political parties, radical individualism and indifference to the banality of commonplace matters. Patriot and nationalist he certainly was, but with his contempt for the realities and compromises of the political game he tended to move more and more into the realms of pure theory. And yet he could not stay away from politics—he had to feel that he was playing an important part. By 1925 he was writing political articles and by 1927 he was back in Berlin mixing with Kubin, Brecht, Dr Goebbels and Toller. Jünger's political opinions were as mixed as the company he kept: in fact he moved from the Stahlhelm variety of nationalism through the youth movement to Niekisch's National Bolshevism, that 'Prussian Communism which hated capitalism, hated the bourgeois West and hoped to graft the methods of Bolshevism onto the chivalric ideals of the Junkers'.[18] Jünger was as friendly with Niekisch as he was with anyone, and helped his wife and child when he was arrested by the Gestapo in 1937. Jünger probably did earnestly desire the alliance of workers and soldier-aristocrats who would abolish the middle classes. He probably did, more than anything else, hope to win over the workers to the national cause, but this did not make him totally committed to National Bolshevism—he just was not capable of total commitment. He was not a political careerist, he was more like one of the irresponsible littérateurs he himself despised. He attacked Socialism, democracy, pacifism, but most of all he attacked the middle classes and the Weimar Republic, calling instead for an authoritarian state under the guidance of a great national leader, if necessary a dictator. In effect there was little difference between his political attitudes and those of the National Socialists. The main difference was that Jünger was a true conservative revolutionary. He really wanted revolution. What he admired therefore was the *early* NSDAP, before it adopted the legality policy, before it became a mass party prepared to make accommodations with the hated middle classes and the almost equally despised capitalistic and commercial centres of power. He admired Hitler and heard him demonstrate his demagogic magic. Yet although he dedicated his book *Fire and Blood* 'to the national Führer', he probably never felt he could accept Hitler, with his obsession about the Jews, any more than he could Ludendorff with his obsession about Freemasons. Jünger seems to have been closer to the original Goebbels wing of the party, because it corresponded more to his own ideal of dynamic revolutionary *élan.* And yet, despite his distant admiration for Hitler and his personal closeness to Goebbels, he never joined the party, though most of his nationalistic collaborators on *Arminius* (for example Blunck, Johst, Stoffregen, Jungnickel, Müller-Partenkirchen, Steguweit, Beumelburg, Fechter, Schauwecker, W. Weiss) did accept the NSDAP as the proper organ of the new nationalism. Apart from his dislike of *all* party political organisations and his predilection for the purity of theory, he disagreed with the NSDAP on various matters. He thought the party was wrong about the *Landvolkbewegung*, that revolution of the peasants which the NSDAP condemned, and he rejected the racial policies of the NSDAP (though for his own special reasons). But all this seemed like hair-splitting to contemporaries for whom Jünger appeared to be as close to National Socialism as it was possible to be. Differences between them disappeared in the light of the far greater number of correspondences and at the time liberal and left-wing critics quite rightly recognised in Jünger a gifted National Socialist and regarded him as one of the intellectual leaders of the party. Most readers and admirers of Jünger landed up in the party, for in it they found the realisation of all he had argued most effectively for. All the not inconsiderable energy he generated, the continual reminders of the war just past and the possibility of the one to come, the impossibility of accepting the republic, the longings for an authoritarian, military-style Germany, all this worked to the benefit of the mass movement. His *Total Mobilisation* (1931) showed how his goals would be achieved, namely through the collapse of the liberal system, the necessary loss of individual freedom, the transition to totalitarian structures, whose prime goal would be the military mobilisation of all collective efforts 'right down to the very seamstress at her sewing machine'. In this same passage he also developed what was to become the policy of *Gleichschaltung* put into practice by the NSDAP when it came to power:

To develop powers of such dimensions, it is no longer sufficient to arm the sword-arm—what is essential is arming to the very marrow, arming right down to life's finest nerve-ends. To realise this is the task of total mobilisation, by which all the energy-capacity of the modern world which is so widespread and so complex can by one single movement at the control panel be fed into the great grid of military power.[19]

This vision of the National Socialist state seemed to many observers, including some in the party hierarchy itself, to be already foreshadowed in Jünger's abstract work *The Worker*, which extended the total state of war to the whole of society and made the individual into someone without rights or privileges, a mere functional cog in a completely planned society. Here again all the National Socialists had to do when they came to power was to turn the blueprint into reality:

The Worker is a vaguely formulated machine-age utopia whose citizens are required to commit themselves to a 'total mobilization' . . . in the undefined interests of the State. The Worker, as Jünger understands him, is a technocrat. His business, ultimately, is war. His freedom—or rather his sense of inner freedom—is supposed to correspond to the scale of his productivity. The aim is world government by force.[20]

Jünger, however, merely wrote the words and conjured up the visions: he played no part in turning them into the horrific reality of the Third Reich. Instead he withdrew once again from politics, declined consideration for the Academy, rejected the possibility of a seat in the Reichstag representing the NSDAP, and asked the *Völkischer Beobachter* not to publish him without permission. Yet undoubtedly he did great service to the party by his war books, for throughout the course of the Nazi regime they poured from the presses in carefully prepared editions. All the reality of the original reports and diary entries had now been refined into glorious visions of fateful events, presenting the younger generations with models for heroic behaviour and inviting them to follow the examples of the earlier generation of front-line fighters who had paved the way for the national awakening resulting in the Third Reich. Many accepted this invitation, joined the armed forces and died.

Joseph Goebbels is thought of now as a man of the spoken word, while his name is almost synonymous with the use of propaganda in

the political sphere: yet his career started off in a much more convention-
ally literary fashion. As a university student he seems to have been
unusually restless, changing universities many times, though he was far
from well-off—indeed he relied heavily on a scholarship from the
Catholic Albertus Magnus Society. In 1920, however, he eventually
settled in Heidelberg, where in November of the following year he
submitted a dissertation on 'Wilhelm von Schütz: a Contribution to
the History of Drama in the Romantic School', and gained the title
of 'Doctor'. For the rest of his life he proudly insisted on being
addressed as Dr Goebbels. In his early years he wrote extensively and
it is only because of copyright and legal problems that his literary
writings remain unpublished to this day. The Goebbels archive contains
many notebooks with unpublished verses, poems, prose passages and
essays. There is one drama with the title *Heinrich Kampfert* and
manuscripts with 'Romantic' titles like 'Those Who Love the Sun', or
'A Roaming Scholar am I'. Many of the early poems have titles
equally redolent of romantic kitsch, and there are also parts of a
religious drama called *Judas Iscariot.* [21]

   In his early years Goebbels made many attempts to break into
writing and publishing (for example, into the circle round Gundolf)—
but without success. Fortunately, however, one of his literary works
is available for study, namely his novel *Michael: a German Fate through
the Pages of a Diary*. In *European Witness*, published after the war in
1946, Stephen Spender drew attention to this novel, not because it
was a forgotten masterpiece, but because a novel written by a
common murderer would excite considerable interest, and here was a
book written by one of the greatest murderers of all history. Published
in 1929, four years before the Nazis came to power, it was never
discussed outside Germany and hardly at all inside Germany. And yet,
as Spender rightly saw, it contains in literary guise 'all the Nazi and
Fascist symptoms'.[22] This is what makes it still compulsive reading to
this day. Goebbels, the master orator, could exercise some of the
same magnetic power over his reader. What Goebbels offers first of all
is comradeship—the cameraderie of the front-line fighter—for his book
is dedicated to his friend Richard Flisges, who had died six years earlier.
In 1918 his friend had come back from the war 'wounded arm still in
sling, grey helmet on head and chest covered with medals'. With this
friend he lives through the trials of the difficult post-war period and
replies to its problems with cries of 'Revolution! Defiance! Resurrection!'
The book is to be a sign of the times, a symbol for the future, showing
in exemplary manner a type of German youth characterised by will,

faith, work, passion and sacrifice – for the fatherland! The language of this short novel is exclamatory and ecstatic after the fashion of Nietzsche's *Thus Spake Zarathustra*; and indeed Nietzsche's name is often invoked (needless to say in a manner and context of which he would not have approved). There are also many literary references, not least to Goethe, but these are merely the external trappings of culture. The essence of the book's message is its anti-intellectualism: its appeal is to the blood rather than the brain. The German youth of the time, in its Faustian creative drive, is described as waiting in its millions for a new dawn, a new way of life which will come like a storm to sweep away the old and bring in the new. And youth is always right, not old age and maturity! So the protagonist returns from the battlefield (which Goebbels himself, because of his physical condition, never saw), and as the representative German 'rises like a phoenix from the ashes' to confront the peace in his beloved homeland Germany. The heroic life of the front-line soldier now lies behind him, the less exciting life of the university student lies ahead. But even here the New Man (according to the developing Nazi doctrine as adumbrated for the hero) is described not only as the soldier, which he has been, but also as the peasant rooted in the soil, which he always will be: 'I stand with both feet on the hard soil of the homeland. Around me is the smell of the soil. Peasant blood mounts up slow and healthy within me.' That is what makes it possible for him to live life to the full, unlike the city-dweller or intellectual. As for the universities, they are full of pale faces and bespectacled high-brows and are certainly not where 'the future leaders of the nation' are to be found. Science and study are denounced as the death of common sense, and intellect as a hindrance to the formation of real character.

When Michael, the hero of the novel, meets a girl called Hertha at the university, the discussion between them is about the combination of poet and politician in one and the same person. The credo expressed is clear: the statesman is also an artist of a kind. The *Volk* is for him what the stone is for the sculptor. The relationship between a Führer and the masses is the same as that between painter and paints. Politics is the creative art of the state, just as painting is the creative art of the painter. 'To turn the masses into a Volk and to form the Volk into a state, that has always been the fundamental essence of all true politics.' From this, it is an easy step to war. War is the simplest form of life affirmation:

Struggle the moment man sets foot on this earth. Struggle till the moment of leaving it, and in between stretches never-ending war for a place at the feeding-trough. One only has real regard for what has to be conquered or defended.

Peace has to be fought for, not with the palm frond, but with the sword; there is no such thing as equality; the natural world is anti-democratic—these are the arguments put forward, and as the debate continues Michael develops his ideas on *Volkstum*, Socialism and capitalism to the point where Hertha points out that even when talking about politics he thinks like an artist, and notes that this is a dangerous combination. But this does not stem the flow of the poet-politician. Again he develops proto-fascist ideas, this time about the role of woman in society. The woman's duty is to be lovely and bring children into the world. When she accuses him of being 'reactionary'. he takes up the challenge by attacking fashionable, liberal ideas of what this means: 'If modern means unnatural, utter collapse, putrefaction and deliberate corrosion of all morality, then I am being reactionary.' The language used in this attack on modernity is particularly significant, especially in the use of the term *Zersetzung* (corrosion) which was to become one of the key concepts for National Socialist attacks on all modern literature.

Many critics then and now have doubted whether there ever was such a thing as a National Socialist *Weltanschauung*. Michael has no doubts that his primitive, crude life doctrine is indeed a *Weltanschauung*, 'not one worked out and arrived at by the power of reason and logic, but one which has grown organically and is therefore capable of resisting all attacks'. His *Weltanschauung* has nothing to do with culture: it relies on belief, including the belief that Another and Greater is on the way, 'who will one day arise among us and preach faith in the life of the Fatherland'. Significantly, too, Michael is convinced that this coming genius will consume him, indeed consume a whole generation of youth, called upon to make the supreme sacrifice for the great cause. The demand for total sacrifice was to become one of the most attractive of all the appeals of National Socialism to the hearts and minds of the young.

Michael the poet continues his struggles with himself and with Christ, though it is clear that he has moved a long way beyond orthodox Christianity. His Christ is a hard unrelenting one who declares war on money and uses a whip to drive Jewish money-changers out of the temple. The fierce tirade against the Jews is in what was soon to become the accepted style in National Socialist Germany. Jews make Michael physically ill; Jews have despoiled his people, soiled his and the Germans' ideals, lamed the force of the nation, contaminated its customs and ruined its morals; with the Jew it is them-or-us! This whole vicious catalogue of the supposed features of the Jew culminates in the statement: 'Christ cannot have been a Jew. I do not have to prove this scientifically, it is so!'

After this it is not surprising that Michael proceeds to compound his own peculiar brew of anti-Semitism and anti-Marxism. Christ was the first great opponent of the Jews and this is why they killed him, because he frustrated their aim to conquer the world. The Jew is the lie personified, while in Christ the Jew nailed truth to the cross. Christ first gave form to the concept of sacrifice; this was corrupted by the Jews into getting others to make sacrifices for them. The true sacrifice is Christian Socialism, Jewish sacrifice is Marxism. From specious arguments Michael arrives at the strange but peculiarly fascist conclusion that the real struggle is that between Christ and Marx, Christ representing the principle of love, and Marx the (Jewish) principle of hate. All this, strangely enough, is argued out within the context of a discussion of Expressionism and Modern Art:

> Our decade is absolutely expressionistic in its inner structure. This has nothing to do with how fashionable the word is. We people today are all Expressionists. People who want to form the world from inside out. The Expressionist builds himself a new world within himself. His secret and his power is passion. His mental world usually breaks against reality.
> The soul of the Impressionist is the microscopic picture of the macrocosm.
> The soul of the Expressionist is the new macrocosm.
> A world in itself.
> Expressionistic sensation is explosive.
> It is an autocratic feeling of being oneself.

Goebbels is said to have had a weakness for Expressionist art and at an early stage in the party's development it seemed possible that Expressionism would be adopted as the artistic mode of the party. The matter was in doubt for some time. In the novel, however, there are no such doubts and this section finishes with the ominous declaration: 'this whole foreign rabble will have to be removed!'

While in the first part of the novel Michael has engaged partly in exclamatory monologues and partly in discussions with Hertha, in the second part, after they separate (she being perhaps still too bourgeois to follow the young poet-revolutionary on his fateful path), he meets up with a Russian student with whom he also engages in significant and wide-ranging talks. At first he is attracted by Ivan's revolutionary fervour and love of Russia, but soon he is just as repelled as he was initially attracted. It has been suggested that this encounter between Ivan and Michael in fact represents a more fundamental confrontation, namely between the Russian and the German, and also indicates Goebbels' own National Bolshevism. In the end Michael, like Goebbels and National Socialism, decides that Ivan is the enemy who must be destroyed. Michael stops being a student. 'Soldiers, students and workers will build the new Reich. I was a soldier, I am a student, a worker I will be.' With his hatred of the cowardly bourgeois this is the course for him, especially for one who wants to make history. He leaves the university and works in a mine. In his simple worker's room he has the Bible and *Faust*. The end of the novel is sudden and un-expected. He hears that Ivan has been the victim of a political assassination and he himself is killed in an accident soon afterwards. A letter from a miner to Hertha Holk tells her that Michael died with a smile and that in his copy of Nietzsche's *Zarathustra* he had marked the passage: 'Many die too late and some too early. Strangely still sounds the lesson! Die at the right time.'

Michael is not much of a novel. It is told in the form of diary entries and consequently has little or no plot and little or no shape or form. The style is exclamatory as it follows the exaltations and depressions of the student hero, who does little but talk. However, Michael does have faith in his own personal 'demon', he does have crude political beliefs which he expresses in 'poetic' language, ideas which in normal circumstances would be dismissed as primitive rubbish, were it not for the fact that they were also the common currency of a nationalistic wave which was to assume total power over a whole nation. And it must be admitted that the novel and its ideas must have had the power to attract those it was aimed at, namely the disgruntled youth of a defeated people. Stephen Spender is correct in observing that *Michael* is genuine in so far as it captures the sense of defeat, of reaction against post-war decadence and of national humiliation. He is right too to look beyond this and sense in *Michael* an ennui with the modern world, which deliberately seeks release through conflict and chaos. Above all he sees in *Michael* the attraction of evil. The hero who has announced the coming of the Great One goes by chance to a political meeting and immediately falls under the spell of an unnamed speaker of sinister power. Like one who has slumbered and had strange dreams and visions, he is suddenly awakened, as Germany too awakens to the call from the Leader:

> That evening I sit in a big hall with a thousand others and see him again, hear him who awakened me.
> Now he stands in the midst of a loyal congregation.
> He seems to have grown in stature.
> There is so much strength in him, and a sea of light gleams from those big blue eyes.
> I sit among all those others, and it seems as if he is speaking to me quite personally.
> About the blessing of work! Whatever I only ever felt or guessed at, he puts into words. My confessions and my faith: here they gain shape.
> I feel his strength filling my soul.
> Here is young Germany, and those who work in the blacksmith's shop of the new Reich. Anvil till now, but hammer before long.
> Here is my place.
> Around me are people I never saw and I feel like a child as tears well up in my eyes.

Goebbels was to become the master myth-maker, creating heroes out of such unlikely figures as Schlageter and Horst Wessel. It is more than likely that here too he was creating a myth, round the moment of his own spiritual awakening to the light of National Socialism. He probably did not hear Hitler speak in 1922, as the novel claims. In fact he was working in a bank and on the Stock Exchange, calling the prices. It was not until 1925 that he actually did meet Hitler. Once he did, however, he never looked back and his career took off like a meteor. Nevertheless it is equally true, as Stephen Spender claims, that *Michael* is the key to his later success:

> One has to go back to Goebbels' first work, a novel called *Michael*, published in 1929, to discover that the real Goebbels is essentially the Nazi Goebbels, from the days when he was a rebellious student at Heidelberg to his dramatic death in the Reichschancellory in 1945.[23]

In the novel the poet hero struggles more or less successfully to write a vast religious drama on the theme of Christ and (as has been noted) parts of just such a Christ drama with the title *Judas Iscariot* are to be found among his unpublished works. Goebbels fancied himself as a dramatist and used to entertain his guests with readings from another drama called *The Wanderer*.[24] This play, though it remained unpublished, did reach the public stage. *The Wanderer* is a play with a prologue, eight scenes and an epilogue and follows the 'stations of the cross' form familiar from the Expressionist theatre. Equally expressionistic is the elimination of individual psychology and the reduction of the dramatis personae to representative figures: the prologue is taken up by a confrontation between poet and wanderer, the first scene (Poverty) has Man and Woman, the second (Church) has Deacon and Chaplain, the third (Industry) Director General and Captain of Industry, the fourth (Stock Exchange) Stock-Market Baron and Private Secretary, the fifth (Sex) Gent and Prostitute, the sixth (Party) Politician and Worker, the seventh (Government) Minister and Counsellor, the eighth (Death) only Death. The epilogue completes the circular form by coming back to the poet and wanderer of the prologue. In this play Goebbels once again returns to his own position *vis-à-vis* Hitler. In the same way as the poet here becomes the mouthpiece of the wanderer, who is the harbinger of a new faith and a new will to take a stand against the sufferings of Germany, so too Goebbels, the Gauleiter of the Berlin NSDAP, becomes the most fervent of his master's voices. The most striking feature about the play is that all eight scenes represent a negative catalogue of the German misery, without the presence anywhere of the slightest ideology. What he does is merely to reject all democratic and Socialist endeavours and, by defamation of them, strengthen the irrational wish for an authoritarian Germany under the guidance of a strong leader. So the Germany of the time is denounced as decadent, and the poet despairs because he believes that everything noble, great and beautiful is doomed to decline. In the chaos, corruption and immorality of the modern world, he meets the wanderer, who is a proclaimer of the Truth and exponent of an unshakable faith in a new life. He gives the poet insight into the life of the time, a life filled with suffering in a society driven by lust for money. The problems of a sterile, dogmatic Christianity are contrasted with a religion of action. The real 'God' of the age is shown to be Mammon, while Death stands grinning over the chaos. The individual scenes are linked by a voice from the darkness, which comments on what the poet has seen, giving guidance where necessary, till in the epilogue the exhausted poet is uplifted by the wanderer, who imparts to him a faith

in morality and bravery with which to return to the people. His mission
will be to awaken the people to this message: 'Be strong and believe!'
This is the call which it is hoped the play will convey to all who are
capable of hearing, moving hearts and opening eyes to the certainty of
a new Germany of honour, purity and political and moral greatness.

Various attempts were made by the NSDAP to set up theatre
groups which would travel the country bringing this kind of message to
the people and it was in the context of one such group that Goebbels'
play was performed.[25] It must be said that such Nazi theatre groups
were far from successful, but by 1932 when *The Wanderer* was
performed in Chemnitz the situation had changed drastically, as a
report from the *Chemnitzer Tageblatt* makes clear. By this time
Goebbels was known as the famous Berlin Gauleiter, agitator in the
grand manner, propagandist and organiser. He was also known as a
dazzling journalist from his articles in the *Angriff*, and in his book,
Struggle for Berlin, which had just appeared. The *Tageblatt* reporter
reminds his reader that Goebbels had been in Chemnitz only a
short time before, addressing a mass gathering of 12,000 who hung
on his lips as they sat surrounded by 1,000 Storm Troopers. How
different from the time six years before, when he spoke in the Marble
Palace before a much smaller crowd and with only a few dozen SA
men as stewards! Then his audience had been made up mainly of
Communists and the evening had ended with the bloodiest political
meeting Chemnitz had ever experienced with not a pane of glass, not
a chair, lamp or beer glass remaining intact. It was against a background
of such conflicting memories as these conjured up in the local press
that Goebbels' play *The Wanderer* was now performed. Of course,
there is not a mention in the play of National Socialism, of Hitler or
of the SA directly; nevertheless the message still came across loud and
clear. The need of the hour, it emerged, was not simply a new faith,
but a *fanatical* faith. Marxism, parliamentarianism, liberalism, all
such democratic solutions have failed, and only the great leader can
guide Germany out of the dark night. According to the newspaper
report Goebbels' play succeeded in putting this simple message across
and the Chemnitz theatre enjoyed a wonderful evening, yet despite its
programmatic nature Goebbels' play did not succeed in finding a
more permanent place in the theatre repertoire. Chemnitz was not
Berlin and the Gauleiter's play never did reach any of the major
theatres. Clearly it shows the same faults as the author's *Michael*.
The language is exclamatory and ecstatic, and altogether the play, like
Goebbels' novel, betrays far too much of its expressionistic origins.

Besides, despite its essentially abstract nature, the play did deal with subjects which held all sorts of special dangers in Nazi Germany. Had poverty disappeared with the end of the Weimar Republic? Had the Christian Church disappeared in an essentially heathen state? Were there no more money-greedy capitalists or stock-market speculators? Was sex a completely taboo subject? Had the party solved the problem of its relationship with the workers? Worst of all, what was one to think of the figure of Death looming over the land? Altogether it is not surprising that Goebbels' expressionistic play disappeared almost as quickly as it appeared.

WHEN I HEAR 'CULTURE' I REACH FOR MY REVOLVER

If the question of the connection between Expressionism and National Socialism is one which the literary efforts of Goebbels inevitably force upon the reader, the same might be said of the works of Bronnen. Arnolt Bronnen has been described as one of the most morally questionable beings of the twentieth century.[1] In the Roaring Twenties this Viennese writer first gained fame through the erotic violence of his *Patricide* (1920), an expressionistic generation-conflict play, which nevertheless even at this stage had the young hero expressing (in language anticipating Blood and Soil) the desire to be a peasant. But Bronnen steadily moved from friendships with people like Brecht to more nationalistic groups, until he finally landed among the National Socialists. In this he has been compared with the expressionistic worker-poet Max Barthel, who from early association with the Haus Nyland circle, moved from the KPD through the SPD to acclaim and acceptance by the NSDAP.[2] After the Second World War Bronnen published his own life history which goes some way towards explaining the psychological and sociological roots of his character. Bronnen's family background (his adoptive father was a Jewish professor) contained all the ingredients of a Freudian clinical case and many of the factors Adorno found in the fascistoid, author-itarian character. His early plays, *Patricide* and *Anarchy in Sillian*, were noticeable for their combination of sex, violence and sensationalism. Following these *succes de scandale* Bronnen progressed steadily to the right, though his playwriting career finished in 1925 with the production of his earlier sex comedy, *Excesses*, a play notorious for the scene involving a woman and a goat. By 1928 he had moved from literature to radio and had written one of the first radio plays, a version of Kleist's *Michael Kohlhaas*. However, it was his *O.S.* (meaning Upper Silesia) of 1929 which finally documented his move into the Nazi camp. In this novel Bronnen describes the fighting of the Freikorps groups in Upper Silesia after the end of the First World War. Tucholsky demolished the novel in a famous review. There is no reason, Tucholsky says, why the right-wingers should not be capable of producing a good, worthy, nationalist writer, or of writing clear concise German. 'Political sincerity is something one can smell.

Lienhard, the *Heimatkunst* writer was genuine. Hans Grimm is a completely honourable man. Bronnen is *not* genuine.'[3] Tucholsky then goes on to quote Lord Northcliffe's saying to the effect that every good news item should contain three elements, namely blood, sex and patriotism, only to expose Bronnen as a writer deliberately contriving a cocktail of these same ingredients, but failing because his is a show of phoney cruelty and violence. The whole concoction Tucholsky denounces as drawing-room fascism. Bronnen, whom Tucholsky ridicules as a dandy with a 'steamed-up monocle', has gone too far. There are levels below which one should not sink and Bronnen with his shameless exploitation of political attitudes has done just that. It goes without saying that reviews of the novel from the other political camp saw it quite differently. Joseph Goebbels in the National Socialist *Angriff* wrote: 'Bronnen's *O.S.* reads as if it had been written by all of us.' Ernst Jünger also admired it.[4] Indeed it may have been the dandy Ernst Jünger who first drew Bronnen into the world of the conservative revolutionary nationalists. Looking back on 1927, Bronnen wrote in his memoirs: 'I came, I saw and was conquered. Ernst Jünger was exactly the sort of individual for whom I always had the strongest sympathy.'

In the meantime Bronnen had installed himself in the Berlin Broadcasting House and thus occupied a privileged position during Germany's turbulent years. He got to know the National Bolshevist Ernst Niekisch, whose *Hitler, a German Fate* he read at an early stage and rejected because it was an attack on National Socialism. Niekisch was to spend several years in Hitler's prisons. He survived.[5] Bronnen made sure that *he* would survive and he did so by making it his business to get close to Goebbels. Goebbels became his patron, and Bronnen devoted himself from then on to the Nazi cause. When in 1930 Thomas Mann was to give a lecture in the Beethoven Rooms in Berlin, his 'German Address: an Appeal to Reason', warning of the threat of fascism and asking the middle classes to make common cause with the Social Democrats in defence of the republic, Bronnen went along and Goebbels sent twenty Storm Troopers to back him up, so creating another Bronnen sensation. When *All Quiet on the Western Front*, the film based on Remarque's novel, was shown, Bronnen was in the cinema with his consort Olga, to disturb the showing by releasing white mice among the audience. Bronnen sat in Dr Goebbels' box in the theatre, drank with him at his table and gained the support and praise of his followers. It was Bronnen who gained Goebbels access to the republic's radio services. When the party eventually came to power, the Jewish question caused him problems because of his parentage, but he solved this by having himself declared born out of wedlock (and therefore not the son of his Jewish father) and produced skull measurements proving his Aryan descent to support his claim. He wrote a Nazi novel called *The Battle of the Ether*. He was with the first German television team, commissioned to cover the Berlin Olympic games. By the end of the war he was in the army, and by his own account attempted to sabotage the war effort and to join the Austrian resistance. After 1945 he became the mayor of a small town, but for some reason he did not enjoy the confidence of the people, so he eventually made his way to East Germany, where J.R. Becher had offered him a job as a theatre critic. He died in East Berlin on 12 October 1959. National Socialism encouraged intellectual opportunism, though it had to be carried off with the panache and air of conviction of a Gründgens. H.H. Ewers failed to be accepted, despite his readiness to write a Horst Wessel novel. Bronnen's opportunism did permit him a modest career under the National Socialist regime, though his close association with Goebbels helped. By 1951 he was calling this friendship the 'tragic mistake' of his life.

Of another famous member of the Expressionist generation it cannot seriously be claimed that he was motivated by mere opportunism; indeed the affinities between Expressionism and National Socialism in his case seem somehow much more deep-seated. Gottfried Benn was an apolitical poet of *poésie pure*, an Expressionist, a stylist, a brilliant essayist and paradoxical thinker: yet when the National Socialists came to power he did not leave Germany, turned upon those who did so and publicly proclaimed his allegiance to the National Socialist movement.[6] Why did he do this? Was he blind, divorced from reality, or was there some fundamental connection between his own thinking and the new wave? One reason was medical— Dr Benn was without doubt deeply impressed by Nazi 'eugenics' and wrote essays which align him with Nazi concepts of racial hygiene. He also seems to have been an outsider, as isolated nihilist who was only too ready to adopt a movement which would fill life's emptiness, only too ready to stop thinking and go with the stream, in order to be accepted into the national community. Certainly too, as far as external symbols of acceptance were concerned, the outsider seems to have been so delighted with his election to the Prussian Academy that he was prepared to throw his colleagues to the wolves, when this became necessary shortly afterwards because of the politicisation of the whole literary scene. Just how political Benn the apolitical poet was prepared to be was evidenced by his speech on Stefan George at the invitation of Hanns Johst, the new President, to commemorate the poet's death in 1933. The title *The New Reich* given by George to one of his collections was of course inviting and it was not surprising that Benn, like Hans Naumann, should attempt to show the similarity between Hitler and George, in their shared belief in Germany's greatness and mission, the principle of leadership, and the value of ancestry, blood and race. This was not so unusual. Even members of the George circle had made many public statements to the same effect, George himself had made too many ambiguous remarks about the Jews and politics, and his poetry lent itself to Nazi interpretation.[7] There were obvious differences—George was Mediterranean, he had an antipathy to Nordic man, he had Jews like Friedrich Gundolf and Karl Wolfskehl close to him and there was no real connection between his intellectual longings and the brutality and barbarism of the Third Reich. In addition he had made his opinion of the Nazis clear by going into exile in Switzerland where he died, before he could be exploited. However, the high esteem in which he was held in early Nazi circles is undoubted, and his influence on National Socialist poetry self-evident. Rust, the Minister of Culture, quoted from George's *The New Reich* at the university celebration for the founding of the Third Reich and curiously it was the psychiatrist Kurt Hillebrandt, a close member of the George Circle, who developed the key Nazi concept of *Entartung*.[8] That Benn in his Academy address should claim George for National Socialism was not so surprising. Benn also played an active part in the *Gleichschaltung* of the Prussian Academy, leaving it a body characterised by the presence of Hans Grimm, Emil Strauss, Erwin Guido Kolbenheyer, Blunck, Börries von Münchhausen and other such national worthies, rather than by the literary luminaries he had joined in the first place. In such company he attended the première of Johst's *Schlageter*, and did not feel too uncomfortable in the presence of this new political constellation. Only a few days later he gave his famous radio talk in which he publicly proclaimed his allegiance to the new state in response to an open letter addressed to him by Klaus Mann on behalf of those who had gone into exile to escape from the new barbarism. Klaus Mann asked him how he, whose name for many was synonymous with the highest intellectual standards and a purity little short of fanatical, could have been persuaded to offer his services to people whom the rest of Europe found lacking in those very qualities. Would the intellectual not always remain an object of suspicion in the 'camp of the awakening Germany'? Benn's reply was based not on reason or logic, but on the concept of experience. He claimed that only those people who had actually experienced directly what was happening in Germany could appreciate what it was like. This was something one should discuss only with all those who had remained in the country, not with *émigrés* who had left the homeland. The latter had missed the chance to feel welling up within them the concept of *Volk*: they had missed the chance to experience the phenomenon of national oneness, they had missed the chance to observe history at work. History is here understood by Benn as something unquestionably decreed by fate. So he was not referring to the well known theatricality of revolutionary events, the magic of torch-light processions and martial music, but to the inner process, the release of what he felt to be a massive creative energy which had brought about a far-reaching human transformation. None of what he said in his talk was particularly new, for he did tend to think in irrational terms of the experience (*Erlebnis*), and was intellectually infatuated with the grand, fateful sweep of history, with visions of cultural developments on a vast scale. What was new was to find Benn associating it particularly with the nationalistic concept of the *Volk*, for Benn was far from Germanic in his myth-prone world-view.

Benn then went on to discuss the concept of barbarism, for in his view Klaus Mann made it sound as if Germany were a threat to culture and civilisation, as though a horde of savages were threatening the ideals of humanity as a whole! Benn's answer to this was once again couched in terms of cultural rather than political history. Benn rejects what he considers to be a vision of history created by nineteenth-century bourgeois minds: history has never heard of democracy or rationalism. The only *modus operandi* known to history is to bring forth at its turning-points a new type of Man, who must fight his way through and force the message of his generation and his kind on to the age he lives in by action and suffering, as the Law of Life decrees. This view of history is neither enlightened nor humanitarian, but metaphysical—it is, Benn argues, based on an irrational principle.

Klaus Mann's words were: 'Come out in support of the Irrational as the first step; the next step is barbarism; before you know it, you've got Adolf Hitler.' Benn's reply to this (after suitably insulting remarks decrying the exiles' 'opportunistic', 'progressive' concept of Man as superficial, irresponsible and hedonistic) is the pseudo-scientific jargon he loves. This time his defence is *biological*, permitting him to use terms he can share with the National Socialists: what is taking place is the emergence of a new *biological* type, a change of direction in history,

the coming of a new national stock. What Benn offers in defence of
National Socialism has nothing to do with structures of government,
what he offers is a grand new vision of the Birth of Man:

> As a concept it may be old or it may perhaps be the last magnificent
> product of the white race, probably one of the world spirit's most
> magnificent creations in our time, adumbrated in the Goethe hymn,
> 'To Nature': and if only you would grasp the further fact that this
> vision is not subject to success or failure; if ten wars in East and
> West were to overwhelm and annihilate the German people, if the
> Apocalypse were approaching by land and sea with its seals about
> to be broken, this vision of humanity would still stand: in order to
> realise it, the nation must be bred and your philosophical inquiry
> about civilisation and barbarism is shown up as absurd in the face
> of an overwhelming historical reality.[9]

Benn then leaves this vision of the 'white race' to turn to politics
and to what he calls the facts of experience. What he experiences, he
claims, is the construction of a new state whose faith is remarkable,
whose seriousness of purpose is extraordinary, whose situation (both
internally and externally) is grave, surrounded as it is by those who wish
upon it a war of annihilation and total collapse. Benn rejects out of
hand accusations of 'hysterical brutality', not least from Marxists, since
in his view the state where Marxism is triumphant has put to death
two million bourgeois intellectuals! This does bring him, however, to
discuss Socialism in a more general sense and in particular the situation
of the worker under the new regime. Here he claims that as a doctor he
comes into contact with many social groups, including many workers,
and he further claims that many who used to be Communists and
members of the German Socialist Party tell him that they are better
off than they ever were. They are better treated at work; supervisory
staffs are more cautious, personnel more polite; the workers have more
power; they get more respect; morale at work is higher, thanks to a new
awareness of their political role. What the Socialist Party was unable
to win for them, they have been given by this new form of Socialism,
namely something motivating their lives. Benn claims to be genuinely
convinced that the new holders of power will continue to win the
workers over; the sense of community of a whole united people (what
the National Socialists always claimed as their prime goal overcoming
all class differences) was no sham. Benn's defence was written at a
very early stage in the National Socialist revolution, when the

Socialist element in the party programme was still being stressed, but nevertheless this part of his defence does seem particularly naïve in view of NS brutality towards those Socialists and Communists who did not eagerly join the National Socialist Party. Attempts *were* made to win over the workers to National Socialism, but gentle persuasion was not the favoured method and the first concentration camps were already full of the kind of people Benn claims were being won over.[10]

From this defence of the new national variety of Socialism, Benn moves on to an equally spirited defence of Blood and Soil. Few would normally think of Benn as a regional poet, and indeed he was far closer to the image of the decadent, big-city littérateur the National Socialists loved to denounce; yet he reminds Klaus Mann that his ancestors came from the country and that he himself grew up 'in the midst of flocks', claiming therefore that he knows the real meaning of 'homeland'. The city, industry, intellectualism, all these, he claims, cast their shadow over his writings, but equally they fade away and there is nothing left but the plain, the seasons and the soil! What about Hitler? Is the *Volk* behind Hitler, or only sheep? Which came first, Hitler or the movement? The latter question for Benn is a revealing one, for in his opinion Hitler and the movement are identical. For him it really is a case of the magical coincidence of the individual and the general which Burkhardt refers to in his *Reflections on History*. Benn sees Hitler completely foreshadowed in Burkhardt's description of the great man's rise throughout the course of world history – the perils at the outset, his sudden appearance in terrible times, his incredible perseverance, his extraordinary facility in everything; and in addition, the suspicion growing in all thinking people that this is the man to achieve what only he can do.

In general, Benn's reply to Klaus Mann is that of an intellectual to an intellectual and not surprisingly it finishes with grand quotations from Hegel, Fichte, Burkhardt and Nietzsche. Not surprisingly, too, the debate has raged from that day to this over whether Benn's confession of faith in National Socialism represented a sudden break with his past or whether there were already elements in his earlier thoughts and writings which predisposed him to move in this direction. Equally and not surprisingly, it is often stressed that Benn's blindness did not last for long, that he soon saw or was made to see the error of his ways. He was subjected to attack in party organs, not least for racial reasons, and had to go through the humiliating business of proving that his name was not a Jewish Benn (like Ben-Gurion), but more an Indo-Germanic Benn like Wedgwood Benn or Ben Lomond!

He was also attacked for his roots in Expressionism. When Benn found Expressionist painting being denounced as debased, anarchistic and snobbish, Expressionism in music being called cultural Bolshevism, Expressionism in literature being publicly condemned, he rose to its defence, because he was also defending himself.[11] His defence was first of all to associate Expressionism with the war. This was a generation, he reminded his readers, whose finest flower had been destroyed by the war. His next defence was racial; he claimed that this was a European movement of Aryans (not Jews). He was careful too to single out Johst particularly as one who developed out of this great collection of talent.

Interestingly Benn tried to construct a German literary ancestry for Expressionism and to some extent the writers and works which he singled out were to become the favoured objects of reverence for National Socialist literary historians. Among these Goethe's *Faust* figures prominently of course, followed by Kleist (not only for his anti-French explosions), Nietzsche and Hölderlin, whose 'mystically apprehended words live on with a genuinely inexplicable power of suggestion'. From this it was but a small step for Benn to those other kinds of mystical ecstasy to be found in Meister Eckhart and Jakob Böhme. After them came further Germanic visionaries like Schiller, Bach and Dürer![12] Expressionism, Benn maintains, was the unconditional, the anti-liberal function of the spirit; it put the pure utilitarian world of science behind it, broke through the world of big business and took the difficult inward path to the creative strata, to the primal images, the myths! Was this to be rejected as abnormal and foreign to the people now that the great national movement was at work creating new realities? Was this art to be discounted as anarchic and formalistic? Benn was convinced that the leaders of the new Germany, 'artistically productive people' themselves, would know that the path which art takes cannot always be one of immediate and direct communication with the people. In fact Benn himself anticipates the answer National Socialism would give to the question of literature in general and the Expressionist generation in particular: namely, that it had failed to assume any historic patriotic mission, and that it had no political instinct. Against that he claims that German literature had always been apolitical (quoting Goethe and Hölderlin as examples), and that it was only the First World War which had changed this, resulting in all the Marxist 'dialectical rubbish' and functionalism which he rejected. Benn was, of course, being completely naïve in arguing for the freedom of the creative writer. His confession of faith in Expressionism was fulsome and sincere, possibly because he was arguing for himself; but it also shows how blind he was to the realities of the National Socialist mentality. Expressionism had no chance and the 'Expressionism Debate' was continued not inside National Socialist Germany but in Russia and elsewhere. In May 1936 the SS paper *Das schwarze Korps* and the *Völkischer Beobachter* attacked Benn as degenerate, Jewish and homosexual. In 1937 *Cleaning out the Temple of Art*, a book by SS man Wolfgang Willrich, included a particularly vicious attack on Benn. Fortunately for him, in this case as in so many others, there were divisions in the Nazi camp and Himmler came to his defence, arguing that it was well known that Benn had changed his views and that since 1933 and even earlier his behaviour from a nationalist point of view had been impeccable. Himmler considered it unnecessary and pointless to 'run amok' against a man who had wholeheartedly supported Germany at an international level.

By March 1938 Benn had been excluded from the Reichsschrifttums-kammer and had had the customary writing ban imposed upon him by the regime. Of course he never had been as apolitical as he claimed the poet of the Expressionist generation was. As his essay 'Art and State' of 1927 indicates, he was an opponent of the Weimar Republic, but in an anti-capitalistic, anti-democratic, aristocratic way. Almost inevitably at the time he had come into conflict with left-wing colleagues like Becher and Kisch. Even his essay on the conquest of Nihilism was not completely apolitical, for it appeared in the National Conservative journal *Der Vorstoss*. By 1933 Benn was capable of viewing this conquest of nihilism as the 'ultimate stage of the white race'. He could see in Nazism 'a new anthropological quality and a new human style', identify the Führer with the 'creative element' and the 'highest intellectual principle' and hail the new era as 'one sprung from drunkenness, nourished by impulse'.[13] The Röhm Putsch marked the beginning of his awareness that Klaus Mann had been right, yet it cannot really be said that he was ever aware of what National Socialism really meant, nor did he ever see any necessity to revise his fundamental position. His may have been a temporary aberration, but it was not one he himself ever subjected to critical analysis. If he had been taken up by National Socialism as Weinheber was, if Expressionism had become the literary doctrine of the new Germany, perhaps his development would have been different. Instead he found himself despised by the Nazis as an un-German formalist and intellectual. From 1 July 1937 onwards he was in the War Ministry, wryly observing Hitler's preparations for war. He had taken the 'aristocratic form of emigration' into the army.

Fascist theatre did not have to wait till 1933 to reach the stage in Germany. On 30 January 1932, exactly one year before the take-over, a play by the Duce Benito Mussolini, put together with some help from the professional writer Giovacchino Forzano, had its première in the German National Theatre in Weimar.[14] The fact that it was first put on in Weimar was no coincidence. The performance in the place where thirteen years before the Weimar Constitution had been ratified was intended to act as a deliberate provocation to the republican state and to demonstrate the strength of the national movement. Thuringia had since the end of 1929 been under NSDAP rule and the theatre director Franz Ulbrich was also trying to make his name with a theatre appropriate to the government which controlled the region. So the production of Mussolini's Napoleon drama *A Hundred Days* was a grand theatrical occasion, before an auditorium adorned with swastikas. Adolf Hitler was present and with him Italian diplomats, members of the Berlin Embassy, the Dresden Consul General, reporters from all the major European newspapers and theatre directors from London, Frankfurt and Leipzig who were also planning productions in the near future. Also present was Elisabeth Förster-Nietzsche, a lively old lady of biblical age responsible for concocting the *Will to Power*. The whole period of the Wars of Liberation was a favourite with National Socialist authors, though it was not customary in Germany to show the foreign invader as the hero. Nevertheless this audience could appreciate the evident attack on parliamentary democracy and the case being made for a leader with dictatorial, Caesarian powers. The most successful scene, however, was the one in which the defeated French stood before Blücher. This reminder of Germany's great past and the hope it gave a defeated Germany of glories to come brought the audience to its feet. The play was later performed in London in 'an adaptation for the English Stage' by John Drinkwater. The review in *The Times* of 19 April 1932 was highly favourable, though there is no mention of fervent acclaim.

In a manner which was to become familiar in National Socialist Germany a film was made of this successful theatre production with Werner Krauss in the leading role as Napoleon. The leader is the man of destiny who has no desire for war. Indeed he offers the crowned heads of Europe peace, but when he is forced to fight he does so. When he loses the battle of Waterloo (owing to another's incompetence), he asks parliament for 'extraordinary powers of absolute rule for a fixed period for the purpose of saving the nation'.[15] The leader also demands absolute loyalty and is prepared to allow a whole generation to go to its death if necessary. His sacred mission is to break up the little states of Europe, and bring all nations together into one great community. This is how he would bring peace! As with so many National Socialist plays and films the scenario was to prove incredibly close to reality, for like the Napoleon of the film Hitler was to unite Europe under German hegemony and bring death and destruction to many countries besides Germany before his ultimate defeat.

A recent volume on Expressionism described Bronnen as the 'Judas of the self-betrayal immanent in the movement'. All the most dubious and dangerous tendencies, it is claimed, were unleashed by Bronnen and put on the stage. Expressionism turned to exhibitionism, pathos to rhetoric, the revolutionary turned provocateur, the programme became propaganda. The same latent fears about Expressionism might equally well be expressed about Hanns Johst, whose play *Schlageter* (1933) marked the end of that same development from Expressionism to National Socialism, and from the historical treatment of military heroes of the past to the realistic treatment of fascist heroes of the present. In his commentary on Johst's play Günther Rühle describes the 'Schlageter Case' as one of the 'most neuralgic events of the Weimar Republic'.[16] Hitler himself had singled out Schlageter as a hero on the second page of *Mein Kampf* and Johst had been interested in the affair since 1923, but did not start to write the play until 1929 under the influence of the widespread Schlageter memorial services. At that time Johst was also influenced by his reading of Mœller van den Bruck's *The Prussian Style*. The final version of the play was completed before the foundation of the Third Reich, but Johst's publisher advised against publication during the Weimar Republic, fearing that it would be banned, and it did not appear in print until after the seizure of power. Because of Hitler's known interest, both in Johst's work and in Schlageter, it was not surprising that he asked that Johst's play be dedicated to him, which it was 'in loving devotion and unwavering fidelity'. The première took place on 20 April 1933 in the Staatliches Schauspielhaus, Berlin, for Hitler's first birthday as Chancellor, and almost exactly ten years after the execution of Schlageter by the French at four o'clock on the morning of 26 May 1923 on the Golzheimer Heide outside Düsseldorf. The National Socialists had taken over the reins of government only a short time before on 30 January 1933. They also took over control of the theatre with remarkable speed. On 4 February 1933 Johst was given a position with the National Theatre together with Franz Ulbrich, who put on

Schlageter as his first production. The theatrical overlord for Prussia was the new Minister President Hermann Goering. In this first patriotic, national drama Albert Bassermann played the part of the general, Veit Harlan that of Friedrich Thiemann, while the daughter Alexandra was played by Emmy Sonnemann, whom Goering later married. The performance of the play was clearly intended as deliberate opposition to the 'decadence' of the Weimar Theatre. Present at the first performance, in addition to prominent National Socialists like Dr Goebbels and State Commissar Hinkel, were invited representatives of the new literary cadre, which had taken over from the rejected intellectuals of the Weimar Republic, men of the stature of Emil Strauss and Peter Dörfler, Will Vesper and Hans Friederich Blunck, Wilhelm Schäfer, Jakob Schaffner and Magnus Wehner. At the end of the performance there was no applause: instead, after a brief silence, the audience rose as one man to sing the first verse of 'Deutschland, Deutschland über alles', followed by the first verse of the Horst Wessel song. Only then did an explosion of applause come, forcing author and actors to take curtain-call after curtain-call, which they did giving the new Nazi salute. This was clearly more than just a theatrical success, it was a national event. *Schlageter* became compulsory school reading and went on to be performed throughout the land, although for party political reasons it was taken out of the repertoire as quickly as it had been taken up. Plays of this kind dealing with the real history of the early Nazi movement could too easily come into conflict with the requirements of day-to-day party politics. By the end of 1933 the whole question of the occupation of the Ruhr was once again a particularly delicate one because of the diplomatic and political manoeuvring between Nazi Germany and France; and so a work like *Schlageter*, dealing with real people and real problems, had to be dropped in favour of the cloudier mysticism of the *Thing* play. Plays of that kind, however, did not appeal to Johst and he did not attempt them. *Schlageter* was the last play he wrote, and by the end of the same year, he had left his post in the State Theatre after internal squabbles, to become President of the Reichsschrifttumskammer, President of the Deutsche Akademie der Dichtung, Reich Culture Senator and first holder of the NSDAP prize for Art and Science. His career henceforth was to be that of the highest cultural official in the National Socialist hierarchy and not that of a dramatist or writer.

At first sight the figure of Albert Leo Schlageter does not seem to possess the qualities which go to make a great national hero. As Weiskopf put it: 'The real life Horst Wessel was a hooligan and pimp, only in later legend was he transformed into a lofty figure of pure light. The same applies to Leo Schlageter.'[17] After an army career as an artillery officer he took part in various Freikorps activities as a member of the 'Heinz Organisation', one of those bands of soldiers who had grown accustomed to war and could not stop fighting, either against the 'external enemy' in the Baltic and Upper Silesia, or against the 'inner enemy' whenever revolting workers needed to be shot down during 1921-2. He took part in acts of sabotage against the French, as leader of the 'Essen Group' blew up a railway bridge killing some French soldiers, was captured by the French, tried before a military court and executed for spying and sabotage. There seems to have been no doubt that there was treachery and betrayal among the German group, indeed Schlageter may not only have been betrayed by his own comrades, he almost certainly betrayed them in an attempt to save his own skin. Needless to say, treachery is only tangentially a subject for discussion in the play. In fact it is quite clear from reactions at the time that all sides in the Weimar Republic needed a 'national' hero and, despite the unpromising nature of the human material, Schlageter had to serve. The Weimar Republic was even exposed to an incredible alliance between Communists and right-wing Nationalists, when Radek praised the nationalist martyr in a speech, and thus initiated the so-called Schlageter Policy, bringing Communists and Nationalists together to make common cause in their fight against the French. Political confusion and party expediency were commonplace features of the Weimar Republic, but no greater confusion could have been caused than by the spectacle of 'the strange phenomenon of Communists and Nationalists sharing the same platform, writing in the same newspapers, and even conceding some merit to each other'.[18] What Radek was attempting to do was to react realistically to the confusion in the minds of workers, caused by the appeal of nationalism as a solution for economic and political problems. That it was not only simple work-people, or unscrupulous Communist politicians, who were prepared to see in Schlageter some kind of national saviour, can be deduced from the manner in which one of the greatest thinkers of the age, Professor Martin Heidegger, Rector of the University of Freiburg, addressed the Schlageter memorial service at his university on 26 May 1933, ten years after the execution. From this and other such rhapsodic eulogies one begins to appreciate some of the reasons why Schlageter became a mythic hero in his own time. The particular event with which Schlageter's name is associated was the occupation of the Ruhr valley in the spring of 1923, bringing French troops, some of them coloured, to the sacred German soil. In response the republican government advocated passive resistance, while Schlageter's nationalist group took more drastic action. His lonely death was linked by the author with the rise of National Socialism and a 'new beginning' for the German people.

> Using a known historical figure of the recent past, Johst successfully dramatises the struggle of the Nazi party's fight for power. He brings this struggle to life and effectively preaches the message that the Nazis had preached so loudly and often so violently since the beginning of the movement. The beliefs and spirits which motivated these men find dramatic expression in this play.[19]

Johst himself describes his play as a *Schauspiel*, indicating perhaps that, despite the death of the hero, the mood is not tragic; on the contrary the open ending, engaging the audience as it does, was clearly intended to suggest a greater and more glorious future. The play is set in the post-war period in a largely middle-class setting of domestic interior in which university, politics and army are represented, but workers, foreigners and others are excluded. There are no judges or court officials, and Schlageter's trial is not dealt with. Any conflict in the play will be shown as existing *within* the German republic itself, and not as resulting from any external enemy. In the first scene Schlageter, the returned soldier, is presented as a student, his speaking manner is *'sachlich'* in the characteristic post-Expressionist style of the Weimar Republic, his language is the slang of the soldier-student and accordingly witty, snappy and anti-literary. Significantly, Schlageter is attempting to study book-keeping and economics, subjects exposed as deeply suspect, if not indeed ultimately responsible for Germany's present parlous state of affairs. His comrade, Friedrich Thiemann, flier and professor's son, puts the anti-intellectual case, speaking with the words which were felt to be so revealing for the National Socialist mentality that they were thereafter variously attributed to different political leaders: 'Whenever I hear the word "culture" I reach for my revolver.'[20] Thiemann in fact rejects not only culture, but all abstract concepts, especially ideas like liberty, equality and fraternity. Taking their place will be a combination of blood, *Volk* and sacrifice. In the end it is Schlageter, 'the first soldier of the Third Reich,' who makes the supreme sacrifice for his beloved Fatherland. The final visionary scene reveals the symbolic stance of Schlageter, bound with his hands on his back 'as if with the whole world on his shoulders'. Light effects are added to sound effects to reinforce the impact, as Schlageter, with his back to the audience, cries:

> Germany!
> One last word! One wish! Command!
> Germany!!!
> Awake! Burst into flames!!!
> Ignite! Burn furiously!

Johst has left the realm of normal prose behind and the punctuation indicates the expressionistic nature of this ecstatic utterance. Schlageter's last words are more than a wish: they are an order. Meanwhile the fire that he tries to ignite in Germany is matched by the order to fire which is given by the commander of the firing squad. Again significantly and symbolically, the flash from the guns passes through Schlageter's heart into the darkness of the theatre, to be reflected and picked up by the audience. What appears to end in triumph for those who have brought about the death of Schlageter will lead to the ultimate triumph for Germany herself, when as a result of Schlageter's sacrifice she does awaken!

From this description of the conclusion of Johst's play some idea of his artistic intentions can be deduced. Johst developed a theory of the open end, making the audience an integral part of the whole. According to this theory members of the audience would abandon their distanced position as mere observers of events on the stage and would become actively involved in the action, in a manner which is the exact opposite of Brecht's later theory of alienation. But as can be seen, this does not mean that the play culminates in the proclamation of party-political slogans or direct references to specific causes: it will not be a crude work of propaganda of that type. Instead the theatre, by its formal quality, should offer an emotional event appealing not to reason or logic, but to 'deeper' spiritual realms and releasing energies for action. The play becomes an 'experience' transmitting the hero's attitudes to the audience:

> The theatre we want has to be a theatre of experience. Only then can it be more than a mere pantomime, dancing and acting on the stage. Only then can it be elevated formally into a truly cultic expression of mass feeling.[21]

The question still remains regarding the extent to which Johst was expressing deeply held beliefs. F.C. Weiskopf has doubted this:

> He is an opportunist through and through, though that is exactly
> what makes him capable of producing literature which, faithful to
> national-socialist basic principles, places feeling above reason, clouds
> of words above clear concepts, the blood above intellectual
> perception.[22]

This kind of reaction is understandable, but it is perhaps unjust, for there is little doubt that Johst did believe in what he was doing. As his confessional work *I Believe* indicates, he did try to work out a consistent theory of theatre as cult, community and national experience, and his development over the years does show him going back from his own expressionistic beginnings to the Greeks, Storm and Stress drama and Kleist, in order to build up a consistent though conservative 'ethos of restraint', culminating in heroic, mythologising drama of the *Schlageter* type. In effect, however, what he was trying to do proved impossible. He attempted to go beyond Naturalism to create larger-than-life drama, yet his play is a curious mixture of naturalistic dialogue and symbolic intention. He tried to go beyond reason to myth, yet his whole play, while denying logic, is built up of one discussion scene after another. He tried to create drama which would culminate in the metaphysical act, yet his play is a denunciation of all culture and all theory. Johst accused the theatre of the Weimar Republic of cultural Bolshevism in its neglect of the hero, yet in his own traditionally constructed, four-act play, he failed to create a traditional hero, who arrives at insight into his own fate and acts in a convincing manner. On the contrary Schlageter is strangely passive:

> One thing has to be established right from the start; Johst's
> Schlageter figure offers no genuine dramatic hero. For that (and
> one cannot help being reminded of *Florian Geyer* from last night's
> Volksbühne production) it is too passive in conception. In this play
> too the real action is moved outside the play itself, and what we
> experience is just emotional and intellectual discharges.[23]

What remains is far being being a great play (even National Socialist critics were aware of its many weaknesses), yet it is representative in many ways, not only of the fact that some Expressionists did move from left to right, from pacifism to adulation of the front-line soldier, but also of the ways in which the apolitical aspirations of Expressionist intellectuals for sacrifice and belonging could be perverted by the frustrations of the Weimar Republic into cultural suicide. This play is revealing as a document of German history at that time, one which through the literary context in which it stands unfortunately also indicates the tradition of idealistic thinking National Socialism could draw on, twisting and shrivelling it into something totally its opposite.[24]

PART TWO

1933-1945 — INSIDE GERMANY

4 GERMANY AWAKENS

Of all the 'cultural' acts associated with National Socialism, none evoked a more immediate or more negative response throughout the world than the Burning of the Books on 10 May 1933. Romain Rolland, the French winner of the Nobel Prize for Literature, wrote an open letter to the *Kölner Zeitung*, as an admirer of German culture and idealism, to denounce as childish what the German authorities themselves called an *auto-da-fé*. Rudolf G. Binding replied with a letter entitled 'A German's Answer to the World'. In London H.G. Wells presided over a Society of Friends of the Burned Books, and in Paris a German Freedom Library for Burned Books was set up. This attempt to eradicate the 'un-German spirit' was felt to be symptomatic of a barbaric new regime, for it was quickly recognised, following Heine's famous words in *Almansor*, that it was but a small step from burning books to burning people. The identical ritual observed at all universities and the use of the term *auto-da-fé* was clearly intended as a reminder of the Burning of Books by the Inquisition in Madrid in 1634. At the same time there were also reminders of Luther's burning of the papal bull; indeed the ceremonial posting of twelve theses 'Against the un-German Spirit', planned for 12 April, also seemed deliberately modelled on Luther's historic precedent. The student context pointed to another 'burning' incident in German intellectual history, namely the Wartburg Festival of 1817. But of course the banning of books and the elimination of intellectual opposition was no new development for Germany. In the Weimar Republic certain writers and groups considered undesirable by the Establishment were subjected to considerable harassment and there had been many famous test cases against left-wingers and pacifists, particularly on charges of *lèse-majesté*, espionage (for publishing the true facts about German rearmament and re-militarisation) and pornography. The difference now was the stringent, sweeping and racist manner in which *all* opposition was eliminated. As soon as Hitler was appointed Chancellor on 30 January 1933 laws had been quickly passed which initiated the first steps towards total control over literary output. The Law of 28 February for the Protection of the Nation effectively abolished all constitutional rights, and specifically forbade all Marxist writings, arranging for their removal from bookshops and libraries. However, the Law for the Establishment of the Reich Cultural Chamber and the Law for the Protection of German Blood and German Honour, which were ultimately to ban outright all Jewish authors and their writings and bring all other writers, publishers, booksellers and librarians under state control, were not to be enacted until September 1933. What was needed at this stage, in addition to bureaucratic measures, was some more public demonstration which would permit the extension of National Socialist control over literature, while preserving some semblance of legality. A 'spontaneous' expression of the people's will was what was required. What the people demanded, namely the elimination of un-German writings, could then be retrospectively legalised by the executive. This was exactly what was arranged. Despite its apparently spontaneous nature the action was far from unplanned and improvised. German universities of the Weimar Republic were a fertile breeding ground for nationalistic, reactionary beliefs:

> The younger generation found völkisch philosophy 'youthful' and more modern than the national liberal ideology. To them it was revolutionary tempered with social moderation; in no way could it be regarded as 'bourgeois' in the derogatory meaning of the word, implying stuffy, narrow-minded, materialistic — moderation and reason in politics were rejected.[1]

This particular 'action' was carried out by the Deutsche Studentenschaft, an organisation which from its foundation in 1919 had been anti-Semitic and reactionary.[2] A special office for press and propaganda concerted things in universities around the country through a series of circulars which used explicitly Nazi language. The action called for was a *Säuberung*, a Nazi euphemism meaning everything from clearing out to elimination. The prime target was specifically Jewish and 'corrosive' writing, the aim was control by removal, burning and blacklisting. There was clearly also intended to be a close link between the burning of 'undesirable' and 'harmful' literature, and the indoctrination of the universities along fascist lines, including the removal of uncooperative teaching staff, especially if they were Jews. The movement thus prepared over the period from 12 April till 10 May 1933 was described publicly as a campaign of enlightenment. Needless to say it also claimed to be merely reacting against the Jewish spirit, which was said to have unleashed a wave of unspeakable horror stories about the new Germany. It was to become a common Nazi ploy to denounce the truth (especially if it came from outside Germany) as 'horror stories'.

This is what the student officers did, claiming that their response to such stories could not be confined to a silent protest, but must take the form of action directing thought and attention to those fundamental German values being undermined by Jewish contamination. This 'action' would involve not merely a pyre on which certain books would be burned, but also twelve theses which the students would nail up. In the event the idea of having such a 'pillar of shame' at every university in addition to a bonfire came to nothing, and the nailing of the theses became a symbolic reading. On examination not all of these twelve theses are equally significant, some indeed are almost meaningless, but the general thrust of the list is clear. Literature was to be exclusively German and this meant the total exclusion of all foreign elements, especially Jewish. Intellectualism and liberal decadence were denounced and in addition universities were to be the exclusive preserve of German students and German staff. Thesis number seven contained the important point for future action, namely that un-German books be removed from libraries and bookshops. Some time before the ceremonial burning, lists began to appear in newspapers and elsewhere of books deserving to be burned according to these criteria. That these lists were hastily conceived is clear from the faulty spellings of authors' names and gaps and outright mistakes, but they do make the targets even clearer: not only all writers who were known to be Jewish or had Jewish connections, but also anybody with any pacifist or pro-Bolshevist associations. The existence of such blacklists immediately called forth the opposite, namely white lists, since booksellers and librarians (not to mention authors themselves) needed to know whether they were approved of or not. The organisation of the ceremony may have been well planned, but from what actually happened it is clear that far from sufficient thought had been given to criteria for inclusion in the list of books for burning. Still the *auto-da-fé* was supposed to be a spontaneous action and it would have been wrong to have too carefully prepared lists before the event. These could be worked out more thoroughly by the bureaucratic machinery after the will of the people had been brought to explosion point.

The spontaneous action now took its course. For days after 26 April 1933 the newspapers started to report that students were confiscating books from bookshops and libraries. In some cases, to make sure that there would be no resistance, they presented themselves in these places in SA uniform. Then on 10 May 1933 in all university cities, students, professors and a large public gathered for the official ceremony, undeterred by the rain. Books were brought in for burning, in Berlin in furniture vans, in Frankfurt in ox carts. According to newspaper reports the Berlin book-burning was a particularly jolly and festive occasion. In most places students, professors and party officials addressed the gathering. In Berlin Alfred Bäumler, the first Nazi professor of political education, proceeded straight from his inaugural lecture to the event with a large body of students following. In Bonn Rust, the Nazi Minister of Culture, was followed by Hans Naumann,[3] a professor of German literature, who addressed the crowd, while in Göttingen the crowd was harangued by the newly elected Rector and by Gerhard Fricke, also a specialist in German literature. Most other universities had similar speeches and speakers. That the event itself was well rehearsed can be seen from the way in which the spontaneous event was given dramatic, rhetorical form. During the burning of the books SA and SS bands played German folk songs and marches, until nine student representatives, who had been allocated works according to nine separate categories, committed the books to the flames with the stirring words:

First Speaker.	Against class struggle and materialism, For Volk community and Idealism! I commit to the flames the works of Marx and Kautsky!
Second Speaker.	Against decadence and moral decay For discipline and morality in family and state! I commit to the flames the works of Heinrich Mann, Ernst Glaeser and Erich Kästner.
Third Speaker.	Against political irresponsibility and political betrayal. For dedication to Volk and State! I commit to the flames the works of the pacifist Friedrich Wilhelm Foerster.
Fourth Speaker.	Against the exaggeration of unconscious urges based on destructive analysis of the psyche. For the nobility of the human soul. I commit to the flames the works of Sigmund Freud.
Fifth Speaker.	Against falsification of our history and denigration of its great figures.

	For respect of our past!
	I commit to the flames the writings of Emil Ludwig and Werner Hegemann.
Sixth Speaker.	Against un-German journalism of a Jewish, democratic kind.
	For responsible cooperation in the work of national reconstruction!
	I commit to the flames the works of Theodor Wolff and Georg Bernhard.
Seventh Speaker.	Against literary betrayal of the soldiers of the First World War.
	For the education of the people in the spirit of truthfulness!
	I commit to the flames the works of Erich Maria Remarque.
Eighth Speaker.	Against conceited debasement of our German language.
	For the cultivation of the most precious property of the people!
	I commit to the flames the writings of Alfred Kerr.
Ninth Speaker.	Against impudence and presumptuousness.
	For awe and respect before our immortal German Volk spirit.
	Devour, flames, the writings of Tucholsky and Ossietsky.

The whole nation had to be made aware of the significance of this gesture and to this end radio, film, sound recordings and all the propaganda resources of the modern communications media were employed, so that those not actually present could hear over and over again the announcer's voice, the recitation of the authors' names, and the reason for the commitment of their books to the fire, the announcement of the Minister's speech, the rehearsed vocal choruses, the address by Dr Goebbels, the song 'People, to Arms', to stirring music by Arno Pardun. 'People, to Arms', contains the lines:

Many years dragged by with the people subjected and deceived.
Traitors and Jews had their profit, they demanded sacrifices in legion.
Born among the people a Leader emerged to lead us, gave us back
hope and faith in Germany. People to arms! For Hitler, for freedom,

for work, for bread. Germany awake! Death to Jewry! People to arms, people to arms.

When he stepped up to the microphone Goebbels said:

Fellow students, German men and women! The age of extreme Jewish intellectualism has now ended, and the success of the German revolution has again given the German spirit the right of way . . . You are doing the proper thing in committing the evil spirit of the past to the flames at this late hour of the night. This is a strong, great, symbolic act, an act that is to bear witness before all the world to the fact that the November Republic has disappeared. From these ashes there will arise the phoenix of a new spirit . . . The past is lying in flames. The future will rise from the flames within our hearts . . . Brightened by these flames our vow shall be: The Reich and the Nation and our Führer Adolf Hitler: Heil! Heil! Heil!

There seems to have been no internal German reaction against this symbolic destruction of 'un-German' literature and thought. Resistance was hardly possible given the might of the Nazi forces, and besides, the action was not only dramatically staged and orchestrated, it also demonstrated the usual Nazi mixture of the acceptable with the unacceptable. Who was not against decadence and moral decay? Who was not for discipline and morality in family and state? Who was not against political irresponsibility and betrayal? The national *Volk* community and idealism could be defensible goals against divisive class struggle. The heroic front-line soldier was often held up as the ideal against hated pacifism. Not surprisingly, nationalists like Hanns Johst saw absolutely nothing wrong with this kind of action. As he saw it, an event with the dimensions of the NS revolution could not stop short at the desks on which literature was produced; it was one of the most urgent tasks after the assumption of power that a radical shake-up of German literature take place to purge it of all undesirable elements. The purges he looked for did indeed take place. All reading-rooms belonging to the trade union movement and all public libraries were searched and all Socialist and Communist literature removed. The aim of the book-burning, according to Goebbels in his fiery speech at the *auto-da-fé*, was to demonstrate by a great symbolic gesture that the spiritual foundations of the November Republic had been destroyed. In his view the phoenix of a new spirit would rise victoriously out of the ruins showing that the new revolutionaries were not only great in destroying the old values, but also equally great in creating the new. Whether this was ever satisfactorily demonstrated remains to be seen. The immediate consequence was the appearance in the *Börsenblatt* of the first *official* blacklist of books to be rooted out of all libraries.[4] Other lists quickly followed covering the areas of politics, social sciences, history, et cetera, and these lists were regularly brought up to date. With its facility for creating vast bureaucratic organisations, the new National Socialist state then proceeded in time to deprive the German *Länder* of their traditional cultural sovereignty, to centralise control of literature and to make it assume the role of a weapon which would protect the Aryan race and strengthen national resilience. Department VIII (Propaganda Ministry), together with fifteen other departments, had already been set up on 13 March 1933 under the direct leadership of Dr Goebbels, and this was the only Cabinet Office controlling literature. It was by far the most powerful of all NS organisations in this field. The Reichsschrifttumskammer (RSK) was one of seven departments of the Reich Culture Chamber (RKK), the others being concerned with other cultural manifestations like music. The RKK was set up by Goebbels in November 1933 and had the function of controlling the various professions involved in the production of culture. In effect it meant that everybody had to be a member of one of the chambers, otherwise it was not possible or permissible for that person to practise his or her craft. Goebbels had been given direct orders from Hitler to set up the RKK in order to place all cultural activities at the service of the nation, thereby giving the artist a directly political task. All Jews were automatically excluded from membership. The professional organisation of the book trade — Börsenverein für den deutschen Buchhandel — was forced to join the RSK, as was the Reich Association of German Writers. Yet another state organisation supervising literature was the Department of Public Libraries. In effect the regimentation of literature was completed in three phases:

(1)   the period of struggle prior to 1933 when racist Nazi writers fought democratic literature with chauvinistic and anti-Semitic slogans;

(2)   the period of purges and control machinery between 1933 and 1936;

(3)   the totally NS period after 1936.

As far as party organisations (as distinct from state bodies) were concerned, the most important was the Reichsstelle zur Förderung des deutschen Schrifttums. This Reich Centre for the Advancement of German Writing was the largest of all the state and party organisations and at times was in direct competition with Goebbels' Propaganda Ministry. The foundations of this organisation were laid during the time of the Weimar Republic when the Fighters for German Culture strove to bring about what seemed a supra-party coalition of anti-modern, anti-intellectual and anti-democratic forces. Founded in 1929, it was led by Alfred Rosenberg, who gathered under his leadership NS artists and writers, journalists and scholars, as well as well known personalities from various camps in the cultural life of Germany like the *Heimatkunst* movement, the Nationalists, the ultra-conservatives and the pan-German racists. The aims of the original Fighters for German Culture were clearly laid down in the first paragraph of its statutes. This read:

> in the midst of the current cultural decline, the Fighting Union for German Culture has as its goal to defend these values which are essentially German and to promote each and every ethnic expression of German cultural life. It is also the aim of the Fighting Union to enlighten the German people about connections between race, culture and science, and about moral and intellectual values.

Rosenberg was to make his name with the publication in 1930 of his *Myth of the Twentieth Century*, yet his influence was also to decline steadily in cultural matters the more Goebbels' star ascended.[5] During the first stages of the establishment of the Rosenberg Centre, however, he was the master of a mammoth body with thirty-eight separate departments employing a vast number of qualified staff. Generally speaking, between 1933 and 1945 no book could be published in Germany which had not been checked by Rosenberg's experts. This fact should be kept in mind when there is any discussion regarding literary resistance and inner emigration. At the same time it should be remembered that after the initial stages of suppression or exclusion of rivals and opponents of the regime, the purpose of this official machinery was not merely to muzzle literature and reject what was undesirable, it was also to *promote* literature. Rosenberg was a notorious Jew-hater, who detested what he felt to be decadent big-city literature; on the other hand he was also committed to giving the full support of his organisation to literary works of a traditional German kind.

In addition to the Rosenberg Centre, the Parteiamtliche Prüfungs-kommission (PPK) must be named. This Party Supervisory Commission was rather different in function. Rosenberg's organisation was supposed to promote literature. This latter body, under the direction of Reichsleiter Bouhler, had the task of compiling the party index. What it had to do was check the party's philosophical and political publications in order to eliminate any misconceptions regarding the ideology. In addition it had to compile an NS bibliography, check all academic publications, and check all schoolbooks with a view to making sure that the NS ideology was properly and forcefully enough presented. All NS bodies were subject to in-fighting and it is not surprising to see Bouhler and the PPK attaching themselves ever more closely to Goebbels and gaining in significance as Rosenberg's star waned.[6] Of the many other bodies dealing with literature in the NS state none could compare in power with the organisations of Goebbels, Rosenberg and Bouhler, though they all served specific purposes in the network of party and ideological control, like the specialist bodies controlling books for the Reich Youth Organisation, the NS Teachers Organisation, et cetera. The aim of the whole process was *Gleichschaltung*, or as Hitler put it in *Mein Kampf*: 'Every idea and every thought, every theory and all knowledge must serve this one purpose. In this light everything has to be checked, and used according to this purpose.' This was achieved by every method possible, by forcing everybody to be a member of the RSK, by banning unwanted writers, by pre-censorship, by post-censorship, by regulating paper supplies, by import and export regulations, by controlling publishing houses, by indexing prohibited and permitted books, by propaganda and publicity, by banning all criticism and so on. Writers, publishers, booksellers, librarians were all subject to the same strict control. The creative writer in particular was a notoriously elusive and unreliable figure who had to be made aware, by force if necessary, of his role in the new society. Hitler himself, as *Mein Kampf* revealed, was the first artist of the Third Reich, and like him the new writer had to be educator and warrior, propagandist and preserver of the new faith. Writers were urged to be front-line fighters of the new Reich, soldiers of the mind. The break with the past was to be complete: Germany was to be no longer the harmless land of poets and thinkers, but the land that could fend for itself. The first task was to remove Jews and Jewish sympathisers and all the cosmopolitan cultural Bolshevists. Hitler also denounced the representatives of the old Germany he disapproved of as charlatans, madmen, artistic scribblers, dwarfs and stammerers, while Rosenberg vituperated against them as artistic mestizos, intellectual syphilitics and bastard drug addicts. Once these rootless modernists, repulsive parasites, political turn-coats and opportunists had been removed, the path would be free for the new literature appropriate to the new Germany. Decadent foreigners could claim on the basis of what was done to writers in Germany and the public burning of the books that the new Germany was barbaric; in reply the new state did everything to demonstrate that it was far more of a patron of the arts than any previous state had ever been. Books were promoted by means of prizes and conferences; a National Book and Film Prize was set up by Goebbels' Ministry, a National Prize for Arts and Sciences was even established by Hitler personally. Promotion of books reached a climax during the Week of the German Book, at the Berlin Book Weeks, and during the Writers' Days in Weimar. It is, however, not surprising that few people then or since have been convinced by this outward show and the general belief has gained hold that between 1933 and 1945 absolutely nothing of literary value was produced or could have been produced inside Germany. Ernst Loewy puts it like this: 'There has hardly ever been a type of literature with such blatant ideological overtones as that of the NS period . . . The characters are mere mouth-pieces of the spirit of the times.' It is this contention that we must now examine, looking not only for literary quality, but also at the possible appeal of NS literary works for NS followers and believers. The assumption is that there were real Nazis who genuinely believed in Hitler and in the party. If there were such true believers, what did they write? And what did the true believers read and enjoy?[7]

The age of Expressionism was an age of poetry. Little magazines seemed to appear overnight and with them poets from all parts of Germany, eager to enjoy the new freedom of the post-war period and publish their poetry. Much of it was ecstatic, formless nonsense; some of it was extremely formalistic and difficult; but from all quarters great poets emerged. It is easy to assume that this literary flowering also died with the Weimar Republic in 1933. Nothing could be further from the truth. The arrival of the new regime was proclaimed by its leaders as the beginning of a new age of poetry. A new kind of poet would be called for, who would sweep away the false, in-comprehensible poetry of the previous decade and proclaim a new unity between poet and people. And the new poets did announce themselves in great numbers and burst into print, and into song. Where is this mass of material? Has it all completely disappeared without trace and was it all the worthless expression of a false philosophy in the first place? Not surprisingly after the horrors of the Nazi period examples of real Nazi poetry are no longer readily available and it is only with difficulty that a general impression can be formed of it.[8] The natural expectation is that it was all kitsch, that Nazi poems were cheap imitations of traditional folk song or nature poetry, combining Blood and Soil longings with brutality and sentimentality. Hermann Glaser gives one sample of such horrific lyrics in his survey of Nazi culture:

Wetzt die langen Messer
auf dem Bürgersteig!
Lasst die Messer flutschen
in den Judenleib.
Blut muss fliessen knüppelhageldick,
wir scheissen auf die Freiheit der Judenrepublik.
Kommt einst die Stunde der Vergeltung,
sind wir zu jedem Massenmord bereit.

Hoch die Hohenzollern
am Laternenpfahl!
Lasst die Hunde baumeln,
bis sie runterfalln!
Blut muss fliessen . . .

In der Synagoge
hängt ein schwarzes Schwein.
In die Parlamente
schmeisst die Handgranate rein!
Blut muss fliessen . . .

Reisst die Konkubine
aus dem Fürstenbett,
schmiert die Guillotine
mit dem Judenfett.
Blut muss fliessen . . .[9]

(Sharpen the long knives on the kerb-stones! Let them sink into the Jews' bodies. Blood must flow thick and fast, we don't give a shit for the Jewish Republic's freedom. When the time comes to pay off old scores, we'll be ready for any mass murder. Up the Hohenzollerns, from the lamp-post! Let the dogs dangle till they drop. Blood must flow . . . A black pig hangs in the synagogue. Chuck a hand-grenade

into the parliament buildings! Blood must flow . . .
Tear the concubines from the princely bed, grease the guillotine with
the fat of Jews. Blood must flow . . .)

In fact such verses give a false impression, however direct their
expression of National Socialist anti-Semitism, contempt for elected
delegates and dislike of reactionaries. After all, the lyric was considered
as a cultural weapon in the formation of a mass political party, and
this kind of poetry was far more likely to repel than attract. An audience
had to be reached by much more noble sentiments. Hitler himself
could be put forward as the model. His most famous saying, 'Unsere
Jugend soll sein, zäh wie Leder, hart wie Kruppstahl, flink wie
Windhunde!' ('Our Youth has to be tough as leather, hard as Krupp
steel, fast as greyhounds'), was only one of his pithy and much quoted
sayings. This particular quotation became the slogan for the Hitler
Youth. Even his prose was turned into Hölderlin-like verse. But
according to Orlowski[10] all the basic ingredients of NS poetry were
already contained in the poem 'Deutschland erwache!' by Dietrich
Eckart, the poet whom Hitler admired so much, who was the founder
of the anti-Semitic paper *Auf gut Deutsch*, the first editor of the
Völkischer Beobachter and the man to whom Hitler dedicated his
Mein Kampf:

Deutschland erwache!
Sturm, Sturm, Sturm, Sturm, Sturm, Sturm!
Läutet die Glocken von Turm zu Turm!
Läutet, dass Funken zu sprühen beginnen,
Judas erscheint, das Reich zu gewinnen;
läutet, dass blutig die Seile sich röten,
rings lauter Brennen und Martern und Töten,
läutet Sturm, dass die Erde sich bäumt,
unter dem Donner der rettenden Rache!
Wehe dem Volk, das heute noch träumt!
Deutschland erwache!
Sturm, Sturm, Sturm, Sturm, Sturm, Sturm!
Läutet die Glocken von Turm zu Turm!
Läutet die Männer, die Greise, die Buben,
läutet die Schläfer aus ihren Stuben,
läutet die Mädchen herunter die Stiegen,
läutet die Mütter hinweg von den Wiegen,
dröhnen soll sie und gellen die Luft,

rasen, rasen im Donner der Rache,
läutet die Toten aus ihrer Gruft!
Deutschland erwache![11]

(Germany awaken!
Storm, storm, storm, storm, storm, storm! Sound the bells from
tower to tower! Ring till the sparks start to fly, Judas is coming
to take over the Reich; ring till the ropes go red, all around
nothing but burning and torture and killing, sound the storm-bells,
till the earth heaves, under the thunder of the vengeance that
saves! Woe betide the people still dreaming today! Awaken
Germany! Storm, storm, storm, storm, storm, storm! Sound the
bells from tower to tower! Ring out the young men, old men and
boys, ring out the sleepers from their rooms, ring the girls down the
steps, ring the mothers away from the cradles, the air must hum
and scream, rage, rage in vengeance's thunder, ring out the dead
from their tombs. Awaken Germany!)

Here again, it is easy to dismiss such poetry as epigonal imitation of
antiquated nineteenth-century models or as mere versification of an
ideology; but this is to overlook much of the intention and the impact
of the verse. It was not for nothing that Goering recited these lines in
the Reichstag by way of introduction to the debate on the Enabling
Law that was to give the NS party total power over the country; and
he made everybody stand while he did so. The listener so solemnly
addressed was being invited to join up with the great movement, to
abandon his liberal individualism and unite with the totality. It is
noticeable too that no specific occasion is mentioned in the poem.
There is no recognisable historical moment — instead, everything is
generalised. It is not clear at all why the storm bells have to be sounded,
why Germany has been slumbering, or who the enemy is that threatens
the homeland, though the reference to Judas does suggest who the
foreign foe might be. *Sturm* was the title of a famous Expressionist
journal, but this poem is far removed from Expressionism, despite the
exclamatory nature of the diction and the multiplicity of exclamation
marks. By contrast with that of the Expressionist poet, the imagery is
also extremely limited and traditional, while the metre is regular and
predictable, though it is 'markig' and 'zackig', in a stirring, staccato
manner, consistent with the theme of the poem. The rhyming couplets
are also predictable and somehow familiar. Indeed the familiarity of
the rhymes gives the clue to the poem's literary sources, for the

rhymes Wache and Rache act almost as a deliberate quotation from and pointer to the period of German political and poetic history singled out for favour by the new movement, namely the age of national upheaval during the Wars of Liberation 1811-13. In 1812 Arndt wrote his 'Song of the Fatherland', and in his 'Oath of Allegiance to the Flag' he also expressed similar sentiments, in almost identical words. But it was Theodor Körner who took over the same formula and turned the sentiment into an imperative, *commanding* Germany to awake and fight the foreign foe, France. Eckart was not being a mere epigone, he was deliberately and consciously evoking cultural and political echoes with these words. The ideological intention of his poem is also quite clear. A great deal of noise is necessary to stir the sleeping German giant because the Reich has allowed itself to be surrounded, and now on all sides can be seen 'burning and torturing and killing'. The situation is basically that of Löns' *Wehrwolf*—determined action is called for, the Reich can only be saved if all levels of society unite as one—young and old, men and women, boys and girls. Why a call to save the nation from an encircling enemy should also be linked with revenge is not made clear in the poem. In the earlier poems by Arndt the need for vengeance was explained by the justness of the cause, but now all such rational explanations have faded, leaving only feelings of resentment and aggression. Indeed the last lines of the poem become extremely violent, culminating in madness, as a kind of *furor teutonicus* is invoked and even the dead warriors of former times are called up to wreak vengeance. Significantly, however, the poet makes it clear that despite such deliberate echoes of the past he is addressing himself to the Germany of his own day, which must no longer be a romantic land of dreamers. 'Woe betide the Volk which still dreams today!' Victory, or total defeat and destruction, are the alternatives normally envisaged in NS lyrics. These are what Ketelsen has called 'texts of the last hour'.[12] The feeling of urgency imparted is deliberate, the suggestion is that if Germany does not make the correct choice, it is doomed. These words, and many like them, were written before the party came to power, but even later (and especially in wartime) the same alternatives of victory or total defeat were to be endlessly repeated in Nazi poetry.

Nazi poetry of this kind is agitation-poetry. The aim is to call together all like-minded people into the national community. Over a whole range of lyrics from this period the words of the appeal stayed essentially the same, and sometimes whole lines were taken over from Eckart's poem into later poems. In this way the message throughout the mass of NS poetry remained immediately recognisable. Such poetry does not rely on originality and variation for effect: on the contrary the recipient must be made to feel at home in a complex of received ideas. Analysis and logical argument are avoided and instead the appeal is to basic emotions. No new solutions for real problems are offered. Instead the timid, whose resistance is to be broken down, have to have their faith in a Germany of the future strengthened. Germany, it is suggested, is in danger, yet despite everything the situation is not so hopeless as it seems. There is hope. No mention is made of economics or any such modern problems: all the complexities of the modern age can be solved by the simple step of joining the marching men and following the leader. Poetry of this kind is not for the lonely reader in his room, it is poetry of the street, of the mass demonstration, to be accompanied by flags, music and all the panoply of power. Worker or petty bourgeois can put on the same uniform as everybody else, and sing the same text to the same melody. He can submit to the 'Magic of Columns of Four', as the poem of Anacker invited him to do.[13] This is poetry of the 'we', not of the 'I', so the competitive spirit of the liberal bourgeois society is overcome and the isolated, lonely, helpless individual becomes part of the national community. Unity means strength—not the strength of one class of society or of one party, but of the whole nation.

The marching song suggests the discipline and control of a formation. This is the appeal of the most famous of all Nazi marching songs, the one which bears as its title the name of its author, the leader of the Fifth SA section in Berlin: Horst Wessel.

Die Fahne hoch! Die Reihen dicht geschlossen!
SA maschiert mit ruhig festem Schritt.
Kameraden, die Rotfront und Reaktion erschossen,
marschiern im Geist in unsern Reihen mit.

Die Strasse frei den braunen Bataillonen!
Die Strasse frei dem Sturmabteilungsmann!
Es schaun aufs Hakenkreuz voll Hoffnung schon Millionen.
Der Tag für Freiheit und für Brot bricht an.

Zum letzten Mal wird nun Appell geblasen!
Zum Kampfe stehen wir alle schon bereit.
Bald flattern Hitlerfahnen über allen Strassen.
Die Knechtschaft dauert nur noch kurze Zeit.[14]

(Hoist the flag! Close ranks right up!
The SA is marching in step, quiet and firm. The spirits of

comrades shot by the Red Front and by the reactionaries, are
marching alongside us.

Free the streets for the brown battalions! Free the streets
for the SA Man! Already millions filled with hope look to the
swastika. The day of freedom and bread is breaking.

For the last time assembly is sounding!
We all stand ready to fight. Soon Hitler flags will flutter over all
the streets. Serfdom will last but a short time longer.)

Horst Wessel, the twenty-two-year-old author of these lines, was
often compared with Körner. Brecht made the comparison extremely
ironically. According to him the two great national upheavals of
modern German history, that of 1813 and that of 1933, brought forth
two legendary heroes, two young men who were so alike in so many
ways. Both of them, Horst Wessel and Theodor Körner, were students,
both had middle-class parents, both were models of manly beauty.
They both composed political songs, which were very weak in literary
terms, but which exercised a powerful political effect. They both
fought, and they both fell in battle. This is as far as the similarities go,
for (as Brecht points out) the differences are also striking. Körner
fought against the French, while Horst Wessel was fighting his own
countrymen. Körner was fighting for a backward nation against a
progressive one, while Wessel fought for a reactionary class against a
revolutionary one. It is clear that Brecht the Communist could have
little sympathy for Horst Wessel the SA man, and he rounded off his
demythologising attack by including a parody of Wessel's famous
marching song in *Schweyk in the Second World War*:

Der Metzger ruft. Die Augen fest geschlossen
Das Kalb marschiert mit ruhig festem Tritt,
Die Kälber, deren Blut im Schlachthof schon geflossen
Sie ziehn im Geist in seinen Reihen mit.[15]

(The butcher calls. With eyes tightly closed
the calf marches with step quiet and firm.
The calves whose blood already fills the slaughter-house
march alongside him in spirit.)

Brecht was clearly quite correct in his assertion that Horst Wessel was
the deliberate creation of a Nazi legend by Goebbels and the propaganda

machine.[16] Nevertheless legends—even false ones—do have powers of survival, and the Horst Wessel Song and the legend surrounding its author are among the few quasi-literary survivals of the National Socialist period. Account has to be taken of this.

Horst Wessel's marching song is simple enough in itself. It has to be remembered that it was written around 1928, and therefore before Hitler came to power. It was also written long before the Röhm Putsch and the virtual elimination of the SA, at least as one of the power centres of a 'united' movement. The metre is steady, with regular pauses and with well marked, alternating rhymes. On the whole the Horst Wessel Song is not quite so loud as Eckart's 'Storm', which was noisy enough to make 'the earth rear up under the thunder of vengeance'. It has a steadier beat (and on certain ceremonial NS occasions was often played slowly, with full orchestral effects). Nevertheless a glance at the text shows that it is still exclamatory; the first line alone has two exclamation marks. This is more than a simple indication of the style: the exclamations are in fact also commands, as one would expect in a military-style formation. So the famous words 'Die Fahne hoch!' mean: '*raise* the flag!', the flag itself, as in so many NS poems, being the visible symbol for rallying the troops, but also for the formation of a community, excluding all conflict of interests. As Karl Kraus pointed out, there were no metaphors in poetry of this kind—they were all translated into reality. So, however banal they may appear on the page, they have to be imagined as actually happening, as indeed they did in countless NS demonstrations. Thousands of flags were raised aloft, thousands of marching men did close ranks, as the SA marched quietly but firmly, exuding discipline and control as well as quiet confidence. This was the appeal to the timid to join a mass movement.

As is customary in NS literature, the world is split into a simple friend-or-foe division. If you want to be a friend, then you join the ranks of the SA. The enemy is unusually clearly designated in the third line: Rotfront—that is to say the paramilitary organisation of the Communists. The inclusion of 'Reaktion' among the enemies of the SA also shows the early date of the poem. As has been seen, very early NS poetry did still reveal traces of its revolutionary origins, for example by calling for the Hohenzollerns to be strung up to the lampposts; and here the enemy in similar fashion seems to be located among the 'reactionaries' as well as with the Communists. The last lines of the first stanza echo the last lines of Eckart's poem. In the latter the dead were called up from the tomb, here the comrades who have been shot and killed in the fighting are understood to be heroes whose spirit lives on to help the living in their fight. How these heroes died is not explained. In fact they must have died, not in battle like Körner in 1813, but in the political street-fighting of the 1930s in Berlin. Somehow the impression is conveyed that they are all front-line fighters and must be honoured as such. The second stanza then mentions the streets which are to be cleared, though the repeated word 'free' is deliberately more evocative; freedom is invoked as one of the goals of the marching men in the last line, with the 'poetic' image of the dawn of a new day of freedom and bread. Freedom is not an idea normally associated with National Socialism. Here it presumably means freedom *from* something—freedom from Communism. Bread suggests not only that National Socialism will overcome the times of hardship and hunger, unemployment and economic crisis: in this poetic context it also gives the verses a religious aura.

Eckart's poem was described as one of the NS 'texts of the last hour'. This description applies equally well to the Horst Wessel Song, because the third stanza sees the roll-call being taken for the last time. Once again there is no explanation of any kind why this should be so, but it does add to the sense of urgency, calling upon the people to join the movement before it is too late. And it is here that the tone becomes even more solemn and prophetic with its vision of Hitler flags fluttering everywhere over all the streets. The comrades are ready for the final struggle, prepared to make the supreme sacrifice and they are going to be victorious. In the same way as freedom is about to dawn, so serfdom is about to come to an end. To the present-day reader this idea may seem contradictory, because he may well associate serfdom with the Nazi state itself, but as with freedom the poet is dealing with a two-edged concept and the word he has chosen (though perhaps deliberately archaic and therefore 'poetic') is indicative of the resentment of a defeated Germany, which was about to free itself from its oppressors. The last stanza is a repetition of the first and reinforces the feeling of circularity and encapsulation.

As Brecht put it in his Horst Wessel essay,[17] 120 years had passed since the Wars of Liberation and one of the problems for the propagandist in the modern age was to find a suitable hero. Difficulties arise not because the expectations of the petty bourgeois audience have grown any greater, but simply because the goods to be sold have shown a disturbing drop in quality. How the young hero dies is a difficult area for the myth-maker. This was not too great a problem 120 years before, because Körner had died in battle. Unfortunately Horst Wessel died as a result of a private affray. In fact at the time he was living with a prostitute in rented rooms in a particularly sordid part of Berlin, indeed he was probably living off her immoral earnings and he was most likely killed by a business rival, in other words, by another pimp. Brecht has many ironic comments to make about the appropriateness of a pimp as a NS hero, but it is perhaps more important to observe the various stages in the successful creation of a legend.

First of all, it is important to note that the Horst Wessel Song is not Blood and Soil poetry, indeed it is quite clearly a product of the big city. Its theme is the struggle for the streets. Not only is it part of the hated asphalt literature, it is closely involved with Goebbels himself, the Gauleiter of Berlin. Accordingly it was not surprising that Goebbels took a personal interest in this case. His involvement started with visits to the bedside of the dying Horst Wessel, where by all accounts Wessel pleaded with the Gauleiter to accept Prince August Wilhelm von Preussen into the SA. This was done and the Prince became an activist for the party. Just as in the song it is claimed that heroes in the fight will not die, so Goebbels in his first articles after Wessel's death wrote not only that Wessel's spirit would live on, but that equally the spirit of others prepared like Wessel to make the supreme sacrifice for the cause would also live on. In the same way Goebbels predicted that the song would live on, not merely as the marching song of the Fifth Storm Troopers for whom Wessel intended it, but for all who would join and follow Wessel's example. Wessel's song contained the line about 'the millions who already look full of hope to the swastika', and Goebbels picked up and developed this vision. The body was brought home in ceremonial fashion, his comrades kept the vigil by his bier, a golden laurel wreath was placed upon his head and the whole house was shrouded in flowers. The next step was to ensure a 'worthy' burial. This meant a parade of the whole party, with funeral march, public speeches, all guaranteed to attract maximum attention, and elicit counter demonstrations from opposition parties. Because the authorities naturally attempted to ensure a quiet burial, Horst Wessel's sister was cast in the role of 'the Antigone of the Brown Movement', and she even approached the Reich President Hindenburg, an old friend of the family from the days when Wessel senior had been a padre in the army. Only a service by the graveside was granted. Nevertheless a party order was issued that all party members had to observe mourning in the fullest sense because this 'case was considered as symbolic for the life and inner development of the SA in Berlin'. At the cemetery thousands of supporters were assembled with thousands of Communists outside determined to disrupt the ceremony. Inside the walls Goering, Goebbels,

SA leader Pfeffer and Prince August Wilhelm von Preussen (the latter in SA uniform) gathered round the grave. The visible symbol of the reconciliation of SA and Reaction had taken place to satisfy Horst Wessel's 'last wish'. Representatives of SA groups and the student associations to which he belonged stood guard to receive the coffin adorned with the swastika. Goebbels heightened the atmosphere with his customary fanatical half-sentimental, half-religious form of address. The flag was lowered over the grave, and then came the words: 'Die Fahne hoch!' This was all deliberately symbolic, as were the gestures that followed from Goering, the students, the SA and others. Goebbels' speech over the grave was one of his greatest. The actual burial with its drive through the streets did result in violent demonstrations on the part of the Communists (who by this time were being accused of murdering Horst Wessel). The shock-wave from these Communist demonstrations did not remain without effect, as became evident in the elections to the Reichstag five months later. The NSDAP leapt on 14 September 1930 from 12 to 107 seats, an incredible victory for the party. The *Völkischer Beobachter* of 15 September 1930 received the news of the great election victory with a line from the Horst Wessel Song! 'The streets free for the brown battalions!' Horst Wessel had not died in vain: he was the party martyr. His song became the second anthem of the Third Reich. His death was celebrated every year, streets were named after him, statues were erected, plays and novels were written. In 1937 the Karl Liebknecht House, the headquarters of the Communist Party, were taken over and renamed the Horst Wessel House, and from then on served as the seat of the SA group for Berlin-Brandenburg.

But what, apart from writing this little twelve-liner, had Horst Wessel actually accomplished? The song was an invitation to join the party, but it could also sound like a threat. In the same way as Goering introduced the debate of the Enabling Law by reciting Eckart's poem, so too the Horst Wessel Song was heard for the first time in the Reichstag itself when in February 1931 the 107 NS members walked out, and from outside roared the Horst Wessel Song. It would not be long before they were singing it inside the Reichstag itself

Horst Wessel himself was stylised and mythologised in various ways which were significant for the development of the party in Berlin at that time. First of all he had been a student of law (though he never did much studying) and this placed him in a certain social category with a certain attraction for academic people and reactionary student groups. In the same way more was made of the fact that his father had been in the army than of the fact that he was a minister of the Church. In the press the father's picture appeared in full officer's uniform with the Iron Cross, and the traditional university duelling scar on his lower face. All this was reassuring to the middle classes the NS were trying to win over. At the same time Horst Wessel had been killed while living in a working-class area of Berlin and this was also manipulated for propaganda purposes. It was suggested that Horst Wessel, like the hero of Goebbels' novel, had sought to live like a worker himself, indeed it was claimed that this was the area of his greatest success, namely in winning over Communists to the SA, and that this was the reason why he was assassinated in the line of duty. The suggestion was that the Communists got so angry because so many of their best men were being won over that they had him removed. Since then there has been great controversy over the success or otherwise of the NS party in converting the proletariat. In legend as distinct from reality Goebbels claimed success in this area. In the same way as Hitler was the 'drummer' (the demagogue with the power of persuasion) so too Horst Wessel had the 'gift of the gab', bringing the message of the *Volk* community and national comradeship to the Reds. Horst Wessel was a front-line soldier, only his front line was to be found in the workers' districts of Berlin. He carried out the command of *Mein Kampf* to win the battle for the streets. He saw the reality of life in the big city, but he had faith, hope and courage and this is what his song was able to transmit. He was a true idealist with a vision. Like a true poet, he was not only a leader of men, but also a prophet—one whose prophecy of millions looking to the flag would come true. In his own inimitable manner Goebbels summed up all of these elements in his speech by the graveside, which he made sure was given the widest possible publicity. In it Horst Wessel was addressed as Sturmführer, worker, student, singer and German, and explicitly compared with Theodor Körner the student, singer and freedom-fighter. Goebbels praised Horst Wessel as the man who, by his struggles and his death, had regained the capital city of Berlin and who had reawakened in modern youth the volunteer spirit of Langemark in the First World War, the will to fight, to sacrifice and trust. Goebbels finished with a quotation from a worker-poet: 'Germany must live, even if we must die'—once again a curious echo of the live-or-die motif from Eckart's poem. It is almost the unconscious expression of a desire for the destruction, which was indeed (thanks to Goebbels and Hitler) to be Germany's fate.

Following Goebbels' efforts the legend continued to grow and different literary versions added additional ingredients, though, as they were dealing with a party saint, a tight rein was kept on what was actually published about Horst Wessel, especially as some of the areas of his doubtful life had to be carefully handled. *The SA Conquers Berlin. A Factual Account* (1934), by Wilfred Bode, is an interesting contemporary version, for one thing because it contains a discussion between Horst Wessel and Dr Hans Gerkenrath, a Germanist and expert in medieval art. The issue is quite simple: how can Wessel the student defend the life of squalor and brutality he leads? Horst Wessel admits that he is a man of culture, who loves literature and music, and in particular he says: 'I have buried myself in Goethe and I love German Romanticism, Schlegel, Tieck, Novalis—I adore Hölderlin and I know my Nietzsche and my Kant.' But he claims to speak for German youth when he says that he cannot seriously contemplate a secure existence, career prospects or cultural pursuits. He knows that many people will be repelled by the 'rough manners and the rough language and rough appearance' of himself and his SA comrades, but argues that to build a new dwelling-place for German culture from the ground up it is necessary to do a lot of 'clearing out', and that has to be done in the streets: 'The SA is marching for Goethe, for Schiller, for Kant, for Bach, for Cologne Cathedral and the Bamberg Rider, for Novalis and Hans Thoma, for German culture, whether you believe it or not.' The apparent barbarians are the defenders of culture! The same point is made in the Horst Wessel novel by H.H. Ewers. Hitler must have forgotten, when he suggested this literary version of the 'Battle for the Streets', that the man he was engaging to write a *vie romancée* of Horst Wessel was a notorious specialist in grotesque and erotic perversities with titles like *Morphium*, *Vampires* and *Dead Eyes* to his credit. Goebbels must also have been prepared to overlook this, because he made all the necessary documents and letters available to the author. Ewers was certainly a professional writer and a smooth version of the life was guaranteed from his pen. This, together with some sickening compliments to Dr Goebbels and to Hitler, is exactly what Ewers provided. Nevertheless even this work has its value, if only for the theory of the song which he has Horst Wessel develop in it. It was, for instance, a well known fact that the NS political lyric consciously stole successful songs from other parties. One of the best known examples of this practice was the Socialist song 'Brüder zur Sonne, zur Freiheit', which was transmogrified into 'Brüder in Zechen in Gruben' with the lines:

Hitler ist unser Führer
ihm dient nicht Gold oder Sold.

(Hitler is our Führer, he is in nobody's pay.)

This is also the process which H.H. Ewers identified in Horst Wessel's songmaking. Not only does Wessel steal the idea of the Communist kazoo band and have great success with it, he also steals the kind of songs the Reds sing. There is, however, a crucial difference! The Communist songs come from the head—his songs will come from the heart. It is possible to win Communists over by debate, by argument and counter-argument; but in order to hold on to them 'German emotion' has to penetrate their hearts. 'Something strange, mystical, mysterious' has to be present in the song. The Communists talk about security of tenure, high wages, shorter working hours, games, sport and enjoying leisure time, but this is not enough. As an example of the mystical extra ingredient which Horst Wessel incorporated into his song, Ewers draws attention to the flag, which Hitler himself is said to have conceived—it has the black, white and red of Bismarck's Germany, allowing the red to predominate because the Nazi Party is still thought of as a party of real revolution! And then there is the swastika, the old fire wheel which has the power to inspire fear. According to Ewers all the leaders of the party are artists in some way—Goebbels, Hitler and Horst Wessel, too. They have the power to give artistic expression to what all feel. It goes without saying that H.H. Ewers closes his novel with a reference to Eckart's 'Storm' poem: 'Horst Wessel has rung the bell and awakened the sleeping Germany and now millions sing his song.'

Other novels, 'factual' accounts and dramas based on the life of Horst Wessel were written, but many of them encountered considerable difficulties with the Propaganda Ministry. This was also the case with the film of Horst Wessel's life which was made, using a film script by H.H. Ewers. After one showing to a select audience Goebbels had it withdrawn from circulation and recast, avoiding all factuality and projecting instead merely a totally generalised account of the making of an SA man. It then went into circulation under the title *Hans Westmar, One among Many—a German Fate from the Year 1929.*[18] In the final outcome the whole structure of this re-made film was over-simplified. All Communists were deceitful, ugly and cowardly and all Nazis were magnificent blond knights—noble, brave and pure. By the end the hero who has gone among the people reaps his harvest of success and the clenched fists of the Communists unfold to form the Nazi salute. In this sign they will conquer – assuming of course that they are pure-blooded Germans. Jews, like the grotesque Communist Party speaker or the drunken party secretary, are all too obviously excluded, foreigners are disdained and the corruption of Berlin night-life totally rejected. In a cabaret called 'Chez Ninette' only French is spoken and the sacred 'Watch on the Rhine' is desecrated into a jazzed up, pantomime version. Decadence and Communism are presented as the enemies to be fought by the SA. All in all the film was too crassly polemic and crudely systematised into the friend-or-foe formula, and it enjoyed little success. Goebbels had just as little success with another Horst Wessel film called *A Song Goes round the World*. The singer of the song in the film, an internationally famous radio tenor, was a Jew called Josef Schmidt, and the director Richard Oswald was definitely *persona non grata* with the Nazi hierarchy.

The very first bards of NS political poetry had been Dietrich Eckart and Horst Wessel. Around 1930 a second group formed under the name Junge Mannschaft ('Young Team').[19] These were party poets who generally occupied official positions within the hierarchy. Among this number were Heinrich Anacker (who was still very actively writing and publishing after 1945 and well into the 1970s), Gerhart Schumann, Herbert Böhme and Baldur von Schirach, named Reich Youth Leader by Hitler and later Gauleiter of Vienna. In 1946 he was condemned to twenty years' imprisonment for war crimes. Also important was Hans Baumann, who enjoyed enormous success until 1945. None of these writers developed anything approaching an individual voice: they were party workers delivering texts for party purposes and they would have considered it against the ethos of the organisation for them to have spoken out in any individually differentiated way. It is for this reason that it is possible to single out one of this group – Hans Baumann – as representative of many, and also because he became famous beyond the strict confines of the party audience by reason of his one song 'Es zittern die morschen Knochen' – a song which, like the Horst Wessel Song, went round Germany and from there round the world.[20] Hans Baumann made his poetic debut in 1933 in Munich with a volume called *Macht keinen Lärm* (*Make no Noise*), dedicated to the 'people working silently on the cathedral of the Reich'. The insistence on silence both in the title and in the dedication is misleading, for some of the songs are at least as noisy as Eckart's 'Storm'. The first part of the collection is of a quieter nature and it is only in the second part (entitled 'Germany') that the development is clearly marked from the traditional quiet inwardness of the German poet of the past to the active, committed poet of the present. The year 1933 is the dividing line between old and new, and Baumann is not motivated by political opportunism. Only eighteen years old, he clearly does have complete faith in the movement and its leader. The song which made Baumann famous is the one which follows. For this one, as for all his songs, he composed the music himself:

Es zittern die morschen Knochen
der Welt vor dem roten Krieg.
Wir haben den Schrecken gebrochen,
für uns wars ein grosser Sieg.
Wir werden weitermarschieren,
wenn alles in Scherben fällt,
denn heute gehört uns Deutschland
und morgen die ganze Welt.

Und liegt vom Kampfe in Trümmern
die ganze Welt zuhauf,
das soll uns den Teufel kümmern,
wir bauen sie wieder auf.
Wir werden weitermarschieren . . .
Und mögen die Alten auch schelten,
wir lassen sie toben und schrein,
und stemmen sich gegen uns Welten,
wir werden doch Sieger sein.
Wir werden weitermarschieren . . .

Sie wollen das Lied nich begreifen,
sie denken an Knechtschaft und Krieg —
derweil unsre Äcker reifen.
Du Fahne der Freiheit, flieg!
Wir werden weitermarschieren,
wenn alles in Scherben fällt;
die Freiheit stand auf in Deutschland
und morgen gehört ihr die Welt.[21]

(The world's rotten old bones are trembling at the great/Red war; we've broken the terror, a great victory is ours. We'll march on, even if everything falls to pieces — today Germany belongs to us and tomorrow the whole world will. And even if from the struggle the whole world lies heaped in ruins, we won't give a damn, we'll

build it up again (Refrain). And even if the oldies complain,
just let them scream and shout, and even if worlds try to stop
us, we'll be sure to come out on top (Refrain).
They're incapable of understanding our song, they think of
serfdom and war—while our fields ripen. You, flag of freedom,
fly! We'll march on, even if everything falls to pieces;
freedom rose up in Germany and tomorrow the world will be free.)

The repeated lines in this poem 'today *Germany* belongs to us—tomorrow
the whole world will!'—were later adapted to read 'the world *listens* to
us' (*gehört—hört*). But the first version was quite clearly the author's
original inspiration, written in the full flush of enthusiasm for 1933,
which had seen the seizure of power by the NSDAP. Germany did
belong to them. Was it also the original intention of the party to
conquer the world? There certainly is a latent threat in the lines and
this is how it must have been understood. The world is also mentioned
in the first stanza of the song: 'The rotten old bones of the world tremble
at the Red War.' This problem has been solved at a blow—'we have
broken the terror, for us it was a great victory'. Quite clearly the 'Red
War' is yet another reference to the war against Communism inside
Germany. At the time of the German-Soviet non-aggression pact
this line too had to be modified into the 'great' war, but here again the
original inspiration is clear, for the young poet was thinking of Germany's
mission to fight the red foe, to break the 'terror'. NS poetry tends (as
has been said) to follow the friend-foe pattern, and this is the case
here with the enemy specifically mentioned. But the threat of further
aggression is continued in the lines of the refrain, which promises that
'we will march on' (although where to or against whom is not
specified). The 'even if' clause is also typical of the Nazi all-or-nothing
mentality: in this case, the onward march will continue even if everything collapses all around. The same apparently unconscious drive for
destruction is contained in the next stanza, also in the form of an
'even if' clause: 'even if from this struggle the whole world lies heaped
in ruins, we shall not give a damn'. The point was often made about
Hitler's *Mein Kampf* that he never concealed his intentions, or even
his methods. The same applies to this poem, in which the collective
feels that blame for the destruction of the world could not possibly
attach to it. The Nazis were the ones who did more shouting and
screaming than anyone else, yet of course it is the others who are
blamed for this in the poem. It is the old and old-fashioned who are
accused of the violence that the party of the young practises.

The Nazis are peasants thinking only of their ripening fields and do not understand why others should interpret their song to mean slavery and war. No NS poem is complete without a flag and the flag they hold up is the flag of freedom. But in fact, of course, this song is a song of war, as the military beat of the metre clearly indicates: freedom perhaps for Germany, but slavery (again the archaic word 'serfdom' is used) for the rest of the world. Günter Hartung is quite right when he interprets this poem as a perfect example of that kind of propaganda which accuses the enemy of doing exactly the things it is guilty of itself.

This is a successful marching song though even more generalised than Horst Wessel's song, which was written for the SA and mentioned the SA explicitly. 'Marching' and 'singing a marching song' are also themes of the song itself. The general feeling imparted is one of confidence – the confidence of victory, victory already gained and to be gained in the future again and again. Once again the German encirclement myth is suggested, so Germany must defeat the world which threatens to defeat it. Those who thought of war and slavery when they heard this song proved to be right. Those who feared the vision it conjures up of a world in ruins were also right, for this was to be Germany's fate – only it was not the Nazis who rebuilt a destroyed Germany. Equally, if freedom's flag was eventually raised over Germany it was not done by the NSDAP.

The poetry examined so far is basically SA marching poetry of an almost Storm and Stress kind from the earliest days of the movement, that is from the period before the actual accession to power or from the days immediately after it. It must not be thought that all NS poetry is of a crude, warlike, aggressively racist kind. Much of it, it is true, revolves round the figure of the leader and the ideology associated with him, but there is also a great deal of entirely different poetry. Nature poetry of a traditional kind was much favoured and did not need to go all the way into the Blood and Soil category; and significantly, over the grave of Horst Wessel, Goebbels quoted a worker-poet. This was another area much favoured by NS poetry projecting as it did an idealised concept not of the worker, but of work; not of the trade unionist, the unemployed proletariat or organised member of a left-wing party, but of German craft. Goebbels gave some idea of the form the new poetry would take in his speech of 15 November 1933 in the Berlin Philharmonie with which he opened the Reichsschrift-tumskammer. In this speech, 'German Culture before New Tasks', the man who gained his doctorate with a dissertation on German Romanticism attacked liberalism from a particularly 'romantic' point of view, and offered rootless bourgeois intellectuals a chance to attach themselves to the revolution.

> Their attention is drawn . . . to an ideal realism, to that heroic life-concept, which today re-echoes through the marching steps of the brown columns, which accompanies the peasant as he pulls his ploughshare through the soil in his fields, which has given the worker a sense of a higher goal in his struggle for existence, which stops the workless from despairing, and which fills the work of reconstructing Germany with an almost soldierly rhythm. It is a kind of steely Romanticism which has made German life worthwhile again, a Romanticism which does not hide from the hardness of life or strive to escape from it into blue beyonds, a Romanticism which has the courage to face problems and to look them straight in the pitiless eye, firmly and without wavering.[22]

All the NS artistic concepts are combined brilliantly in this speech: the idealised realism, the heroic view of life, the marching men, the peasant and the worker forming one *Volk* community. The common goal is the task of rebuilding Germany, the successful revolution, the hope for the future in place of despair. But the phrase which was to prove indicative of future developments was 'steely Romanticism'.[23] It was to be expected of the NS cultural leaders that they should claim to continue the true German cultural heritage, but nevertheless significant that the choice should fall on Romanticism. This is consistent with the rejection of the rationalism of the Enlightenment, with the focus instead on mythology and myth and with a preference for semi-feudal corporate forms of society. History and Nature and the Divine were the favoured themes of Novalis. All of these themes were to prove amenable to NS treatment, elevated into eternal values and adapted according to need. Goebbels' 'steely Romanticism', therefore, did not imply an exclusively aggressive political poetry: it encompassed also a gentler kind of lyric for formal occasions, solemn celebratory poetry associated with family gatherings like Christmas and Easter—especially if the original religious aura could be associated with more Germanic cults like Winter and Summer solstice ceremonies, weddings and funerals. Poetry of great simplicity could be written, at the same time suggesting a community spirit without specific party political reference. In this way it was possible to create a sense of continuity with the great poetry of the age of Goethe, the poetry of the nineteenth century (excluding Heine, though his style was often imitated) and the poetry of the youth movement from the turn of the century. Goebbels' appeal was therefore an appeal to defend 'German' culture of a traditional kind, 'high' lyrical poetry as against the sordid modernity and Americanism of the Weimar Republic. The whole so-called 'German Movement' from Herder onwards could be invoked as something worthy of defence against foreign invaders destructive of the traditional depths of the German soul. That such anti-modern poetry could include supposedly 'un-German' forms is adequately demonstrated by the proliferation of sonnets like Anacker's 'The Reich' or E.W. Möller's 'What is the Fatherland?'[24] Hans Baumann was able to continue writing after 1945 without any need for radical change of style. Indeed he did this so successfully that his play on the theme of military obedience, *In the Sign of the Fish*, submitted under a pseudonym, won the Gerhart Hauptmann Prize for 1959. It was not only the writers of the inner emigration who could carry on writing in Germany after 1945 without changing step.

5 NOVELS AND DRAMAS IN THE THIRD REICH

While there was a considerable amount of poetry devoted to work in NS Germany, responsible agencies were constantly remarking on the absence of novels about this theme. This is perhaps understandable, because it had been dominated by Socialists and left-wingers, and NS writers avoided social spheres in which conflicts of interest had clearly not automatically disappeared with the advent to power of the NSDAP. Factories still had workers and managers and capitalist controllers, and in the twentieth-century world of the machine and ever-advancing technology, it was impossible to conjure up a vision of the pre-industrial age, in which the patriarchal relationship between master and apprentice still allowed everybody to live and work in harmony. Attempts at this kind of novel were made, but it cannot be said that they were very successful. More successful were novels which turned worker into SA man. In such novels (for example *The SA Conquers Berlin*), only the surface appearance of class conflict is maintained; in fact the worker in the brown shirt is given an excuse to work off his aggression against well dressed bourgeois opponents. The class war is personalised and trivialised, the appearance of anti-capitalism is only a cover for attacks on Communism. Instead of the solidarity of the working-class movement, the novel offers the companionship of group violence, that close-knit feeling of belonging given by the gang. The fight is what counts, not the reason for it or any abstract ideal. As in the Horst Wessel Song, all who die are heroes and martyrs. Novels of this kind were all part of the civil war leading up to the real war. The Communists were the enemy to be eliminated or won over and there was more joy over a convert than over a killing.

This attitude is best demonstrated not with an SA novel but with a Hitlerjugend one.[1] *Quex of the Hitler Youth* became not only one of the most successful novels of the time, it also provided the book for the first real Nazi film. The basis of the novel by Aloys Schenzinger was the murder of young Herbert Norkus by the Communists earlier in 1932, the year of the book's appearance. As with Horst Wessel we are dealing once again with one of the movement's early martyrs, but what makes the novel really interesting is the fact that it has a firm basis in reality. First of all, it is a Berlin novel, far removed from Blood and Soil and firmly rooted in the world of unemployment so realistically captured in Fallada's novel of the same year *Little Man — What Now?* In addition it is a gang novel somewhat after the fashion of Erich Kästner's *Emil and the Detectives*. There were such gangs in Berlin at that time, generally called cliques. In a sense the clique was a proletarian development from the middle-class *Wandervogel* movement, and its members did leave the city to go camping and sailing, but basically they came together not in order to make country excursions, but for reasons of survival and self-defence. By virtue of being young unemployed they were engaged in an endless struggle against the police, welfare and prison authorities. They were of necessity anti-establishment and anti-authority. On the other hand some of the cliques were highly organised, some did have Communist connections, and some were so successful that the Hitler Youth walked in fear and trembling. They were much more successful in their resistance to National Socialism than middle-class groups like the Scholls' White Rose. Schenzinger had found a real-life theme for this novel, depicting, of course, the situation in reverse: the success of one Hitler Youth group against a 'wild clique' called North Star in Berlin-Moabit, as seen through the eyes of one boy torn between the 'sordid' attractions of the working-class gang and the organisation and discipline of the Hitler Youth. The model is Horst Wessel — his song, his flag, and his success in winning over the working classes to the cause. While the novel was lively enough, it became even livelier in the film version. Unlike later Nazi films, *Quex* is realistic from start to finish, showing Berlin with its sad, grey, working-class districts and pubs, in the tradition of the German silent film — Brecht's *Kuhle Wampe* and other successes like *Mother Krause's Trip to Happiness*. The director Hans Steinhoff had learned from the best of these progressive films of the Weimar Republic and deliberately took over their style, their sets and their actors. This was yet another example of appropriation of enemy material and its adaptation for party purposes. The result was a Nazi masterpiece. What the film shows is the climate of terror caused by the violence of the battle for the streets between SA and Communists. The hero (called Quex because he is quick as quick-silver and Völker to indicate his *völkisch* significance) stands between the parties, but, through nothing less than a quasi-religious revelation, he sees the light. Despite the resistance of his Communist father, he joins the Hitler Youth. Quex is called upon to betray his former comrades and is killed by the Communists when distributing pamphlets with the slogan 'Hunger and Misery in Soviet Russia'. If Horst Wessel's song was an appeal to join the SA, this novel and its film version were an appeal to join the HJ, an appeal directed particularly at the young and uncommitted, to workers and Communists. The film was proclaimed as being 'about German youth's spirit of sacrifice': youth was the Germany of the future. By joining the HJ, they could leave the corrupt, hopeless life of the clique behind; climb out of the proletarian misery; feel liberated; have a duty, be of service to the *Volk* community and to Germany. Young people distressed by the modern world, filled with a feeling of aimlessness, are given a sense of purpose, a positive mission: 'the rebuilding of their shattered fatherland by a youthful army marching towards the glorious future'. What this novel offers is a sweeping vision of the new Germany. This was a film directed at all young people. Baldur von Schirach, the Hitler Youth Leader, was at the première: indeed he had composed the verses 'Forwards, forwards sound the bright fanfares' for it, to music by Otto Borgmann. Hitler too was there to honour the dead young warriors, a Bruckner symphony was played and the film took its course. After 1945 Schenzinger continued his career as a writer in the Federal Republic, specialising in factual novels about scientific and technological subjects.

It has been argued that all the representative works of Nazi literature were written before 1933 and that after that date the initial *élan* was lost and the promised generation of national geniuses failed to appear. Certainly this would appear to be true, at least as far as narrative prose is concerned. No new style or development in technique or language can be observed. The wave of war novels continued without throwing up a major new writer and as far as Blood and Soil was concerned, the traditions of the earlier *Heimatkunst* were continued, for example by writers like Friedrich Griese, who seemed to demonstrate by their own longevity that Blood and Soil was something incredibly healthy. Born in 1890, Griese had already written his successful novel *Winter* by 1927, showing graphically the survival of the fittest, when the cruel weather wipes out a whole decadent village population except for the strongest and the healthiest couple. He was acclaimed and honoured throughout the Nazi period, and was still writing in the Federal Republic right up to his death in 1975.

Literature of Blood and Soil (*Blubo*) was cultivated so extensively that it almost swamped everything else and some control of its excesses had to be exercised from above. It is, of course, easy to ridicule novels and stories of this kind, but this is to overlook both their possible appeal and their purpose. As far as the appeal is concerned, it has to be remembered that there are many different parts of the German-speaking world, each one of them (especially the most marginal and furthest removed from the cities and centres of government) proud of its regional characteristics, its dialect, its individual contribution to Germanness and *Volksstum*. After all even a thinker like Heidegger turned down an invitation to a chair at the University of Berlin in order to stay in the 'provinces'. However, where earlier novels of this kind did still contain internal conflict, for example between the peasant and the landed gentry, or over the incursion of modern industrial methods into the world of farming, by 1935 all conflict had been smoothed over and hollowed out, and what was left, while not idyllic, was rather bare. Perhaps there was an ulterior motive behind the apparent vagueness and irrationality of the Blood and Soil creed, perhaps Hitler and his advisers were thinking in terms of a long-range agricultural policy, making Germany self-sufficient as far as foodstuffs and farm produce were concerned, a necessary calculation for times of war. The formula 'Blood and Soil' is now so indissolubly a part of National Socialist terminology that it is almost impossible to disentangle who put the two ingredients together. August Winnig has been named for the first use of the phrase as a chapter heading in his book *The Reich as Republic* (1929), after which it became popular in *völkisch* circles. The Artamane Kenstler took it over in 1929 for the title of his new journal, before it was finally appropriated by Darré, the Reich Peasant Leader after 1933.[2] Darré made clear in his speeches and essays, which were brought together in the volume *On Blood and Soil* (1939), that he was thinking of more than foodstuffs. The peasant was the 'life motor' of the people, the producer of healthy children with the right racial characteristics. Hence for such a prudish movement as National Socialism, Blood and Soil literature is curiously sexual in its stress on the fecundity of the peasant woman. The cult of the blood is a cult of the mother, as *The Mothers* (1935) by the Austrian novelist Karl Heinrich Waggerl indicates. Another Blood and Soil writer, Josefa Berens-Totenohl, made the connection clear in her speech of 1938 with the title: 'Woman as the Creator and Sustainer of the People'. When Darré linked this with the concept of a *Volk* without Living Space, Blood and Soil became the literary expression of an expansionist policy, not, however, as Grimm envisaged it into Africa, but rather anticipating expansion into the East of Europe.[3] The result was that there was little colonial literature, but a great concentration on books about the Eastern borders of the German Reich. Orlowski has drawn attention to the German-Polish literature and to the wave of books about the Sudetenland by highly subsidised authors like Heinrich Zillich (the most militant of the border Germans), Wilhelm Pleyer, Bruno Brehm and others.[4] In style and content *Blubo* meant a form of regression, which could look strange in the context of the industrialised twentieth century. Not all regression is fascist and reactionary; in fact forms of primitivism had been features of the avant-garde literature and art which the Nazis had themselves denounced. Avoidance of naturalistic detail and the quest instead for the absolute essence resulted in many cases in a kind of abstraction close to that of the Expressionists, many of whom (for example Brust and Barlach) had produced work of this kind. Avoidance of personal psychology, preference for types and symbolic figures as the mouthpieces for political and religious concepts, the demonstration of cosmic and vitalistic forces, the search for absolute values in the midst of relativism and nihilism – all these were characteristic features of the Blood and Soil novel, but could equally well be descriptive of expressionistic works. Expressionism too was fascinated by the city as a late development for Germany which had remained agricultural and semi-rural for so long. Indeed the vision of the metropolis and the possibility of escape from it to the green fields had developed after Kaiser's *Gas* trilogy into one of the clichés of the age and was by no means confined to fascist thinkers. For these reasons it has been argued with some force that Blood and Soil literature after 1933 was far from new: on the contrary with its myth-prone avoidance of reality and its ahistorical, asocial tendency, it was clearly part of a major trend in German literature from the turn of the century, through *Heimatkunst*, Neo-Romanticism and Expressionism to the 1930s. The major difference was that linguistic experiments were avoided and that intellectual content was simplified and where necessary redirected. When Blood and Soil literature was finally reduced to hymnic ecstasies, ecstatic grunts, grand gestures and primeval screams it was time for the authorities to call a halt and the much-acclaimed movement was over.

It is, of course, a mistake to separate Blood and Soil novels too rigidly from historical novels, of which there was a spate after 1933, so much so that official NS quarters often complained about this literary flight from the present into the past.[5] In effect, however, there were many reasons for favouring the past, not the least of them being Hitler's own predilection for historical panoramas in his speeches. Hitler liked to think of the two thousand years of history which had gradually gathered together all the scattered Germanic tribes and welded them together into one *Volk*. History for him was therefore a demonstration of *Volkwerdung*, the making of a people. Once the Third Reich was established history could be considered to be over. The past was merely an incomplete present. Hitler did, however, stress the importance of great men in this process of the creation of a nation, hence for him the role of the historical writer was to present Germanic heroes to the young of the present, so that they might be filled through them with an unshatterable national feeling. Hans Friedrich Blunck filled this role completely. Blunck had been a student of law, a follower of the youth movement, an officer in the war, and an administrator (town clerk of Hamburg) before finally becoming a writer. From 1933 to 1935 he was President of the RSK and later holder of many honours and titles in NS Germany. After the war he was brought before the denazification committee in Kiel, classified as a 'fellow traveller' and fined 10,000 marks, despite his defence that he had been an 'anti-fascist chairman of the Reichsschrifttumskammer'! A writer like Blunck appears on the surface to be nothing more than an old-fashioned nationalist; there are for example no direct references to National Socialism in his *Great Journey*. He is more properly seen as the literary representative of that 'Nordic Racism' of which the *Lebensborn* concept of breeding for a Nazi elite was the most sensational product.[6] The Artamanen Himmler, Darré and Höss, the commandant of Auschwitz, were all believers in the Nordic idea.

The action of the novel is set towards the end of the fifteenth century in Iceland and in Germany. At the centre of the action is the German Diderik Pinin, the Statthalter of Denmark in Iceland. From there he discovers Greenland anew and sights the coast of America. The reader discovers that a German was the first discoverer of America! If Diderik Pinin is a prime example of 'the might of the German man', then the female protagonist Deike Wittens is the ideal picture of German womanhood. The reason for the hero's actions is his longing for a 'pure' land in which all peasants will be happy. This concept of a Utopian society is in fact a pointer to the present, for (as Blunck saw it) the society which Hitler was building corresponded to this ideal society. The Third Reich was the realisation of all the longings of centuries gone by. What drives Diderik Pinin to discover America is the idea of procuring land for the peasants of Germany, Sweden and Iceland. So even in those days Germany was a *Volk* without living space. Why this should be so is not discussed, nor is the fact that settling Germans in America will mean displacing the native population. Because Diderich's son is studying in Erfurt the Germany of Reformation days also becomes an element in the action. This son is the other kind of German, the prophet, the preacher, the fighter for his beliefs. Dierk also presents a picture of a divided Germany living in 'serfdom' under foreign rule from Rome. Dierk preaches the gospel of a Reich of Germans without a

Roman pope, of an uprising of the humble, the collapse of the mighty, and the protection of all men of all classes, peasants and seafarers alike. In this way the Reformation is presented not as a religious renewal, but purely as a German national movement. The reader is given a picture of the German which, by appeal to history, justifies the NS claim to be a master race and justifies in effect the suppression of non-Aryan races. History, in this kind of novel, is made by the will of single, powerful individuals; history is a matter of leaders and led; a strong hand is necessary; dictatorship (it is suggested) can be the best form of government. Essentially the view presented is undemocratic, nationalistic and irrational. There is no analysis of society: instead the novel directs the reader away from reality towards a mystical, Utopian solution to Germany's problems.

What, one may ask, does a National Socialist love story look like? The answer is given by Hans Zöberlein in his *Conscience Commands. A Novel from the Confusions of the Post-war Period and the First Uprising* (1937).[7] Like most NS novels of this kind, it focuses on the favoured period from 1918 to 1923 in the development of the hero up to acceptance into the party. What made the novel one of the most widely read of the period is the fact that it is a story in which the love interest runs parallel to the process of political development. The hero, significantly called Hans Kraft ('Power'), has been a front-line soldier till, like young Siegfried rising from the blood-bath, he returns from the war to civilian life and to thoughts of love and marriage. It is only after his decision to take part in political activity in the form of Freecorps action against the Bavarian Soviet Republic that he meets a suitable girl. Her heart is in the right place, she approves of what he is doing and shows her 'Nordic' inclinations by singing Solveig's song. They are able to demonstrate their love of nature by walking in Bavaria and bathing in its lakes. It is in an open-air swimming pool that evil is introduced into the idyll, with the appearance of some Jews who molest Berta sexually. She makes her attitude clear: 'These Jewish swine are ruining us, they're polluting our blood. And blood is the best and only thing we have.' The whole scene is a combination of anti-Semitism and eroticism, for it ends with the German couple swimming naked together in the lake. In a similar episode later, Hans is approached by a Jewish temptress, but all such attempts to undermine fascism fail. The novel ends about the time of the march on the Feldherrnhalle, with the couple becoming one, not by Christian marriage, but by a quasi-religious ceremony celebrated in Nature, before they repair to a village inn where breeding can commence. Zöberlein himself had been a front-line soldier; he was severely wounded and was awarded the Iron Cross First Class and other decorations. He helped to put down the revolution in Munich, joined the NSDAP at an early age and (like Hans Kraft) worked as an architect in Munich. The novel is therefore largely autobiographical. He was also in the SA and became a brigade-leader, holder of the Blood Order and of the Party's Golden Badge of Honour. Because of his participation in the Penzberg murders of 28 April 1945 he was condemned to death in 1948. This sentence was later commuted to life imprisonment, he was released early and died on 13 February 1964. Zöberlein was regarded as one of the main exponents in literary form of the front experience. His war novel *Belief in Germany* has an introduction by Hitler himself. He was also a film writer and as such was responsible for the film *Shock Troop 1917*.

According to Johst, there was nothing in the theatre of the Weimar Republic but 'ladies' underwear, sex, drunkenness, mental illness, decadence, materialism and bias'.[8] His opinion was fairly represent-ative and 1933 therefore meant for convinced National Socialists an exciting chance to clear out the temple, sweep away all the decadence and bring in the new. There was consequently an atmosphere of great expectation and euphoria. As Goebbels put it on 6 April 1933: 'the age of spiritual decomposition' was at an end, a new age of reconstruction could begin. In fact a wave of plays did come forward and among them one written as a radio play for the 'Nation's Hour' as well as for the stage roused a great deal of interest.[9] *German Passion* (1933) by Euringer was in line with the quest for a new theatrical form, which had crystallised round the concept of the *Thing* play, *Thing* being the ancient Germanic place of gathering for free men in the open air to hold court.[10] Holding court implied the possibility of reviewing the faults and crimes of the Weimar Republic, while performing in places associated with Hun graves, battlefields, and burial places of German heroes gave the whole a quasi-religious, mythical, heroic aura. And besides, the 'monumentality' of the new theatrical form appealed to the party leaders because it meant that a presentation of this kind would be a visible and public demonstration of the power and unity of the new Germany, the new movement, the new people's community. Instead of an audience in a theatre, there would be like-minded Germans coming together as one in a cultic celebration far removed from the artificiality of curtain and proscenium arch. In fact, of course, the *Thing* plays were not completely new and natural, they tended to lean on the architectural model of the Greek arena and even as far as the plays themselves were concerned, sources like the *Oresteia* were

drawn on (for example by Möller) for models of cult theatre. Euringer's
title also indicates another source, namely the medieval mystery play,
and here the *Ludus de antichristo*, which had been recently performed,
was a particularly important model. Similarly religious plays of the
Oberammergau variety had been and still remained popular in the
fullest sense, yet, despite their anti-Semitic implications they were not
suitable for National Socialist purposes unless fairly drastically
modified, for example by superimposing a national message over the
Christian one, as was done by Eggers in his *Job the German.* There was
also a long and well established tradition of open-air theatre in Germany,
associated with the Church and with organisations like the youth movement, but in this sphere the repertoire had tended to be drawn from
classics like *Götz von Berlichingen*, not that this play was by any means
an ideal one from the official point of view. There was far too much of
the individual and too little of the folk in it. *The Battle of Hermann* by
Kleist and Hebbel's *Nibelungen* were also nationalistic enough and
certain historical dramas also provided suitable fare, but these were
still far from being ideologically safe as audiences were notoriously
liable to draw a false (democratic) message, for example from a
Schiller pageant like *Wilhelm Tell.* Nevertheless, through such open-air
productions a great deal of appropriate theatrical experience had been
gathered on how to address mass audiences, how to move, position and
light large casts, how to employ gestures and choreographic movement.
National Socialist commentators liked to stress that they were drawing
on this fund of experience and on true German regional dialect and
folk theatre. They did not like to admit that here as elsewhere they
were also taking over and adapting the theatrical experiments of those
they despised and rejected. However it is now quite clear that the
Thing play also drew very heavily on the dramatic and linguistic
devices developed by the Expressionist theatre and forms of mass
theatre developed by the Socialist and Communist parties in the Weimar
Republic.[11] Such plays had also employed simplified plots, allegorical
and symbolic figures and vocal choruses, chants, music, bands, banners
and marching men. The single most striking feature about Nazi plays of
this kind was their size and scope and the number of people involved,
both as actors and audience. The barrier between actors and audience
was broken down, and a form of participation-theatre evolved, in which
the audience could join the actors in chanting the words and singing the
choruses. So-called stadium plays were put on before full-scale *Thing*
plays could be written for the *Thing* amphitheatres. In *Aufbricht
Deutschland! (Germany on the Move. A Stadium Play of the National*

Revolution) by Gustav Goes, there were two thousand marchers on the grass for the climax in the first Potsdam production. In the Berlin production there were 17,000, formed by columns of SA, army, police and other units. The words were spoken by actors in sound-proofed rooms, with their voices transmitted over loud-speakers, while the thousands of actors mimed. Getting the words across was to be one of the perennial problems with mass performances of this kind.

The theme in this stadium play was the victory of the national uprising, and so the focus was on the period from the German collapse at the end of the war, through revolution and civil war, economic crisis, inflation and unemployment, up to the seizure of power by the NSDAP. Peace speaks as an allegorical figure promising the whole world an idyllic future, but for Germany this figure is unmasked as the Peace of Versailles. Goes composed three such plays—all of them projected the same image of a Germany, which throughout the war years did no more than defend her own borders from an encircling enemy. The legend of the stab in the back, of the undefeated army at the front and the treachery of the politicians at home, was constantly insisted upon. Revolutionary disturbances were caused entirely by the plots of the Communist Internationale and the only salvation was the national one.

Euringer's *German Passion* operates on the same monumental scale as Goes' *Germany on the Move*. Originally written for radio, it rapidly became the model for the new *Thing* play and was as successful on stage as in book form. In 1934, one year after the Heidelberg Festival, it had reached a print figure of 30,000 copies and had gained several awards, including the Stefan George Prize. The theme is very much the same as Goes' stadium plays: the coming of the Third Reich. Its sources were quite clearly *Faust* and the theatre of Expressionism, with its visionary effects. NS literature tended to operate according to a friend-or-foe pattern and this obtains here. In the same way as Mephisto and the angels fight over Faust, so Euringer has an evil spirit and a good spirit struggling over the future of the German people. The duel is brought to a close by the unknown soldier who rises from a mass grave, wearing a crown of barbed wire round his head. The passion of Christ and the ascension have become the path of the German people to salvation in the Third Reich. The aim is clearly to give this political, secular progression a religious aura, making all rational critical discussion impossible. The front-line soldier standing for all the fallen is victorious over the evil spirits of the post-war period. He is the Leader who will guide the German people through the morass of November-criminals, democrats, Jews, pacifists, Marxists and weak-kneed Christians, in effect through all the products of democracy which is the evil spirit bringing Germany low. Euringer was deliberately exploiting Christian models for the new national purpose. The true faith now fuses the ancient concept of the passion of Christ with the expectation of salvation from the Leader, the Messiah come to save the German people. However, this was obviously rather a difficult area and while Euringer was given full credit for his experimental advances in the right direction, his *German Passion* was also criticised for its 'mystical religiosity' in theme and 'tinges of Catholicism' in style.

A further step in the direction of cultic, choric theatre was offered by Kurt Eggers in his *Job the German* (1933). In this 'mystery' the German is shown as the pawn between two mythical powers, Light and Dark, Good and Evil. As in Euringer's *German Passion*, the Goethean model is apparent, but this time the almost total absence of any realistic, historical framework led critics like Julius Petersen to see similarities not with Faust, but with Goethe's festival play in classical form *Epimenides*, symbolising Germany's liberation. Euringer's play could not be performed properly because the *Thing* amphitheatre was not ready on time. The same fate befell Eggers' *Job*, which also had to be performed in a hall. By the beginning of June the first *Thing* amphitheatre was ready near Halle and at last a national, cultic, heroic drama could be performed in the open air. The author chosen for this great task was Kurt Heynicke, whose poem 'Volk' in the Expressionist anthology *Menschheitsdämmerung* was well known in the twenties. By the thirties he had moved completely into the *völkisch* camp. The theme of *Neurode*, his 'Play of German Work', was an incident from the recent past, the founding of a work-community on a National Socialist basis, in the Silesian township of that name. Needless to say in this choric play the economic problem cannot be solved by the solidarity of a workers' collective, the right to work does not affect the traditional relationship between labour and capital; in effect the 'trouble at the mine' fades on the advent of the new Leader. Heynicke's second festival play, the *Way to the Reich* (1935), is an even more blatant example of wish-fulfilment, for its industrial problems are resolved in an expressionistic manner by the 'Birth of the New Man'! War and the National Socialist expansionist programme also had to be accommodated in plays of this kind, and this need was met by Eggers, who in his *Thing* play *Annaberg* (1933) provided the model heroic death. Annaberg, the hill in Silesia held by Polish insurgents and stormed by Freecorps troops, was a popular theme in nationalist literature and it is not surprising that it should also be treated in this form. *The Great Migration. A Play about the Eternal German Fate* (1934) not only takes up the same theme (the roving fate of the Germans from earlier times to the *Wandervogel* movement) but also indicates the direction in which the German people will *now* migrate, namely to the East!

None of the new *Thing* plays discussed so far was completely satisfactory in the eyes of the hierarchy. They were too religious, too allegorical, too wordy, or too abstract. Some attempt, however, was made to establish an official political and aesthetic position not only to stem the flood of amateurish efforts submitted, but also to assist the birth pangs of what was to become 'the National Drama of Nazi Germany'. This official position was expressed in an address 'On the Volk-play of the Future', given in 1934 by Dr Rainer Schlösser after consultation with Baldur von Schirach and Eberhard Wolfgang Möller. From this discussion emerged *The Frankenburg Dice Game* (1936), the most successful example of the genre.[12] The son of a sculptor in Berlin, Möller had studied philosophy and theatre history and had been deeply influenced by Paul Ernst, a friend of the family, whom he always called the law-giver. The Paul Ernst Renaissance of the thirties was due in no small measure to Möller, who started it with his production of Ernst's comedy *Pantalon and his Sons*. Möller's home background was imbued with the nationalist spirit and he also had close links with organisations interested in border and overseas Germans. His first plays tended to deal with themes from these areas. Möller's first theatrical success was *Douaumont or the Return of Private Odysseus* (1929). Douaumont was the name of a much fought-over fort in the First World War and Möller's play is the tale of a soldier returning to an alienated world behind the lines, to claim a place for those who had died at the front. It was the first German play performed in England after the war. By the 1930s Möller was countering the social dramas of the Weimar Republic with plays like *Californian Tragedy* and *Panama Scandal*, which were clearly directed against money-grabbing, speculation and corruption, but also against parliamentarianism and the neglect of national matters. The year 1932 saw the conception of *Rothschild's Victory at Waterloo*, a play first performed in 1934, and immediately acclaimed as 'the first comedy of the Third Reich'. The Jew Rothschild personifies the capitalist profit-motive and is attacked because for him dying soldiers are merely the pawns in a London stock-market *coup*. Around 1930 Möller had had talks with Brecht, especially about the concept of the didactic play, and himself attempted something along those lines. Like Brecht, he was reaching out beyond the confines of the realistic social play. Reinhardt, Piscator and others were also engaged in expanding the traditional scope of the theatre by staging their plays in circus rings and sporting arenas, while modern composers like Orff and Egk were looking back to earlier musical forms in the cantata, oratorio and school opera. Hence the turn to the *Thing* play was no mere atavistic regression, it was in line with the most modern trends. Cooperation with Rainer Schlösser and Baldur von Schirach led Möller to an appointment in the Propaganda Ministry and close association with Goebbels. He carried out a commission from Baldur von Schirach to write a Führer book for the Hitler Youth, and also accepted a commission from Goebbels to write a *Thing* play for the opening of the Dietrich Eckart Stage and the opening of the cultural programme of the Olympic Games in Berlin in 1936. The play which he wrote, *The Frankenburg Dice Game*, is important because it was 'subject to high governmental and aesthetic scrutiny; consequently it may be viewed as the most complete example of the state-supported program'.[13]

The historical basis for Möller's play was an incident from 1625 in Frankenburg (Upper Austria), when Protestant peasants resisted forcible re-conversion to Catholicism and were rounded up. When the ringleaders refused to come forward, thirty-six were chosen, of whom half could save their lives by a cast of the dice. Whoever lost was hanged immediately. As a result of this violent deed, the peasants revolted and the last Peasants' War broke out, leading to the deaths of thousands of peasants. This is the historic crime which is uncovered, the dead are called up from their graves and, in accordance with the *Thing* tradition, a court of justice is held. The very title of the play has immediate echoes of Kaiser's *Burghers of Calais* in which a similar lottery for life takes place and Möller admitted that this was one of his sources, together with other expressionistic plays like Sorge's *Beggar* and Reinhard Goering's *Captain Scott's South Pole Expedition*, plays which pointed the way to unnaturalistic, quasi-abstract theatre. The première took place on 2 August 1936, the day after the official opening of the Games and following the sacramental play *Olympic Youth* by Carl Diem with music by Werner Egk and Carl Orff.[14] The form the choral parts should take proved particularly problematical, because vocal choruses were so closely associated with the Communist gatherings and agitprop productions of the Weimar Republic. On high authority this was not permitted. In addition the size of the stage made it necessary for the actors to perform in buskins. Ideally, judgement in the case enacted should have been given by the highest possible authority, namely Hitler. As this was not possible, Möller felt it necessary to give the play a symbolic figure as supreme judge. As it happens, Hitler, who was supposed to have been present beside Goebbels, Goering and representatives of the diplomatic corps, got as far as the door and turned back, fearing embarrassing Austrian demonstrations.

Möller's *Frankenburg Dice Game* was to prove the high point of the short-lived *Thing* play movement. What had started off with great expectations and euphoria was practically over and done with by 1937 or, at most, left to mere regional development. Particularly disastrous was the failure of the much-vaunted programme to build *Thing* theatres all over the country. At one time Otto Laubinger, the President of the Reichstheaterkammer, spoke in his speeches of four hundred such arenas, but the enthusiasm for this vast building plan waned rapidly. There was also much criticism of the very concept of the *Thing* play, especially when so many amateurish efforts were submitted. The *Frankenburg Dice Game* was an attempt to halt the collapse of the movement, but even it fell foul of the inter-party rivalry between the Goebbels and the Rosenberg circles. Rosenberg and Himmler did not approve of the mystical, religious theme and suspected Möller of being a disguised supporter of the *actio catholica*. The Catholic Church meanwhile denounced the play for its treatment of what seemed exclusively Catholic atrocities and injustices and claimed that the Protestants had even more of such crimes in the past to account for. After that the *Thingspiel* movement lost its designation as 'important to the Reich', and by 1937 Goebbels had officially proclaimed it dead. 'Immediately all the singing, marching, banner-waving and torch-bearing ceased, and all the people's choruses were silenced.'[15] There had simply been too many problems — acoustics and spectator visibility caused difficulties, the thematic restraints were too great, the presentation was by necessity too abstract, too symbolic and allegorical, and therefore too static. The Nazis wanted a sacramental theatre, but Germanic myths proved too thin, while Christian symbols, while powerful, were basically inadmissible. The *Thing* play attempted to act as a substitute church, a political platform and a national theatre. In its attempts to subvert Christianity it ran into trouble. It could not be political because no analysis or critique of the ideology was allowed—it was only effective when attacking the old opposition, whereas its revelation of the new Germany failed. Perhaps, as Kemmler has argued, the strange marriage of the successful political mass meeting and the theatre was always doomed to failure; perhaps no *Thing* play performance could ever match the

intensity of the Nuremberg rallies.[16] But even the rallies had to be cut
and streamlined as people became bored with hours of marching men
and endless speeches. In addition the German weather could not always
be relied upon to be aware of the national interest.

Möller himself was directed away from the *Thing* play movement
by the new goals set by the central office. The new party line which
Schlösser had indicated in an essay about 'Nordic Culture' was the
quest for tragedy. This was not to prove a fruitful quest, though the
hierarchy attached great importance to it and the most important
dramatists in Nazi Germany pursued it vigorously. Curt Langenbeck
firmly believed that drama should make the theatre and not theatre
the drama, and worked to this end with plays like *Alexander* and
Heinrich VI – a German Tragedy. He followed them up with essays on
tragedy and with elevated dramas like *High Treason* and *The Sword*,
which moved from history to myth. Unfortunately the latter play
roused the displeasure of the authorities because it could be interpreted
to mean that the Führer should commit suicide. Another much-admired
writer of tragedies, Hans Rehberg, who was a friend of Gerhart
Hauptmann, had the protection of Johst and Goebbels. His historical
dramas on the theme of Prussia and Frederick the Great were admired,
produced and performed by Gründgens, but also caused great
difficulties for the system. After 1945 he continued to write plays but
without success. Möller himself was not particularly successful in his
quest for tragedy and his play *The Destruction of Carthage* particularly
roused the wrath and suspicion of Rosenberg, who thought he detected
in it a pointer to the coming fate of Germany. Despite this, Möller's
career continued successfully. His songs, like 'Germany, Sacred Word',
were in the fixed repertoire, and his experience of war as a reporter
strengthened his belief in Germany's mission to lead Europe and to be
the defensive wall against invasion from the East. It also confirmed the
view of tragedy which he expressed in his last play *The Sacrifice* (1941).
After the end of hostilities he was in various camps between 1945 and
1948. On his release he continued to write and publish in West Germany.
He died in Bietigheim on 1 January 1972.

With Blood and Soil drama, as with the *Thing* play, the Nazis
attempted not to reproduce reality, but to create a new German myth,
that of the peasant as the spring out of which the new, pure German
race would arise. Walter Darré compared the renewal and revitalisation
of the German people with the saving of the Hannover breed of horses
from near-extinction by carefully planned breeding. Richard Billinger,
who was born on an Austrian farm near the German border and was

destined for the priesthood, turned instead to the theatre and became
one of the most successful exponents of Blood and Soil drama, with
works in which the characteristic themes, like 'the city-country
antithesis, the mythical dark powers of the earth, the individual fate
within the folk collective, the eternal unending progression of country
life and the irresistible force of inherited blood', found dramatic form.[17]
He became widely known for his wild peasant drama of ritual sexual
murder *Rauhnacht* (*Night of the Spirits*, 1931) which won the
prestigious Kleist award. After the war he continued to write dramas,
but never achieved his earlier successes. In *The Giant* (1937) the striking
feature of Dub the peasant is his refusal to change. He refuses to drain
the ancient swamp in his land, does not smoke, will not buy a car and
prefers to travel by horse and cart. A spirit haunts the swamp and takes
revenge on all who betray the land. Dub's daughter leaves the land for
the city. When she returns ruined she accepts her fate, follows the call
of the spirit and drowns in the bog. Her mother was city-bred and
therefore incapable of adjusting to life on the land; and she too had
gone to her death in the swamp. Anuschka the daughter has inherited
her mother's city blood! Maruschka, on the other hand, as a true
country-woman, has mysterious powers which surpass rational
explanation. Nature too has magical powers, but the real essence of the
play is the contrast between the healthy, good, natural life of the country
and the corrupt, unhealthy life of the city. Prague is the city which
exercises this tremendous pull—Anuschka is drawn to it, only to be
seduced and abandoned. Only then does she realise 'that the famous
Prague, the great city is not the *giant* that lives in her dreams'. Though
there is no explicit propaganda in this play the ethos, with its
acceptance of the power of the blood and of fate, is completely
consistent with NS ideology. The play was filmed in glorious Agfacolour
by Veit Harlan, with the famous Kristina Söderbaum in the leading role.
By now, however, the play had been changed into a glorification of the
greater German Reich and tragedy comes about not because of fateful
forces, nor because of the conflict between rural and urban life, but
because the peasant has polluted German blood with a woman of inferior
race. The success of the film was overwhelming, bringing international
prizes for director and leading actress. In Paris 350,000 customers queued
to see the film over twenty weeks. By contrast Blood and Soil dramas
on the stage proved no more successful than *Thing* plays and by the mid-
thirties they had faded from the repertoire. In spite of a great deal of
government support, performances in the best theatres and productions
in the care of directors like Reinhardt, Jürgen Fehling and Leopold

Jessner, the thematic scope they offered proved simply too restricting. In addition, after the party had come to power there was less pressing need to win the ideological support of the peasantry. By 1938 the country was at war and what was needed was industrial productivity to feed the war machine, not countryfied kitsch.

It is very easy to demonstrate that National Socialism failed to produce any great artists or any great art. This is, however, to approach it from the wrong angle. As Cadigan rightly saw, Hitler was well aware that despite his success in overthrowing the Weimar Republic, without the support of millions of Germans and Austrians his thousand-year Reich could not last more than a few months. Decrees and physical coercion could sustain the power base only for a short time unless the people willingly accepted his propaganda, and all the arts combined had to be employed to gain this willing acceptance. Goebbels and his colleagues developed the necessary bureaucratic system of reward and punishment, but they too relied on the cooperation of believers who could project through their poetry, their prose and their dramas the essence of the National Socialist ideology. National unity and collective solidarity were attractive ideals in an age of economic, social and political chaos and the authors exploited their appeal to the full. National superiority, economic prosperity and brotherhood did seem preferable to slavery, poverty and humiliation. Law and order were offered instead of civil strife and anarchy in the streets; military power was made to seem more attractive than internal aggression, strong leadership than the inefficiency and corruption of the Weimar Republic. What Germans were being promised was a renewed sense of their spiritual heritage through a return to their traditional and conservative roots. The promise was never realised, the dream turned to nightmare and Germany was destroyed:

> It was this strange brand of idealism, of course, that led ultimately to the devastations of war throughout Europe and the still unbelievable inhumanity of prison camps such as Auschwitz.[18]

6 INNER EMIGRATION

The Reichstag Fire was immediately followed by a great exodus of writers and intellectuals. Not everybody left, however, and it is now generally believed that some kind of 'inner' emigration took place among those who decided to stay. It is not clear who actually invented the term 'inner emigration' and its history is particularly bedevilled by the fact that various people emerged after 1945 claiming to have been against National Socialism all the time, though they had continued to write and publish inside Germany and therefore of necessity had their position as writers and their works approved by the official organs of the state. Frank Thiess claimed to have invented the term, but Feuchtwanger seems to have used it even earlier in one of the final chapters of his novel *The Oppermanns*. By inner emigration Feuchtwanger clearly means active resistance inside Germany, whereas Thiess is talking about passive resistance. Exiles like Feuchtwanger may have understood the term in one sense, while non-exiles used it differently—either way the term was in the air. Certainly Kurt Kersten, reviewing Weiskopf's novel *Lissy* in 1937, saw this tale of a young woman, who is gradually disillusioned by the reality of the new Germany as an example of inner emigration, meaning opposition culminating in illegal, underground resistance. Bruno Frank's novel *The Passport* (1937) also covers resistance (though as its hero is a prince the social sphere is a different one) and it too was characterised in the *émigré* press as an example of inner emigration. Clearly exiles believed at the beginning that active resistance was possible inside Germany and only gradually came to realise the near impossibility of it. As they did so they began to use the term more pessimistically to indicate a passive stance. An early example of this is Klaus Mann's novel *The Volcano*, started in 1937, in which he talks about inner emigration as a form of silent suffering, and spiritual isolation. In general there seems to have been an awareness among *émigrés* that perhaps there were many like themselves inside Germany, who had lost their real homeland and as a result felt cut off and isolated. The question was, how many upholders of *this* real Germany were left inside National Socialist Germany? Was there, as Thomas Mann later claimed, in one of his speeches in October 1945, an inner emigration of millions of Germans inside Germany, waiting for the end, hoping, that is, that Germany would be defeated though not actively doing anything to bring defeat about? And who were these millions of Germans? Not, presumably, the ill-educated, petty bourgeois post-office officials and white-collar workers who usually got the blame for the collapse of the Weimar Republic. And what had happened to the five out of eight Germans who had consistently voted against Hitler, the Socialists and others? Whoever the millions were, it is significant that there was such a belief in a broad stratum of latent opposition to the Hitler regime, a belief that Hitler's success rested on the enthusiasm of only some part of the German people for the Führer. And this was a belief which seems to have been shared by Hitler and his closest circle because of the unremitting measures taken against assassination and conspiracy. Support and acclamation existed (or could be organised and manipulated), but despite Hitler's successes and the extension of the German frontiers, the war was never wholeheartedly supported, the masses of workers had not all been converted, the churches did not approve of the actions of the pagan regime, intellectuals were always suspect, and so the terror had to continue and indeed escalate. In these circumstances some form of inner emigration was to be expected.

After 1945 the term inner emigration became the target of bitter controversy and as a result developed a restricted meaning. Whereas before it had often been freely employed in exile journals to indicate all good Germans not infected by the deadly virus of fascism who combated it actively or passively, after 1945 the term became restricted to those writers who had stayed on in Germany and who had engaged in passive resistance through the medium of literature.[1] The term now marked the gulf between the non-exiles and the *émigrés*, and the gulf was a large one. By the nature of Nazi censorship those who had stayed behind had also been completely cut off from contact with colleagues who were scattered over many different countries and exposed to a vast variety of differing conditions. By the same token those same exiles had been able only to look from afar at those in the homeland, seeking any signs of resistance or even the slightest indications of doubts on the part of those nationalist colleagues who had perhaps once welcomed the Nazi take-over. Not surprisingly the exiles had also been prone to certain illusions, for example the expectation that the Nazi regime would be of short duration, that there would be a workers' uprising or that the intellectuals would make contact with the masses! After

1945 they were still looking for signs of this kind and found it hard to accept what had actually been written inside Germany. Only gradually did they begin to accept what they at first rejected as a flight into the idyll, into history, into 'pure' poetry, only gradually was it realised that writing idylls, historical novels, or 'pure' poetry could be forms of protest against Nazi brutality. It was not always easy for exiles after 1933 to come to the right conclusions about developments inside Germany. Exile writers often accused their colleagues inside Germany of intellectual treachery and opportunism and in some cases their accusations were justified. Very often there were indeed great similarities between 'Christian writers of the inner emigration' and equally talented Nazi sympathisers like Rudolf G. Binding, Hans Grimm, Erwin G. Kolbenheyer or Josef Weinheber.[2] There certainly was, as Klieneberger has pointed out, an excessive amount of patriotic sentiment in Schröder's *German Odes* or in Gertrud von le Fort's *Hymns to Germany*, or here and there in the work of Schneider, Klepper, Bergengruen and Wiechert. The latter also had more than a small share of Stahlhelm Romanticism in his stories and novels, and there was, too, plenty of reverence for the Prussian tradition in such works as Reinhold Schneider's *The Hohenzollerns*, and Wiechert's *The Simple Life*. The Nazis attached a great deal of importance to the idea of the Reich and this was also a feature of various works by Schneider, Bergengruen and Gertrud von le Fort. In the same vein Wiechert came close to the Blood and Soil school of Griese and Blunck, while Gertrud von le Fort wrote of motherhood in a fashion not far removed from that of the Nazi panegyrists. It took very close reading to notice the difference between writers of the so-called inner emigration and National Socialist followers and sympathisers, for after all they had all received the same stamp of approval from the same censors. At the same time closer examination revealed that there were also great similarities not only between inner emigrants and National Socialists, but also between inner emigrants and exiles. Inside and outside Germany the same traditional styles were continued, the same historical themes were treated, and indeed, apart from certain obvious differences consequent on the presence or absence of censorship and of an oppressive regime, it can be claimed that there was often no fundamental literary difference between works written inside or outside Germany. It is therefore not surprising that confusion was worse confounded on the collapse of Nazi Germany in 1945. The discovery of the full extent of Nazi crimes against humanity made resolution of the problem even greater, for while it was difficult enough to ascribe blame for the rise to power of National Socialism in the first place, it was even more difficult to allocate blame for the concentration camps and all the other atrocities committed against millions of Jews. Were all Germans equally and collectively guilty or was there a Nazi Germany and, concealed inside it, another innocent and good Germany? Had life been more difficult for the good Germans who stayed on and lived and worked inside Nazi Germany than for the exiles who had left? Was it more honourable *not* to have left the homeland (despite the fact that this would have meant certain death for many writers)? In the light of such questions it is not surprising that a great debate developed after 1945, or that works and authors of the period 1933-45 should have come under close scrutiny to establish the nature and extent of their resistance to National Socialism. New techniques had to be developed for analysing a literature written in a 'slave language', where the message of resistance to the new Germany was to be found between the lines, by implication and suggestion, in hints, symbols, parallels and all sorts of similar devices. What could not be expected in works by writers of the inner emigration was any kind of analysis of the social, economic and political interests responsible for National Socialism, for most authors of inner emigration characterised and explained the Third Reich and the historical process which had led to its triumph as a tragedy, a demonic embroilment, an accident of history, an inevitable fate. In other words they attributed it to forces and factors outside human control, to something for which no one could be held directly responsible. Similarly the response of the German people to the Third Reich tended to be explained away in terms of weakness, blindness, human error and fallibility, madness, stupidity, desperation, fear. This tendency to escape into the sphere of the irrational was not acceptable to most exiles and not surprisingly there was a storm of protest and a demand for the roots of evil to be more openly exposed, and for the guilt to be more readily acknowledged and accepted. After 1945 it was this whole guilt question which most seriously divided the exiles from the non-exiles. It was not really the fact that one group of writers and intellectuals had lived through 'the German tragedy' by being there, and not deserting, while another had not: it was the readiness or otherwise to accept German guilt which brought about the big split between those who had remained inside Nazi Germany and those who had not.

On 8 May 1945 Thomas Mann spoke to his 'German listeners' on BBC radio. He spoke of the German disgrace which defeat had revealed for all to see, he spoke of *our* disgrace . . . 'for everything German, all who speak German, write German, have lived German are equally affected by this revelation which strips us of our honour'. This radio talk elicited a reply from Walter von Molo, the immensely popular and much-filmed patriotic author of works like a Frederick the Great trilogy and the Friedrich List novel *A German without Germany*.[3] Frank Thiess also responded by writing an open letter in which the guilt of *all* Germans was rejected. It was as much the way in which he talked of the problems of those who had lived through the Nazi period inside Germany, by contrast with those who had observed Germany's fate from the 'comfort' of exile, which set the tone for the bitter exchanges that followed. Thomas Mann took up Walter von Molo's original reply, but it is clear that he was also aware of the Frank Thiess comments. He drew attention to the oaths of allegiance which various writers were known to have given in Nazi times (although this was done under some duress), and then came the famous accusatory statement:

It may be superstitious belief, but in my eyes, any books which could be printed at all in Germany between 1933 and 1945 are worse than worthless and not objects one wishes to touch. A stench of blood and shame attaches to them. They should all be pulped.[4]

Wilhelm Hausenstein attempted a reply with an article called 'Books free from Shame', in which he listed many books produced inside Germany during the years in question, which no one would be ashamed to touch, but to no avail. The war of words continued unabated, the gulf between the exiles and those who had 'stayed on' became greater and greater, and the doubts about the validity of the resistance of the inner emigrants also mounted.

Since these immediate post-war days tempers have cooled and some attempts have been made to look more dispassionately at what was written inside Germany. Some writers did fall silent, some were forced into silence by exclusion from the officially sanctioned bodies, some moved into different spheres of literary and creative activity. Erich Kästner was one famous writer who had no sympathy whatsoever with National Socialism, who saw his books burned, suffered exclusion from the Reichsschrifttumskammer, yet who did manage to continue in a related sphere, writing film scripts and harmless children's books.[5] Other writers doubtless practised similar techniques of evasion, not only in the film world, but also into radio and journalism. As far as journalism is concerned it was noticeable that all journals and newspapers were not immediately and totally *gleichgeschaltet*, upon the seizure of power. There were certainly massive restrictions and tight controls, new journals could not be established, all literary and art *criticism* was broken off in November 1936 to be replaced by non-critical *reports*, and, where all else failed, newsprint rationing kept a tight rein on divergent views. However, despite all this it has been possible to argue that certain literary journals were able to continue much as they were before 1933 – that is, on a non-Nazi line. The most daring of these was the *Deutsche Rundschau*, a journal established in 1874 by Julius Rodenberg and guided from April 1919 until April 1942 (when it was banned) by Rudolf Pechel. This editor was far from being a left-wing intellectual or fellow traveller. He had been an officer in the Imperial Navy and by background, training and inclination he was a conservative nationalist. Pechel in a sense was an example of what the exiles were always looking for, a man who had been close to the NSDAP, but whose eyes had been opened by the reality as distinct from the rhetoric of the new Germany, and who had gradually moved into the opposition camp. Pechel was close to Nazi intellectual circles, was a member of the June Club presided over by Artur Moeller van den Bruck and had had every opportunity to observe the party from close quarters.[6] He even met Hitler personally through the auspices of the June Club. However, instead of being enthused and converted by these experiences, he turned against the whole movement, and made his journal into an organ of opposition. To avoid endangering staff he was by the end doing all the work of the journal with the help of his wife alone, and by this kind of effort managed to keep it going into the fourth year of the war. What Pechel relied on was camouflage. One of his most famous articles was about Siberia and consisted of a review of a book about terror tactics in the Soviet Union. Every sentence was equally applicable to Nazi tactics of oppression in Germany. Another technique was that of employing historical parallels, for example the journal would publish essays with titles like 'In Praise of a Charlatan', 'The Demonic Nature of Power' or 'Image of a Tyrant'. Pechel was arrested on 8 April 1942 and spent three years in concentration camps and prisons. He survived these Nazi brutalities to emerge as a sick man. His book on German resistance, one of the first, was published in 1947.

A political journal with some interest in literary matters was *Widerstand. Blätter für Sozialistische und Nachrevolutionäre Politik*, edited by Ernst Niekisch. *Widerstand* means resistance, but as used here has clearly nothing to do with resistance to National Socialism. What Niekisch meant when he started the journal was resistance to the Treaty of Versailles and to the pro-western policies of Stresemann. Niekisch was a National Bolshevist and as such was anti-western, anti-urban, anti-capitalist and anti-Communist. Above all he very early became one of Hitler's most outspoken opponents and in 1932 published his brochure with the title *Hitler – a German Fate*, followed by other equally anti-Hitler works. Under these circumstances no journal with which Niekisch was associated could last long in Nazi Germany, but remarkably it did keep going until December 1934. The *Neue Rundschau* was more of a purely literary journal than either *Deutsche Rundschau* or *Widerstand*. Thomas Mann had published in it before 1933, and his essays and literary works continued to appear in it *after* the seizure of power. The director of the *Neue Rundschau* was Peter Suhrkamp, who also took over the S. Fischer publishing concern after Bermann-Fischer went into exile. Suhrkamp was arrested in April 1944.[7] Other literary journals like *Hochland*, *Corona* and *Das Innere Reich* have also been claimed for the inner emigration, though no consistent policy of resistance can be discerned in them. The best example of literary resistance was the *Frankfurter Zeitung*, though considerable doubt has been cast on exactly what was possible within the *feuilleton* pages of a daily newspaper.[8] Nevertheless even if no actual resistance was present in its pages, it did by its insistence on a high level of excellence in style, syntax and vocabulary remain a 'bastion of the language' and in this (if in no other way) demonstrated its distance from National Socialism. The exponents of such literary excellence could be described as *bürgerlich*, conservative and nationalistic, but nevertheless there was no doubting their ability. Stefan Andres' *We are Utopia* was serialised in its pages, as were stories by Elisabeth Langgässer,[9] Werner Bergengruen and Hermann Hesse, as well as lyrical contributions by poets of the quality of Marie Luise Kaschnitz. In effect the paper used every device to express its true feelings about National Socialism, even to the extent of exposing it to ridicule by quoting NS linguistic absurdities, for example, in calling the Japanese 'yellow Aryans', or the tomato the 'Nordic fruit of the South'. The newspaper was finally banned outright when it published an essay on the seventy-fifth anniversary of the birth of the leading Nazi poet Dietrich Eckart, leaving out none of the truth and determinedly undermining the party myth about his life and works.

Here as elsewhere in any consideration of inner emigration the question arises as to why the authorities permitted such material to be published at all. The same question also arises with writers in the traditional, classicistic, humanistic, conservative, religious vein, who, while clearly not National Socialists, nevertheless continued to write and be published, indeed in some cases to enjoy great publishing success inside Germany during the National Socialist period. Such writers were Hans Carossa,[10] Rudolf Alexander Schröder, Werner Bergengruen and others. The answer must surely be that by tolerating them and the journals in which they were normally published, the educated middle classes who formed the main body of their readers would be persuaded that the new regime was well disposed to culture and that it respected traditional values and traditional forms of literature. In this way too cultured, middle-class writers could be manoeuvred, willingly or otherwise, into becoming tools of the NS propaganda machine. The fact that their works could be published and sold proved to observers in Germany and abroad that National Socialism itself was equally respectable and cultured and operated as a counter-measure against the horror stories about the new Germany's intellectual and cultural barbarity. Part of the calculation was doubtless simply to allow the older generation to fade from the scene gradually, as NS poets and writers emerged. In practice, nearly all the writers who maintained a respectable distance from National Socialism, who remained cool and uncommitted if not actually hostile, sooner or later had difficulties of various kinds with the regime, ranging from withdrawal of permission to work professionally to imprisonment, torture and death. The NS regime did not like uncommitted writers any more than it did unpolitical scientists or doubting academics. The division of the world into friend or foe operated in this sphere as in any other.

While at first sight there is often little apparent difference between the style of writers well or less well disposed to the regime, there are some distinguishing features. Consciously or unconsciously, the pressures of the age were at work. For one thing writers tended to move away from the more obvious literary genres. One form that suddenly enjoyed increased popularity was the literary diary. Communicating openly with a diary meant of course that the diary was unpublishable until after the collapse of the regime or that it could only circulate privately among friends. Diaries of this kind were kept by Oskar Loerke and Jochen Klepper; they were forms of writing for the drawer and not for publication, as were the memoirs of Werner

Bergengruen or the notes and aphorisms of Ernst Jünger, who from the start of his literary career had tended towards the diary form. Yet even in writing of this kind there were few outspoken denunciations of the new Germany, for documents in a drawer can be found by the secret police. Instead there was a tendency towards the veiled remark, the significant pause, the double or multiple meaning. It also involved reliance on the sensitivity of the reader to pick up a literary allusion, a biblical reference or a historical parellel with relevance to National Socialism. This was the only development in the literary artistry of the time. No new forms, no new style emerged, only progressive refinement in techniques of making oblique statements.

While the National Socialists had banned all progressive, avant-garde or socialistic literature, they actively encouraged writing of a traditional kind. This meant among other things encouraging the historical novel. They themselves had used it to show the descent of the National Socialist state from what they claimed had existed in the Germanic past, namely the unity and greatness of the German people. The historical novel was one means of showing what had been achieved thanks to National Socialism; the stylised heroes of the past were models for the German heroes of the present. For them history was not in any sense a critique of the present, but rather a validation of it. Nevertheless the historical novel could be used to expose the deficiencies of the present and when employed by writers of the inner emigration it did come closer to the anti-fascist novel which had developed outside Germany: there it had grown out of the resistance to fascism engendered by the experience of National Socialism and exile. By writing novels of this kind inside Germany it is claimed that such writers were not only preserving the integrity of the German language and the threatened traditional values, they were also adding a political dimension to their work. No novel of this kind could help to bring about the defeat of National Socialism, but that is not to say that it did not have other qualities, for example it could counter false history and defend culture. While there are differences between writers of the inner emigration and exiled writers there are nevertheless sufficient similarities between them and their circumstances to permit a theory to explain why the historical novel should have experienced a revival both inside and outside Germany with the coming to power of the Nazis. The exiles had to come to terms with life in an often hostile environment, while the inner emigrants had to cope with the even more hostile environment of a homeland which meant for them censorship, surveillance, danger even to life and survival itself. Those who had left Germany no longer had their own country before them as a living experience. They had no present to write about, and so they wrote about the past. Those inside Germany had even less choice. They dared not write about the Germany they rejected, and so (apart from the exotic and remotely aesthetic) this too left only the past. Both groups might deny that their concern with history was a form of escapism, but both had reasons for avoiding the present — as for the future, it could be presented either in the form of Utopias or, more pessimistically, as visions of total disaster and chaos. Going back to the past was of course also a useful device for criticising the form of government of which they disapproved by holding up a counter-image.

Goebbels and his officials were, needless to say, not unaware of the boom in historical writing and though it was just as much a feature of committed National Socialist writing, they were suspicious of this literary flight into the past. Did this trend mean simply a quest for historical colour and costume as distinct from the local and regional colour of the Blood and Soil variety, or did it mean an attempt to avoid the problems of the present; or again were the costumes and characters of past ages really being used for purposes of concealed criticism and resistance to National Socialism? One of the best examples of the relationship of such novels to the Third Reich can be found in the works of Werner Bergengruen. By his own reckoning, and he discussed the various possibilities extensively in his *Writer's Desk Memories*, the historical guise was merely one of the more obvious and successful methods for concretising and actualising not only the problems of the time, but the fundamental and basic problems of mankind. He was clearly not interested in history as such, but rather in history as a means of literary camouflage. The results can be seen in a work such as *The Grand Tyrant and the Law*, which is only superficially a historical novel. In fact the historical milieu turns out to be largely fictional, providing a somewhat creakily constructed allegorical framework for the basic moral and spiritual message to be imparted. Neither this novel, nor the Berlin novel *In Heaven as it is on Earth* with its more explicitly religious title, was conceived with National Socialism in mind. Both were started before 1933, both were not

> thought of from the start as polemics, although as a consequence of the weighty events during the writing of them, both were of necessity and as a matter of course caught up in the struggle against tyranny and were quite clearly and consciously employed as weapons in the forefront of spiritual resistance.[11]

The Grand Tyrant was first printed in serial form and Bergengruen reports in his memoirs the editorial changes to which his text was subjected. First of all the title was altered to *The Temptation*, the word 'tyrant' being completely removed everywhere and replaced by 'regent', or some such harmless term. Obvious similarities between the novel's tyrant and Hitler also had to be removed (for example love of monumental buildings or lack of children) and as was consistent with the traditional view of 'art' which the National Socialists favoured, all political allusions had to be eliminated—leaving only a 'pure' literary work. In fact even in such a purified version and despite Bergengruen's claim that he never intended his tyrant to be Hitler in disguise, nor his 'fisher of men' to be Himmler, there must still have been plenty of echoes of Hitler and his bloodhounds. His intention had been originally to write on the larger theme of power and its temptations, the error of the powerful in seeking to set themselves up as God, and the ease with which the powerless and the oppressed allowed themselves to be seduced, but by 1933 this theme had become an acutely political one. Yet Bergengruen never attempted to elaborate any theories about the roots of National Socialism or fascism, nor did he ever have any solution to offer once tyranny had established itself, other than the appeal to religion and conscience. If he was anti-Nazi it was from the extremely national-conservative quarter, though it must be remembered that, as in the case of Jünger, Niekisch and others, this was by no means unusual. The Socialists and Communists had no monopoly of opposition to National Socialism. When Bergengruen's novel was published as a book complete and unadulterated with its original title, its success was enormous. How can this be explained? If it was indeed a novel with a secret message, how did it ever get past the massive party machinery with its competent and trained literary readers? To this there are various answers. For one thing censors are notoriously stupid and blind, and in view of the fact that the *Völkischer Beobachter* actually praised the book as 'the Führer novel of the Renaissance Age' it is tempting to take this as an example of Nazi stupidity. But, of course, the novel *could* be read in this way. As has been seen, too, the novel also corresponded to the Nazi ideal of the pure work of art in a high literary style. However, the book could also be read differently. The author could also calculate on another type of readership with a literary sensitivity highly developed by the atmosphere of the time and the place. Such readers needed only the tiniest of clues to set them on the track of hidden meanings even in something as apparently harmless as a description of the weather. Altogether, regardless of how the book was read it still remained fairly harmless, for despite its success it was not sowing the seeds of opposition among the masses, no active resistance was encouraged, a literary treat was guaranteed in a barren age, and much moral and spiritual comfort was imparted. Despite Rosenberg's known suspicions Goebbels made a clear decision not to ban the book.

Bergengruen's second novel of this type encountered rather more difficulties when it came out in 1940. It was classified as 'totally un-desirable' by the official agencies, no reviews or discussions of it were permitted, yet despite this, it reached sales of 60,000 copies in one year and only then was it banned. In his previous novel Bergengruen had dealt with the problem of power and its temptations, without in any way challenging the Führer principle: the *status quo* was left intact, his tyrant was still there at the end, and there was no indication that his leadership was being challenged. For *In Heaven as it is on Earth* he turned to the problem of fear. Clearly this was also a theme with possible relevance to National Socialist Germany, for the very idea of fear was a direct challenge to the heroic Master Race mentality. Here was a novel in which it was shown to be present at all levels of society. Once again Bergengruen's position was clearly a Christian one and the solutions he offered were to be found in God's will and His mercy and nowhere else. Still no action was taken against the author. Apart from such novels Bergengruen also published novellas, some of which (like the *Three Falcons*) reveal incredible, almost excessive mastery of the highly sophisticated narrative techniques of this traditional German narrative form. Here again was 'pure' art and apolitical literary virtuosity. By contrast his poems, often printed and distributed anonymously and illegally, revealed much more of Bergengruen's attitudes towards the Third Reich. It was these poems, later collected and published under the title *Die heile Welt* (*World Intact*, 1950), which gave the post-war era one of the slogans characterising the restorative tendencies of the Adenauer period. In none of these poems did Bergengruen attempt to rouse his readers or listeners to active resistance, yet equally they never left any doubt about his rejection of the evil of the age. He did in fact play a more active part in the resistance by distributing the pamphlets of the White Rose and the sermons of Bishop Galen, yet somehow he never attracted the closer scrutiny of the Gestapo and Goebbels seems to have been prepared to tolerate him to the end.

The same can be said of Reinhold Schneider. Like Bergengruen he is said to have distributed thousands of duplicated sheets of poems, but was never caught by the vigilant Gestapo. His selection of poems published by Insel in 1939 was classified as 'undesirable', as was his history of England. Even so various collections and selections of his poems continued to be published despite charges of 'defeatism' and 'instigation to high treason'. Schneider's literary weapon was the pure form of the sonnet and opinions vary as to its efficacy. Certainly his sonnets gave comfort, but comfort was a commodity recognised as useful to the army and to a people at war. There was no reason to forbid them. In 1938, shortly before the *Kristallnacht* Schneider published his historical novel *Las Casas and Charles V*, about the Dominican monk (1474-1566), father of the oppressed and conscience of the West, who has an audience with the Emperor Charles and argues against colonial exploitation. This is an example of the remarkable similarity between the novel of inner emigration and the exile novel, because Schneider's historical subject-matter is the same as that used by Döblin in his South American *Amazonas* trilogy (1937/8), contrasting the exploitation of the Latin American population by the Spanish colonialists with the message of peace of the true Christians. In both historical works there was a clear parallel between the substance of the novels and the expansionist power politics of Hitler's regime. As in Bergengruen's novel there is no criticism of the Emperor, who even decides in favour of Las Casas and orders new laws abolishing slavery. In the light of National Socialist practice this seems an unduly optimistic ending, though there is no suggestion that Schneider himself expected Hitler to act in this way. Indeed, according to his own account, it was the discovery of the Nazi concentration camps and other similar practices that changed his own life, led him to become a Christian and later moved him to join the Catholic Church in 1938.

While there were some indications in his diaries and elsewhere which suggest that Schneider was aware of the possibilities of literary resistance in historical guise, it is clear that Friedrich Percyval Reck-Malleczewen wrote with this definite intention. This Conservative Prussian aristocrat, doctor, musician, author and theatre critic wrote a historical study, *Bockelson. History of a Mass Hysteria* (1937), which while ostensibly dealing with the Anabaptists of Münster in the sixteenth century, was quite clearly an attack on the mass hysteria which had resulted in National Socialism, with the inherent suggestion that any mushroom growth with such flimsy roots must collapse as quickly as it succeeded. This diagnosis of the sickness of the time was expressed even more explicitly in his private *Diary of a Desperate Man* (1936) in which, as he put it, 'anybody who doubts or finds fault with the new doctrine is doomed to execution'. After being spied on for ten years he was arrested on 31 December 1944. He died on 16 February 1945 in Dachau.

By contrast Frank Thiess, an enormously professional writer of novels, essays and film scripts, was a survivor. It was he who stirred up what came to be called 'The Great Controversy' after 1945.[12] His treatment at the hands of the various official organs of censorship varied, but in general he too was 'tolerated'. Goebbels not only felt the need for 'pure' literary products and therefore put up with writers like Bergengruen and Schneider: he was also aware of the need for literary products with some entertainment value in wartime and encouraged such works through his 'Week of the German Book'. Thiess fitted into this category with works like his Caruso novel *The Neapolitan Legend* of 1942, though other efforts, such as his *Reich der Dämonen*, were categorised less positively. The reaction of the authorities was understandable, as this latter novel had the word *Reich* in the title — *Reich of Demons* — and the subtitle proclaimed it as 'the novel of a thousand years'. Thiess' novel set out to present the German race over this period of time, but did so by portraying the varying development of Greek, Roman and Byzantine civilisations, at a time when ancient cults came into conflict with Christianity and the tensions between rulers and ruled were greatest. This permitted comparisons to be made between Germany and the military civilisation of Sparta, between modern leaders and Greek tyrants. While the setting was historical the language was contemporary, employing words like emigration, Gestapo, Führer, et cetera. The authorities gave this work the silent treatment, banning all reviews or comments, but did not initially take any more drastic steps either against the work or its author.

Thiess managed to survive to claim after the war that he had been against the regime, though this had not always been absolutely true. Jochen Klepper, by contrast, seemed doomed from the start. He was married to a Jewess with two daughters from a previous marriage and as a result suffered harassment and loss of employment. The son of a clergyman, he had close Church connections, and indeed worked for the Church press. He was also a member of the Socialist Party, and had worked for a time with *Vorwärts*, although his Prussian background made him also something of a monarchist. By 1933 therefore he was neither one thing nor the other, neither left- nor right-wing. To his ideological and religious confusions were added the characteristic pressures of the new Germany, in particular the threat that he would be forced to divorce his Jewish wife and that she would be deported with her daughter (the other daughter having already left for England). Fortunately for Klepper, the Minister of the Interior, Frick, took an interest in his case and gave permission for the step-daughter Renate to leave Germany. After frantic efforts to obtain a Swedish visa for her, Klepper found that the exit permit had expired. Last-minute efforts to save his wife and step-daughter from deportation also failed and Klepper committed suicide together with them on the night of 10 December 1942. 'This was a suicide under the cross, the symbol of love.'[13] Some impression of the mental and physical strains of the time can be gained from Klepper's diary jottings for the years 1932-42 in *Under the Shadow of your Wings*. His historical novel, *The Father* (1937), was his most extensive work. Remarkably, although the author lost his writer's permit after its publication, the novel itself was favourably received in National Socialist quarters and judged to be an attempt to place National Socialism in the Prussian tradition of Frederick William I. This may have been a deliberate misunderstanding, put out by the Nazis so that they could lay claim to a distinguished and respectable work, which fitted their purposes. Certainly the novel enjoyed every encouragement from official quarters and sold in large numbers. The more sensitive reader, however, could not fail to notice that the author was not acclaiming, but criticising, the Third Reich.[14] Certainly the Führer principle was present to a degree, but the ideal held up was the Prussian one of responsible leadership, with a firm Christian and moral base. Klepper wrote a small booklet on the Christian novel and this is quite clearly his aim throughout *The Father*. Like Bergengruen and Schneider, he also wrote Christian verse, which has retained much of its power to this day. Klepper was indeed as much a dedicated Christian writer as Gertrud von le Fort, whose best poetry and stories were also written at this time, though she never wrote with any direct intention of opposing the regime.

In general it has to be noted that though novels and stories were the order of the day and drama gave little opportunity for concealed critical allusion a great deal of admirable and worthy poetry was written. One writer who did attempt both drama and poetry deserves to be mentioned in this context – Albrecht Haushofer. Haushofer had at one time been a friend of Rudolf Hess and was another example of a National Socialist sympathiser who moved from the Hitler camp into direct opposition to it.[15] Through Major General Beck and the Wednesday Club of artists and intellectuals he made contact with the German resistance and took part in plans to bring about Hitler's downfall. In December 1944 he was arrested and on 23 April 1945 he was shot in Berlin-Moabit. In the hand of the dead man his brother found a notebook with seventy-nine poems written in prison – the *Moabit Sonnets*.

Altogether this was a period remarkable in terms of lyrical productivity.[16] Even more than to history and the past, writers of every shade and hue inside National Socialist Germany turned to poetry. Understandably this has been interpreted as a flight into subjectivity, sentimentality and apolitical escapism, but not all of this poetry can be dismissed in this way. If the sonnet form was an indication of rejection of chaos in the world and resistance to it by means of pure form, then lyrical expression and purity of language were indications of opposition to National Socialist slogans about the military 'magic of marching columns of four'. Among the best known names (although there were many more) are Wilhelm Lehmann,[17] Oskar Loerke, Dietrich Bonhoeffer and Gertrud Kolmar. Rudolf Alexander Schröder wrote both secular and religious poetry and Rudolf Hagelstange a *Venetian Credo* consisting of a cycle of thirty-five sonnets, written and printed secretly in Italy in the last months of the war. In his essay 'Form as Primary Decision' Hagelstange sums up the reasons why so many chose the sonnet form at this time:

> the sonnets offered themselves like blocks of granite one could build with. In their strict form . . . was manifested even externally the reaction against what was shapeless, the will to new laws . . . created against the false spirit, the sonnet became absolutely *the* fashionable form of resistance.

The sonnet as a form of resistance overstates the case. As has been pointed out more than once it was not the sonnet, nor indeed any other literary genre, which brought about the collapse of the Hitler regime; besides, National Socialist poets also practised the sonnet form and revelled in its literary tradition.

The same might perhaps be said of the story which has been acclaimed as the 'major work of inner German resistance' – Ernst Jünger's *On the Marble Cliffs* (1939). Given Jünger's views and the favourable light in which his earlier works were seen and propagated by the NSDAP, this would appear to be an example of resistance from rather an unexpected quarter; but perhaps it is yet another example of a nationalist sympathiser who saw the light and moved away from National Socialism. This short novel has indeed been read as evidence of such a 'transformation'. Here is a book which had no difficulties put in its path by the massive machinery of National Socialist thought control, a book which reached a figure of twelve thousand copies sold in the year of its publication without advertising of any kind, and which continued to be readily available throughout Germany in the years that followed. The authorities were aware of the fact that both inside Germany and beyond its boundaries it was being widely read and interpreted as an anti-Nazi book—yet they did nothing. Was there some policy decision behind this? Did they believe the author's own statements that he had no intention of writing an anti-Nazi work? Did Jünger, despite his story's very obvious parallels with the rise of National Socialism, attempt to throw the authorities off the scent by writing in a deliberately esoteric and obscure manner, leaving 'dark passages' which did not have any obvious parallel with National Socialism? Whatever the reasons, the authorities were not fooled, and Boulher immediately proposed that the book be placed on the index. What happened after that is not known—only that it was not banned. Perhaps it avoided this fate for tactical reasons, because Jünger was such a famous nationalist figure or because Hitler had the author labelled in his mind as a front-line fighter and holder of the Pour le Mérite and refused to change his image of him. Also Goebbels was said to be flattered and amused because Braquemart was modelled on him. All this is mere conjecture. The simple fact remains that the author and his book encountered no difficulties inside Germany.

Various arguments have been adduced in favour of reading Jünger's story as resistance literature.[18] It is, for instance, a tale about a tyrant, although, as has been seen with Bergengruen, Schneider and others, this was by no means a unique choice of theme, nor one which unduly worried the Nazi literary guardians. What does make Jünger different from the others is that he does not deal with his theme in a historical setting, nor even against an exotic, geographical background. Instead he moves freely between past and present, North and South, openly constructing his plot and people for his own expressive purposes. Despite this, various elements in the story immediately suggest contemporary Germany. Jünger's is a story of despotism and rule by terror. It also shows an almost ideal state, a Utopia, being undermined and brought to a state of collapse. There are many echoes of the rise of National Socialism, for example in the violence employed by the ruling clique and the inability of a cowed populace to offer any resistance, the behaviour of the quasi-military thugs, the cult of primitivism, the liquidation of former allies, the linguistic brutality. In effect a multiplicity of elements of this kind certainly make it possible to read the first part of the novel as an account of the end of the Weimar Republic, when the people lost all sense of direction and became ready to accept a 'strong leader' and submit to his will; when justice collapsed, the bureaucracy was infiltrated, revolutionaries and anarchists destroyed the system, and the new leader paralysed society by alternating terror and relief, or by creating chaos before offering himself as protection from it. Yet though all this fits the historical framework very well, what Jünger offers as the moral of his tale is not quite so obvious. If he has gone through some kind of 'transformation', he is still not very clear about the values he is putting in the place of the old militaristic ones. Certainly he is not in the same religious category as Bergengruen or Schneider, though he does seem to be advocating similar virtues of order and responsibility. Nor does he invite the reader to resist, indeed resistance is dismissed as devoid of any hope of success.

Another criticism levelled against Jünger is directed at the aestheticism of his work. He is accused of being 'precious' both in expression and in point of view. What he offers in this novel has been described as a 'flight into an artificial world'. Yet this was no new element in Jünger's work. He was always the dandy, the meticulous scholar, the precision worker. The difference now is that he seems to be using exquisite words and images as a deliberate counterweight to the ugliness of evil and the chaos of society. The result is a strange, almost Romantic mixture of love and death, order and chaos. The style is supercharged with symbol and hieroglyph, allegory and myth, to a point where no clear meaning can emerge. Jünger seems to be playing a dangerous game, letting the reader suspect that a seditious statement is being made, but expressing it in a mysterious way. There is never any doubting Jünger's courage, but he also seems to be demonstrating his need to be different, his need for elitist, snobbish isolation, his need to keep the hierarchical distance. It is significant that in the novel his hero preserves his position as a mere observer and never joins any of the conflicting parties and certainly does not ally himself with the lower classes. His attitude remains fundamentally undemocratic and anti-Enlightenment. Emmerich has described the world of the *Marble Cliffs* as nothing other than 'the calligraphical, mystical escape-realm of inwardness', while Lämmert talks of Jünger's *dégagement* – that is, unwillingness to take sides.[19] There are strong arguments for accepting this to be the case, for Jünger himself claimed that his novel had no particular political message. After 1945 he more than once denied that his novel had any 'tendency' and his diaries too confirm that he never had any thought of resistance when he wrote the novel and put all such readings down to the imagination of the reader. 'The Chief Ranger was supposed to be Hitler, or Goering, or Stalin. Of course I foresaw that kind of thing, but I *never intended it*,' or: 'Non, ce livre n'était pas contre Hitler.'

Despite the author's own protestations, *On the Marble Cliffs* is still read as if it were an example of inner emigration writing. One of the most recent non-German Jünger specialists has no doubts about this whatsoever:

> *Auf den Marmorklippen* is clearly an act of resistance and an accusation, a thinly veiled criticism of totalitarian nihilism. It describes the factional strife within this movement which, in Germany, reached its climax in 1934 when Hitler crushed an opposing faction with ruthless violence. The author shows up the terroristic practices by graphically describing a camp of torture and murder.[20]

But there have been just as many critical voices claiming the opposite. Largely because of Jünger's earlier career and strongly held beliefs there was a reluctance to accept the theorist of 'total mobilisation' as the author of a resistance novel. Before 1945 and during the years of the National Socialist regime there was no such reluctance. The reception of the novel between 1933 and 1945 both inside and outside Germany clearly shows that this was how the work was understood, and indeed there was general amazement that such a work could have been published under NS censorship, let alone be made available freely in thousands of copies. Perhaps the quaint old-fashioned guise did help, after all characters from a pastoral world like the Chief Ranger, the Monk and the Shepherd do not immediately call to mind a Germany which, by 1939, had for long been a modern industrial nation with big cities, and masses of industrial proletariat employing advanced technology for war or peace. Of all this there is no trace whatsoever in Jünger's book. Perhaps this was why the army printed twenty thousand copies of this resistance novel in Paris in 1942.

While no one would ever seriously suggest that Jünger's novel was fascist, it does reek of Blood and Soil. Curiously the same could be said of the works of Ernst Wiechert, another conservative author who was wooed by the National Socialists.[21] Wiechert seemed the kind of writer of whom they would approve. In 1932 he had won two awards — in the words of the first, for his novel's 'confession of faith in work and fidelity, its human purity, its literary power and artistic perfection'.

He even expressed the desire to write a 'cantata of the German soul', a book to be called *The Third Reich*. In effect he shared many of the basic attitudes of the National Socialists. His themes were theirs—blood (that is the significance of racial purity within the family); closeness to the soil as against the rootlessness of the city; the struggle against the chaos caused by the men of revolution; clean, brave Germanness; heroism not in words but in being; the defeat of the materialism of the modern age; the defence of what is right. Essentially the earlier Wiechert looked backward to a better time in the past, when the lives of the bourgeois were not so barren and when the workers were not so grasping and self-centred. As a result he tended to be classed among those writers like Grimm and Kolbenheyer, who did not get the respect they deserved from the left-wing intellectual clique supposedly controlling the literary scene in the Weimar Republic. Wiechert himself denounced the commercialisation of art in the Republic and criticised the academies, societies and clubs which went in for divisive literary debates and squabbles instead of working to bring about a harmonious national community. Almost one year after the seizure of power he published an essay on 'The Duties of the German Book Trade in the National Socialist State', in which, while not approving of extreme measures, he nevertheless went a long way towards agreeing with the aims and goals of NS literary policies. Between the years 1939 and 1944 Wiechert was fairly sure of general approval for his literary endeavours; after all, as he was later to say:

> I did not want to write polemics, I just wanted to carry on writing my books as I had done till then. Not Blood-and-Soil books, but Soil books, the only difference being that on my soil love grew, not hate or Germanic grandchildren of the Gods. And that this soil was as ancient as the first book of Moses.[22]

In general, Wiechert's self-diagnosis was accurate, though he perhaps played down the religion of blood and the sword, the idea of war as a means to purification, in a word all the commonplace nationalist concepts, which assumed such a large part in his early works, alongside the curative power of the natural world and the agnostic's developing awareness of the New Testament doctrine of love. By 1936, however, Wiechert was suddenly under heavy fire from the *Völkischer Beobachter* for his book *Of Forests and Men*. Where had he gone wrong? For one thing in the year of the great German successes, the year of the greatest optimism of the people, he had complained that modern German youth

no longer knew what *Weltschmerz* meant, and he had praised pessimism.
The article in the *Völkischer Beobachter* was not criticism of Wiechert
as a writer, but an exploration of his *Weltanschauung*, which was not
positive enough about National Socialism. It claimed that his characters
showed the influence of Slav blood, evidence therefore of racial
contamination, that he had dared to name Jewish models like Heine
with approval, showing that he was himself contaminated with the
Jewish spirit, that he preferred sickness to health, and insisted on the
individual stance instead of accepting the NS folk community. This
was quite a change! Until 1935 most journals had written very
positively about his works and he was viewed very favourably. Wiechert
himself was well aware of this:

> In 1933 it was still the case that the powers that be thought anybody
> who could write *Doskocil* must be one of us . . . Even in 1935 the
> path was still open for me, and I knew very well that it would be a
> dazzling path externally, if I would only grasp the hand which was
> still stretched out to me.[23]

But Ernst Wiechert had not taken the hand that was held out to him.
True he continued to write as he had done before and that was a way
which the Nazi authorities did not find unacceptable. What they did
find unacceptable were his public acts of defiance. Nevertheless what
he wrote continued to be successful, and his novel *The Simple Life*,
published after a spell in concentration camps, sold over a quarter of a
million copies between 1939 and 1941. Unlike most novels of the inner
emigration considered so far, this was not a historical novel, nor was it
set in the immediate present. Wiechert set his action in the period after
the First World War and dealt with the problems of the soldier returning
from the chaos of war and seeking order. This he finds not in the
modern city, but far removed from it, in the simple life close to nature.
There was much in this that the National Socialists could accept — the
experience of war, the closeness of the soil, the rejection of the corrupting influence of the metropolis, though they perhaps could not accept
criticism of the reactionary military mentality, nor Wiechert's
sentimental pessimism and fatalistic acceptance of things. Nevertheless
the novel clearly struck a popular chord. Wiechert's public actions were
another matter. In April 1935 he had addressed the students in the
Auditorium Maximum of the University of Munich and appealed to
them to listen to the voices of their conscience and not let themselves
be seduced. In 1937 he gave a public reading in Cologne from his *White*

Buffalo, an Indian legend on the theme of justice and the struggle
between truth and falsehood. This was applauded so enthusiastically
that the Gestapo interrupted the reading. The existence of this story,
his protest against the arrest of Niemöller, the printing of his 1935
address to the Munich students in the Moscow *émigré* journal *Das Wort*,
his 'No' to the *Anschluss* with Austria plebiscite, were all factors which
led to Wiechert's arrest in the spring of 1938. After two months of
exploratory confinement in the Munich prison, he was transferred to
Buchenwald towards the end of 1938. Here he does not seem to have
been given the full treatment: nevertheless, even modified Buchenwald
was horrific enough. After this taste of what it could be like, he was
released as a living proof of Hitler's (or Goebbels') generosity and made
to deny at the Weimar Conference stories about ever having been in a
concentration camp. Later he recorded his experience of the KZ in the
story *Forest of the Dead*, which like everything else written before the
end of the war he buried in his garden. It was not published until 1946.

The Wiechert case is symptomatic for the development of literature
inside Germany during the period 1933-45. Immediately after 1933
the old-established literary journals were still in existence and they still
continued to publish and review the established literary figures of the
nationalist-conservative school in just the same way as they had done
before the Nazis came to power. On the Nazi side there was a multiplicity of different government agencies dealing with literature and
culture, and hence no coordinated party policy was always available.
Problems were dealt with from case to case; in general, however, it was
recognised that the party needed the support of the older generation
until it could produce a new generation of writers of its own. Once the
regime was established, fewer and fewer concessions were made, and
one by one the members of the older generation were called to order.
Even then the hierarchy seems to have decided to leave books alone and
only to deal with people. Bergengruen, Wiechert, Jünger, Schneider,
Thiess were all permitted to publish their books and enjoy the benefits
of high sales. Any public declaration against the party, however, any
real sign of open protest or resistance, as distinct from literary
camouflage, was immediately dealt with. The Nazis themselves do not
seem to have considered inner emigration a source of serious danger to
them.

7 RESISTANCE

In the light of the apparatus of the police state in Germany, and later in Austria, the question immediately arises whether any kind of literary resistance was possible.[1] Resistance as such was never on the same scale or of the same type as resistance in occupied countries or even in a fascist state like Italy. Inside Germany large-scale sabotage was not possible, trains were not blown up, the army was not attacked and there was never any suggestion of extensive underground forces launching clandestine operations. Nevertheless Hitler was notoriously terrified of conspiracy, assassination attempts on his life were not unknown and his personal security was rigorous. As far as the written word was concerned it is also well known that even the slightest manifestation of opposition provoked retaliation — wall messages, illegal newspapers, political pamphlets were treated as major offences and the perpetrators of them were ruthlessly hunted down. Arrests were on a sweeping scale, whole families were taken, court cases against such 'resisters' often involved scores of people, all of which contrasts markedly with the comparative lack of interest shown in the inner emigration, whose duplicated poems were said to be circulating illegally in large numbers. So there is no need to wonder whether there was resistance or not. In the eyes of the Nazi authorities it existed, the simple proof is the number of people who were arrested after 1933 for offences against the regime. A Marxist like Brecht also knew that there were two kinds of Germans, and in the poem which he dedicated to the resistance fighters in the concentration camps he made it clear which he thought were Germany's real leaders:

Also seid ihr
Verschwunden, aber
Nicht vergessen
Niedergeknüppelt, aber
Nicht widerlegt
Zusammen mit allen unverbesserbar Weiterkämpfenden
Unbelehrbar auf der Wahrheit Beharrenden
Weiterhin die wahren
Führer Deutschlands[2]

(So you may have disappeared, but you're not forgotten,
been clubbed down, but not refuted.
Together with all those incorrigibles who fight on,
those unteachables who insist on the truth, you
remain Germany's true leaders.)

When Günther Weisenborn, who had himself been active in the resistance
and spent years in Nazi prisons, published an article after the war with
the title 'There was a German Resistance', he received hundreds of
letters from people who had been involved in it like himself and had
suffered for it, and these included many writers and intellectuals. He
also later met Ricarda Huch, the poetess who had refused to remain a
member of the nazified Academy, and discovered that she had been
assembling material on resistance. Shortly before she died she invited
him to continue her work; he did so and published his results in the
book *Der lautlose Aufstand*[3] (*The Silent Revolt*, 1953), in which he
showed the nature and extent of German resistance, whether by
Socialist and Communist workers, church people, army officers, middle-
class groups, intellectuals and writers, or simply by individuals. Much
of the information came from Gestapo sources and police and court
reports. According to his estimates there were around 300,000 people,
most of them German, in concentration camps at the beginning of the
war, and approximately one million people had actually passed through
the camps by then. The war years brought even greater numbers
(including non-Germans) and final estimates go into the millions. So
there certainly were Germans who did not agree with the policies and
practice of National Socialism and showed their disagreement
sufficiently to be severely punished for it. The *other* Germany existed.
It could be decimated but never totally destroyed. Nor did it consist
entirely of those in high army circles involved in the attempt on
Hitler's life on 20 July 1944, or of those wonderful young idealists
associated with the White Rose group who saved the honour of the
German university after the disgrace of the Burning of the Books by
Nazi students.[4] After the war, former resistance fighters and concentration camp inmates were regarded as heroes in the German Democratic
Republic but largely ignored in the Federal German Republic. After all,
it was argued, resistance had accomplished nothing. The resistance
fighters had not broken the Nazi regime, the Allied armies had. In the
West conservative writers of the inner emigration were highly regarded
and awarded literary prizes, while writers of more radical persuasion
were hardly mentioned. As a result it was easy for the general assumption

to spread that the other Germany had no existence and that as far as literature was concerned there never had been anything of an outspoken, anti-Nazi kind.

What has to be realised is that anti-Hitler literature did not only start after 1933.[5] As early as 1923 Ernst Toller had written a bitter farce called *Wotan Unbound* with Hitler in mind, but Toller was something of an exception and it was some time before most writers and intellectuals were prepared to take Hitler seriously and not merely present him as a figure of fun. Nevertheless it is important to be aware of what anti-Nazi literature there was in the Weimar Republic, for only then is it possible to understand the reactions of the Nazis to certain writers when they came to power. Joseph Roth, for example in his *Spider's Web* (1923), revealed the fascination Hitler had for nationalistically minded ex-officer types. Lion Feuchtwanger, too, in his novel *Success* tried to grasp the reasons for Hitler's success, but was still inclined to view his political career as some kind of Bavarian excess, without significance for Germany as a whole. Even the old Expressionist Georg Kaiser was aware of the Nazi menace and in his historical play *Leatherheads* (1928) tried to show what the Nazi street fighters were really like. Unfortunately his play contained all the weaknesses of his later abstract style. By contrast, post-Expressionists exploiting the possibilities of the 'New Objectivity' tended to be cynical and disinterested. Erich Kästner, for instance in *Fabian*, his Berlin novel of decadence and inflation, showed the street-fights between the Reds and the Brownshirts, but had his hero say: 'I'm watching and waiting. I'm waiting for the victory of the decent people then maybe I could make myself available.'[6] Fallada too in a novel like *Little Man – What Now?* (1932), did not take sides. Not until *We All Die Alone* did he tackle a resistance theme based on Gestapo documents. Both Kästner and Fallada stayed on in Germany after 1933, avoiding involvement with National Socialism. Horváth in a play like *Sladek* (1928) was capable of showing the petty bourgeois gradually being caught up in fascist brutality, but preferred to let the action speak for itself, though to judge from this and other works, there is no doubt where he stood.

Gradually, as Hitler became more powerful in the early thirties, writers and intellectuals became more alarmed. After the September elections of 1930 Thomas Mann addressed the nation with his appeal to reason, deploring fanaticism as un-German. He himself had been a slow developer politically, and in his literary works was never outspoken on fascism. *Mario and the Magician* (1930), which has often been read as if it dealt with Hitler and his hypnotic fascination, went back to a holiday experience in 1926 and, if anything, refers to Italian fascism and not to German. Mann's defence of the republic simply came too late. Mention is often made of the left-wing radical group associated with the journal *Die Weltbühne*. These Jewish intellectuals were aware of the danger inherent in the divided left wing, in which Socialists and Communists spent more time and energy attacking each other than they did attacking the Nazis, and hence they came round to support for the united front policy in defence of the republic, a goal that was never realised. The best-known of this group was Tucholsky and, though he too was slow to see the danger of Hitler and his party, he eventually became one of the Führer's bitterest opponents, using the wit of his pen to ridicule the man with the funny moustache in poems, songs, sketches and essays. Satire and the grotesque were his weapons and political cabaret the medium he used for his attacks. The Hitler camp detested him thoroughly. He himself despaired, saw himself as a prophet crying in the wilderness and finally committed suicide in Sweden. After Tucholsky the most famous of the *Weltbühne* circle was Carl von Ossietsky, the editor. He too attacked and made fun of Hitler and suffered for it after 1933, when he was taken first to Sonnenburg and then to Esterwegen concentration camp in the peat bogs of north-west Germany. The sufferings of this famous pacifist became the centre of an international outcry which led to his being awarded the Nobel Peace Prize for 1935, which infuriated the Nazis even more. He died as the result of his treatment at their hands on 4 May 1938. Many literary figures had played their part in the mass movement for the peace martyr including Romain Rolland, Heinrich and Thomas Mann, H.G. Wells, J.B. Priestley, Virginia Woolf and Aldous Huxley. Ossietsky became a symbol of the 'other Germany', as Wickham Steed indicated in *The Times*:

> This is a proof of what Germany can be, a real German character and real culture, an example of those upright and fearless men who will, one day, demand and obtain for their fatherland an assured and rightful place in the family of nations.[7]

Another literary figure of the Weimar Republic hated by Hitler was the Jewish anarchist Erich Mühsam who, like Tucholsky, ridiculed the Nazis in verse and song. His drama *All Weathers – a Folk-play with Singing and Dancing* (1930) made fun of the 'Workers' Racial Party', but Mühsam knew by then how serious the situation was and called for a united front and a general strike to stop the Nazis. He too was a particular target after 1933, was imprisoned and tortured to death. On 10 July 1934 his battered corpse was found hanging in a latrine at Oranienburg concentration camp.[8] Equally active were left-wing writers and pacifists like Kurt Hiller, Fritz von Unruh, Heinrich Mann and Walter Benjamin. While by this time the anti-Semitic, chauvinistic nature of the movement was clear for all to see, the economic roots of fascism had attracted little comment. This area was, however, examined by Erich Reger in his novel *Union of the Firm Hand* (1931), dealing with the history of the Krupp Works, and by Bernard von Brentano in his book *The Beginning of Barbarism in Germany* (1932). While the perspective of such works was clearly left-wing, there were also attacks upon Hitler from the other political pole, most noticeably from National Bolshevists like Ernst Niekisch. Ernst von Salomon's *The City* (1932) gives some idea of what a National Bolshevist novel looks like.

The official organs of the Socialist and Communist parties tended to be rather timid. In the cultural field anti-Nazi forces gathered within the framework of the bodies put together by the organisational genius Willi Münzenberg, the BPRS (Bund proletarisch-revolutionärer Schriftsteller – Union of Proletarian Revolutionary Writers) and the ASSO (Assoziation revolutionärer bildender Künstler Deutschlands – Association of Revolutionary Artists).[9] In this sphere, by far the greatest impact was achieved by the satirical drawings and the photo-montages of John Heartfield in the *AIZ* (*Arbeiter-Illustrierte-Zeitung*), ridiculing 'His Majesty Adolf'. As far as literary forms were concerned the most effective were marches, 'Red Songs' and satirical poems, with Erich Weinert emerging as the greatest exponent of the aggressive poem and the witty song. His public performances were widely acclaimed. Brecht too tried his hand at Agitprop verses with the four 'Antifa' poems written before 1933: 'The Führer has said'; 'When Fascism got Stronger and Stronger'; 'The Song of the SA Man' and 'The Song of the Class Enemy', in which, like Weinert, he advocated a proletarian united front from below. The Communist Party also developed its own theatre parties to put on topical sketches and shows. Among the best-known were the Red Mouth-Piece and the Red Rats, with sketches like *Nazis Among Themselves.* More fully developed anti-fascist dramas were written by Friedrich Wolf in *The Lads of Mons* (1931) and *Peasant Baetz* (1932), or by Gustav von Wangenheim, whose play *The Mousetrap* (1931), written for Troup 31, a collection of unemployed actors, set out to show how the Führer won the support of the lower middle classes. The KPD also tried to exercise some influence on the minds of the workers, with their series of anti-fascist

Red-One-Mark-Novels, of which the most important was Willi Bredel's *Rosenhofstrasse* (1931). Comrades like Bredel, Wolf, Wangenheim, Weinert, Becher, Brecht, Seghers, Scharrer, Grünberg, Uhse, Regler, Kantorowicz were all active in the 1930s in the fight against fascism and remained active in exile and in the Spanish Civil War. Events were soon to prove wrong those who ridiculed them for wasting their time on a 'puppet' like Hitler.

As early as September 1933, in the first number of the Prague exile journal *Neue Deutsche Blätter*, Ernst Fischer set out the three possibilities open to writers opposed to the new Germany:

> They can stay in Germany under cover, attack fascism from linguistic ambush or by artistic masking device, in the expectation that sooner or later their mouths will be shut and the pens smashed from their fingers. They can work anonymously for the illegal press inside the country or for the anti-fascist press abroad. They can cross the frontier and address themselves to the Germans from abroad.

This gives a fair idea of what resistance literature meant, namely literature which was anti-fascist and not merely non-fascist, and which also aimed to have some effect inside Germany itself. Various permutations were possible; literature written, produced and read inside Germany; anti-fascist literature smuggled into Germany; literature written in Germany but smuggled out; the literary activities of resistance fighters in concentration camps and prisons; and even opposition literature produced legally but written in a form not spotted by the censors.

When the National Socialists came to power on 30 January 1933 the democratic forces were ill-prepared. Not even the workers' party organisations had contingency plans for going under cover and continuing illegally, and all had been so successfully bureaucratised that the police authorities had party membership lists and knew where to go to make their arrests. Trade union and party leaders were quickly rounded up and put away. The Professional Writers Organisation was wound up. Some late attempts to organise resistance were made. In the weeks before 27 February (the day of the Reichstag Fire) a meeting of left-wing writers was organised and the long-planned Congress of the Free Word met in the Kroll Opera House in Berlin, but nothing was accomplished. The BPRS, which had been so active towards the end of the Weimar Republic, was a prime target for the Nazis and leading members had to leave the country. Those who failed to do so were arrested. A first report called *Brains behind Barbed-Wire*, printed in Switzerland in 1934, gave a list of writers persecuted and imprisoned in the first year.[10] Among the names were BPRS members Willi Bredel, Ludwig Renn, Franz Braun and Klaus Neukrantz, but also other non-members like Erich Mühsam, Kurt Hiller and Carl von Ossietsky. Anna Seghers, Egon Erwin Kisch and Kurt Kläber had also been arrested, but subsequently set free. In 1934/5 Brecht wrote his *Five Difficulties in Writing the Truth*, in which he dealt with the problems of writing and distributing oppositional literature in conditions such as those prevailing in Germany. By then he was himself in exile and his pamphlet had to be smuggled back into Germany between false covers. What Brecht from outside Germany probably failed to understand was just how difficult the non-creative side of any subversive operation was; how difficult it was to print or distribute anything, when simply being in possession of an oppositional pamphlet could be punishable by death.

BPRS writers close to the Communist Party were the first to regroup after the first wave of arrests. They put out pamphlets, stuck slogans on walls, and provided contacts abroad with inside information on conditions in Germany. Most important was the activity of the Berlin group of the BPRS, which even managed to issue an illegal newspaper, *Stich und Hieb*, between 1933 and 1935. There were, of course, other Communist newspapers and works newssheets. In Berlin there was also the *Red Flag*. *Parry and Thrust* was different from these in that the title did not immediately indicate a Communist affiliation. It is difficult to form a firm impression of this paper for, because of the danger of handling it at the time, only the first number and parts of the second have survived. However, it was also different from other underground political papers, in that it contained comments on the cultural scene, satirical passages, sketches, short stories and other literary offerings including verses and jokes. Jan Petersen's story *The Street*, which appeared in the second number, was picked up and re-printed in several other clandestine papers. Although later often republished by the exile press, its first and most immediate impact was on readers inside Germany who could identify with the experiences recounted in it. This Berlin BPRS group was rounded up by the Gestapo in 1935 and all its members arrested, except for those who, like Jan Petersen, had emigrated. However, other BPRS groups were formed in other cities to carry on the work of resistance. According to one account of the people involved, there emerged

a new type of writer . . . so diametrically different from the way the
wanted notice of the petty bourgeois portrays him. He has become
hard and disciplined, one day he is down in a cellar editing an
illegal newspaper – a dead man on holiday – another day he is
composing crude verses, yet again he is running them off or sticking
them on walls, in the meantime sifting the material which is to form
the basis for a larger novel or a bigger piece of reporting. No theatre
première envelops him with its applause, no prizes are awarded him,
no fees await him, no press proclaims his name.[11]

The writer in exile did not have to put up with hardships and difficulties
of this kind and all of this did have an effect on the kind of literary
material produced. Oppositional poetry often meant *Klebeverse* – two-
or three-line rhyming slogans for distribution by sticking on walls, lines
which were immediately comprehensible and as memorable as
advertising slogans, but containing a political message of illumination
and enlightenment. So the Nazi slogan 'Volk ans Gewehr' ('People to
Arms') and the slogan about guns before butter were fused into:

Die Margarine wird teurer
Die Butter noch mehr
Volk ans Gewehr![12]

(Marg gets dearer, butter even more so, people to arms!)

The limitations of such extremely brief poetic forms are obvious. The
impact had to be immediate. There was no room for subtlety of
thought or argument. Even vocabulary and metre had to be of the most
basic kind. There was little scope for development. Art lay in the
concealment of art.

Concealment was also the major element in the so-called *Tarnschriften*,
which were smuggled into the country.[13] After the elimination of the
party printing facilities in Berlin by successful Gestapo raids, various
clandestine printing materials were smuggled into the country in the
form of print-ready stencils, printing blocks and so on. Nearly 80 per
cent of all printed material smuggled in was party material – the
writings of masters of Marxism like Marx, Engels and Lenin or other
training material for Communist Party cells needed for briefing on
changes in the party line, for example during the Hitler-Stalin Pact, or
the Spanish Civil War. There was also a steady trade in literary classics
and works of some newer Marxists like Brecht, Renn and Rudolf

Leonhard were also smuggled in. More important than such *Tarn-schriften* were literary works smuggled *out* for publication abroad. The authors of these works, the authentic voice of anti-Nazi resistance, saw it as their duty to make the world aware of the existence of the other, secret Germany, the democratic Germany that was not Hitler's. Their aim was to mobilise the world outside against Hitler's Germany and to awaken sympathy for the inner German resistance. The most important figure was the Berlin editor of an exile journal, which set out 'to let the voice of freedom suppressed in Germany speak'. The journal was the *Neue Deutsche Blätter*, a literary and critical monthly which appeared in Prague between September 1933 and August 1935. This journal had as a regular feature a column called: *A Voice from Germany*. Other exile journals attempted to have the same. The mysterious Berlin editor of the *Neue Deutsche Blätter* was Jan Petersen, who made something like ten trips between Berlin and Prague to bring out around sixty contributions for the journal. The important thing was to keep up a flow of authentic material from Nazi Germany in the form of eye-witness accounts, autobiographical stories, tales from the everyday life of the workers and little people which cast a light on the reality of Nazi terror. However, the importance of these contributions was perhaps marred by the party line which foretold the imminent collapse of the Nazi regime and still revealed Communist reluctance to co-operate with the Socialists against the common enemy.

Jan Petersen (or Hans Schwalm) occupies a unique position in the history of resistance literature in Germany. Born in 1906 in Berlin, he had trained as a turner and toolmaker. In 1930 he became a member of the Communist Party and was from 1930 to 1933 co-organiser of the BPRS. He carried on this work under cover after 1933 until 1935. In 1935 he took part in the First International Writers' Congress for the Defence of Culture in Paris as a representative of the other Germany, appearing on the platform as the 'Man in the Black Mask'. He was a sensation! The last words of his speech were:

> The land of poets and thinkers has turned into a land of hypocrites and hangmen. But Germany is not Hitler! The Germany of tomorrow, the Germany of Freedom is on the move, it has struck such deep, underground roots, that even the bloodiest terror cannot tear them up! This is the Germany we write for! This is the Germany we're fighting for![14]

He was exaggerating the strength of the forces of freedom in Germany.

His group was rounded up in his absence, he was ordered not to return to Germany and he emigrated to Switzerland. Even there he was not safe, for the Nazis tried to have him extradited, so he moved on to England where he became Chairman of the Writers' Section of the Free German Cultural Association in London and member of English PEN. He was interned in Canada from 1940-1 before finally returning to the German Democratic Republic, where he was acclaimed and awarded the National Prize in 1959. Petersen was the author of *Our Street. A Chronicle Written in the Heart of Fascist Germany* (1933/4), *Gestapo Trial* (1939) and *Germany Beneath the Surface. Stories of the Underground Movement* (1940). With these writings in mind Petersen has been called the 'first significant literary chronicler of the resistance movement'. It was the success of his story *Street* in *Parry and Thrust* which encouraged Petersen to write his more extended chronicle, while still actually active with a resistance group in Berlin. This chronicle *Our Street* was intended not merely as a story with local significance, restricted to one street in a working-class district, but as a picture of how fascism affected working-class districts in all German cities.[15] It is fictionalised, of course, to protect the real people involved, but the proclaimed intention is also to be as 'authentic' as possible and the dead named at the beginning are real anti-fascists murdered in Charlottenburg. At the same time this book was intended as a 'memorial to the bravery of *thousands, tens of thousands* of nameless heroes, who carry on the fight despite the threat of imprisonment and execution'. In effect therefore the book claims that resistance inside Germany was no limited matter involving only a few good Germans, but rather a continuation of the Battle for the Streets, which had been such a feature of the Weimar Republic. After 1933 the fascists knew where the opposition lay and attacked this street and its Socialist occupants ruthlessly. What the chronicle shows is the day-to-day life of the people who live in it, the kind of people who are the backbone of resistance to fascism. It was written to show something different from the official picture of the new Germany, to show that there *was* another Germany. If writing the chronicle was difficult enough because of the dangers involved, getting it out of a hermetically sealed Germany was even more difficult and the manuscript was eventually smuggled out in a dramatic way and published. What Petersen offers is something entirely different from the literary excellence and refined art of the inner emigrants. His is not a historical novel, but a chronicle of the present time as it is happening, recording events from 21 January 1933 until the middle of 1934. The sections are dated as in a diary, and important

political points like Hitler's nomination as Reich Chancellor, the
Reichstag Fire, the plebiscite over Germany leaving the League of
Nations, and the workers' uprising in Austria form the framework for
the events of the street. Petersen also gives variety to his documentary
account by inserting dramatic scenes, colloquial exchanges in Berlin
slang, comments and reflections, dreams and visions. There is no plot
as such, only a string of episodes allowing the people and the street to
come to life. The political bias of the book is not merely obvious, but
also openly declared, for it is not only dedicated to the liberation of
the German people and the victory of Socialism: it also specifically
concentrates on the illegal resistance of the Communist Party. The
need for the formation of a People's Front with the Socialists and for
contacts abroad is, however, stressed. Despite the clearly stated political
intention, the main impression that comes across is the brutality of
the SA. Although the author is aware of the attractions of fascism for
the unemployed and the petty bourgeois, National Socialism is exposed
as a reign of terror. Resistance of the kind shown in Petersen's account
was possible only at a very early stage in the national 'revolution'.
Petersen shows not only the forces massed against the workers, but
also the other sources of support for fascism in Germany, most notably
the legal system and the law courts. The second part of his chronicle is
concerned more with the political show trials in Germany than with
street fighting. In the case brought against the Communist Hüttig for
shooting the Nazi Ahé, Hüttig is condemned to death, although even
the *Völkischer Beobachter* admits that he was probably not even in the
vicinity at the time. Fourteen others get 94 years' hard labour and 18
years in prison! The Maikowski trial ends with 53 defendants condemned to 39 years' hard labour and 95 years in prison. The *Völkischer
Beobachter* is quoted for its comments on the 'mildness' of the verdict:
'No death sentences for the red bandits.' Petersen's street is finally
renamed the Maikowskistrasse after this dead Nazi 'hero'. Resistance
fails and fascism triumphs.

   Petersen's book has many weaknesses, and although the author
constantly took advice from a professional colleague (now known to
be the literary critic Louis Kaufmann), the style is often that of a semi-
educated amateur, although to some extent this increases the impression
of authenticity. The party line is also something of a handicap, as the
author dwells on apparent contradictions within the SA and looks for
the signs of the internal collapse the Communist party line predicted.
Despite these flaws the world-wide impact of the book in various
languages was enormous. One commentator put the world total at

800,000 copies by 1966, many, but by no means all, of which were published in East Germany after 1945, where the book came to be treated as a classic of resistance literature.

While Petersen's *Our Street* was perhaps the 'only Anti-Nazi book written in Hitler's Germany and published abroad', there were other similar books which carried on the process of telling the world outside what conditions were really like and which therefore belong to the literature of anti-fascist resistance, although they had to be written after their authors had escaped from the concentration camps and had reached the safety of foreign shores. Hans Beimler, a metal worker and Reichstag Communist Party member, was arrested in 1933 and sent to Dachau. Showing incredible daring, he effected a sensational escape and published *Im Mörderlager Dachau* in Moscow in 1933 as one of the very first concentration camp reports. It appeared in English under the title *Four Weeks in the Hands of Hitler's Hell-Hounds*. Hans Beimler made his way to Spain, where he was a very successful military leader until he was killed in action in 1936.

Willi Bredel came from a worker's family in Hamburg. By 1917 he had progressed through the Socialist youth movement to Spartakus and by 1919 he was a member of the Communist Party. In 1923 he took part in the Hamburg workers' revolt for which he received two years' imprisonment. He was a member of the BPRS and in 1930 again received two years' imprisonment. During this time, as has been noted, he developed as a writer of party novels. In 1933 he was arrested, escaped to Czechoslovakia after his release and in 1935 made his way to the Soviet Union, where he was active in exile literary circles. In 1937 he took part in the Second International Writers' Congress for the Defence of Culture and from 1937 till 1939 was Commisar with the Thälmann Battalion of the International Brigades in the Spanish Civil War. He too returned to East Germany after 1945, became a member of the Central Committee of the SED, winner of the National Prize and President of the Academy of Arts in East Berlin. Like so many others Bredel was arrested after the Reichstag Fire in February 1933 and imprisoned in the Fühlsbüttel concentration camp outside Hamburg, where

> in solitary confinement and darkness, during the nights in which I was whipped, during the other nights in which I had to listen to the screams of my imprisoned comrades, I worked in my mind on a book on this place of death . . . This novel I took with me to freedom, as as contraband in my head when I passed through the old prison door.

After his flight from Nazi Germany he wrote the book in a remarkably short time and it came out under the title *The Test* (1934). He also wrote *The Informer and Other Stories* (1936). There were as many stories and sketches about the Nazi informer as there were about the 'Beef Steak Nazi' who was brown on the outside and red on the inside. Bredel followed this up later with his *Your Unknown Brother: Novel from the Third Reich* (1937), about one year in the life of a resistance fighter from 1934 till 1935 after he has been in a concentration camp.

When he wrote *The Test* Bredel was no untutored writer like Jan Petersen. He already had considerable writing experience and comparative success behind him.[16] He did share with Petersen the same Communist and BPRS background and therefore the same political perspective. The remarkable thing was that he decided to write his book as a novel and not directly as an eye-witness report. Why this should be so is something the author himself comments on, but first of all he stresses the authenticity of what he has to say. Of course the reality of the concentration camp world in 1933 was still a long way removed from the unspeakable horrors of the holocaust and the death camps of ten years later; nevertheless the reality which Bredel had to report was horrible enough. In his foreword he explained his basic attitude:

> The crass realism of these records has sometimes caused offence; however, I have not regarded it as my duty to embellish the facts or beat about the bush, even when they are a lasting disgrace for the culture of our people. In order to be able to shape the truth — and nothing but the documentary truth — while telling my story, I chose the form of the novel.[17]

Earlier he had also pointed out that he had not invented any of the characters in his novel. Like Petersen, he changed the names of prisoners and people still in need of protection, but kept the real names of the guards and persecutors. After the accepted manner of socialist realism, the novel also had one positive figure as a model of heroic behaviour in the face of torture and death — the Communist Reichstag member Matthias Thesen, who was kept alive in the camp for eleven and a half years without trial only to be murdered in the last hours of the Third Reich.

The title of the novel refers to how a man is tested by unheard of and unspeakable conditions. Bredel has respect for other sources of strength, but in the long run it is the Communist faith which helps man to survive and the solidarity of the comrades which gives hope for the future. This too is the reason why Bredel moves beyond the episodic, incident-by-incident chronicle of the Petersen approach. By writing a novel he can still impart the intensity of the experience through his first-person narrator, but the novel form also gives shape and form to the whole, permitting reflection on the meaning of this totally new experience and on the consequences to be drawn from it for future action. Bredel had been in prison before, but a Nazi concentration camp was something entirely different from the prisons of the Weimar Republic. This was something the world had never seen before, something which 'tested' the person to the core of his being, tested his beliefs and tested his image of the opponent. From the point of view of the party it meant re-thinking, realising that the new Nazi Germany was not just some continuation of the 'dictatorship of bourgeois capitalism', but something totally new. It was also clear that this terrorist dictatorship would not crumble in a short time under the weight of its own contradictions, to make way for the inevitable and real Socialist revolution after the false national revolution. The Communists had been wrong in their assessment of fascism in Germany and the test now consisted in whether the party could draw the right conclusions from this mistake which had left it with most of its leaders in the clutches of the dictator. But not only did the Communist have to test his view of fascism: he had to test his opponents and his fellow prisoners (including the Socialists), test the informers and above all test himself. In the end the crisis is overcome and the narrator emerges from this experience stronger than ever in his belief in Communism.

Written according to the author's own account in four weeks, the novel is nevertheless extremely effective both on the autobiographical, subjective level of a personal experience of suffering, and also on the objective level as a literary work with a didactic as well as aesthetic purpose. It has none of the obvious blemishes of haste which mar the impact of Petersen's *Our Street*. It had an impressive success outside Germany in the thirties, was translated into seventeen languages within a short space of time, and in the Soviet Union alone was brought out in an edition of one million copies.

Another author who reached a wide audience with his account of life in a concentration camp was Gerhart H. Seger. A lithographer by profession, Seger was also a journalist and a writer. From 1923 till 1928 he was general secretary of the German Peace Association which of itself made him a target for the Nazis who hated all pacifists. After experience as a newspaper editor he also became a Socialist member of the Reichstag. As such he was arrested in 1933 and imprisoned from March till December. His book *Oranienburg* bore the subtitle 'First Authentic Report, by an Escapee from a Concentration Camp' and was particularly effective because it was written by such a respected political figure and non-Communist. It appeared in English under the title: *A Nation Terrorized*. The most 'popular' concentration camp report was written by Wolfgang Langhoff, who actually refers in his book to Seger's *Oranienburg*. This actor and director was a well known theatrical figure in the Weimar Republic, who was also active in the workers' movement, appearing at big rallies and demonstrations put on by the Communist Party, reciting poems and doing dramatic readings which were enthusiastically received. He had been a member of the Communist Party since 1928. He too was arrested in 1933 and spent thirteen months in the Börgermoor concentration camp. After his release he escaped to Switzerland, where he became prominent again in the Zurich Schauspielhaus and also in the 'Free Germany' movement. After 1945 he lived first of all in Düsseldorf before settling in East Berlin as theatre director, national prize winner and leading light in the cultural life of the country, though not without some friction between himself and government circles. His book *The Moor Soldiers, Thirteen Months Concentration Camp* came out in Switzerland in 1935. Its most striking feature is the picture it imparts of the party organisation inside the camp, and of the solidarity of the prisoners against the SS oppressors, although because of the usual expectation of dissension within the Nazi ranks and the quest for the good Nazi his attempts at understanding the psychology and political motivation of his captors are occasionally naïve.[18] What Langhoff was describing was a very early stage in the development of the concentration camp system. As he said in a preface written for a post-war edition, Börgermoor was like an idyll compared with the gas chambers of Auschwitz, or the torture hells and mass graves of Bergen-Belsen, Buchenwald and Mauthausen ten years later. That, despite the torture and killing, this camp aimed to re-school Communists and dissenters is indicated by the number who were actually released. The commandant even allowed the inmates to put on a show, the 'Circus Conzentrazani', the most famous item of whose programme was the song which was to become a standard element in all anti-fascist shows around the world. This was the Börgermoor Song, written and composed in the Prussian State Concentration Camp I, Börgermoor/Tapenburg, with words by Johann Esser, a miner, refrain by Langhoff and melody by Rudi Goguel.

1. Wohin auch das Auge blicket,
   Moor und Heide nur ringsum.
   Vogelgesang uns nicht erquicket,
   Eichen stehen kahl und krumm.
       Wir sind die Moorsoldaten
       Und ziehen mit dem Spaten
   Ins Moor . . .

2. Hier in dieser öden Heide
   Ist das Lager aufgebaut.
   Wo wir ferne jeder Freude
   Hinter Stacheldraht verstaut. (Refrain)

3. Morgens ziehen die Kolonnen
   In das Moor zur Arbeit hin.
   Graben bei dem Brand der Sonnen
   Doch zur Heimat steht der Sinn. (Refrain)

4. Heimwärts, heimwärts jeder sehnet
   Zu den Eltern, Weib und Kind.
   Manche Brust ein Seufzer dehnet,
   Weil wir hier gefangen sind. (Refrain)

5. Auf und nieder geh'n die Posten
   Keiner, keiner kann hindurch.
   Flucht wird nur das Leben kosten,
   vierfach ist umzäunt die Burg. (Refrain)

6. Doch für uns gibt es kein Klagen,
   Ewig kann's nicht Winter sein,
   Einmal werden froh wir sagen:
   Heimat, Du bist wieder mein!
       Dann ziehn die Moorsoldaten
       Nicht mehr mit dem Spaten
   Ins Moor![19]

(As far as the eye can see nothing but moor and heath all around, no bird-song regales us, oak-trees stand bare and crooked.
   We are the moor-soldiers who march out to the moors with their spades

Here in this bleak heath the camp has been built. Far from pleasures of any kind we are stowed behind barbed-wire. (Refrain)

Every morning the columns march out to work on the moors.
They dig in the heat of the sun, but their thoughts turn to home.
> (Refrain)

Homewards, homewards, goes their longing, to parents, wife and
child. Many a breast heaves a sigh, because we are prisoners here.
> (Refrain)

Up and down go the guards, nobody, but nobody can escape.
Flight can cost your life, for the prison has a fourfold fence.

Yet we do not complain, winter cannot last for ever.
One day we'll rejoice and say: home, you're mine again!
> Then the moor-soldiers, will *not* march
> out to the moors with their spades.)

This is not great poetry, but when sung to the heavy, dark, marching
beat of the melody it could be tremendously moving: in the book even
the guards are moved. The song is banned, but constantly asked for and
repeatedly sung at work, a fine indication of the high spirits and good
morale of the men, despite the degrading brutalities they are subjected
to. Similar concentration camp reports were those of the Social
Democrat Julius Zerfass (written in 1936 under the pseudonym Walter
Horning), and of the Communist engineer Paul Massing (using the
pseudonym Karl Billinger). The latter's *Inmate 880. From a German
Concentration Camp* was printed in Paris in 1935 and translated into
many languages. Some of these concentration camp reports were
smuggled *back* into Germany, as extracts concealed in fake books, and
they had considerable effect there. As Ernst Bloch was to argue in his
essay 'The Nazi and the Unspeakable', nothing could be quite so
effective in exposing the true face of fascism and undermining its mass
following as the little grain of truth in a fact.

That women could be as brave as men in the face of torture and
brutality and as courageous in speaking the unspeakable was shown by
Lina Haag. She was active politically with her husband, the youngest
Communist member of the Württemberg government, and in 1933 they
were both arrested. She spent the next four and a half years in prisons
and concentration camps. After her own release from Lichtenburg she
never gave up her efforts to secure her husband's release and even got
as far as seeing Himmler personally. After seven years he was released
from Mauthausen only to be called up and sent to Russia. He eventually
survived that and came back from a Russian prisoner of war camp in

1948. Lina Haag's moving account, *A Handful of Dust*, was not published until 1947.[20] Also not published till after the war was Luise Rinser's *Prison Diary*. As a Fischer paperback, over one hundred thousand copies have been sold to date.

Wolfgang Emmerich has raised the question whether the concept of resistance literature should be expanded to include the use of literature as a means of resistance inside concentration camps and prisons.[21] Certainly there are many examples of literary works being employed in such circumstances to encourage the inmates, to impart a feeling of solidarity, reinforce individual identity or to give hope and encouragement. The aim of the concentration camp system was to crush and demoralise. The Börgermoor Song could show the SA and the SS that the prisoners were not subhuman. Besides, as Langhoff, Petersen and others show, there was a persistent belief at least in the earliest stages that perhaps the Nazis were not all bad; that with some the National Socialism was only skin-deep; that even real Nazis could be reached and possibly even re-converted. The authorities did permit dramatic performances of literary works by the prisoners at Buchenwald and Sachsenhausen though again it must be stressed that these were work camps and not places of mass murder. In some camps and prisons, inmates found literature a means of keeping their sanity, as well as strengthening their will to resist. Apart from literature as reading matter there are a surprising number of cases of literary works being actually written under impossible circumstances.

Possibly the most remarkable story in this connection is that of Theresienstadt in Northern Bohemia, a concentration camp which has become famous in all accounts of Nazi inhumanity and brutality, not only for the resistance of the inmates despite the conditions to which Jews from various countries were exposed, but also because of the Czech and German literary activity which took place there.[22] Theresienstadt had been built as a fortress under Kaiser Joseph II towards the end of the eighteenth century. It never had to be defended in any war, but did occasionally serve as an Austro-Hungarian military prison. On the orders of the German occupying forces the city (that is, the fortress and the civilian areas associated with it) was turned into a ghetto. What had been built for a few thousand now had to contain up to sixty thousand Jews from Czechoslovakia, Austria, Germany and elsewhere. An average of 130 people died daily in the streets of the township which was ostensibly self-governing, but in reality guarded by Czech trustees under SS control. In addition to the ghetto there was also a so-called Little Fortress where political prisoners were kept guarded by the Gestapo. Czech cultural life was extremely active in Theresienstadt, but German literary activity, at first banned and then encouraged for those living under a constant threat of death, was also lively. The prisoners were often from the older generation and hence the literary products of the place tended to be traditional and conservative. Nevertheless, thanks to professionals like Kurt Gerron, the German camp cabarets were of a very high standard, as was the poetry written both by writers who had already made a name for themselves (like Camill Hoffmann and Ilse Blumenthal-Weiss) and by younger writers. H.G. Adler, himself a poet, has written accounts of literary life in Theresienstadt and has attempted to collect and preserve the poetry that was written there. For obvious reasons, the works produced were mostly poems or the shorter literary genres, but even whole poem-cycles were also written in prisons and camps like Theresienstadt and in one case a complete novel was not only written, but by a miracle survived to be published after the war. Haushofer's cycle of *Moabit Sonnets* has already been mentioned, but some attention might also be devoted to two narrative works: *Esther*, a story by Bruno Apitz, and *PLN*, a novel by Werner Krauss.

Bruno Apitz demonstrated that it was possible to carry on some kind of literary activity even in a camp like Buchenwald, in which 56,000 prisoners from eighteen different nations died at the hands of their Nazi oppressors:

> There were no human conditions in
> these camps.
> In them the prisoners were only
> alive, in the sense that they
> had not died yet.[23]

Nevertheless, compared with other camps Buchenwald did enjoy certain advantages. The political prisoners ran their own internal administration, the party leadership was not German but international, and as a result could draw on a varied supply of books, and there was a camp library, with a remarkable range of reading matter, including Heinrich Mann, Ilya Ehrenburg, and even Karl Marx. After the start of the Second World War the camp became more and more a work camp, there was a 'legal' camp orchestra and regular concerts were permitted. There were illegal concerts as well and the programmes at these were intended to ensure the international cooperation of all nations in the camp in the fight against the Nazis. The song 'Hold your Head High', composed by

Kropinski to words by Bruno Apitz, gives some idea of the encouragement that could be given:

> In den schweren Jahren,
> Kamerad, erinn're Dich,
> galt das Wort, das schicksalharte:
> Steh' gerade oder brich!
> Sind auch viele schon zerbrochen,
> wir stehn hinterm Stacheldraht
> aufrecht, Jahre oder Wochen—
> hoch den Kopf, Kopf hoch, Kamerad!

> (In the difficult years, comrade, the words that mattered
> were those as hard as fate: 'Stand up straight or break!'
> Even if many have broken, behind the barbed wire we stand up
> straight, for weeks or years—hold your head up high,
> comrade, up high!)

The words 'Head up, comrade' in the refrain were repeated in Polish,
French, Russian, German, et cetera. Apart from secret gatherings at
which such verses were sung, 'literary evenings' with selected programmes
of special texts for invited guests proved especially effective. Political
and satirical sketches, passages from Büchner's *Danton's Death* and
items like the banned Marquis Posa speech from Schiller's *Don Carlos*
formed the basis of such programmes. So, much music and literature
survived even in Buchenwald and helped the prisoners to stand up to
inhuman treatment, resist terror, and believe that fascism would be
conquered and that their suffering would come to an end. Even the
officially permitted Buchenwald Song expressed this positive attitude
to life:

> O Buchenwald, wir jammern nicht und
> klagen, und was auch unser Schicksal sei,
> wir wollen trotzdem, 'ja' zum Leben sagen,
> denn einmal kommt der Tag: dann sind wir frei.

> (O Buchenwald, we never moan, we never complain, and
> whatever our fate may be, we're determined nevertheless
> to say yes to life, for sometime the day will come when
> we'll be free.)

In Buchenwald poems were written by Karl Schnog, Bruno Apitz and others, including non-German authors. Narrative and dramatic pieces were also written, but the most significant larger work was the story 'Esther' by Bruno Apitz. As an opponent of Hitler from the start, he spent nearly the whole duration of the regime in imprisonment. In 1933 he was in prison for four months, was arrested again in 1934 and condemned to two years and ten months' hard labour. After completing this term in Waldheim prison, he was moved to Buchenwald in 1937 and remained there until his release in 1945. Bruno Apitz had started to write before 1933, but these attempts, including two dramas and a novel fragment, remained unpublished. He was regional chairman of the BPRS in Leipzig and devoted a lot of his time to Agitprop theatre, apart from being something of a creative artist and a musician. His many-sided abilities were to prove invaluable in prison, for in addition to exercising his literary and musical talents he also became an expert at making plaster models, something which got him an 'easy' job in the pathology lab. Apitz wrote his story *Esther* in 1944, basing it on the real-life experience of a prisoner in the Netzweiler camp. His Esther is one of a hundred Greek Jewesses, brought to an all-male camp for the camp doctors' racial experiments, following which they are all to be gassed. In the camp Esther meets Oswald, the Kapo, and a remarkable love develops between them, culminating in a 'festival of love'. Oswald proposes joint suicide by means of morphia, but she refuses. She says 'yes' to life, though there is little chance of survival for her; and indeed the last section of the story indicates that she goes to her death at the hands of the Nazi murderers. As a tale of love in the face of death, therefore, it does incline to the romantic, even sentimental, and the 'festival of love' climax even suggests the 'sex in the death-camp' motif, which was to play such a large part in glamourising and falsifying National Socialism in post-war kitsch. There are clear elements of love-of-life and the will-to-resist in the story, but essentially it is a private love affair. Resistance by Esther and Oswald would be pointless: only joint action by all the prisoners as the Nazi empire began to collapse could have any hope of success. To that extent, the story does anticipate Apitz' larger and weightier post-war novel *Naked Among Wolves* (1958), though here too the sentimental idea of bringing a child into a concentration camp teeters over into the improbable. That Apitz was not unique among resistance writers in stressing the private life of the individual in imprisonment rather than attempting a wider statement is demonstrated by Günther Weisenborn, who wrote parts of his *Memorial* on paper bags in the Gestapo prison in Prinz-Albrecht-Strasse,

Berlin, after being condemned to death for his involvement with the Red Chapel resistance group.[24] He carried on writing in Luckau prison, when the death sentence was not carried out. He too asks coming generations not to forget 'those hundreds of thousands who stood upright and fought against blood-soaked terror and went to their deaths fighting at the guillotine front'. After the war his play *Illegal*, based on his own experiences with resistance groups, was the first indication that there had been resistance inside Germany. It made some impact but was easily swept aside by Zuckmayer's *The Devil's General*. Apart from writers belonging to organisations like the BPRS there were also others who, while politically uncommitted, rejected National Socialism from the start and yet remained in Germany. The most extensive of the groups formed by such writers was the so-called 'Rote Kapelle', the name given to it by the Gestapo. Otherwise known by the names of its organisers Schulze-Boysen/Harnack, it was by no means exclusively a red chapel, but gathered together independents, intellectuals, Socialists and workers as well as (later) some Communists. One-fifth of the group were artists, writers and journalists. Among its most notable members were the writers Adam Kuckhoff, Günther Weisenborn, John Sieg and Werner Krauss.

From his initial career and background one would not expect Werner Krauss to be the kind of person to engage in resistance. Krauss seemed born to be a scholar, and indeed followed the traditional lengthy training of the German academic, studying law, politics, literature and art history in Munich, Berlin and Madrid. He took his doctorate in 1929 with a thesis on 'Life and Letters in Medieval Spain', then became a professor of Romance Languages at Marburg till 1940. In 1940 he was seconded to Berlin as an interpreter and in 1941 joined the Schulze-Boysen/Harnack resistance group. He was arrested and condemned to death in 1942, the sentence being later commuted to hard labour. Krauss served his sentence in Plötzensee, where he managed to write two books, one a novel called *PLN*, the other a scholarly work on Gracían. After the war he became a professor again in Leipzig, was awarded the National Prize of the GDR and rose to be the Director of the Institute of Romance Languages and Literature in Berlin, publishing many scholarly works.

Of interest in the present context is *PLN*, the only literary work by this scholar. According to his own account, this novel was written with bound hands, while he was in prison, first in Plötzensee and later in the army prison at 61 Lehrter Strasse. It was smuggled out by a fellow prisoner. In December 1945 Krauss gave the manuscript so rescued to a friend Erich Lissner, who had it published by the Vittorio Klostermann publishing house. Unfortunately, despite the sensational manner in which it came to be written, it did not enjoy great success with the public and has since been largely passed over in silence in standard histories of literature. There are various reasons for this, quite apart from the climate of the Adenauer period and the acclaim given to Christian and conservative writers of the inner emigration rather than to real resistance fighters. The most obvious reason for the novel's lack of success is its style and structure. Writing in prison, in constant fear of execution or discovery, Krauss was compelled to write very obliquely and as a result adopted a style similar to the extreme mannerism of the baroque Spanish writers of his scholarly work. The title *PLN* (*Postleitnummer* or postal code), derives from a postal code plan of the Reich Postal Minister who is the hero of this absurd novel, subtitled 'Passions of the Halcyonic Soul'. The structure of the novel is extremely elaborate, involving a string of episodes and separate strands instead of any consistent plot. Style and structure together do conjure up, however, the atmosphere of an absurd chaotic world. That this halcyonic Reich is the Third Reich, that Muphti is Hitler, Oleander Goering, Koben Goebbels, is fairly clear; the general picture is of a despotic, archaic, mythical realm. But that is about all that is clear, though closer study of the text does reveal an attempt to lay bare the economic and social roots of fascism. It has also been claimed that Krauss is one of the few authors in Germany to attempt to analyse how the German people came to submit to the Nazis and why they did not offer much resistance, although in the novel he does exploit his own personal experience to show the activities of a resistance group. All these levels have to be hunted out and the mystifying style—intended to make it difficult for the enemy to make sense of the text should it fall into their hands—also makes it difficult for the well disposed reader. The style of the novel has been compared with that of Cervantes' *Don Quixote*, Grimmelshausen's *Simplicissimus* or even with Rabelais' linguistic excesses; embellishment takes over and the essence remains hidden, though the satirical *roman-à-clef* certainly rewards closer comparison with other 'oblique' exposés of the Third Reich like Brecht's *Arturo Ui*, while Kafka has also been mentioned in connection with the novel's representation of alienation, claustrophobic atmosphere, fear of death, loss of human contact, et cetera.

Krauss' *PLN* was written during the Nazi regime, but was not published till after its collapse. Adam Kuckhoff is another writer often mentioned in the context of resistance literature, because he actually published his main work in Germany after 1933 in the normal way and yet still managed to smuggle into it many features critical of national developments. Kuckhoff was a manufacturer's son who only gradually developed an interest in Marxism. The articles he wrote for *Die Tat* in 1927 show traces of this in the attitude expressed to war, rearmament and the restriction of liberty of expression in the Weimar Republic. In 1927 he also published a major essay on Georg Büchner, in which he demonstrated his sympathy for the ideas of Marx and Lenin, as regards the role of the masses, violence in history and the revolution of the proletariat. Only one of Kuckhoff's later resistance pamphlets, one dealing with the heroic struggle of the Soviet partisans in the face of Nazi atrocities, has survived. According to his wife there were other such illegal, anti-fascist writings, including poetry. His last political poems have also not survived, though he is said to have recited them after his trial. Kuckhoff was arrested and condemned to death for his activities in the Red Chapel resistance group and for his appeal to 'workers of brain and hand, *not* to fight against an invaded Russia, but to defend it as the homeland of the working-class'.[25]

As early as 1915 Kuckhoff had written a drama about Russia, the home of all workpeople, which achieved its first production in 1918. His novel *The German of Bayencourt* (1937) was a reworking of this play. Essentially this novel, with the central figure caught between two nations, is about war and people's attitudes to it. Kuckhoff cleverly constructed his novel in such a way that the action and its setting permit the subsidiary characters to voice subversive, anti-imperialistic and anti-chauvinistic ideas, which the author or his central figures could never express directly. In 1914 the Socialists and the working class had failed to unite against the war. In 1933 the anti-fascist intellectuals and workers failed to stop Hitler. Kuckhoff struggles to find reasons for this failure. In the face of a Germany rearming and preparing for war Kuckhoff wrote a novel which was anti-militaristic and anti-fascist — if the reader knew how to listen to what the marginal figures were saying. In other words, as Brekle has pointed out, the author was using one of the Brechtian tricks from the *Five Difficulties in Writing the Truth*, namely 'scattering the truth over many'. He did the same with his crime story *Strogany and the Missing People* (1941), smuggling in (as Brecht advised) 'descriptions of horrible conditions at unlikely places'. Kuckhoff was different from the writers of the inner emigration, in that there was no doubt about his active anti-fascist commitment and about his real involvement with a resistance group, the Red Chapel. He paid the penalty and was executed.

Opposition to Hitler was wide-ranging and heterogeneous. It was neither the monopoly of the Communist Party nor of a few army officers. There was no single resistance movement; instead there was a bewildering confusion of groups, cells, circles and conspiracies. Participants were drawn from most social classes and institutions, and in some cases action against Hitler could be the outcome of one individual's personal decision to do something to stop the dictator, as J.P. Stern has shown by highlighting the case of Johann Georg Elser.[26] There must have been many like him. There *was* another Germany.

Against the reality of a mad system of evil, a system reinforced by the resources of a totalitarian state which became a huge alienated apparatus of destruction converting human beings into objects, things, these Germans, many of whom come over as strong and distinct subjects, even though their opposition was realised as a bewildering welter of contradictory and even irresolute actions, tactics and attitudes, were united in the attempt to confront inhumanity with the humane and uphold what they felt or knew to be good or right.[27]

PART THREE

1933-1945 — OUTSIDE GERMANY

8 THE SPANISH CIVIL WAR

The Spanish Civil War broke out on 17 July 1936 when a number of
generals and other military leaders, with General Franco at their head,
revolted against the liberal government. This revolt had the immediate
support of Italy which was interested in control of the Mediterranean.
For various tactical and diplomatic reasons Germany avoided the
Italian level of commitment, although in view of its long-term war aims
it also afforded Franco considerable help, especially as Spain could
prove a useful training ground. Because of the non-intervention principle
which most European states had accepted, Germany 'commanded' an
expeditionary corps of volunteer fliers, technicians and others to move
into Spain. By November of 1936 a Condor Legion had been formed
in Seville under German command. To keep up appearances Spaniards
were nominally in charge. Limited French and Russian assistance did
get through to the republican side, but on nothing like the scale of the
resources made available to Franco by Germany and Italy. With help
from Foreign Legionnaires and Moroccans flown to the mainland in
German aircraft, Franco's forces were able to press north as far as San
Sebastian, while the east of Spain continued to be held by the
republicans. In November 1936 Madrid was surrounded by Franco's
forces, but managed to hold out against the siege until 1939. While
Franco had the support of the military, the fascist falangists and the
clerical Carlists as well as the German Condor Legion and the Italian
militia, the republican forces gained support from democrats,
Socialists and Communists from many lands, who poured into Spain
to form International Brigades. In this way the Spanish Civil War
assumed an importance far beyond any internal significance it might
have had for the future of Spain alone. It became a symbol of the fight
against fascism, and a forerunner of the inevitable war brewing between
the Axis countries and the rest of Europe, indeed the world. Spain was
the great cause, a chance to take part in the popular front, a chance to
demonstrate that fascism could be stopped. As far as the Germans were
concerned the Spanish Civil War was a German civil war, in which
hostilities were continued where they had been broken off in 1933.
Germans faced Germans, the only difference was that the fronts were
now more clearly marked. Motivated by the determination to halt in
Spain what they had failed to halt at home, the Thälmann and Ernst

André units were the first armed German opposition to Hitler's army. Hemingway appreciated this when he wrote 'To the Real Germany' in *Das Wort* (1939):

> This summer I was with the Ebro offensive of the republican army. There I saw Germans sitting in Heinckels and Junkers: they came in superior numbers, flying over peaceful villages, dropping their bombs, pulverising the peasants' houses, burning the harvest, then they turned tail and ran and flew back to Franco as quick as they could, when the first republican planes appeared on the horizon. Meanwhile down below, over the banks of the Ebro moved the Thälmann and other German battalions, regardless of the danger. They took on everything, knowing that capture meant death, but they did what they had to do, attacked and won . . . They were the real, admirable Germans, Germans of the kind we love, Germans of the kind there are millions living in Germany, we are sure.[1]

In fact the great cause failed, the people's front was not united and Franco, after splitting the country into two, finally brought about the capitulation of Barcelona and Madrid, and the end of the bloody war, leaving Europe with fascist governments in Italy, Germany and Spain. Whether the Soviet Union could have done more to help the republican cause remains a hotly debated issue, but Moscow was in any event busy at the time with its own internal problems, culminating in show trials and spy hunts. This was to be the testing time not only for Spain, but also for faith in Russia as the great hope for the free world.

'For intensity of emotion, neither the First World War nor the Second World War exacerbated the feelings of people to the extent of those events in Spain from 1936 to 1939.'[2] This is how Frederick R. Benson introduces his masterly study of the literary impact of the Spanish Civil War. In it he did not ignore right-wing writers, but on the whole it is clear that they were not the ones with the greatest literary contributions to make at this time. In this connection he mentions Stefan Andres' short religious novel *We are Utopia*, 'an extremely moving portrayal of conversion and martyrdom', but immediately goes on to say that the literary efforts of Catholic intellectuals and hence of those inclining to the right were not significant. By contrast with the few like Dwinger, who reported from the Spanish front on the Franco side, many leading German authors threw themselves into support for the republican cause.[3] Kantorowicz mentions some twenty-nine. Benson was aware of the numerical significance of this German literary presence in Spain on the anti-Franco side, but because of his decision to concentrate on six writers only (including Arthur Koestler and Gustav Regler), he passed over most of them in silence. It is to the many-sided activities of the German literary engagement in the Spanish Civil War that this chapter is devoted, to those early fighters, Germans against Germans who have not received the credit due to them either in the East, because of their dangerous exposure in Spain to contamination by Trotskyism, anarcho-syndicalism and other 'deviations', or in the West because they were Communists. Not all exiles returned, and those who did were not made particularly welcome. Their works were either not reprinted, or they were heavily censored.

Important as they were at the time, the Writers' Congresses and other public activities launched to help Spain will not be discussed here.[4] Instead the focus will be on the authors themselves and on what they actually wrote. Clearly there was a great upsurge in journalistic and publicistic activity as writers endeavoured to make the world aware of the issues. Some idea of the range of journalistic activity involving well known literary figures can be gained from the special Spain Number of *Der Deutsche Schriftsteller* produced in July 1937 by the SDS in Paris for circulation inside Germany. The representative character of the issue is revealed by the fact that, of its thirteen German authors, seven were actually at the front on the republican side. The thrust of this special number was, needless to say, the appeal to all Germans to fight the threat to the world represented by the Spanish situation. Perhaps the most important of all the essays was Thomas Mann's 'For Republican Spain', for the simple reason that he was not too closely associated with left-wing radical opinion. Mann felt it his duty as a humanist to enlighten a public exposed exclusively to the Goebbels propaganda machine as to the true state of affairs in Spain. By contrast his brother Heinrich's essay was much more explicitly political. He called for the creation of a German People's Front to match the equivalent movement in Spain and bitterly attacked Hitler, Mussolini and Franco as threats to international peace. Essays by Kurt Kersten, Gustav Regler and Egon Erwin Kisch provided valuable background information to the history of the struggle in Spain, while the brilliant reporter, Arthur Koestler, gave an eye-witness account of the siege of Alcazar, in which the fascists held four hundred women and children hostage. Alfred Kantorowicz offered a similar account of life in beleaguered Madrid, while the contributions by Bodo Uhse, Anna Seghers and Ludwig Renn kept up the high literary standard of the whole number. Apart from articles of the kind collected in this special number, other works of an essayistic character exercised considerable influence at the time. Thomas Mann's pronouncement, 'I stand with the Spanish people,' carried considerable weight internationally, as did another essay called 'Spain', in which he saw the main issue as the need to support the republican cause 'in the name of humanity'. While then he was fundamentally optimistic about the ultimate outcome, despite the desperate plight of the Spanish people, even after the collapse of the republican cause Thomas Mann never lost this optimism. This was made clear in his address to the mass rally against Franco in New York at the beginning of the Second World War, in which, despite his disappointment, he still expressed his conviction that Hitler's Germany and Franco's fascism would be defeated.

Despite his total commitment to the republican cause and his absolute rejection of fascism, Thomas Mann tended to avoid explicit political statements. Heinrich Mann's articles on behalf of republican Spain were entirely different, as the many he published, mainly in the exile journal *Die Neue Weltbühne* or in his *Der Mut* (1938), clearly demonstrate. He was outspoken in his attacks on fascist intervention, which he saw as an assault on civilisation, and attempted to demonstrate the capitalist roots of the outrage and the economic and political reasons for German military involvement in Spain. Speaking on behalf of 'the other Germany', which could not countenance such violence and brutality, Heinrich Mann pleaded with the German people, its military leaders, its intellectuals and others to turn against the NS system which had sent German soldiers into Spain, bombed defenceless cities and destroyed an ancient Basque city like Guernica. With hindsight it seems naïve of him to have expected any success at this stage from an appeal for German workers, peasants and middle-class citizens to unite with Communists and Socialists into one German People's Front against National Socialism. Just as naïve, but nevertheless just as sincere, were his more general appeals for the formation of a People's Front of international solidarity against the fascist enemy. History was to prove him wrong, the republican cause was defended heroically but chaotically, and the united front was rent by internal squabbles, while the non-intervention policy of certain governments left republican Spain at the mercy of the armies and air forces of Germany and Italy. Not surprisingly his later articles became progressively gloomy. Heinrich was certainly much more active than his brother Thomas in his journalistic activity, but also much more doctrinaire and therefore perhaps less effective because of his readiness to identify the causes as capitalism and high finance, and the cure as a proletarian revolution leading to Socialist humanism after the Russian model. As Benson pointed out, journalism of this kind did not enlighten the public: it polarised it.

However involved Thomas and Heinrich Mann were with the republican cause, they were writing at some distance from Spain in their respective places of exile. Erika and Klaus Mann, by contrast, did visit Spain and were able to report from first-hand experience, even to the extent of exposure to real danger when they had to escape from the encircled city of Valencia and survive the almost constant bombardment of Madrid and Barcelona. They, too, did not write from an objective standpoint. On their return they published their impressions in an essay entitled 'Back from Spain', and what clearly impressed them more than anything else was the spirit of resistance of the Spanish people, against all the odds. In this they may have been holding up the idea of 'resistance' as a model for others inside and outside Germany to follow in the fight against fascism, but they also had other intentions, for example to counter reports of Red 'barbarism' and put the charge back where it properly belonged, with the fascists. 'Spain is the model' — this was the moral they drew from their first visit, and the message of encouragement they proclaimed to all fellow exiles, who might otherwise have inclined to despair and defeatism. Another publicist active on behalf of Spain might be mentioned in this context, namely Ludwig Marcuse. In an essay 'Miguel de Unamuno. The Second Don Quixote' in *Das Wort* (1936) he took issue with the famous Spaniard, who had quite suddenly thrown in his lot with the fascists. Marcuse tries to demonstrate that this was a case not unlike that of Hauptmann, where one who had seemed to be a fighter for the cause of the people turned out to be no more than a vague idealist, divorced from reality. Unamuno's nostalgia for an agrarian state, instead of acceptance of a form of society appropriate to the modern age of technology is exposed by Marcuse as rooted in the fascist tendency to look to the past instead of adopting the Marxist view which alone offers such a downtrodden people as the Spanish hope for the future.

Some of the literary commentators on Catalonia were as famous as Marcuse, but without Communist connections. Rolf Reventlow, son of the authoress and noted *bohémienne* Gräfin Reventlow, wrote *Spain in this Century*, a book made up partly of personal experiences, partly of historical survey. Willy Brandt came to Spain in 1937 as a reporter for Norwegian newspapers and was particularly interested in Catalonia. Augustin Souchy, the German anarchist, is interesting for his comments on the role of anarcho-syndicalism in the Spanish Civil War, especially as from orthodox Communist commentators one only hears it being viciously denounced. Something of the same kind is also to be found in Hanns Maassen's *Brigada Internacional*. A German eye-witness account of anarchist Spain at the front and elsewhere is offered by Clara and Paul Thalmann's *Revolution for Freedom*, which is especially illuminating about the cross-examination and execution of suspected informers, traitors and fifth columnists, and highly illuminating about the Stalinist spy craze, which gave the Communist bureaucracy in Spain such a bad name.

Not least of the problems debated among writers was whether literature was still possible in an age of open aggression, whether the word still had any power, or whether guns could only be met by guns. Many German writers decided that the word could still be effective, and this explains the optimism with which they set out to address themselves, first to a German and then to a wider public, with informative essays, eye-witness reports, personal accounts, statements, appeals and essays. They were writing on behalf of the Spanish people, but they also set the issue of Spain against the wider context of the struggle against fascism to be fought by all liberal forces. The struggle was also that of intellectuals and writers against the powers of darkness, of humanism against barbarism. Resistance to fascism *was* possible, success of even the most limited kind gave hope to opponents of the regime inside Nazi Germany and to all exiles from it. So they reported with enthusiasm the first military successes of the republicans. What was to become a major problem for such anti-fascist writers was how they should record the mounting catalogue of defeats for the good cause.

The war in Spain was among other things a war with slogans. The anti-fascist slogan was *venceremos* ('we will win'). How effective such slogans and such propagandistic efforts were in putting the republican case across is perhaps doubtful, especially in view of the predominance of Communist writers arguing the united front case, regardless often of the reality of the situation. It is perhaps not surprising that some attempts were also made to present the republican case on the stage, the traditional German literary medium for such purposes, but here too success was limited and no major author or work emerged. Even Brecht's *Senora Carrar's Rifles* (1937) reached an audience limited mainly to Germans in exile. Ludwig Renn wrote a playlet with the title *My Mule, my Wife and my Goat* (1938) and the militant Communist Friedrich Wolf composed three dramatic sketches on Spain, which he put together under the title *We are with You!* (1937), though he had already touched upon the Spanish struggle in *The Trojan Horse* (1936), his play on the theme of industrial sabotage. Mention might also be made of the dramatic contributions of Erich Weinert, *Dialogue at Dawn* and *To Them Nothing's Sacred* (1938).

Brecht's *Senora Carrar's Rifles* was written for a group in France. Like most Brecht plays it had a literary source—John Millington Synge's tragedy *Riders to the Sea*.[5] It also had a specific setting—the British blockade of Bilbao. Brecht originally intended to call his play *Generals over Bilbao* and only changed the title shortly before the first performance. His named collaborator for this play was Margarete Steffin, who probably provided the Synge source. Another of Brecht's lady companions, Ruth Berlau, the Danish Communist, actually went to Spain to fight and he gave her the job of finding material for him. The time and place of the action are given in the stage directions as 'an April night 1937, in an Andalusian fisherman's house'. The wife Teresa Carrar is baking bread. The story line is simple and basic. In the time it takes for the bread to bake, she is transformed from a woman who refuses to let the guns hidden in her house be used for further fighting, because her husband has been killed, to one who is brought to realise that neutrality is impossible in the face of such a violent aggressor. The key-word of the play (and the one which describes not only her dilemma, but the world's dilemma) is non-intervention. She tries to save her two sons by keeping them out of the fighting, but Brecht shows that fascism can only be fought with its own weapons, thereby taking up the ideas of the First and Second International Writers' Congresses. This view is expressed, however, not in abstract terms, but through the fateful decision of one mother for her children. While there are references in the play to the 'Reds', Senora Carrar is by no means an idealised, Socialist Realist heroine; in fact she has no political, philosophical or religious reasons for her pacifist stance. She has simply lost her husband and now thinks only of survival for herself and her children. The other point of view is put first by Senora Perez. Representing the tragically split Spanish family, she has lost four of her seven children in the war, and finally loses her daughter with the republican forces while another son is fighting on Franco's side. A war of this kind splits families in two, and yet this old lady has no doubts about what must be done, and never loses her will to resist. The religious dilemma is presented through the padre, who is neutral by reason of his faith, though his sympathies are with the people and the republican cause. Yet he cannot give Senora Carrar any guarantee that she and her sons will be safe if she remains neutral. The only character on the right path from the start is the worker Pedro, who is unwavering in his belief that might must be met with might. He has only left the front because of the desperate need for the guns Senora Carrar has in her keeping. It is with him that she departs at the end, taking the freshly baked bread and the guns, to fight for her son casually killed by a fascist boat, simply because he looked poor and therefore dangerous. In place of the tragic acceptance of fate of *Riders to the Sea* Brecht offers the practical proposal to eliminate the fascist plague by action.

Figures like Senora Carrar are not unusual in Brecht's work and she has not surprisingly been compared with Mother Courage as well as with the female protagonist in *The Mother*. Like Teresa Carrar, Anna Fierling in *Mother Courage* attempts to survive the war with her children; but the Thirty Years War was rather different from the Spanish Civil War. In the earlier war there was no cause for Mother Courage to follow, whereas in the case of the Spanish war, right and wrong were clearly delineated, and joining the anti-fascist camp was the only possibility. Mother Courage does occasionally see that war is wrong and senseless, but paradoxically still hopes to 'make a living' out of the trade with death. Even the loss of her three children does not result in any heightened awareness on her part. Senora Carrar by contrast becomes aware of the consequences of her policy of non-intervention and takes the correct decision: 'mother-love emerges from selfishness with the readiness to sacrifice even one's children in the fight against the class enemy'.[6] In the same way in *The Mother* Pelagea Wlassowa sees the consequences of her actions and becomes a revolutionary.

As far as the form and structure of the play are concerned it is noticeable that in this exile drama Brecht abandoned the experimental forms of epic theatre and returned to more traditional Aristotelian techniques, presumably for immediate propaganda effect with unsophisticated audiences. Brecht never explained why he wrote *Senora Carrar's Rifles* in the 'Aristotelian' mode, but the note 'Direct Effect of Aristotelian Drama' gives some idea of what he may have intended:

> If a certain social situation is very ripe, then plays of this kind can bring about practical action. This sort of play is the spark which ignites the powder keg.[7]

The difference between this Aristotelian work and similar non-Aristotelian plays can be established by comparing *Senora Carrar's Rifles* with *Saint Joan of the Stockyards* and *The Good Woman of Sezuan*. Joan

Dark and Shen Te want to relieve the misery around them, but do-gooders only compound the suffering and reinforce the system responsible for it: 'Only violence helps, where there is violence.'[8] This is emotional drama, in which the audience is invited to identify with the problems of a mother, to suffer with her when her dead son is brought in, and agree with her when she takes her decision to fight. As has been seen, the roles of the parallel and contrasting figures (the old woman, the padre, the worker) are clearly marked, and dialogue and discussion leave everything on the surface, with no hidden meanings or obscurities. Focus on the individual dilemma did have its problems in that the general issues could be lost sight of, but Brecht envisaged putting on this short play alongside a documentary film so that wider issues of the war would be opened up. Brecht also moved further towards epic theatre by providing the play with a prologue and an epilogue, for a Swedish production. The prologue takes place in a French internment camp (of the kind where many Spanish freedom fighters ended up). Senora Carrar, her son and Pedro the worker are interned there, and are asked whether it was worth while fighting, since they have been defeated—like the Czechs, who also offered resistance. The answer given is that to ask the question is to accept defeat.

The play was a success. It was first performed in Paris in 1937 and subsequently in Copenhagen and in Prague. By all accounts Helene Weigel was magnificent in the leading role. However, it was played almost exclusively to German exile groups and did not reach a wider audience. It was only a one-acter and did not have the weight of Brecht's major parable plays, written in exile. Martin Esslin dismisses it as 'effective theatre, but rather over-simplified politically and clearly a pot-boiler'; and indeed all the signs indicate that this is so. The red flag forms part of the action, and the International Brigades march past the fisherman's cottage, the German Thälmann column at the head singing 'Far is the Homeland', followed by the French, Poles, Italians, Americans and Spaniards, all singing their national songs of resistance. At the same time the play has something of the quality of its Irish source and the simplicity of the language and basic situation has a wider appeal than mere identification with the cause of the workers against their oppressors.

Spain is also the theme of two of the scenes in Brecht's sequence *Private Life of the Master Race* published in Prague in 1938. The first of these has the title 'In the barracks the news of the Almeria bombardment becomes known'. This is a very elusive little scene in which external signs reveal the undercurrent of feeling in the German army against intervention in Spain. The second, much more extensive scene, called 'Getting Work', is dated Spandau 1937 and involves a worker, who after a long spell of unemployment has at last found a job in an aircraft factory. Naturally he would do anything not to lose his job, but he discovers not only that it is war work but also that he is thus indirectly responsible for the death of his brother-in-law, who has been killed in action as a flier in Spain. Of course he would like to find another job, but all work in Germany is directed to war. Like Senora Carrar, he would prefer to offer no resistance, hoping only to survive; but like her he has to discover, through his wife, that active resistance is the only course. Brecht does not involve his audience in any elaborate plot or complicated characters: the action, in the traditional 'Aristotelian' manner, simply presents the realistic dialogue of everyday people who dislike being forced to make a decision or to take a political stand. The simple point is made in the last words: 'Then do something that *will* be of some help!' Neither of these little scenes is particularly weighty—indeed Brecht may be accused of sharing the same *naïveté* as his other Communist colleagues in over-estimating anti-war feeling in the German army and expecting the workers in Germany to be capable of concerted action against the Hitler regime. In performance these particular scenes were often omitted: the significant point is merely that he does include the Spanish theme as a characteristic feature of life in Nazi Germany.

Brecht was not the only professional dramatist to attempt to bring the Spanish problem on to the stage, but in comparison with his dramatic efforts those by other contemporaries seem lightweight. Ludwig Renn's *My Mule, My Wife and My Goat* (1938) is a mere sketch, dedicated to 'the field dressing station of the 45th Division, to be performed before soldiers and peasants behind the front of the republican people's army'. In it the simple peasant who wants to return to his mule, his wife and his goat comes to realise the absolute necessity of the fight against fascism; the stage fills with flags and all sing together the song of the people's front. Despite the popular humour, and the satire against Franco and his dog, the didactic intention makes the play only too obviously a piece of agitprop theatre. Pure propaganda also are the three little sketches which Friedrich Wolf wrote for Soviet amateur groups. The first scene, 'In Alicante', demonstrates the support given to the republican cause by a Russian supply ship. In the second scene, 'Outside Madrid', a traitor is caught and the role of the International Brigades praised, while the third scene at the front shows enemy soldiers being won over—hence the title—'We are with you!'—

which provides the linking theme of solidarity in the fight against
fascism for these otherwise only loosely connected scenes. Altogether
it is fairly obvious that the author in far-away Russia had no real
knowledge of the Spanish scene and was content with his simple
propagandistic framework. The frequently inserted revolutionary
songs, the party-political slogans and the phrases from People's Front
vocabulary make this an all too obviously doctrinaire work, following
the author's 'art as weapon' formula. It is a play strictly for the
converted. The same applies to the short sketches written by Erich
Weinert, the 'original political poet'. In the first scene Communist
and Social Democrat, together in the same fox-hole, discover under
fire that united they are invincible. In the second, fascist lies about Red
atrocities are unmasked and the truth revealed. Such plays are of only
historic interest for their party-line fantasies of winning the enemy
over and projections of a phoney united front. Only Brecht's one-acter
is of interest beyond the events of the time.

A feature of the plays about Spain discussed so far is the number of
times that anti-fascist songs are introduced. Certainly such songs were
among the most successful of all the literary genres attempted, but this
did not exhaust the possibilities of lyrical expression to which the
Spanish Civil War gave rise. One of the most expansive works devoted
to Spain was the epic poem 'The Journey to Teruel', by J.R. Becher,
published in his *Novels in Verse* (1946). This verse epic in terzinas
reveals by its form the author's familiarity with the literature of the
Soviet Union, which has many examples of this mixed genre. The tale
he tells is of Killian, a peasant from Bayrisch-Zell, and his development
into a man capable of political thought and action. Dachau confirms
his decision to fight for a better world by joining his comrades in
Spain. There he fights and dies for the good cause and a better social
order. Clearly this is a propagandistic work, but one with higher
pretensions, as the sophistication of the verse form and the mathematical
precision with which the novel in verse is divided into two equal halves
indicate. Louis Fürnberg's balladesque poem *The Spanish Wedding* is also
something of a verse epic. It is dedicated to the 'Spanish nightingale'
Garcia Lorca, who as the singer of Spanish liberty was killed by the
falangists in 1936. This work was started in December 1944 and
completed in April 1945, at a time when (according to the preface)
'the Soviet Union had bled, made sacrifices and finally conquered for
the whole of mankind'. The work has its source in a Reuter press release
about a grand royal wedding in Spain, celebrated with fairy-tale
splendour. The author contrasts this with Constantin Simonov's reports

from the same time of the horrific discovery of the Auschwitz extermination camp. These contrasting events are Fürnberg's point of departure, the aim clearly being to show that the guests at the wedding and the murderers of Auschwitz are the products of the same social order, for the victory of fascism in Spain, the horrors of the extermination camps and the suppression of countless peoples of the world can be reduced to one common denominator. Only the first five songs of the verse-epic deal with the struggle in Spain and the fate of Garcia Lorca. Thereafter Fürnberg takes his readers from Madrid and Spain by way of England, Poland, France and Yugoslavia to Stalingrad in order to show the growth of resistance to fascism, before eventually returning in the last section to the Spanish Wedding. Altogether, despite the subtitle, it is hard to see why it is described as 'balladesque', for the songs of varying length (the longest 159 lines) explode the accepted form of the ballad. What is left is a work of political poetry with a clear Stalinist slant.

Unlike Becher and Fürnberg, who did not visit Spain, Erich Weinert, the most prolific of the poets of the Spanish Civil War, was directly and personally involved from the 1937 Writers' Congress in Madrid onwards. As cultural commissar he poured out a steady stream of songs, poems, translations from Spanish and various languages — an impressive range of poetic activities of which his book *Cameradas* gives some idea. Perhaps the best known of his lyrical efforts is the 'Song of the International Brigade' (1936), which was translated into many languages and sung around the world. The first stanza goes as follows:

Wir, im fernen Land geboren,
Nahmen nichts als Hass im Herzen mit.
Doch wir haben die Heimat nicht verloren,
Unsere Heimat ist heute vor Madrid.
Spaniens Brüder stehn auf der Barrikade,
Unsre Brüder sind Bauer und Prolet
Vorwärts, Internationale Brigade!
Hoch die Fahne der Solidarität![9]

(We who were born in distant land, brought nothing with us but hate in our hearts. But we have not lost our homeland, today our home is Madrid. Spain's brothers man the barricades, our brothers are peasants and workers. Forward, International Brigade! Raise the flag of solidarity!)

Here Weinert combines the internationalism and the patriotism of those
fighting against Franco, speaking especially for the Germans who had
no homeland and therefore fought all the more desperately. It was Hans
Beimler (not Weinert) who coined the slogan: 'The only way back to
Germany is by way of Madrid.' Unfortunately Madrid was not to be
the grave of fascism. Weinert's poem is effective propaganda filled with
the will to resist and fight, but it cannot be described as great poetry,
nor can any of his other songs to the Eleventh Brigade, the Edgar
André Battalion, the Thälmann Song or the Song of Red Spain. These
verses are still to be heard to this day in the Democratic Republic of
Germany, but are rarely heard in the West, except by record-collectors,
who like the voice of Ernst Busch singing the revolutionary songs he
sang for the fighting men at the front. The best-known of all the songs
was the 'Thälmann Column' with text and music by Paul Dessau. Ernst
Busch made recordings of the most popular songs in Barcelona in 1938
and the collected texts were published in *Canciones de las Brigadas
Internacionales.* They have been reprinted legally and illegally many
times. Weinert wrote a word of greeting for the song-book. His own
talents were not restricted to such fighting songs and he devoted a wide
variety of other verse forms to Spanish themes, though here too many
are devoted to the role of the Soviet Union in the Spanish conflict, and
to Stalin. Weinert is firm in his faith in Communism, but even the
optimism deriving from such faith was gradually worn down by the
adverse course of the war, and he was forced to face the consequences
of defeat. Weinert is the poet of the propagandistic song, but all his
other poems too have a propagandistic purpose, which accounts for the
simplicity of form and expression and the predominance of the folk-
song manner. They are less effective on the page than they obviously
were when he presented them in person.

Unlike Weinert, Rudolf Leonhard was not himself close to the fighting
in Spain, but he did manage a short visit despite his poor health and
recorded it in a volume of poems and diary entries. Leonhard, like
many comrades at the time, was rather naïve in his belief that the
workers in Germany would soon revolt against their Nazi oppressors.
Nevertheless, there is no doubting the fervour of his poems aimed at
winning hearts for the Spanish cause—poems in which he appeals to the
countries of the world to overcome their apathy and resist fascism.
J.R. Becher was another poet who, like Leonhard, regretted being
unable to be in Spain in person. Such was the theme of many of his
poems on Spain, which when taken together form a cycle on
man's inhumanity to man, with particularly drastic examples of the

barbaric face of fascism in Spain. His hate-filled language tends towards what Benson has described as the 'pornography of violence', in its recital of horrors. Unlike the other German writers in Spain Erich Arendt did not belong to the interbrigades. After escaping from the fascists on Majorca he got back into Spain again and made his way to Barcelona. The poems on Spain which he wrote at that time for various journals and newspapers did not appear in collected form until the publication of the *Bergwindballade* (*Mountain Wind Ballad*, 1952), whose four sections indicate by their different titles the general areas he covers, namely 'The Homeland is Far . . .'; 'We have a Friend Behind us'; 'Land of Suffering'; and finally the 'Song of Resistance'. While Weinert had preferred the simpler folk-song mode, Becher had adopted the stricter form of the sonnet; Arendt too uses this sophisticated form, and even the double sonnet. Unfortunately Arendt, a Communist Party member from 1926, also felt compelled to follow the party line and praise the role of the Soviet Union, so once again the volume contains glorifications of Stalin and Russia, in a way which cannot be said to correspond very closely to the facts of history. His last section on resistance is also excessively optimistic about the liberation of Spain from fascist rule, as the 'mountain wind' of the title (symbolising the resistance fighter in Franco's Spain) indicates. While his work is not widely known Arendt's poetry was recognised in the German Democratic Republic, where he was awarded the National Prize for Literature not long before he died in 1953. Another who committed his poetic talents totally to the support of the Spanish Republic was the exile poet Max Zimmering, whose Spanish poems were published under a title strangely similar to that of Arendt, namely *Im herben Morgenwind* (*In the Harsh Morning Wind*, 1953). But there were many German writers in exile, who felt moved to lyrical expression by the Spanish cause, yet never wrote enough to make up a separate volume. Published elsewhere were Walter Ulbrich's song of the Chapayev Battalion and the very well known song by Karl Ernst on the Thälmann Column. Stefan Heym wrote a poem in memory of Hans Beimler, and there were many less well known writers like Ludwig Adam, Ludwig Detsinyi and Hugo Huppert. Better known as a song-writer was Walter Mehring, who composed a 'Hymn to the Victor of Guernica'. Without a doubt, however, the best-known of all poems about Spain was Brecht's 'My Brother was a Flier'.

Mein Bruder war ein Flieger
Eines Tags bekam er eine Kart

Er hat seine Kiste eingepackt
Und südwärts ging die Fahrt.

Mein Bruder ist ein Eroberer
Unserm Volk fehlt's an Raum
Und Grund und Boden zu kriegen, ist
Bei uns ein alter Traum.

Der Raum, den mein Bruder eroberte
Liegt im Guadarramamassiv
Er ist lang einen Meter achtzig
Und einen Meter fünfzig tief.[10]

(My Brother was a flier, one day he got a card, he packed his
trunk and went south. My brother is a conqueror, our people
lacks living space, and getting a plot of land is one of our
ancient dreams. The plot my brother conquered lies in the
Guadarrama Mountains six foot long and five foot deep.)

In this poem Brecht takes up again the theme of German Air Force
activity in the Spanish Civil War, but he has reduced it to the simplest
language, to point up the striking contrast between the dream of
conquest and the reality of death in a foreign land. This simple poem
is far more effective than all the more elaborate party-line attempts to
deal with the theme of Spain in elaborate but conservative forms like
the sonnet.

So far examination of the German lyric and drama on the Spanish
Civil War has shown how little success authors had in these genres.
Apart from a few songs and Brecht's playlet, most of the lyric and
drama of the Spanish Civil War lies covered with the dust of time.
Prose narrative forms were much more successful. As might be expected
of authors who were themselves actively engaged in the fighting, shorter
forms were preferred, possibly because extended narratives of novel
length needed more time for reflection and preparation. Many of the
shorter narratives which appeared in newspapers and army magazines
have since been collected into anthologies like *The Flag of Solidarity*
and *Cameradas* by Erich Weinert, *The Death of Don Quixote* by Rudolf
Leonhard and *Red Citadels. The Spanish War of Liberation 1936-1939*
edited by Hans Marquardt. There is also some narrative work in Alfred
Kantorowicz' *Chapayev – the Battalion of Twenty-one Nations.*
Generally, writers wrote about the fighting they experienced. Bodo
Uhse, who had come to Spain in the autumn of 1936 and joined an

International Brigade, wrote *The First Fight*, which was smuggled into Germany disguised as Schiller's *Wallenstein*. While this describes in more or less documentary style the baptism of fire all the volunteers from many different countries underwent in the defence of Madrid, Uhse's second story, *Spanish Episode*, is rather more fanciful and inclined to wish-fulfilment. The story *The Sacrifice* by Eduard Claudius is also devoted to the battle of Madrid, which the author himself experienced as a member of the Edgar André Battalion. The story tells of the action of a young soldier who sacrifices his life for the cause. *Araganda* by Hans Marchwitza, one of the first volunteers in Spain, is another story about the fierce fighting in defence of Madrid. Here too one of the young soldiers gives his life for the cause, though the main theme is the solidarity of the International Brigades. In his second story, *Outside Teruel*, the same enthusiasm and optimism, despite the hardships, emerge from the common struggle and the readiness to die for a good cause. Kantorowicz and Peter Kast wrote stories of a similar kind with little pretension to literary or lasting value. Erich Weinert likewise wrote extensively in narrative forms, which were more in the nature of documentary accounts of real events or personal experiences than literary creations, taking the story from the first battles right up to the dissolution of the Eleventh Brigade and the escape over the frontier into camps in France. Rudolf Leonhard's stories are less autobiographical, but even more propagandistic, and as a result tend to be repetitive in their treatment of standard themes. Manfred Georg was another reporter who turned to story-telling, though his narratives are now only of historical interest. Certainly he is not in the same class as the 'mad reporter' Egon Erwin Kisch, whose reports from the front have been collected under the title *Under Spanish Skies*. 'The Three Cows', a story which has been reprinted many times, tells how a peasant from the Tyrol sells his three cows, travels to Paris and from there to Spain, where he takes up the cause of the Spanish people in the International Brigades. Despite the propagandistic intention and the glorification of Russia, which is held up as the model of a just society, the story in lively dialogue form is extremely effective. In this story, as in his others about Spain, Kisch is the supreme example of what Lukács called the 'revolutionary reporter', because of the way he combines documentary reporting and historical reminiscence with a gripping picture of contemporary circumstances. In his hands reporting becomes a literary art form.

While Kisch was able to write from first-hand experience of Spain, others had to demonstrate their feelings from afar. This was the case with Alfred Kurella who in 1937 published in Moscow a collection of stories called *Where is Madrid?* in which he tried to demonstrate how close he felt to Spain, despite the geographical distance between them, for the struggle against fascism was by no means unique to Spain. The same feelings for Spain were expressed by Franz Carl Weiskopf from his Czech standpoint. Some of his stories and anecdotes were published in 1945 in *The Invincibles* by Aurora Press, the German exile publishing house in New York. Anna Seghers was another who demonstrated her feeling for Spain in narrative form, despite geographical separation. Like other authors so far discussed Seghers never concealed her left-wing bias; but there were also so-called bourgeois writers who wrote about the fate of Spain. The best example of this is the *Legend of the Gallows' Rope that Broke* by Franz Werfel, which, despite the pronounced religiosity of its narrative, still arrives at the same conclusion as all the other stories considered so far, namely the need to fight against fascism. Non-intervention is once again shown to offer no guarantee of safety from Franco's troops and execution squads. In journalistic literature on Spain the eye-witness, documentary approach predominated among writers who were actually on the spot in the country. Their aim was to tell the world what was actually going on. The same applies in the first instance to the larger volumes of prose produced. Yet the documentary approach did cede in the end to fiction and several significant novels were written. Among the first and most significant in the first category of reporting is the book *Spies and Conspirators* by Franz Spielhagen, in which the author attempts to expose the preparations for the Spanish Civil War. Using documents confiscated by the republican police in Barcelona, he unmasks the people pulling the strings behind the revolt of the Spanish generals. Hitler and Mussolini not only helped these people when they first revolted against the Loyalist government, they were the main sources of political intrigue. This is particularly true of Hitler who, as Spielhagen reveals, had for long exercised great influence on the financial, commercial and diplomatic life of the peninsula. This book had no literary pretensions— it was aimed at enlightening the German public from an admittedly left-wing perspective. The same is true of Anna Siemsen's *Spanish Picture Book*, which, while presenting an illustrated account of her travels in Spain, is quite explicit about the horrible atrocities committed by the fascists and the threat this represents for the rest of the world. Rudolf Leonhard's *Spanish Poems and Diary Entries* also comes into this category of eye-witness accounts, as the Goya quotation 'This I have seen' (which is its motto) indicates. Hubertus, Prince of Löwenstein, is particularly interesting, because his impressions are recorded under the title *A Catholic in Republican Spain*, a book in which he tries to show that the republican government is not against the Church, but only against those abuses of Christianity which are to the advantage of the upper classes, the nobility and the bankers. The true enemy of the Church is fascism. Peter Merin's book *Spain between Death and Birth* is very informative, because of its historical perspective, but cannot compare with Franz Borkenau's *The Spanish Cockpit*, an eye-witness account of the 'Political and Social Conflicts of the Spanish Civil War', a classic book by an anti-Communist German commentator (though written in English). While all of these accounts are important because their authors travelled through republican Spain and reported what they saw, Arthur Koestler went one step further. Within a few days of the action by the generals in Spain, Koestler had been advised by the party what his function was to be. He already had considerable journalistic experience, including clandestine activity on behalf of the Communist Party, and he had travelled widely. His new task was to produce anti-fascist propaganda. In August 1936 he sailed for Lisbon posing as a reporter for a right-wing Hungarian newspaper, and as a correspondent for the *News Chronicle*. His real mission was to collect evidence of Italian and German aid to the nationalists. He did this by interviewing the highest level of nationalist officials. Unfortunately he was recognised by a German journalist and only just managed to escape. The result of this adventure was the book which first appeared under the French title *L'Espagne Ensanglantée. Un livre noir sur l'Espagne.* The German title was *Menschenopfer unerhört.* The subtitle *A Black Book about Spain* indicates the extent to which it was modelled on Willi Münzenberg's *Brown Book on Reichstag Fire and Hitler Terror.* It is a book filled with horrors, a testimony to inhuman brutality including the slaughter of women and children, attacks on hospitals and the shooting of defenceless prisoners by Franco's troops. Koestler's *Black Book* is good propaganda but bad journalism, for there is no doubt that some of the horror stories were added and embellished for propagandistic effect.

About the middle of 1937 Koestler returned to Spain once again as a foreign correspondent. However, when the republican troops retreated from Malaga he stayed behind, because he wanted to be an eye witness to the behaviour of the Franco forces. He was arrested after the fall of Malaga and as the author of the notorious *Black Book* he was condemned to death, without examination or trial. For ninety-four days he waited in prison, and was only released thanks to the world-wide protests and appeals on his behalf. Fortunately, the fascists wanted to effect an exchange and Koestler was included as one of the twenty-one rebels exchanged for the wife of a nationalist flier. Koestler published his experiences first of all in serial form in the *News Chronicle* and then in the book *Dialogue with Death*, later expanded into the *Spanish Testament* by the inclusion of sections from the *Black Book*. The German edition with the same title (which followed in 1938) deals only with the period from the fall of Malaga until his release from prison. What is really so fascinating about Koestler's account is not the objective recital of horrors as prisoners all around him are tortured and killed, but the subjective insight into the world of the prisoner waiting for death, with his changing feelings as the waiting lasts not hours and days, but weeks and months. As a result the reader is gripped: he cannot escape from the power of such writing, and can only see the 'Spanish Problem' from this perspective. Koestler did more with this book to enlighten the British reader about the realities of Spain than anybody else had done before him. The German public inside Germany, of course, never saw Koestler's book, and since 1945 remains broadly unaware that Koestler, by then an apostate from the Communist faith, had once upon a time been among the most famous German commentators on the Spanish tragedy. This is a pity, for here was a German writer who did not always write as a political agitator with all the crudity of that approach; here was a writer who had shown his commitment and bravery by going to both parts of the Spanish struggle and who had been released from captivity by the combined efforts and solidarity of all anti-fascist forces; here was a writer who was the only German literary figure of international standing to emerge from the Spanish Civil War. This international standing was confirmed by the appearance of the novel *Darkness at Noon* (1940), dealing with Russia, but rooted in the Spanish experience. About Koestler, Friedrich Luft wrote:

> He was one of the child prodigies of the Berlin journalism of the Twenties. He was a Communist. How he freed himself from this dogma during the Spanish Civil War he has described in his sensational book *Darkness at Noon*. How our age might be stirred up against the danger of political dictatorship and intellectual subjection, has remained his subject matter ever since.[11]

In addition to basically journalistic and eye-witness accounts of the kind described so far, mention must also be made of other no less extensive accounts produced by German writers active in the ranks of the International Brigades. Typical of such accounts is *We, Born in the Far Homeland*, by E. Mohr, which tells of the formation of the Thälmann Column. Hanns Maassen's *Sons of Chapayev* not only deals with similar material, it is also something of a companion volume to Alfred Kantorowicz' *Chapayev – the Battalion of Twenty-One Nations*, a book with an extremely interesting publishing history not only in Spain, but also later during attempts to reprint it in the German Democratic Republic. An equally adventurous fate awaited *Encounter at the Ebro* by Willi Bredel. Described on the dust-cover as a novel, the title-page describes it as 'Notes of a War Commissar'. The manuscript was buried under ruins following a bombing raid in Barcelona, and only discovered later by chance. After it was already set up in print by the Malik Press the Nazis occupied Bohemia and the print was destroyed. Fortunately one set of proofs existed and this reached Paris, where the book was finally printed in 1939. It too has since been reprinted in the GDR as *Spanish War I* (*The History of the Eleventh International Brigade*) and *Spanish War II* (*Encounter on the Ebro. Writings. Documents*). The original slim little narrative has developed into two fat volumes, padded out with Bredel's diary-notes, journalistic essays on Spain plus pictures and documents, but the resultant work is flat, emasculated and uninteresting. More interesting is *The Spanish War* by Ludwig Renn, the world-famous author of novels about the First World War. After his release from Gestapo imprisonment in 1933, Renn fled to Switzerland and from there went to Spain, where he was particularly invaluable to the republican side as a training officer and military expert. He became commander of the Thälmann Battalion, Chief of Staff of the Eleventh International Brigade and finally director of the republican military academy. As Jürgen Rühle commented in his study of writers and revolution:

> Altogether in the Spanish theatre of war Renn follows the same discipline and the same code of honour which characterised the imperial German Officers' Corps. Service without complaint, obedience without question, being somebody not just looking like somebody, the only difference being that the Communist Party now gives the commands and receives the obedience.[12]

Renn follows the party line at all times and this makes his narrative rather flat and colourless. Nevertheless he occupied such a high military position that he could not help having a better view of the situation than any other participant in the war, and despite the sober (probably censored) prose there is no doubting the author's passionate commitment to the cause of the republic.

Also conceived and written at the front (this time from the point of view of a battalion medical officer) was Theodor Balk's history of the Fourteenth International Brigade, which he expanded later into *The Lost Manuscript*, published in exile in Mexico in 1943. This version covered the whole war, including the disillusioning experience of defeat and the retreat of the Internationals across the border into France, where internment in concentration camps awaited them. In his *Spanish War Diary* Alfred Kantorowicz went even further in his pessimistic view of the final outcome, because he saw all too clearly the squabbles inside the republican ranks, the havoc created by the terror of the Communist Party machine, the Stalinist persecutions in Russia paralleled in Spain and the fear of spies and treachery of every kind. This did not make him popular in the GDR after the war, but then, as he rightly saw, those who had taken part in the actual fighting in Spain tended not to be viewed favourably in that country, possibly because what they had seen and wished to report did not tally with the party line. Kantorowicz found that his *Spanish Diary* could be published only in a heavily censored form: certainly the version which appeared later in the West under the title *Spanish War Diary* is different in many respects from that published in the East. By then Kantorowicz, living in the West, was being denounced as yet another apostate and renegade from the true faith—a fate he shared with other old warriors who, rejected by the party, eventually went into exile yet again like Otto Brunner. The main value of Kantorowicz' book lies in the fact that it stands up for those who fought in Spain. Like nearly everything Kantorowicz writes it is bitter and quarrelsome, but at the same time the work of an honourable man and not without literary merit. Gustav Regler was another who, like Kantorowicz, was no longer wholehearted in his dedication to the Communist cause by the time hostilities broke out in Spain. In Moscow he had seen his friends arrested and executed in the Stalinist purges, and had experienced the treachery and spy mania of the time. His departure for Spain was therefore an escape from the prevailing conditions. In his autobiography *The Owl of Minerva* he reports his parlous state on arrival in Madrid in 1936, his appointment as political commissar of the Twelfth Brigade, his part in the fighting around Madrid, his friendship with Hemingway, and the battle of Guadalajara. After being severely wounded on 11 June 1937 in the battle of Huesca he spent four months in hospital before being sent to

America on a fund-raising campaign. The tour was successful, but in the meantime the war had been lost; by March 1939 the republicans were defeated. Regler made his way to Perpignan and records in his autobiography what he was able to do for the last of the Brigade survivors struggling into France. His novel *The Great Crusade* was written partly in France and then completed in Mexico, where he settled in 1940. Yet even this novel is not so far removed from the journalistic eye-witness accounts noted so far, because it deals with six months in the lives of members of the International Brigade during the victorious campaign of 1936-7. Hemingway highlighted the documentary nature of the book in the preface he wrote for it.

> The greatest novels are made up. Everything in them is created by the author . . . But there are events which are so great that if a writer has participated in them his obligation is to try to write them truly rather than assume the presumption of altering them with invention. It is events of this importance that have produced Regler's book.[13]

The Great Crusade has been compared with Malraux' *L'Espoir* and Hemingway's *For Whom the Bell Tolls*, but despite its narrative qualities it does not have the same appeal. Concentration on the fighting and the fighting men results in a restricted perspective, which is not helped by pretentious reflections and general comments. As one critic has put it, 'it has so many preachy passages that it falls short as a literary work. One guesses that Hemingway used his influence to see that it was published at all.'[14]

While Regler leaves his narrative half-way between documentary and novel, other writers produced full novels on the Spanish theme. One of the first to do this was Eduard Claudius, already mentioned in connection with his story 'The Sacrifice'. Born in Buer/Gelsenkirchen in 1911, Claudius was arrested by the Nazis in 1933 on the grounds of his anti-fascist activities. He fled to Switzerland in 1934, and from there made his way to Spain. He was wounded several times, made his way back to Switzerland illegally, was interned, fought with the partisans in northern Italy and after the end of hostilities returned to the Soviet zone of Germany, where he received the National Prize for his *People at Our Side*. He later became his country's diplomatic representative in Syria and Vietnam. His Spanish novel *Green Olives and Stark Mountains* appeared in Zurich in 1944. At its centre is a worker from the Ruhr called Jak Rohde with considerable experience as a loyal member of the party and fighter in the class war. In Spain he discovers that the green olives and the fruitful land belong to the nobles and grandees, while the stark mountains and unfruitful stony soil are left to the poor peasants to work. The war is therefore a just one for national and social liberation, quite apart from its significance in the struggle against fascism. The hero, however, while a representative of the other, better Germany, has to suffer the lost battles and defeats of the International Brigades until eventually, like the author himself, he is seriously wounded and sent back to France out of the fighting. But France is about to fall. He is tempted to withdraw from politics and unavailing struggle into domestic happiness with his beloved Thea, but she too comes to realise that the fight for a better world must go on. Claudius did not share the doubts of Kantorowicz, Regler and Koestler. His experiences in Spain did not make him lose faith in Communism and as a result he is still acclaimed in the East as the exemplary worker-poet and trusty fighter for the party and for the cause of the proletariat in its struggle against oppression. *Green Olives* is also approved of as a significant Socialist Realist contribution to political literature on Spain. It demonstrates what the theory demands, namely a model personality in the midst of the realities of the revolutionary class struggle. The world *can* be changed, the oppressed *can* be set free: that is the message. Sometimes the style can become too sententious and sentimental, the party message too overpowering, but by any calculation this novel was still a considerable achievement for a young worker. Very similar in its treatment of the starkness of Spain is Gorrisch' novel *For Spain's Freedom*, later renamed *I'm Thirsty* after the film based on it. The latter title is closer to the theme of the book, which is the Spanish soil thirsting for a social order worthy of human beings. The grandees control the water and water is life. The basis of the novel is the story of a young Spaniard who sees his fields turning to dust, kills the guardian of the well and thereby starts the revolution. While this is clearly an instinctive act, his further progress is charted as he develops intellectually and politically. When he is severely wounded, he leaves Spain for Russia where he will not only be restored to health, but will also train to become a water engineer. This is yet another example of Socialist Realism, but of a rather more naïve kind. The author follows the party line: Russia is the model and the tone is propagandistic, showing the development of the positive hero along the approved lines in the traditional manner of the *Bildungsroman*. The same is the case with Bodo Uhse, who wrote the novel *Lieutenant Bertram* (1944). In this case, however, the unlikely development is from officer in the German Air Force to fighter on the republican side. However, it is written with some authority because it reflects the author's own development from membership of the Nazi Party to membership of the Communist Party. Uhse had arrived in Spain as early as 1936 and could therefore base his novel on first-hand experience, although it was not until he was in exile in Mexico that he had the time to build on ideas and preliminary work from this time. The novel falls easily into two parts. The first is devoted to the preparations for war in Germany, focusing on the ambitious young Bertram, who sees the Air Force as a means of social advancement. The young man enters the milieu of the new master race, which thinks in terms of fame and glory through war. In the second part of the novel German faces German over Spanish soil. While the new Germany sees Spain as the training ground for the Great War to come, the other Germany sees it as the means of wiping out the shame of fascist aggression. The realities of Spain, the cruelties and atrocities inflicted by his side, and the injustice of the priests, the generals and the rich bring about a change in Bertram. The destruction of Guernica adds to his feelings of revulsion and the climax comes when he is shot down and feels that he is 'falling from the clouds to the ground, falling from lies to truth'. This is not presented as a sudden and miraculous revelation, it still takes Lieutenant Bertram some time before he fully grasps the significance of his transformation. Nevertheless this turning away from fascism is the climax of the novel, which was extremely successful in translations in various languages.

While Claudius, Gorrisch and Uhse were all committed Communists before they arrived in Spain and wrote in the corresponding style, the same is not true of Karl Otten, who had been living from March 1933 till August 1936 on Majorca. His novel *Torquemada's Shadow* was written shortly after he left Majorca while the impression of his experiences on the island in the first weeks of the war was still fresh. On 20 June 1938 Otten offered the manuscript of his novel to Gottfried Bermann-Fischer, who had moved Fischer Publishing to Stockholm. The book was printed in Holland, just as the Germans moved in, publication became practically impossible and most copies were lost or destroyed. Some reviews did appear in 1938 and 1939, indicating that copies did reach the public, otherwise the book was forgotten until after the war, although the author had in the meantime become famous for his anthologies of Expressionist writers. The major difference between this novel and others considered so far is that the author does not deal with the International Brigades, but with events in Majorca at the time of the fascist revolt on the mainland. The simple people on the island are suddenly forced to decide what to do, and while they hesitate the fascists on the island, together with the falangists, seize power and terrorise the population. Otten is far removed from Socialist Realism, and still close to the visionary Expressionism of his earlier years. He does not attempt a documentary account of the killing of three thousand people by Franco's followers on the island in the first seven months. Instead he combines report, evocation and lyrical description into what he describes as a new 'constructive' novel form. Otten was also a pacifist and in his novel he only reluctantly arrives at acceptance of the need for armed resistance (his peasants even throw falangist guns into the sea). However, Hitler, Mussolini and Franco had made the idea of peaceful resistance impossible and so even Otten reluctantly accepts the need to fight. Significantly too Torquemada, whose spirit haunts the novel and who has returned in the shape of the leader of the Blue Shirts, is at the root of this resolve, for it was Torquemada who sent thousands of Spanish Jews, baptised and unbaptised, to the stake. This is the spirit which must be fought. As one of Otten's characters says: 'We are all Jews!' Otten the visionary saw beyond Majorca and Spain to the coming fate of Europe. In his book *Writers in Arms*, Benson does not mention Otten's lost novel, but he does discuss extensively *Les grands cimetières sous la lune* by the famous Catholic writer Bernanos. Bernanos had long-standing Spanish connections and was living in Palma in the home of wealthy falangist friends during the period Otten describes. On his return to France he recorded his personal impressions of the purges and the brutality of the Italians on the island: 'His central theme is an attempt to tell the truth about Majorca, about the civil war, and also about the impending disaster facing his own country at the hands of false élites and dictators.'[15] His narrative of death, mutilation and the failure of the Catholic Church was not favourably received and he did not succeed in awakening France to the dangers about to engulf it.

Another novel which looks at the Spanish problem from a different perspective is *The Children of Guernica* (1939) by Hermann Kesten. As the title indicates, the theme is the destruction of the Basque city by German planes which Picasso made the subject of his famous picture: an act of aggression which sent a shudder of horror throughout the whole civilised world and one recognised at the time as a symbolic foretaste of the total war that was to descend on the defenceless civilian populations and cities of Europe. The framework for the narrative is Paris, one of the stations in the author's journeyings in exile. The story-teller is an exile, who hears the tale from a fifteen-year-old Spanish boy. This narrative device distances the story and raises it to a higher, non-realistic plane, but at the same time the author does not always overcome the difficulties of such a technique, for the fifteen-year-old often narrates in a manner far beyond his literary range. The novel has other weaknesses. Writing in Paris without first-hand knowledge of Spain, Kesten wisely restricts the perspective to the family scale. While this can give some insight into the divisive nature of such a war, the author's desire to reduce everything to human terms and avoid direct political comment also reduces the overall impact of the novel. A Civil War on the Spanish scale cannot easily be put on a parallel with family problems.

The striking feature about all this literary activity in connection with the Spanish Civil War was the solidarity of the writers, whether liberal, Socialist or Communist, their realisation of the need to resist fascism and their readiness to do everything in their power to achieve this end. This meant that the writer had to leave his ivory tower, take a stand and express it clearly. Literature and culture were under attack and writers and intellectuals had to use their own weapons to fight back. Many also demonstrated that they were prepared to use weapons other than the pen, by enlisting and fighting with the International Brigades. Clearly too the congresses and public declarations were important, as were journalistic and propagandistic activities. Some (like Renn and Regler) also allowed their name and their fame to be used on fund-raising tours. The most extensive of these tours was that undertaken by Ernst Toller: it was vastly successful in terms of money raised, though by then the cause was lost, and Toller's own life ended tragically in suicide. It has to be admitted that there were no great masterpieces among the literary products which emanated from the war. The plays were small-scale, the poems too explicit and agitprop in style, and the narratives on the whole too documentary and rooted in Socialist Realism. No new forms emerged in drama, lyric or novel, experiments were generally avoided and the result was a cautious clinging to tradition. Nevertheless, as Benson showed by his selective treatment of six literary figures, the impact of the Spanish Civil War on the literary imagination was deep and long-lasting.

9 EXILE, THE FIRST PHASE

Before 1933 the nationalist writers had claimed that they were the representatives of the real Germany and that they had been wrongly excluded from their rightful place by the decadent, un-German cultural Bolshevists of the Weimar Republic. After 1933 they took over all places of power and prestige inside Germany—and 'un-Germans', in so far as they were permitted to do so—left the country. In all centuries, and in all countries artists and writers had experienced exile before, but generally speaking only one person at a time—a Li-tai-pe or an Ovid—had been involved.[1] After 1933 exile was no longer an isolated fate, but a general experience. Germany had seen troubled times in the eighteenth and nineteenth centuries, but never before had there been such a mass exodus of figures from the world of science and learning, from the professions and the arts, nor had Germany faced a situation where two cultural rumps (one inside and one outside) claimed to represent the country. Certainly Germany has never been the same since. All the arts, the professions, all spheres of business and publishing, the newspaper and film industries, not to mention medicine and science have been critically affected by this massive intellectual haemorrhaging. While it is difficult to be precise, conservative estimates quote a figure of around 400,000 people leaving the country after 1933. Around 2,000 of these were active in the arts in some way.

Even before 1933 certain significant literary figures had already chosen to live and work outside Germany and Austria. Joseph Roth lived in Paris and worked for German newspapers. Tucholsky also found Paris more congenial than Berlin, before finally settling in Sweden. Some, like the leading Expressionist Herwarth Walden, had followed their fascination with Russia and the Revolution and had left for the Soviet Union. Walden is now thought to have met his death in Saratov in 1941. France had always exercised an attraction for German writers—René Schickele, the bilingual writer from Alsace moved in 1932 to Sanary-sur-Mer, which was later to attract many more German writers in exile—and Switzerland too had for long been the traditional refuge for German radicals, while Czechoslovakia was a liberal haven for many. Those already living abroad were not immediately followed by refugees after Hitler's accession to power. Some who were in immediate personal danger did leave—these included Robert Neumann,

Alfred Kerr, Heinrich Mann and Walter Mehring. Some had accepted invitations to lecture abroad, while others, like Thomas Mann, who were already abroad never returned. Thomas Mann certainly did not plan to leave Germany and had to be persuaded by his family to stay away.

As has been already noted many were perhaps too slow to take the Nazi menace seriously, but by the late 1930s enough writers and journalists were aware of what Hitler and his party stood for, and had written articles, books and plays proclaiming the danger he represented for Germany. Yet apart from those personally threatened who left the country, there were many more who clearly hesitated, hoping perhaps that the German people would come to its senses at the last minute, or that Hitler's powerful conservative backers could still restrain him. Whatever the reason, the fact that Hitler had been named Reich Chancellor was not enough by itself to make these writers leave the country. The Reichstag Fire and the wave of arrests and atrocities which followed provided convincing proof for most that Hitler really meant what he said. Some Communists were interned for brief periods, others disappeared into Nazi prisons and hastily prepared concentration camps for longer spells. The reporter Kisch was the first to cover this wave of arrests in his documentary *In the Dungeons of Spandau*. But even without such reports the message got through to the literary and political intelligentsia very quickly; by 28 February the flight was on: by the autumn of 1933 it was all over. The National Socialists had apparently removed from the country all literary opposition to proclaimed policies, leaving only scattered underground activity. Some writers slipped across the frontiers with valid passports and little more, while others left more openly with the new Nazi exit visas. Some few did not leave until 1938. Georg Kaiser, the most famous dramatist of the Expressionist movement, stayed on until then; Nelly Sachs was in Germany till 1940, when she left for Sweden. Once the Nazis had removed possible opposition writers from the country their next step was to deprive them of citizenship. This they did with their customary bureaucratic thoroughness, listing authors for exclusion like they listed books for burning. At first the German authors deprived of citizenship took mention of their names in such lists as a mark of honour, in just the same way as Oskar Maria Graf had demanded that his books be burned like those of all the other honourable Germans. However, the Nazis knew what they were doing and authors in exile without passports or papers soon found that they were approximating to Goebbels' description of them as 'cadavers on

holiday'. For the world outside Germany the vital piece of paper with
the proper stamps and visas for those 'in transit' was the only official
proof that anyone existed as a person. Writers in exile claiming to
represent the real Germany found they did not exist. Nevertheless if
the *Ausbürgerung* lists are taken as an indication of those the Nazis
considered to be their enemies, then writers had some reason to be
proud, because a remarkable number of them were included, indicating
that the Nazis considered them sources of real danger to be silenced.
People like Lion Feuchtwanger, Alfred Kerr (the brilliant journalist of
the cutting phrase), Heinrich Mann, Ernst Toller and Kurt Tucholsky
were included in the first list of 23 August 1933; leading Communists
like Johannes R. Becher, Rudolf Leonhard and Theodor Plievier were
in the second; the brothers John Heartfield and Wieland Herzfelde,
who had plagued the Nazis with their cartoons and satires, were in the
third, while Brecht was in the fourth.

By the time the Law for the Establishment of the Reich Culture
Chamber was brought in on 22 September 1933 there was not a single
author of international standing left in Germany, except for those who
were in prison, or who (like Benn) had thrown in their lot with the
Nazis. The aim of the new German government had been to crush all
opposition leaving only those writers whose work would be in line
with the literary policies of the new Germany. The 'steely Romanticism'
Goebbels called for would then be free to flourish, while the decadent
Weimar culture would have been either stamped out or scattered
abroad to wither and fade away. The new Germany and the new
literature would have time to consolidate, while arrest or banishment,
terror and strict control made opposition impossible both inside and
outside the country.

In fact, however, this was not what happened. By the autumn of
1933 remarkable feats of literary organisation had been accomplished.
In Amsterdam Fritz Landshoff, a former director of Kiepenheuer,
completed an agreement with the Querido Press and a first list of works
by German authors in exile was presented. Also in Amsterdam the
Allert de Lange concern took on a German section.[2] Outside the
Netherlands, Switzerland proved another area where works in German
could be published, thanks to the outlets controlled by the Social
Democrat Emil Oprecht. When Bermann-Fischer moved out of Germany
in 1936, he operated first from Vienna, before finding suitable working
conditions in Stockholm. Russia was also another country friendly to
German anti-Nazi writers, although the vagaries of the Communist party
line, culminating in the Soviet-German non-aggression pact, the show

trials and the Stalinist purges, were later to prove that many Communists who thought they had found sactuary there had gone to their deaths. Apart from being a period when publishing houses were founded in various countries, these were also years of optimism, when it seemed a great deal could still be accomplished to counter National Socialism by the power of the pen, exposing the true face of the new Germany to the world and sounding the alarm about the danger of war. The Weimar years had been denounced in nationalist quarters as the age of the un-German art of journalism. While, as Karl Kraus and others demonstrated, there was some justification for this accusation, the lusty newspaper life of Germany in the twenties and thirties was preferable to the desert the Nazis created. Fortunately journalistic expertise was useful in bringing the best of the banned Weimar journals quickly back to life abroad. The *AIZ* (the *Workers' Illustrated News*) successfully transferred to Prague, and the two most prominent weeklies of the Weimar Republic also enjoyed a rebirth. The first number of the new *Tagebuch*, edited by Leopold Schwarzschild, came out in Paris on 1 July 1933, while the new *Weltbühne* came out in Prague about the same time. By September 1933 the first literary monthlies established in exile were coming out—*Sammlung* in Amsterdam, the *Neue Deutsche Blätter* in Prague. Professional writers' organisations, destroyed by Nazis in the course of *Gleichschaltung*, were also set up again in exile in addition to such journals, weeklies and monthlies. The Schutzverband Deutscher Schriftsteller (German Writers Association) was re-established in Paris in 1933. One of its slogans was 'Gesicht nach Deutschland' ('Facing towards Germany') and its members made it their business to continue up-to-date discussions about Germany. They organised public events, for example lectures including one on 'The Germany of the Future' by Heinrich Mann, they supported friends and 'illegal' colleagues inside Germany, and they published their own journal *Der deutsche Schriftsteller* in exactly the same format as the original journal which had been 'gleichgeschaltet' and sent hundreds of copies of it to colleagues in Germany. One year later a fat brochure with the title *German for Germans* was also smuggled into the country.[3] The next illegal number to make its way into Germany from this source was the Spanish one. Altogether the slogan 'Germany is in our Camp', taken up by Alfred Kantorowicz, the general secretary, as the title of one of his collections of speeches and essays gives a fair idea of the tenor of SDS convictions. The climax was the opening of the *German Freedom Library* in Paris on the first anniversary of the Book Burning with a stock of 13,000 volumes. Nevertheless, despite these obvious successes, the optimistic frame of mind which these activities encouraged was delusory. The journals were not to last very long, despite the laudable work they were able to do in the short period of their existence. The writers' professional bodies were a prey to internecine strife and, like many other such anti-fascist centres, even the Freedom Library was exposed to a Communist take-over. The exiles and *émigrés* were still subject to too many delusions about the nature of National Socialism. In particular they still tended to think of their period of banishment from Germany as one of short duration, convinced that they were merely 'on holiday', 'going away' for a few weeks or months to 'let the Germans come to their senses'. Nobody could imagine that once the Nazis came to power they would not let go, and that they would go from success to success. The idea that the new Germany would not last long was held regardless of political party or inclination. It was thought that the regime would collapse because of its own incompetence or because of that of its new leaders, that the democracies would bring pressure to bear to bring down the Nazis, or that the workers inside Germany would start the long-awaited revolution. This latter illusion for long represented the Communist party line, though there never had been any evidence that the workers were on the point of revolting. In any event the traditional hostility between Communist and Socialist party organisations made such joint action impossible. Proof for the exiles' conviction that the new Germany would not last is the fact that most of them did not go very far, but instead settled round Germany's perimeter. As Brecht put it in his poem 'On the Designation Emigré':

Unruhig sitzen wir so, möglichst nahe den Grenzen
Wartend des Tags der Rückkehr, jede kleinste Veränderung
Jenseits der Grenze beobachtend.[4]

(Restless, we squat as close as possible to
the borders, awaiting the day of return,
taking note of even the tiniest of developments
on the other side of the border.)

The SDS slogan 'Facing towards Germany' also indicated that when they wrote or spoke they were still directing their remarks towards the homeland, in the belief that they could still exert some influence on the course of events inside that country. They were still writing in German for Germans inside Germany, to bring about the downfall of the Nazis and so they settled temporarily in Czechoslovakia, France and the Netherlands. German-speaking countries like Austria and Switzerland were particularly favoured, though they were not to know that Austria was soon to be annexed into the new greater Germany or that Switzerland, the traditional land of exile for German political refugees, would prove so vulnerable to pressure from Nazi Germany and develop 'The Boat is Full' policy which would keep so many of them out. Italy was a fascist country and hence not favoured, though some writers like Stefan Andres and Armin T. Wegner found refuge there. Fascist countries like Hungary and Poland were generally out of the question. At this time Paul Zech, a writer of the Expressionist generation, was the only one to go overseas; he went to South America, where despite great difficulties he wrote several significant works, including an exile novel which has only recently been published. Karl Wolfskehl (an important figure in the George circle) emigrated first to Switzerland, from there to Italy and finally, in order to get as far away from the new Germany as possible, he went in 1938 to New Zealand, where he was to remain until his death ten years later in 1948.

Looking back on the situation at that time, Klaus Mann in his autobiography *The Turning Point* summed up the literary programme as most exiles saw it: they had to warn the world about the menace of the Third Reich, and enlighten it about the true character of the regime, at the same time they had to make it clear that there was another, better Germany, and they had to maintain contact with that Germany, in its illegal and secret operations. There was a resistance movement and it was their duty as writers to provide it with the intellectual ammunition it needed for its struggle inside Germany. It was also necessary to remember the roots of that other Germany in the great traditions of the German spirit and of the German language, for which there was no place in the new Germany, and it was the duty of the representatives of the better Germany outside its borders to keep this memory alive and to build on the great tradition. The policy statement of *Sammlung* followed similar lines. Germany was a country which had 'gone astray' and become ashamed of its great tradition of humanism. The function of *Sammlung* was to gather together those who were against the barbarity, brutality and anti-humanism of the new Germany. The *Neue Deutsche Blätter* meanwhile attempted to understand what fascism meant for Germany. Was it an anachronism, an intermezzo, a return to medieval barbarity? Had a mental disease befallen the Germans? Was it an anomaly in the course of Germany's true historical development? Were the National Socialists a gang of criminals who had suddenly seized the land by cunning? The journal's answer to this series of questions was the categorical statement that German fascism was the organic product of 'a capitalism sick unto death' and no accident. From this, the conclusion was drawn that National Socialism had to be fought. Writers were engaged in a war to the death and anti-fascist writing was the only kind worth while. Not surprisingly, from that time on there has been a natural inclination to describe all exiles as anti-fascists. But not much is gained by such an approach, especially in the light of the vast diversity of the literature which was actually produced outside Germany between 1933 and 1945. Nevertheless the fact that writers at this time were themselves giving thought to the nature of National Socialism and fascism is important. Indeed this debate was not carried on marginally or unconsciously, instead the whole question of the function of literature in an Age of Fascism became one of the most central of the time.

As has been observed, the German professional writers were able to transfer their journals apparently without difficulty to locations outside Germany and carry on with their activities as they had done before. Poems continued to be written, novels to be published and normal literary routines seemed to have suffered only a minor hiccup. It was a Dutch writer, Menno ter Braak, who first drew attention to the fact that there was no essential difference between the literature being produced in exile and that written before Hitler, apart from minor changes of place and publisher. Menno ter Braak was quite clear in his own mind that there *should* be a difference and that German literature in exile had to offer more than a mere continuation of what had been there before. Various literary figures including Hans Sahl and Ludwig Marcuse took part in the debate that followed. What ter Braak said was true. Many major works like Musil's *The Man without Qualities* had already been started *before* their authors left National Socialist Germany, but this did not necessarily mean that such works had to be broken off, or that if continued they would remain unaffected by the events of the time. Besides there was some justification for consciously carrying on the progressive literary traditions of the Weimar Republic. If Germany could not be divided into a good Germany and a bad, its literature equally could not be divided into before or after Hitler. 1933 did not have to mark a complete break with the past, or necessitate a completely new start. At the same time there had never been anything so monstrous as the National Socialist regime in German history and each writer and intellectual was forced to clarify his own position with regard to it. All exiles and *émigrés*, Jews and non-Jews, political and apolitical poets shared the common fate of exclusion from the homeland, but this did not make them all alike – far from it. At first it was easy for all exiles and *émigrés* to feel that they were all in the same boat, but gradually changed circumstances forcibly made them aware of their differences. The debate sparked off in the *Neues Tagebuch* by ter Braak helped start this process of clarification.

In the poem already quoted, Brecht questions the label '*émigré*' attached to people like himself. This was a false designation, Brecht claimed, because it meant somebody who had taken a free decision to go to another land. But people like himself had not simply gone somewhere else in order to stay there, possibly for ever. They had fled, been driven out, banished. Brecht's poem concludes:

> Jeder von uns
> Der mit zerrissenen Schuhen durch die Menge geht
> Zeugt von der Schande, die jetzt unser Land befleckt.
> Aber keiner von uns
> Wird hier bleiben. Das letzte Wort
> Ist noch nicht gesprochen.[5]

> (Every one of us passing through the crowd with
> tattered shoes bears witness to the disgrace which
> is besmirching our country at present. But not one
> of us will stay here. The last word has not yet
> been spoken.)

The only thing the exiles had in common was that they were German: the difference was between those persecuted for racial reasons and those forced to leave for basically political reasons, though clearly there was often no strict dividing line between the two. Jews forced out of Germany were unlikely ever to return (especially once the extent of the crimes against the Jewish people became known). They were also less likely to think in terms of a future Germany after Hitler, with themselves playing a part in the life of the country. For them exile was more likely to be permanent, they would seek to find a country which did offer them a future, where they could put down new roots. If they were representatives of the other, better Germany then they were lost to that Germany. Assimilation had failed, Socialism had not halted the Nazi menace, Zionism remained as a possibility of Jewish renewal. Non-Jewish literary and political exiles were more likely to think as Brecht did. Germany remained for them the centre of their interest and of their activities. Though the number of Jewish

emigrants in 1933 was still comparatively small, early works of exile
literature often show Jewish characters in Germany who are completely
assimilated, who have been German for centuries, who have fought
bravely in the First World War, have gained prominent positions in
business and the professions, and have conservative to nationalist views.
They have no desire to leave Germany. The successive measures
brought in by the National Socialists open their eyes and make it clear
to them that anti-Semitism is a central element in the Nazi Party
programme and not mere window-dressing to attract votes. At first it
was also NSDAP policy to force Jews out of the country; it was only
later that the solution to the Jewish Question involved annihilation
camps. As a result of the waves of Jewish *émigrés* many countries
which accepted them ended up with a German-Jewish population of
considerable size and influence. Not all Jews forced out of Germany
came from the professional classes, but certainly there was a large
proportion of culturally interested, book-buying people among them.
Such people were to prove an important public for the literature
produced in exile over the years to come, though they were gradually
lost as assimilation into the other language and revulsion against all
things German increased, and the belief in a better Germany was lost:

> Without this public the émigré publishing houses could not have got
> their production going so quickly, without this public the works of
> the exiled writers would have been the poorer by one important
> sounding-board.[6]

Exiled writers themselves were far from politically homogeneous. The
range was wide and included everything from anarchists, Communists
and Social Democrats to middle-class liberals and right-wing conservatives.
Some were unclassifiable in any political sense and insisted on
preserving their unattached position as individuals. Some even reconsider-
ed their position in exile and opted for National Socialism. The most
notorious case of this kind was that of Ernst Glaeser, a prominent
figure in the Weimar Republic and leading member of the BPRS who
became famous with his early novels *Class of 1902* (1928) and *Peace
1919* (1930). In 1933 his works were banned and burned for their
'decadence' and 'moral turpitude' and he went into exile in Switzerland.
His novel written there, *The Last Civilian* (1936), charts the rise of
National Socialism in a small town and is particularly successful in
showing what makes the new movement attractive to certain sections
in Germany. On its appearance the novel was an immediate success and

it was translated into twenty-four languages. However, it was noted
that the Nazis did not ban this or other exile works by Glaeser, for
reading between the lines, it was possible to detect the author's
admiration for the drive and strength of the Nazis compared with the
often resigned fatalism of the opposition to it. In exile Glaeser himself
began to develop a philosophy of 'Umfall' (sudden change of mind),
and confessed that he felt hopelessly lost without Germany. He was
'lying dead on the marble steps of his successes', and in 1939 he
returned, eventually to be put in charge of a German army newspaper
in Italy. After the war he was still a prominent figure in the literary
life of West Germany. In 1945, for example, he gave a speech in
Heidelberg on 'Germany's Heritage and Obligations', and in 1960 he
published another novel on the *Glory and Misery of the Germans*. Like
Paul de Lagarde, Langbehn and so many others he was obsessed with
the problem of the 'German character', and devoted whole novels like
The Last Civilian to it, especially where the German character showed
a fatal attraction for Hitler and fascism.

Renegades like Glaeser were the exception rather than the rule,
sympathisers with the new Nazi Germany were few and there were not
even many outright conservatives and monarchists among the writers
in exile, though the greatest of them all, Joseph Roth, did develop in
this direction. The fact that writers like Glaeser, who moved from the
extreme left wing to more conservative political positions, had more
influence in the emerging Federal Republic of Germany than left-
wingers is probably the most significant feature of his career. By
contrast the predominantly left-wing body of exile writers found little
echo on their return. In exile, however, a certain cohesiveness was
provided not so much by any clearly defined anti-fascist or anti-Nazi
stance, but by this very awareness that they represented the 'other,
better Germany'. It was this awareness as much as the endeavours of
left-wing bodies and the organisational genius of a person like Willi
Münzenberg that gradually overcame the traditional antagonisms
between Socialists, Communists and others. Weimar literature had
developed a tradition of social concern and readiness to expose the
faults and contradictions within the republic. The early years of exile
continued this tradition—indeed they were marked by an acceleration
of it. Literature became more and more openly political. The 'compulsion to politics' Thomas Mann spoke of was something felt by the
generality of writers in exile to a greater or less degree. This again is a
factor which has worked to the disadvantage of the literary works
produced in this period, given the normal German acceptance that

literature and art have to be removed from (and somehow higher than) 'mere' politics. After 1945 a generation which had had enough of ideological conflicts was only too ready to ignore such works and turn to forms of literature which transport the reader out of the horrors of the real world into a higher, purer realm of ideas, ideals and beauty. As a result Kafka's timeless world was preferred to pictures of the real Germany of the thirties. Thomas Mann was read, but it was the Thomas Mann of the *Magic Mountain* and not the author of the political essays and of the 'Broadcasts to the German Nation'. Brecht was performed, but more often in fairy-tale parables like *The Caucasian Chalk Circle* (without the political prologue) than the specifically anti-Nazi plays.

In this connection it is interesting to examine the literary genres and the extent to which they were exploited by writers in exile. It is easy to assume, for example, that the novel would be the most suitable and most fruitful form, that dramatists would have a difficult time without access to a real theatre and its resources, and that the lyric would probably suffer most of all in what was what Brecht called a 'bad time for poetry'. One must consider too which literary traditions carried over from the Weimar Republic and also which were to possess the best chances of survival in post-Hitler Germany. At first sight prose narrative forms do seem to have been the natural first choice for writers in exile. When they fled from Germany many took the manuscripts of stories and novels with them. In economic terms there was a market for such work, a successful story could reach a scattered market and sell thousands of copies. It could be more easily translated and there were models in this medium to imitate, writers like Glaeser, Feuchtwanger, Remarque, Mann, whose names were known around the world, putting them into the international star class. By the thirties writers were aware of such things as film rights and knew that a novel could appeal to different countries and different cultures. A novel did not have to be about Germany, the novel form made it possible to select interesting settings and move through different time scales, exploiting the fullest possibilities of place and historical location. This is not to say that the novel could not also have a deeper or more serious purpose, for example in putting a political message across, but in the novel it was possible to do both—to tell a story and to impart a message—while at the same time retaining a popular format. One can imagine that when a publisher set up provisionally in exile, he could get going with fairly basic facilities, and when he came to consider his potential customers he would think primarily of novel-readers rather than readers of drama or poetry. In the Weimar Republic things had been rather different. There

were many famous examples of the *texts* of famous and controversial
plays selling in thousands of copies, and there had always been a public
for poetry, even of the most difficult and esoteric kind. The Expressionist generation had been noted for the flood of poetry that poured on
to the market through the medium of the many little magazines that
sprang to life at that time. Even in the post-Expressionist age that
followed there was still a market for the more functional poetry of
the New Objectivity. Now all that had apparently gone and there was
no longer an assured public for the poetry of the lonely poet in exile.
The same applied to literature for the stage. An unperformed new play
script would not sell and theatrical production had difficult pre-
conditions like an audience of people who could be gathered together
in the same place at the same time, not to mention performers, and all
the resources of the stage, all of which cost money. There were still
some theatres where German plays could be performed, most notably
in Switzerland, in Austria for a time, in Czechoslovakia, in the Russia
of the Volga German community, and elsewhere, but these were
exceptions, and generally speaking the dramatist had to be prepared to
make concessions, to arrange for translations, to adapt to the differing
theatrical traditions of non-German countries. Brecht's life in exile was
one continuous sequence of negotiations of this kind. Nevertheless,
despite all the difficulties a remarkable number of significant plays were
written in this period, and not only written but also performed in
most unusual places. In the same way despite all the predictions about
the difficulty if not impossibility of writing poetry in this time, much
significant poetry was written under most trying circumstances. This
too must be examined. That it was impossible to make a living in exile
from writing plays or poems is obvious.

   First, however, prose works brought out in exile against the new
Germany of National Socialism must be considered. The first impulse
was to expose the full horrors of the concentration camps and the
persecution of the Jews in Germany. This explains the existence on the
publishers' lists of works already noted like *In Murder Camp Dachau*
and *Oranienburg*. Even more successful than such authentic, eye-witness
accounts were the products of the publishing concern, Éditions du
Carrefour, set up in Paris by the propaganda genius Willi Münzenberg,
who had been a most successful organiser of Communist propaganda
in Germany. A real man of the people, Münzenberg rose up through
the ranks, took part in the Spartacist uprising in Germany and eventually
became leader of the Communist Youth International. Not long afterwards he created the International Workers Relief (IAH — Internationale

Arbeiterhilfe), 'which became the parent body of the publishing house, daily papers, journals, illustrated weekly, film company, book and film clubs, and proletarian theatre groups which comprised his propaganda empire'.[7] Like everybody else Münzenberg was shaken by the failure of working-class resistance to Hitler, but he realised that a party which had polled six million votes could not have disappeared without trace. In Paris he determined to use his organisational abilities not merely to rouse world opinion against National Socialism, but also to reach these other Germans he was convinced still existed inside Germany. Hence when he set up his many commissions, committees and congresses, he not only denounced the new Germany of the National Socialists, he also constantly drew attention to those inside Germany who were suffering for their opposition to the regime, and stirred up international protest against the maltreatment of the thousands of Germans in concentration camps. From the beginning in Paris he followed a popular front policy, and as a result was able to unite all shades of opinion in his Committee for the Relief of Victims of German Fascism. Between 1933 and 1936 Münzenberg's Éditions du Carrefour published approximately one hundred books and pamphlets, including notable successes like Koestler's *Menschenopfer unerhört, A Black Book on Spain.* Éditions du Carrefour also controlled a number of newspapers, the most successful of which was the *AIZ.* Without doubt the most successful and sensational of all Münzenberg's publications was *The Brown Book on Reichstag Fire and Hitler Terror.* By 1935, 600,000 copies had been published in twenty-five languages, of which 15,000 had been smuggled into Germany disguised as Reclam editions of the classics. The additional mark of his genius was in linking publication of a book with another parallel event, a model frequently followed since then. So, for example, *The Brown Book* was linked with a *counter*-trial in London *before* the Reichstag trial in Germany, permitting international counsel to review *all* the evidence, thereby discrediting the Nazi show trial and forcing the German court to bring in a verdict of not guilty against Dimitrov, Popov, Tanev and Torgler. Münzenberg's counter-trial made it clear that Goering and Goebbels were the real criminals behind the Reichstag Fire, because they needed such an event to consolidate their power and as an excuse for attacks on Communists, Socialists, trade unionists, Jews, and all such targets. Münzenberg followed up the first Brown Book with a second— *Dimitrov contra Goering*, thirty thousand copies of which were smuggled into Germany. A *White Book* was devoted to the Bartholomew's Day shooting of 30 June 1934 in which Hitler had General Schleicher,

Captain Ernst Röhm and other SA leaders assassinated, while *The Brown Net* exposed Hitler's propaganda and spy network outside Germany. Although Münzenberg did also write for his own publications his main energies were directed into organisation and administration, and he had particular success in enlisting the support of public figures, intellectual luminaries and political leaders. One of the largest of the anti-fascist gatherings convened by him was the Congress for the Defence of Culture in Paris in June 1935. Another campaign, that on behalf of Ernst Thälmann, imprisoned by the Nazis, incorporated not only an appeal for his release, but also a reminder that Ludwig Renn, Carl von Ossietsky and thousands of other Germans opposed to National Socialism were also languishing in Hitler's jails and concentration camps. Münzenberg successfully brought together Socialist and middle-class intellectual support in the fight against Hitler's Germany. This was his approach too when the Spanish Civil War broke out in July 1936. All opponents of fascism had to be united in the common fight against it. By the end, however, he was working without the support of the Comintern and was an outcast as far as the party was concerned. In the summer of 1937 he joined the German Freedom Party, which was to pursue a popular front policy in combating fascism and in laying plans for a reconstructed Germany. Here again the important thing in Münzenberg's eyes was to influence the course of events inside Germany by aiding the forces offering resistance to Nazism. The Freedom Letters of this party were addressed to the 'democratic forces of Germany' (which he was convinced existed) and smuggled into the country by the hundreds of thousands. By this time Münzenberg was beyond the pale as far as the Communist Party was concerned. He had attacked Stalin's policies in Spain, and he had rejected the Hitler-Stalin Pact. As a result he was subjected to virulent character assassination. By 1939 the man who had been such a faithful and successful servant of the Communist Party and of the Comintern was denouncing the Communist Party as the party which had betrayed the German people in their most difficult hour and demanded that it be destroyed along with Hitler. He prophesied that there would be no room in a liberated Germany for dictators, regardless of their persuasion. Here as elsewhere he was concerned about the fate of Germany. Hitler's Germany was not the real Germany, but a Communist dictatorship after the collapse of Hitler would not be the real Germany either. By the beginning of the war in 1940 Münzenberg was no longer the powerful impresario he had been only a few years before and found himself isolated and exposed.

In the confusion of the retreat before the advancing German forces he disappeared and his body was eventually found in the woods of Cagnet in South Western France. He had been garrotted. His murder was never explained.

Münzenberg was more of an organiser and an impresario than a writer, but his concern for Germany was real. He had witnessed the failure of his own party under the onslaught of the Nazis and he never gave up his quest to find out why this had happened, what could be done to reach the elements of resistance to National Socialism he was convinced still existed inside Germany, what could be done for its younger generation, and what was to become of the Germany of the future. As a journalist he was not alone in these concerns and from 1933 onwards a spate of books appeared with titles like *The German Tragedy*, *The History of the Weimar Republic*, *The Birth of the Third Reich*, *Hitler the Conqueror*, *Hindenburg or the Spirit of the Prussian Army*, et cetera. But it was not only in journalistic or historical form that such concern over the nature of Germany and her fate found expression. One of the most successful of all the literary forms of the Weimar Republic had been the novel combining a gripping story-line with consideration of the social and political problems of the age and of the country. No novels of this kind were written inside Nazi Germany because the National Socialists proclaimed that no social or political problems existed any more. Harmony prevailed in the community of a united *Volk*. If the social novel was not a literary tradition which could be continued inside National Socialist Germany, it was one which found its continuation outside Germany in the preference for the so-called Deutschland novel.[8] While this was not the only form developed at this time (others were devoted to the problem of exile itself, others yet again to international rather than national issues, and the historical novel will also have to be considered), nevertheless, the Deutschland novel proved to be among the most fruitful of the novel forms in exile and one which was practised throughout the whole period from 1933 to 1945.

To gain some idea of what is meant by a Deutschland novel one only has to look at Lion Feuchtwanger's *The Oppermanns* (1933), which was not only one of the first and one of the most successful, but also one which was to set the pattern for the future.[9] The novel itself was one of a trilogy, including *Success*, the first volume, which had come out in Berlin in 1930, and *Exile*, which came out in 1939. All three were gathered together under the title *The Waiting Room* to characterise the essential exile experience. Feuchtwanger had laid the foundations

for his world-wide success in the Weimar Republic with the historical
best-seller *Jew Süss*, little guessing how the Nazis would later exploit
the possibilities of this theme.[10] *Success* (*Three Years in the History
of a Province*) was a satirical book about the early history of the Nazi
Party in Bavaria, using the typical Weimar theme of the differential
dispensation of justice. An art historian falls foul of the legal system
and through his story Feuchtwanger is able to link the various spheres
of culture and the arts, business and politics. The second volume about
the Oppermanns shows the state of Germany on the advent of the
Hitler regime and what this means for an upper middle-class Jewish
family. The final volume of the trilogy deals (as the title suggests) with
the theme of exile itself. In choosing a title like *Success* Feuchtwanger
was writing about himself, about Brecht, with whom he was always
closely associated, and about the Bavaria he loved. By 1932/3 he was
on a tour of America. In his absence his works were banned and
burned in the Third Reich and he never returned to Germany. Like
many others he lived first in the South of France at Sanary-sur-Mer.
He was arrested by the Vichy government, but managed to escape the
Gestapo and get to America. His incomparable sales record permitted
him to live in luxury at Pacific Palisades, California, where he eventually
died in 1958. *The Oppermanns* was a typical example of the success
he constantly enjoyed. Within five months it had sold 257,000 copies,
only twenty thousand of which were in the original German. According
to one account the novel started life as a film scenario which
Feuchtwanger wrote for Ramsay Macdonald whom he had met in
London. The Prime Minister sent the screen writer Sidney Gilliat to
Sanary-sur-Mer to help Feuchtwanger with it. However, British government policy changed from an anti-Nazi stance to gentle persuasion and
so the author re-wrote the script quickly as a novel. It is markedly
different from the other two volumes of the trilogy. In the first and
third volumes the events of the twenties and thirties are reported by a
fictitious narrator from the year 2000. Feuchtwanger uses this narrative
device in order to gain greater distance from the present. In *The
Oppermanns* he deals with Germany after 1933 directly. In other words
this is Feuchtwanger's attempt to make the world aware of the true face
of Nazi Germany, and to enlighten it about the danger this represents.
For this purpose he uses a framework of real historical events and
people. The old order is crumbling and the 'waiting room' is a symbol
of mankind's waiting for a new and better order to emerge. In his own
words: 'The aim of the trilogy is to bring to life for future generations
that bad time of waiting and transition, the darkest age Germany has

experienced since the Thirty Years War.' By the time he was completing *Exile* the war had broken out and everything had changed, but
nevertheless Feuchtwanger did not lose his fundamental optimism and
his belief that 'reason would win over stupidity'. It was with this in
mind that he reckoned on a final volume to be called *The Return*. He
never did write it and he never did return.

The Oppermanns deals with an extensive Jewish family, focusing
particularly on the one central figure, Gustav. The time covered is
limited to the period between November 1932 and late summer 1933.
This is not a novel of action, but one offering a picture of a society
(or one section of it) at a crucial point in the country's history. The
characters are Jewish, but also totally German in their disdain for
politics. Indeed the novel demonstrates the tragic flaw of Germany's
intelligentsia and liberal middle class in failing to recognise the threat
to Germany and to their world represented by the rise of National
Socialism. Possibilities of opposing National Socialism are indicated,
but even those who recognise the danger fail to play any active part in
the political struggle. Zionism is one distracting possibility, saving the
business another, but all chances of resistance are missed, although the
novel does indicate that underground political activity, of the kind
undertaken by Communists, is the only solution for Germany. In
general the novel fails to explain why the Nazi Party is successful in
attracting so many followers to its cause. Stupidity is not a satisfactory
explanation. Where the novel does succeed is in its consistent focus on
one German-Jewish family. Perhaps, as some critics have argued, this
did not give the broad perspective or the totality of Nazi Germany;
perhaps the author did underestimate the role of the masses; perhaps
he did overvalue one tiny section in the broad spectrum of the new
Germany and thereby fail to reveal the decisive economic forces at work
behind the rise of National Socialism, but nevertheless Feuchtwanger
was right to focus on the German-Jewish dilemma. Despite what many
people, including Brecht, thought at the time the attack on the Jews
was indeed a central element in the Nazi political programme. At this
stage (between 1932 and 1933) the whole action against the Jews in
Germany was only just getting under way with special laws, the
boycott and other measures, but Feuchtwanger shows the beginning
of the process which was to end in genocide. Gustav, after his return
to Germany and his weak attempts to contact the resistance, lands in a
concentration camp and dies shortly after his release. The rest of the
family scatter to various different cities in Europe to start a new life:

Their homeland, their Germany has proved to be a deceiver . . . So
they start to come to the conclusion, that they would probably
never be able to return; for what can follow the rule of Nationalists
except war and years of blood and the most appalling revolution?
But quite secretly, against their own common sense, they hoped it
would all turn out differently.

This is the source of the novel's success — its true insight into the
situation of Jewish intellectuals and business people, portraying German
Jews as they really were with all their faults and flaws, but also with all
their love of Germany and of all things German. They are the real
Germans, the good Germans, the bearers of German culture and
tradition; the Nazis are the other Germans, the despoilers and
destroyers. The 'true face of the Nazi dictatorship' is twofold. What
it shows on the surface is an impression of order, organisation and
bureaucratic efficiency. But this serves only to conceal irresponsibility
and violence. This is the message that comes across quite clearly. What
also comes across is Feuchtwanger's belief that two-thirds of the
German people are against Hitler, that there is real resistance inside
Germany and not merely of the rather romantic kind which he himself
calls 'inner emigration' in the final section of the novel. He attempts
in this second book of the trilogy to deal with two questions, first, how
the catastrophe engulfed Germany in the first place and, second, what
the general situation was in the new Germany. The blame for the first
lies clearly with the failure of the enlightened middle classes to take
political action. Gustav is busy with his Lessing biography, but the
culture of the Age of Goethe and its ideal of 'Humanität' prove no
barrier to the resentments of a petty bourgeoisie running amok. The
question about the nature of Germany Feuchtwanger answers as
follows:

> The Volk was good. It had produced men and achievements of a
> supreme kind. It consisted of powerful, industrious people. But its
> civilisation was young, it was not difficult to abuse its unfailing
> uncritical idealism, to inflame its atavistic urges, its primitive jungle
> impulses, so that they broke through the thin crust and this is
> exactly what was happening.

This is Feuchtwanger's view of National Socialism. The good people of
Germany are seduced by barbarian leaders and madmen: they are
drowned in a wave of filth. The mention of 'primitive impulses' is not

without sexual echoes, which register the attractiveness as well as the obscenity of fascism. Fundamentally Feuchtwanger believed that the number of Beefsteak Nazis was greater than the number of true believers. This led him (like many others) to the mistaken belief that the regime was becoming more and more unstable, instead of stronger and stronger at this stage.

The *Waiting Room* trilogy covers the history of National Socialism from its beginnings as a crude, putschist, counter-revolutionary group, through the period of the actual seizure of power up to the legislation against the Jews. *The Oppermanns* marks merely the beginning of the Terror; the concentration camp sequence is only a minor part of the novel.

Attitudes to Feuchtwanger in the thirties were extremely mixed, though there was no doubt about his success with the general public. Intellectuals like Tucholsky tended to praise his political attitudes and good intentions, at the same time decrying his literary ability. Hasenclever found him 'good enough for the English'!! Since then Feuchtwanger has been largely ignored by German critics and literary historians, while remaining a firm favourite with the reading public. He was nationally famous during the Weimar Republic and he then became internationally famous as a best-selling writer outside Germany during the war years. After the war he was acclaimed in the GDR and generally ignored in the Federal Republic. In recent years some change can be observed and his works are beginning to be re-issued in paperback in the West.

Feuchtwanger's *The Oppermanns* is imbued from the start with a belief in the real and better Germany, but it does also focus on the fate of the Jews. In this Feuchtwanger was completely in tune with the concerns of the time. In the thirties there was widespread discussion about National Socialism, as to whether it could be reduced essentially to anti-Semitism. As early as autumn 1933 *The Duty of Jewry*, edited by Lion Feuchtwanger and Arnold Zweig, appeared; Döblin published an essay on *Jewish Renewal* and Rudolf Olden edited a *Black Book* on the position of the Jews in Germany. As a result it was quickly realised that there was a danger of over-concentration on the Jews to the detriment of other persecuted sections of the German community and with this in mind Heinrich Mann published *The Meaning of this Emigration*. The correspondence between Kurt Tucholsky and Arnold Zweig, which appeared early in 1936 under the title *Jews and Germans*, also gave rise to a debate on this question both inside and outside Germany. Future developments were to show that anti-Semitism was indeed a fundamental element in the National Socialist programme and that Feuchtwanger and others like him were right to focus on it. He was not unaware of economic arguments for the rise of National Socialism, he did show the part played by capitalists, financiers, landowners and ultra-conservatives as 'wire-pullers' behind Hitler, and the attack of the petty bourgeois on the positions held by upper middle-class Jewry, but he was aware too that none of this satisfactorily explains the violence of Nazi hatred of the Jews.

The influence of Feuchtwanger's model for the Deutschland novel can be clearly seen in *The Temptation* (1937), whose author Franz Carl Weiskopf was born in Prague in 1900 and died in East Berlin in 1955. Weiskopf moved from early political activity in Czechoslovakia to Germany, where he worked for Münzenberg's *Berlin am Morgen*. He was a member of the BPRS, involved with the SDS, and eventually editor-in-chief of the *AIZ*. He took part in the Spanish Civil War, and was in France in 1938, before moving to America where he helped to set up Aurora Publishing. After 1945 he took up ambassadorial positions for the Czech government in Washington, Stockholm and Peking, before settling in the GDR in 1953. Among his many publications were *Before a New Day* (1941), a novel about Slovak resistance against the Nazi occupation *before* it actually happened and *Under Foreign Skies* (1948), the first connected account of exile literature. Weiskopf's novel *The Temptation* was also later issued under the title *Lissy*, the name of the heroine, a pretty and cheerful working-class Berlin girl. The novel takes her through work, marriage, unemployment and the temptation of National Socialism for her husband and others like him, showing also her exposure to the attractions and corruptions of the party, till she is prepared to help the illegal resistance. Like Feuchtwanger Weiskopf deals with the limited period before and after the seizure of power and like him he divides his novel into three sections, each with the appropriate heading. Whereas Feuchtwanger's Germany was reflected through the fates of the liberal middle class, Weiskopf moves in the sphere of the proletariat and petty bourgeoisie. The fates of the characters are influenced by the real events of the time, like the advent of Hitler as Reich Chancellor and the Reichstag Fire. Weiskopf clearly writes from a Communist point of view with consequent weaknesses as far as the novel is concerned. For example, the main reason given for the Nazis' victory is the lack of unity between the working-class parties and for this the Socialists, not the Communists, are blamed. Another reason put forward is the success of Nazi propaganda and demagogy in seducing the unpolitical proletariat and the white-collar workers.

Material benefits are also employed as bribes for the undecided. Apart from the susceptibility of the white-collar workers to Nazi propaganda, which Glaeser also stressed, the novel lays great stress on the effect of the Nazis' pact with conservative centres of influence. This follows the general trend in exile circles for Hitler to be seen as a 'tool of reaction', despite the NSDAP's proclaimed intention to smash 'reaction'. Altogether Weiskopf's novel, like Feuchtwanger's *The Oppermanns*, leaves the impression that in the early stages there was still a considerable amount of resistance to Hitler among the German people, centred mainly on the Communists, but present also among Socialists and those disillusioned members of the NSDAP beginning to see the light. Weiskopf's novel is an appeal for unity in opposition to the Nazis, as if it were not already too late.

Another writer who analysed the link between the lower middle class and the fascist mentality was Oskar Maria Graf.[11] Graf thought of himself as a rebel and his life-story confirms this self-diagnosis. Born in Bavaria, he trained as a baker before turning Bohemian in Munich and elsewhere. As a conscientious objector in wartime he spent the period between 1915 and 1917 in a lunatic asylum and later took part in the November Revolution in Munich. Because of his early peasant narratives the Nazis tried to win him for their cause, but he gained world-wide recognition instead by protesting publicly and demanding that he be burned too when he heard that most of his books had been recommended by the Nazis. His famous protest to the *Vienna Workers' Paper* was picked up in whole or in part by the world press:

> The Third Reich expelled almost all German literature of significance and disavowed all genuine German writings, it has driven the majority of our best writers into exile and made it impossible for their works to be published in Germany. The ignorance of a few arrogant, opportunistic scribes and the unrestrained vandalism of the present dictators are trying to stamp out everything of international stature in our literature and art, and to replace the concept 'German' with a narrow-minded nationalism.

Within a few days his books were burned and his citizenship was revoked. He went into exile in 1933 in Vienna, before moving to Prague where he became one of the editors of the *Neue Deutsche Blätter*. In 1938 he left for America, where he settled in New York. He died there in 1967. O.M. Graf is remembered especially for the

types he created in *Bolwieser* (1929) and *Anton Sittinger* (1937).
Bolwieser, which has been made into a very successful film in recent
years, is restricted to the private and personal sphere of the railway-
station manager in the comparative stability of the twenties. Bolwieser
is the archetypal petty bourgeois with all the sexual and social hang-ups
of his class. When Graf moved on to Post Office Inspector Anton
Sittinger he achieved something more fundamental in his exposure of
the susceptibility of such an essentially apolitical type to the dynamic
drive of Adolf Hitler. Sittinger is a Bolwieser writ large with historical
events between 1918 and 1933 clearly impinging on the attitudes and
responses of such a person. At no point is Sittinger *for* the NSDAP or
the Hitler Terror, in fact he clearly dislikes them as forces disturbing
his beloved peace and comfort, but at the same time he is not for
democracy either. Taken as a representative figure, as Graf intends him,
Sittinger is a danger to the nation. 'The *Sittingers* are the improbable
philistines of whom twenty millions make up that class of the German
population, to which we owe the Führer and his government.'[13] In his
novel *The Abyss* (1936), Graf had already attempted something
broader than the narrow perspective of an individual sociological type,
namely a large-scale panorama of the rise of the NSDAP. The basic
mentality he observes in Bolwieser and Sittinger he had already
identified in the functionaries of the Socialist Party, who are decent,
hard-working and honourable men, but essentially workers who have
lost sight of their proletarian roots, and have settled for petty bourgeois
comfort, reliance on the strength of the party machine, and of the
reformist process, instead of preparing to fight the real menace which
National Socialism represents. The first part of the novel, called
significantly 'That was Germany', shows the Socialist Party giving in
step by step, allowing the republic to be destroyed without resistance.
As a result the millions of Socialist voters lose confidence in party
leaders, who are experts at tactical manoeuvres, but incapable of
action. Symbolically, after the old-guard Socialist functionary
collapses his son moves over to the KPD, fights for the united front
policy, takes part in the February Uprising of the workers in Vienna,
and continues the illegal fight in Czechoslovakia when this fails.

Two interesting variations on the Deutschland novel are *The Reward*
(1933) by Anna Seghers and *Molehills* (1933) by Adam Scharrer. Anna
Seghers will also be discussed in connection with her classic novel of
exile, *Transit* (1948), and with her world-famous novel of escape from
a concentration camp, *The Seventh Cross*. However, she is also interesting at this stage because *The Reward*, as the subtitle indicates, is a

'Novel from a German Village in the Late Summer of 1932' and
accordingly deals with the non-urban area, where the Nazis registered
their greatest campaigning successes. The plot of *The Reward* is very
simple: a young Communist, who has fatally wounded a policeman
at a demonstration in Leipzig, goes under cover with relatives in a
remote village. This basic situation permits the authoress to depict a
cross-section of the political and social tensions in the village, and
especially to expose the falsity of Nazi promises to the agricultural
community. Nevertheless Seghers is clear-eyed in her realisation that
the democratic forces have little to offer and the Nazis are almost
bound to win. Scharrer adopts a more doctrinaire party-line position;
the title indicates that there will be moles working (illegally) under the
surface with some hope of success. A long-time Communist, Scharrer
emigrated in 1933 to Czechoslovakia before moving on to the Soviet
Union, where he remained from 1935 till 1945. *Molehills* is described
in its subtitle as 'A German Peasant Novel', and this is the sphere of
most of his subsequent works—as if the author were intent on
demonstrating that the Nazis had no monopoly rights to the peasant
and the German countryside. The fate of another writer who attempted
the same kind of novel is almost paradigmatic for the dangers of the
age. Ernst Ottwald was also a member of the KPD and the BPRS.
As early as 1932 he attempted a history of National Socialism under
the ironical title *Germany Awake!* In the sphere of the novel he wrote
Awakening and Gleichschaltung of the Township of Billingen, parts of
which were published in the *Neue Deutsche Blätter* in 1933. The aim
was clearly similar to that of Seghers and Scharrer (or of Graf's *Agitation
round a Peaceable Person*), namely to expose Nazi propaganda in the
small towns and the countryside. After emigration through Denmark
to Czechoslovakia, Ottwald made his way to Moscow, where in 1936
he was arrested as a spy. He breathed his last in a camp in the north
of Russia in 1943. Ottwald's wife had already been handed back to
the Gestapo following the Hitler-Stalin pact. She survived. He has since
been rehabilitated.

Concern over the state of Germany was not restricted to Socialists
and Communists, as can be demonstrated by the literary career of
Heinz Liepmann. He first made a name for himself in theatre circles in
Frankfurt and Hamburg, left Germany for Amsterdam, and his name
appeared on the first list of those deprived of German citizenship. What
his novel *The Fatherland* (1933) demonstrates is just how quickly a
country can change. The narrative device which Liepmann employs to
show this is very simple. A trawler comes back to port after having been

away from home for two months, cut off from all news. The returning
sailors (and with them the reader) then discover what the Fatherland
has become during this time. As Böll's foreword to a recent edition of
the novel puts it:

> Liepmann describes the spreading of terror through all sections of
> life: in school, tram-car, neighbourhood, professional life, newspaper
> world, and, in a particularly penetrating and shame-making manner,
> in the Writers' Union.[14]

The 'Kulm' has been at sea for eight weeks, but in that time Germany
has become a foreign land, a strange desert, where arbitrary violence
rules. The stress is on the terror methods employed by the Gestapo
and the SA to stamp out ruthlessly all traces of resistance, and in this
Liepmann is totally effective in putting this picture of the Fatherland
across. That the National Socialist government was aware of the
impact the novel was making abroad is proved by the fact that it
initiated lawsuits against the author in eighteen different countries in
its attempts to have the book banned. In addition a Gestapo agent was
put up to publishing critical comments in the foreign press casting
doubt on the veracity of the book. Liepmann himself had described
The Fatherland in the subtitle as 'A Novel from Germany based on
Facts', claiming that there was not a word spoken in it he had not
actually heard, not a person in it he did not know personally, not an
incident in it that had not been witnessed either by himself or by
trusted friends. Liepmann was believed, especially after the Nazi agent
was exposed, and the novel was very well reviewed, though the
Communist Party faithful were a little doubtful about the importance
Liepmann accorded to the treatment of the Jews and questioned his
willingness to admit the existence of 'another Germany' of real
resistance outside the Communist Party. Liepmann suffered somewhat
from being politically unattached. Following Nazi pressure he was
arrested in Holland and condemned to one month's imprisonment for
'insulting the head of a government friendly to the Netherlands'. His
crime was uncovering corrupt practices in East Prussia involving an
estate made over to Hindenburg, a motif picked up by Brecht for his
Arturo Ui. However, he did not have to serve his sentence as he was
pushed across the frontier into Belgium as a *persona non grata*. The
Dutch government thereby avoided having to respond to a German
extradition order. His *Punishable by Death* (1935) was something in
the nature of a sequel to the first novel as it seems to involve the same

underground Communist hero. The importance of this novel lies not only in its recognition of Socialist as well as Communist resistance, but also in its clear intention to warn the democracies about Hitler's war-like intentions, and to demonstrate to the world at large that the German people were not to be identified with Hitler. Liepmann followed this with *Murder made in Germany* (1934) and *Death from the Sky* (1938). His continuing concern for the fate of Germany is shown by his post-war essays under the title *A German Jew Thinks about Germany*. Liepmann spent the years of exile in France, England and America. Between 1943 and 1947 he worked as an editor with *Time* magazine. On his return to Germany after 1945 he continued to work for German and American newspapers. He died in Switzerland on 6 June 1966.

While it was an obvious tactic for writers in exile to demonstrate that there was another Germany resistant to Hitler, nevertheless they had to take cognisance of the fact that in reality resistance had failed and that National Socialism had triumphed. Novels about Germany therefore adopted various different approaches in partial explanation of why this should be so. One was to characterise National Socialist Germany as a land of distrust and treachery, in which the most representative figure was the Spitzel, the man who infiltrates the opposition and betrays it to the Gestapo. The Spitzel became one of the key figures in the literature of the time, for example in Bredel's collection of stories under that title and in Brecht's sketch. In a similar attempt to get inside Nazi Germany, many novels were written from the perspective not of the resistance, but of the SA itself. This gave the novelist an opportunity to explore the social strata making up the membership of the SA and in particular to focus on the misled worker, who for various (obviously) wrong reasons has joined the SA, and then comes to realise his mistake. Here again the writers in exile were them-selves misled into thinking that Beefsteak Nazis were more widespread than they actually were, and that the SA itself was a possible source of resistance to the regime. Clearly some explanation had to be offered for the fact that the white-collar workers were not solely to blame for the collapse of the democratic forces in the republic and that a not inconsiderable section of the working class had failed to recognise fascism as its own worst enemy. The NSDAP called itself not only a national party, but also a workers' party aiming for a revolution; it had put on its programme the breaking of the slavery to invested capital, dispossession of chain-stores, the nobility of labour, et cetera. The expectation outside Germany was that there would be a great deal of unrest and discontent within the ranks, when those who had believed these slogans and joined the party discovered that major planks in the party platform were being abandoned. A good example of a novel dealing with problems of this kind is *Shot Trying to Escape* (1934) by Walter Schönstedt, who describes it as an 'SA novel'. Born 1909 in Berlin, Schönstedt was a Communist from an early age. This is his only significant work though he did play an important part in West Germany after the war in helping to start the journal *Der Ruf*, the forerunner of the Gruppe 47. He disappeared mysteriously some time between 1951 and 1952. The same theme is also dealt with in *The Uniform* (1939) by Hans Marchwitza, a Communist of the traditional kind, who in 1934 started a family epic on *The Kumiaks* (covering the history of the Ruhr) and carried it on generation after generation in subsequent volumes after 1945. It is easy with hindsight to see how completely wrong writers outside Germany were about the SA. The excesses of the SA did not bring about a move to the left by the workers inside Germany, resulting in open revolt to bring down the regime; the workers had not joined the SA merely because of unemployment and financial pressures; the propaganda of the Nazis *was* effective; nationalism and anti-Semitism *were* more attractive to some than economics and class warfare; no widespread process of disillusion and discontent set in among the SA and besides, Hitler solved that particular problem by eliminating all opposition inside the SA by violent measures which did not destabilise the regime — it even made it stronger. If there were any 'good Nazis' they were eliminated. Nevertheless, despite all these reservations, and although the Communist party line may have been totally wrong-headed, SA novels did still serve a useful purpose, in that they gave the reader outside Germany the feeling that he was penetrating into the real heart of the new Germany, instead of constantly being invited to see the new Germany through the eyes of Socialists, Communists or Jews.

That writers in exile were still subject to many more illusions about the Nazi regime despite their attempts to grasp the nature of the new Germany and uncover the roots of the German tragedy is shown by their reaction to events, as the influence of the new Germany began to extend beyond its own frontiers. The February Uprising of the workers in Vienna against the Dollfuss regime was written up by Anna Seghers in *The Way Through February* (1935) and by Oskar Maria Graf in the sequel to *The Abyss*, though generally these books tended to suffer as novels from the dead weight of information and political fact crammed into them. The struggle for the Saar culminating in the plebiscite of

January 1935 also gave rise to various books, for example Gustav Regler's *Cross-Fire* (1934) and Theodor Balk's *This is the Saar Speaking* (1934), both documentary novels. The result of the plebiscite which saw over 90 per cent of the population voting for union with the new Germany shook exile opinion which had completely misread the situation and incorporation of the Saar also removed the last legal method of importing anti-Nazi literature into the Reich. The first phase of exile was over. Writers no longer wrote exclusively with their 'faces towards Germany', no longer clung to a comforting belief in the imminent collapse of a gangster regime, they no longer believed that the silent majority of better Germans inside Germany was going to erupt in protest. To those inside Germany, whether Beefsteak Nazis or not, Hitler clearly still had a great deal to offer, especially as the expansion of the Reich continued by peaceful means, bringing Austria and Czechoslovakia as well as the Saar into the greater German homeland.

The period from 1935 till the outbreak of war in 1939 was one of increasing pessimism and disillusionment for exiles. The German government exercised considerable pressure on those countries on its borders which had accepted German *émigrés*. Deprivation of citizenship, passport and legal papers was a constant source of difficulty. While there was considerable understanding for Jews who had left Germany, others tended to be treated with suspicion, not least because there was a great deal of sympathy in many countries for Hitler, and for his desire to make the new Germany a bulwark against Communism. Most countries had great difficulty in absorbing the wave of exiles and the general world economic recession meant that many German *émigrés* found they were not permitted to practise their professions in competition with already hard-pressed citizens in their country of exile. The German Reich had important economic links with most European countries and here again it was able to bring extensive pressure to bear against refugees trying to establish themselves abroad. Many governments and firms were not prepared to jeopardise their own economic and political advantage for the sake of largely unwanted exiles. H.A. Walters has documented extensively the hardships writers in exile had to contend with. The general state of affairs was summed up not only by Feuchtwanger with his metaphor of exile as a Waiting Room, but also by Brecht in his *Refugee Conversations* when he discusses the passport:

> The passport is the noblest part of a human being. Nor is it created as simply as a human being is. A human being can be created

anywhere, in the most frivolous manner and without proper reason, but a passport never. This is why it is accepted, if it is good, while a human being can be as good as you like and still not be accepted.

While the first optimistic years of exile had seen the successful establishment of journals and publishing outlets of various kinds, the years that followed were characterised by the opposite. *Sammlung* and *Neue Deutsche Blätter* were forced to close in 1935 and a general process of decentralisation set in. No longer were the exiles huddled closely round the German borders. Instead they became more and more scattered to the furthest corners of the globe, with consequent difficulties in terms of continuity, contact and communication. Efforts to coordinate the anti-Nazi effort continued, international writers' congresses were held, a popular front policy was proclaimed, but no real progress was achieved. Certainly the Communist Party line had changed dramatically and there was now talk of The Great Allegiance and of the Common Tradition of Humanism, proletarian and bourgeois liberal writers and intellectuals swore to coordinate their efforts, Heinrich Mann emerged as a focal figure, and an Appeal to the German People was launched, yet little was accomplished. The Socialists still did not really trust the Communists and the start of the show trials in Moscow in 1936, followed by a wave of confessions and disappearances, seemed to confirm such suspicions. Only the outbreak of war in Spain, the continuing German annexations and the start of the long-awaited war with the Third Reich maintained among anti-Nazi groups a sense of solidarity which would otherwise have been sorely strained.

10 EXILE, THE SECOND PHASE

Everybody in Europe at this time was conscious of experiencing a period of historical change, world-shattering events succeeded each other with startling rapidity, figures of hitherto unknown dimensions like Mussolini and Hitler emerged from obscurity to dominate the political stage, while kings and countries crumbled. It is not surprising therefore that there was considerable discussion of history and of the use of history in the literature of the time. Historical novels and dramas had been popular since the nineteenth century and they maintained their popularity inside Germany after 1933, both among nationalist writers well disposed to the new regime, and among writers of the inner emigration; and historical novels continued to be written by German writers in exile, some of which had indeed been started before their authors left Germany. However, it was not till after 1935 that the whole question of the nature and possibilities of the historical novel within the general framework of anti-Nazi literary endeavour was widely discussed.[1] Many émigré writers were aware of how difficult it was for them to write about a Germany they could no longer see and experience. Some authors were forced to rely on what they had read or heard about the new Germany. It was by relying on sources of this kind that the best of the Deutschland novels of the period came to be written – Anna Seghers' *The Seventh Cross* and Arnold Zweig's *The Axe of Wandsbek*. Anna Seghers tells how she came to write this book: 'At that time I was looking for some kind of material which would show the situation in Germany more or less as it was, one in which various people played their parts in a confined space.'[2] The plot is a basic one concerning seven prisoners who escape from a concentration camp. The camp commandant has seven crosses erected and each prisoner as he is recaptured is strung up. One gets out of Germany and hence one cross remains empty, signifying one tiny victory against the might of the Nazi machine. The one who escapes does so not by his individual efforts or bravery, but because he finds friends and comrades. The political message is not excessively stressed, and the main impact of the book comes not because this is yet another look at concentration camp life or yet another adventurous escape story, but because 'the novel gives a total picture of the Germany of these days and of the forces and feelings that governed the German people at that time'. The picture is indeed a broad one, for the various escapees impinge on a wide variety of people, who respond in different but characteristic ways to their plight. Fear is clearly a feature of National Socialist Germany but there are still good Germans among the population, especially the 'little people', who are prepared not only to overcome their fear, but to help someone in distress, despite the regime. There is also real resistance, though it has to keep a very low profile. The fate of Anna Seghers' book was in itself almost as adventurous as the progress of her successful hero Heisler. She started to write the book in France in 1937 and was finishing it in 1938, when the sound of the German guns could be heard in Paris. It began to appear in serial form in *Internationale Literatur* in Moscow, but publication was broken off following the German-Russian non-aggression pact. The novel first appeared in German, published by El Libro Libre in Mexico, where the authoress was by then living. Translations were soon available and it was particularly successful in America where it became the Book of the Month. The Hollywood film of the book, with Spencer Tracy in the leading role, was a great success, though there was some adverse criticism because the picture of the Germans that came across was too positive. Socialist Realism with a 'positive' hero could be palatable to the reading public outside the Communist bloc.

Arnold Zweig was one of the great literary figures of the Weimar Republic, famous among other things for his *Grischa* cycle of novels on the First World War.[3] As a Jew and a pacifist he was clearly *persona non grata* in the new Germany after 1933 and became one of the earliest German literary figures to settle in Palestine. Zweig gradually moved from his original position as a liberal individualist to that of a committed Zionist and Socialist. By the end of his life he was a Communist. In his exile years he constantly differentiated between the German people and the German leadership in the Third Reich. After 1945 he returned to the GDR, where he was a National Prize Winner, President of the East Berlin Academy of Arts, and a highly respected literary figure of the older generation. Arnold Zweig found the idea for his novel *The Axe of Wandsbek* as early as 1937 in a Prague newspaper, and worked on it between 1940 and 1943.[4] The plot is very similar to that of the original *Grischa* novel, for it too involves the army and a court case. Following the trial of four Communists, the Nazis would like to have the whole matter finished off quickly, but this cannot be done to Hitler's satisfaction because there is no executioner. A good solid citizen, in the shape of a Hamburg butcher from Wandsbek, carries out the executions in return for the promise of 2,000 marks which will save his business from bankruptcy. There are various interwoven strands in this rich Hamburg novel, but what Zweig succeeds in showing is a general picture of life in the different social strata of a city like Hamburg, from the proletariat through the educated middle classes to the business people and others who adapt to the barbarity, evil and lawless violence of the National Socialists. The butcher is a good German, who becomes inextricably involved, who kills, and enjoys a brief period of affluence before his inevitable ruin, just as Germany too allows herself to become involved, goes to war, enjoys success everywhere until the inevitable collapse comes. Long before the event Zweig even envisages an assassination attempt by certain army circles to eliminate Hitler. In Zweig's novel there is no condemnation of the German people as a whole, nor even of a person like the butcher Teetjen. Zweig simply lets the reader feel what it was like to live under National Socialism, to gather some idea of why the mass of the people allowed it to happen in the first place and continued to live with it once abnormality becomes the norm.

This is also the great advantage of the novels written in exile by Irmgard Keun, an actress who made a name for herself on the stage before Tucholsky discovered her talent for literary satire.[5] She was probably one of those people 'to whom nothing would have happened', but she refused to join the Reichsschrifttumskammer, emigrated to Holland in 1935 and lived for a time with Joseph Roth before returning illegally to Germany and remaining there under cover from 1940 till 1945. As she did not leave Germany until 1935 she was able to give her novels the feel of life in Nazi Germany. As Ludwig Marcuse put it, she does not divide the German people into Nazis and the others; instead she shows the masses, the normal people, who are not interested in politics and just want to live. Klaus Mann reviewed Keun's *After Midnight* (1937) under the heading 'German Reality' and drew attention to something in it exiles tended to lack: 'the immediate contact with German conditions, with the atmosphere prevailing in Germany now . . . Along comes a gifted woman and tells us what things look like in this land we cannot set foot on.'[6] The perspective of the novel is limited to that of a young girl, who cannot possibly be familiar with all aspects of life in Germany. However, this limitation is more than compensated for by the crackling dialogue and the sheer wit and style of the narrative. No ponderous anti-fascism here! Irmgard Keun published various other novels before her return to Nazi Germany, but she too shared the common experience of finding that Germany began to seem further and further away until it faded altogether. When this process was complete she went back to Germany.

In general Deutschland novels were tied to the time-span of their author's own experience. So all the novels considered so far deal only with the period from the rise of the NSDAP up to its consolidation in power towards the end of the thirties. Just how closely attached to the author's own experience and family history this could be is evidenced by the most famous example of all novels of this kind, Klaus Mann's *Mephisto*. Oldest son of a famous father, Klaus was born in Munich in 1906 and died by his own hand in Cannes in 1949.[7] In exile he became the key exponent of *The Other Germany*, about which he published a book in New York (1940). The motto he gave the book originated with Harold Nicolson and gives some idea of his easy-going approach to the subject: 'The German character is one of the finest but most inconvenient developments of human nature.' Klaus Mann's open letter to Gottfried Benn has already been noted, and the controversy over intellectuals and the new state of Germany which resulted from it. He edited *Sammlung* from 1933 till 1935 and *Decision* from 1941 till 1942 in New York. Klaus Mann was young enough to be capable of changing languages and he published extensively in English. His main novels deal with the problems of exile, but the one which was apparently drawn so intimately from his early life and assocation with the actor Gustav Gründgens was the one which was to have the most remarkable history of all German novels written in exile. *Mephisto* was first published by the Querido Press in Amsterdam in 1936 and enjoyed a reasonable success at that time. After the war the novel was available in the GDR and in Switzerland. But as far as the Federal Republic was concerned the book was banned, following a suit claiming defamation of character brought against intending publishers by the adopted son of the by then dead Gründgens. This was upheld by the courts. After reading a French edition, Ariane Mnouchkhine produced a theatrical adaptation of the novel for the Théâtre du Soleil in Paris Vincennes in 1979, which was a resounding success wherever it was performed, including Germany. Eventually *Mephisto* did appear in paperback in West Germany and became a best-seller. The success of the book and the play was followed by a film version by Milosz Szabo, which made a world-wide impact. *Habent sua fata libelli*! What this particular case-history makes clear, however, is that the original half-scandalous attraction of the book as the 'novel of a career in the Third Reich', exposing through the medium of the *roman-à-cléf* Gründgens' association with such luminaries of the time as Goering and Goebbels, Gottfried Benn and Hanns Johst, is no longer the source of the novel's attraction, for most people seeing the play or the film now will have no idea who Gründgens was, nor will they know of Klaus Mann's personal relationship with Gründgens or the fact that the sexually ambivalent actor was for a time married to Klaus' sister Erika. What is more relevant to the present success of the book is Klaus Mann's own original statement:

> I feel compelled solemnly to declare that I was *not* interested in telling the life story of one particular man, when I wrote my book *Mephisto, Novel of a Career*. What I *was* interested in doing was to present a *type*, and with it, the various milieus (my novel is not by any means restricted to the 'brown milieu'), the sociological and intellectual pre-conditions, which made such a rise to power possible in the first place.[8]

So this is specifically *not* a *roman-à-cléf*, but once again a Deutschland novel, which gives a broad picture of life in Germany starting around 1925 and finishing in 1936. In fact *Mephisto* was one of the very first novels written in exile to reflect broadly on conditions in the Third Reich. The selection of an actor-director for the central figure proved to be a stroke of genius and one which was more than usually illuminating, for in his Mephisto (the evil counterpart to Faust, the representative German with 'two souls in his breast') Klaus Mann saw the key symbol for the 'totally theatrical, totally mendacious, totally unreal regime'.

Mephisto is one example of reliance on features of Germany which the author knew from close and personal experience. Many writers were only too well aware that memories fade and circumstances change, that therefore what they were writing no longer corresponded to the reality of the Germany they had left behind. This is one of the reasons for the historical novel though, as has been observed, some authors (for example, Feuchtwanger) made no distinction between novels about their own time and novels about the past. Some had been successful in the Weimar Republic with historical novels and simply carried on a mode which had worked well enough for them before. Besides, historical novels with their wider range of local colour and exotic colour and exotic times could have more appeal to an international public than works with more limited, directly contemporary German subject-matter. Some, like Thomas Mann, were even able to continue publishing historical works inside Germany after 1933, much to the distress of their colleagues. Mann, however, considered it imperative to keep contact with his public as long as possible.[9] So *The Stories of Jaakob*, published by S. Fischer in Berlin 1933, reached its twenty-fifth printing in that year, while the second volume, *The Young Joseph*, also published by Fischer in Berlin in 1934, was also successful. Even the collection of essays *Sufferings and Splendours of the Masters*, containing the commemoration speech on Wagner (which had resulted in an official protest from the city of Munich) was published in Germany and, despite the clear disapproval of government bodies, it also sold well. The third volume in the *Joseph* series was published by Bermann Fischer in Vienna, before the publisher's transfer to Stockholm, where the remaining works by Thomas Mann up to 1945 were published. These, including essays for the period 1933-45 like *Germany and the Germans*, did not reach a German audience until after the war. Historical works such as the *Joseph* cycle may seem remote from the problems of the time, but the events of the age could not leave them or their authors unaffected. Historical novels written in exile are not identical with similar works of the inner emigration or even of the Nazis themselves. Many writers gave thought to the effect exile would have on the historical novel, or even to a defence against charges that historical novels represented merely a flight from the present, a flight from the problems of contemporary society or a flight from the Deutschland novel they were no longer capable of writing. As early as 1936 Alfred Döblin was writing about 'The Historical Novel and Us' (meaning writers in exile), pointing out that writers who did not have their own country before them to write about would naturally look for parallels in the past, would reflect on the chain of development linking the past with the present, would look for comfort in history, or even for similar circumstances involving perhaps a seemingly invincible conqueror who had ended in disaster.[10] The situation inside Germany goes some way to explaining why most historical novels favoured a negative central figure, but though Döblin does not discuss this in his essay, it was the kind of problem which *was* discussed in the debate which developed at the time in exile journals and congresses. Most outspoken in his attack on the historical novel was Kurt Hiller, who produced an incredible list of actual and invented historical heroes and heroines in order to ridicule the flight from reality that the historical novel represented. Lion Feuchtwanger, however, as an exponent of both the historical and the contemporary novel, was able to argue forcefully that both genres were equally capable of dealing with the burning issues of the present. Marcuse came to the same conclusion in his essay *The Accusation of Flight* and Lukács, who was to write a wide-ranging study of the historical novel (stressing particularly the role of the people and of revolutionary leaders and ideas), came out strongly in favour of the historical novel for writers in exile, not as a means of turning one's back on the present, but of producing artistic yet militant works against German fascism. The historical novel was a means of enlightenment and orientation in troubled times; it could expose the falsification of the past in which the Nazis indulged, and offer rational explanation in place of mystification. History was not necessarily a fateful force over which man had no control—something shaped by charismatic strong men, history was subject to economic and political forces—something in which both the people and the intellectual had a role to play. The important moral to be drawn from history was the need for commitment to conscious action, instead of withdrawal and retreat. This corresponds with Brecht's view of history and is close to what he attempted in his one major novel of the exile period, *The Business Deals of Mr. Julius Caesar*, which he was writing around 1939, though it was not published until 1957, after his death. Brecht's financial situation was never particularly rosy and he possibly wished to follow the example of his successful novelist friend Feuchtwanger and deal with political topics through historical material.[11] He had been working on a Caesar play which Piscator was to put on in Paris, and when this theatrical project fell through Brecht prepared to turn it into a historical novel. The connection between Caesar and Hitler the war leader was obvious, except that Brecht intended to invert the normal process, demonstrating not that great men make history, but that great men make business. The idea of attacking the Nazi dictatorship by means of a historical novel appealed to Brecht greatly. Unfortunately the needs of historical biography conflicted with the satirical impulse and this project, like so many others, remained unfinished. However, some writers in exile were more successful in the historical mode than Brecht and did complete historical novels with a message. No one could accuse the works of Bruno Frank, Lion Feuchtwanger, Heinrich Mann and Gustav Regler of being mere exercises in escapism. The selection of historical figures (often dictators and tyrants) and the concentration on particular themes (persecution of the Jews, witch-trials, waves of religious hysteria) show that such historical works were meant to warn and to enlighten the world about what was going on in Hitler's Third Reich. Sometimes, as in the case of the most admired of such historical panoramas, Heinrich Mann's *Henri Quatre*, the intention was not so much to draw attention to parallels between the past and the present (coupled with the comforting thought that even the darkest of ages passes) as to offer counter-models to Hitler's personality, his beliefs and to 'his' Germany.[12] Henry IV, 1553-1610, King of Navarre, Calvinist and leader of the Huguenots, has become legendary as a 'good king'. His memory is associated with the Saint Bartholomew's Day Massacre, his battles as leader of the Huguenots with the Catholic League and its confederates Spain and the pope, with his conversion to Catholicism to spare his people further war and bloodshed, with the Edict of Nantes, affording the Huguenots in France freedom of conscience, freedom of worship, secure legal status and much more – not least his work for peace, social reform and reconstruction. Quite clearly Heinrich Mann selected the France of this period with its massacres, wars and treachery as a parallel to the Germany of his own time. But his Henry is also a contrast figure to Hitler, projecting the opposite of all Hitler represented. Henry is a true man of the people, a great lover not a hater, a rich, many-sided, human individual, truly original and truly progressive; his religion is humanism, but he knows that this is something one has to fight for: 'Wer denkt, soll handeln' ('The thinker has to act'). Not that Heinrich Mann thought that a novel, even one of this scope, could change the world. In his collection of essays dedicated to his fatherland, called *Hate. Scenes from Nazi Life*, Mann had exposed Hitler's Germany as fundamentally anti-humanist, because it was fuelled by hate rather than love. In *Henri Quatre* he tried to convey 'the embodiment of ideals – rationality, humanism and the power of goodness'.

In general it must be assumed that novels of this kind were directed to the world outside, and not to the reading public inside Germany. Indeed it must be doubted whether very much of the literature written by German writers in exile ever got through to like-minded people inside Germany or was capable of influencing events or public opinion in any way. Writers in exile realised this and by this time they were not trying so much to do something about Germany as to clarify how it could have happened in the first place. The result was an increasing number of novels focusing not directly on the Third Reich from the time of the seizure of power, but on events leading up to the new Germany. This meant a quest for the roots of National Socialism in the Weimar Republic and earlier. The present was being understood in terms of the past together with all contributory factors that went to explain the failure of the republic and the success of Hitler and of National Socialism. Some of the authors of such works (Oskar Maria Graf, Lion Feuchtwanger, Arnold Zweig) have already been mentioned. One of the greatest of them all, the 'creator of the modern novel', Alfred Döblin, also needs to be seen in this context, because he has for too long remained typecast as the author of *Berlin Alexanderplatz*, the avant-garde novel which enjoyed world-wide success after its publication in 1929. Döblin was a Socialist and a Jew, and as such outspoken in his opposition to the Nazis. He left Germany and became a French citizen in 1936, eventually having to leave France after the Occupation. His return to Germany after the war was not successful: in his own words, 'And when I came back—it was no come-back.' His earlier works had been forgotten and he could not find a publisher for his later ones. He had converted to Catholicism, thereby apparently turning his back on his own Jewish roots and he was a German in French uniform. He died a disappointed man. Since then, as is well known, Grass has acclaimed him as his teacher and critics have finally remembered that Brecht pronounced his novel *November 1918* 'something politically and aesthetically unique in German literature and a source book for every-body trying to write'.[13] What Brecht admired about it was its active involvement in its subject, namely the German revolution. Döblin was going back beyond the Weimar Republic, because as a Socialist revolution which had been smashed by Socialist leaders, the revolution of 1918 in Germany had been a turning-point in the nation's history. Döblin's novel does not paint a picture as simple as this—indeed to some extent his desire to link Socialism with religion makes him lose sight of the main political issue. Nevertheless there is no doubt about the significance of his theme, the problematic start of the Weimar Republic. In exile between 1937 and 1943 in France and the United States, Döblin had time to ponder over the failure of the revolution and the resultant failure to restructure German society and saw himself as a doctor plunging his probe into the past to detect the source of the sickness that came over Germany thereafter. *November 1918* is a vast work of 2,000 pages made up of four volumes: 1 *Citizens and Soldiers*; 2 *A People Betrayed*; 3 *Return of the Front-line Forces*; 4 *Karl and Rosa* (Karl Liebknecht and Rosa Luxemburg); and its publishing history is even more complicated than is the norm for works of this kind written in exile. As a result of these complications it is not as well known as it deserves to be; however, it is now available in paperback and it has gained powerful supporters in academic circles as a work which deserves to be taken extremely seriously.[14] Jan Hans has attempted to sum up the significance of vast surveys such as Döblin's *November 1918*. As he sees it, the picture they impart of the Weimar Republic is generally a critical one. Such books are not concerned to conjure up or reinforce the myth of the Roaring Twenties, showing an intact democracy threatened and finally undermined by attacks from the right as well as from left-wing radical groups. Instead what is projected is a picture of a Germany which accepted republican status either unwillingly or half-heartedly, while at the same time retaining traditional structures of authority and leaving the representatives of the establishment in their positions of power in legal and administrative spheres. Such novels tend therefore to suggest that the so-called 'seizure of power was actually more of a hand-over, merely the last act in a long-term well prepared take-over bid'.[15]

Many of the novels considered so far were conceived from the point of view of the writer 'facing towards Germany'. It has to be remembered that from the start these same writers were also aware of their position in exile from Germany, and that they made the theme of exile itself central to their works.[16] The last volume of Feuchtwanger's *Waiting Room* trilogy was entitled *Exile*, Klaus Mann wrote a *Flight to the North* (1934), Konrad Merz *A Man Falls out of Germany* (1936), Irmgard Keun *A Child of All Countries* (1938) and Fritz Erpenbeck *Emigrés* (1937). The exile experience did not mean simply getting out of Germany and into some other country: it meant being viewed as a possible Nazi spy or fifth columnist, being suspected of being a Communist trouble-maker, and (after the signing of the French-German armistice) being caught in a trap and in danger of being handed over to the Gestapo or interned in a camp. Exile meant extraordinary experiences in an apparently chaotic world in which social and political relationships could change overnight, a world in which nothing was stable or secure. Not surprisingly, the most commercially successful literary works were those which exploited the sensational aspects of such situations—thrillers, spy stories and tales of underground adventure. In such novels exile becomes merely a source of fantastic plots, in which exotic localities and interesting personalities are exploited for their emotional impact, tear-jerking qualities or high drama, regardless of the real problems of the people forced to leave Germany. Erich Maria Remarque and Hans Habe proved expert providers of sub-literary fodder which could be converted readily into successful Hollywood films like *So Ends our Night, Arch of Triumph* and *Cross of Lorraine*. That it was possible to put the same experience of exile to more fundamental purpose was demonstrated by Anna Seghers, who used the story of her own personal escape through occupied France for her novel *Transit* (1944), charting the kind of horrors which Feuchtwanger had recorded in his *Unfriendly France* (1942). Böll called *Transit* the finest of all Seghers' novels; it has also been compared with Kafka, most probably because she is not content merely to capture the individual experience, but instead transforms it into a parable for terrified European humanity desperately trying to escape from the unseen menace which threatens to destroy it. Marseilles in 1940 was in the unoccupied part of France and the Germans are therefore not physically present. The characters who people the novel move through a weird world, exposed to an abstract bureaucratic machinery which feeds on transit visas, official stamps and boat tickets.

Exile was no static condition: indeed things grew constantly worse rather than better. On 14 March 1938 Hitler proclaimed the *Anschluss* and Austria became part of the Third Reich. On the first of October 1938 German troops marched into Czechoslovakia. When Poland fell the Second World War started and Hitler registered success after success, taking over Luxemburg, the Netherlands, Belgium and France. Denmark and Norway followed. The Spanish Civil War ended with victory for the fascist forces and Russia signed a non-aggression pact with Germany. With each of these events another wave of emigration and attempted escapes from the German menace set in, although countries to escape to had become fewer. Great Britain modified its quota and within a few months had taken 70,000 refugees, including some 400 writers and stage people. Russia restricted entry to those with the appropriate political backgrounds, and countries like Sweden and Switzerland had introduced legislation limiting immigration. By far the greatest number made their way to the United States. Although Great Britain for a time became what Jan Hans has called 'the central European land of exile',[17] it did not become a productive centre for German culture; nor did the United States, despite its long history of German immigration, prove fruitful soil for German writers writing in German about German problems, in part because of the American melting-pot theory with its expectation of immediate assimilation. Immigrants were expected to become American as quickly and as completely as possible. In Palestine too the land of origin had to be forgotten, and Jews were not expected ever to want to go back. Russia was rather different. Writers in exile did have extensive publishing facilities—but the Hitler-Stalin pact, the ever changing party line, the show trials, the spy mania, mass eliminations and deportations made it an unhealthy country for many. In his recent study of German writers in Soviet exile David Pike has calculated that of the 130 or so Germans who might reasonably be assigned to the cultural sphere, close to 70 per cent were arrested in the purge.[18] Some were luckily absent from the USSR between 1936 and 1939 – Bredel, Weinert, Wolf, Piscator, Ernst Busch and others – otherwise the percentage would be higher. Mexico developed as an unexpected refuge for many exiles, especially for those whose membership of the Communist Party disqualified them from entry into the United States. Other South American governments were not as receptive as the Cardena government in Mexico, although Brazil, Argentina and Chile did provide a refuge for some notable figures. The journal *Deutsche Blätter* appeared in Santiago de Chile with the subtitle 'For a European Germany, Against a German Europe', but the most important new journal to appear at this time was the *Aufbau* in New York.

This further dispersal of exile literary activity accentuated the difficulties all German writers in exile already had to face. Communication was more difficult than ever before, the German reading public outside Germany was now even more dispersed, and even more acculturated. If many readers had abandoned German, writers too felt the same compulsion and let their books appear in another language. The pressure on them to assimilate and abandon thoughts of Germany or of a return to it after the collapse of National Socialism was great. Yet many did still continue to think of Germany and when they did so it was in terms of the political form it would assume, because for Germany too there was no possibility of a return to what she had been before National Socialism. So the novels of this period tend even more than before to expose the weakness of the Nazi regime, point up examples of resistance to it as indication of the coming end with the hope of a new beginning. A novel like Alfred Neumann's *Six of Them* (1944) was based on the *Time* magazine story of 14 June 1943 dealing with the White Rose resistance group in Munich student circles associated with Hans and Sophie Scholl, although it adapted the facts considerably to highlight the fact that there *were* people in Germany prepared to take up the uneven battle against tyranny and barbarism.[19] Heinrich Mann dealt with the Lidice massacre. Lion Feuchtwanger wrote a novel about the French resistance, which Brecht transformed into the play *The Visions of Simone Machard*, while *Schweyk* ends with Hitler lost in the snows outside Moscow. As early as 1941 Johannes R. Becher had started to write his epic drama *Winter Battle*, one of the first dramatic treatments of the war, dealing with the crucial turning-point in Hitler's campaign, when (like Napoleon) he failed to capture Moscow. Theodor Plievier, who spent nearly eleven years in exile in Russia, wrote his novel *Stalingrad* month by month from November 1942 till September 1944 and published it instalment by instalment as the battle was actually being fought—an incredible feat![20] This final stage of reflection on the state of Germany is marked by a spate of books in which important authors attempted to sum up the age. Sometimes this took autobiographical form, for example in such works as Heinrich Mann's *An Age is Visited* (1946) and Ludwig Renn's *Nobility in Decline* (1944). In *The World of Yesterday* (1944), the book he completed just before his sixtieth birthday, Stefan Zweig also attempted the same kind of thing for Austria, presenting not autobiography, but the world of the mind. The result is a historical picture of the Europe and the great Europeans he had known between 1880 and 1939, revealing the current of events in that cataclysmic era:

> The main thing I could do for the old Austria was to evoke a picture of what it was and what it meant for European civilisation.[21]

Some authors, however, still preferred the novel form, and the most astounding example of such a 'Deutschland Allegory' was Thomas Mann's *Doktor Faustus*. To describe this enormous novel as an allegory is perhaps misleading, for Thomas Mann does not offer a simple search for the roots of National Socialism after the manner of what came to be called an 'Ahnensuche' or hunt for the ancestors, in which all the predictable targets, from Luther to Bismarck and beyond, could be held up for blame. Thomas Mann is clearly concerned with the nature of Germany and where it went wrong, but the reader is not plunged into questions of economics and politics, ideologies and mass meetings, concentration camps and gas chambers. The realities of life in National Socialist Germany are included in the total complexity of the novel, but they quite clearly do not constitute the main areas of the author's concern. The basic idea, the diabolic possession of an artist, was a completely unpolitical one and seems to go back to as early as 1901. Much later the political ingredient was added by the addition of music and Nietzsche. By the late 1940s, when he had decided on this, the name of the philosopher had been misappropriated by the National Socialists in the same way that Wagner's name, along with much of German culture including Goethe's *Faust*, had been. A conversation with Alfred Neumann in May 1943 brought the final crystallisation in the

> flight from the difficulties of the cultural crisis into the pact with the devil, the thirst of a proud spirit threatened with sterility for total release from all restraint at any price, thereby pointing the

parallel between destructive euphoria culminating in collapse and fascistic intoxication.[22]

Thomas Mann was no longer simply resuming his favourite theme of artist and bourgeois; now the allegorical parallel was between artistic genius and horrific political reality.

The technique Thomas Mann adopted was that of montage. Everything he had ever read or experienced, whether factual, historical, personal or literary, was assembled and carefully placed. The Third Reich is the point of departure but overlapping time levels illuminate the course of German history from the Reformation and earlier. As a result the present day remains on the periphery, to be presented largely through the incidental comments of a narrator who is far removed from the centres of political activity in a small town in Bavaria. There are air raids on German cities, rockets are falling on London, the allies invade France, the army pulls out of Russia, and Germany by the end faces unconditional surrender and occupation by the Allies—but none of this is reported extensively. Thomas Mann had no first-hand experience of these matters and must have relied on newspaper reports and War Office communiqués. Although the novel succeeds remarkably in creating an impression of denseness and totality a great deal is omitted. So, for example, almost the whole of the time span of the Third Reich is excluded from the novel, for the narrator Zeitblom is concerned to recount the life of a musical genius called Leverkühn, who collapses into mental darkness in 1930, and Zeitblom does not begin to tackle his story until 1943. As a result most of the outstanding features of National Socialism are not discussed directly. Zeitblom does not entirely agree with Hitler and his followers in the matter of the Jews, but there is no discussion of anti-Semitism or the atrocities of the final solution. Zeitblom's sons are Nazi sympathisers and typically he must fear betrayal by his own family, but there is little trace of the Gestapo in the small town of Freising. Chapter 25 is called the Gestapo Cellar scene, but this is true in only a very oblique sense. The resistance of the Munich students is mentioned, as is the 20 July attempt on Hitler's life, but Thomas Mann is not concerned to demonstrate at length such facets of the German character, any more than he is prepared to linger on the strengths of German rationalism, democracy, Socialism and working-class politics. Parallels between Germany and National Socialism do not mean in Thomas Mann's case a crude demonstration of possible links between high finance and fascism; the novel operates in a social vacuum and moves instead into the sphere of psychology, mythology and demonology. The pact with the devil is not that between bourgeois and Junker after 1848, or between reactionary tendencies and the world of capitalism. Instead Thomas Mann operates on the level of high culture, moving freely from the Faust legend as found in the early German versions and Goethe, to music and the other arts, politics, reminiscences of other Faustian figures like Dürer, Beethoven and Nietzsche, autobiographical references, religion and theology. Not surprisingly discussions of the novel rarely involve consideration of 'the German catastrophe', but focus more often on questions of literary technique, symbolism, sources and structure. As a work of art the novel is a masterpiece in Thomas Mann's characteristic manner, being both extremely conservative and extremely modern at one and the same time; as an 'explanation' of why it all happened, or why the good Germany was conquered by the darker side of its nature it is, as a result of the author's exclusive insistence on cultural matters, far from satisfactory. However, like Hesse's *Glass Bead Game*, which it closely resembles, it did not appear until after the war, hence its mixed reception is part of the post-war literary scene and does not properly belong to the National Socialist era as such.

11 THEATRE IN EXILE

In general most critical attention has been directed to the novels of German literary exiles. As far as the drama is concerned, Brecht has captured most of the limelight, though his works are not usually discussed in the context of where they were actually written or in which language they were first performed. One or two other dramatists were known in the thirties; Wolf's *Professor Mamlock* travelled the world in stage and screen versions, but since then such works have been forgotten or dismissed as *passé*. Brecht's fairy-tales and parables survive, while directly political anti-Nazi plays languish in limbo. Yet despite all the well known difficulties of writing plays in exile, links with the lively theatrical life of the Weimar Republic were not abruptly broken off in 1933, and many theatrical forms developed in that period proved capable of continued life in exile. According to a recent survey there were no fewer than 420 dramatists living in exile in 41 different countries, while the archives of the Academy of Arts in East Berlin reveal that they wrote 724 stage plays, 108 radio plays and 398 film scripts.[1] Clearly it is simply impossible to stop dramatists from writing dramas. Some of this material has recently been made available (at least in abbreviated form) in *Deutsche Exildramatik 1933-1950*, a particularly valuable book, because it draws attention to the many worthwhile dramatists who have slumbered in the shadow of the giant Brecht for too long.[2] What emerges from a survey such as this is not only the fact that so many plays were written regardless of the difficulties in the path of production, but also that conditions in exile had their effect on the drama that was written. In particular avant-garde and openly political epic experiments were avoided and there was a general turn backwards to more traditional Aristotelian forms. Brecht and Piscator had made considerable impact on the theatre of the Weimar Republic with expensive and elaborate musical, documentary and political works, but such self-indulgences were no longer possible and something much more modest had to be attempted. One of the most impressive examples in the Piscator-Brecht mode of epic-reflective drama was Ferdinand Bruckner's play *The Races* (1933). Bruckner had been one of the most successful dramatists of the Weimar Republic and especially because of plays like *The Criminals* (1927) and *Elisabeth of England* (1929/30) he enjoyed an international reputation, which he

never regained after leaving Germany in February 1933. *The Races* was
written immediately after his decision to leave Germany and is
remarkably successful in creating a feeling of the contemporary
atmosphere in Germany. As the title indicates, the racial issue is at the
heart of the play, but there is little plot and the essence of the action is
the impact of National Socialism on young people. Of the five main
figures, all but the Jewish girl Helene are medical students at an unnamed German university. The time of the action is March to April
1933. Rosloh is an eternal student who has consistently failed all
examinations, but as a long-standing Nazi he rises to power in the
university with the rise of National Socialism, while Jewish staff and
students are removed. Siegelmann, the Jewish student, is beaten and
abused and forced to leave the country. Helene, Karlanner's girlfriend,
is the daughter of a Jewish soap manufacturer who is close to the
National Socialists. This gives the dramatist the opportunity to exploit
the generation conflict between father and daughter, with the added
complication that the rich Jew refuses to admit what National Socialism
means for less advantaged members of his race. Helene and Karlanner—
Jewish girl and German boy—also have far-reaching discussions when
he is carried away by the intoxication of the new German movement.
What Bruckner demonstrates is how young idealists become brutal
Nazi thugs. Karlanner takes part in the Nazi 'action' against Siegelmann,
but when Rosloh tries to force him to denounce Helene, he murders
Rosloh and lets himself be taken away by the Nazi troop that comes
for him. But more important than the melodramatic action is the
insight Bruckner imparts into the attraction of National Socialism for
this 'lost generation' of Germans, living through the consequences of
the war, the effects of the Versailles peace treaty, the impact of
inflation and the general depression. *Germany* is the key-word that
uplifts them, the Germany of music, discipline and philosophy, the
Germany of a people united in one community of mind and comradeship. By contrast, being a Jew means 'democracy, materialism, liberalism,
republicanism, pacifism'—in the inflammatory words of the lawyer in the
beer-parlour. The myth of the Führer is also conjured up—Hitler the
painter, the Rembrandt, the simple soldier, who suffered for Germany's
greatness. Schlageter too is invoked, as the 'first hero of the new nation,
German youth's unexcelled example', and after a visionary outburst
from the state prosecutor all join in when Rosloh sings:

Dem deutschen Führer unser Herz
Es schlägt für ihn in Freud und Schmerz.

Das deutsche Volk ist aufgewacht
aus Knechtschaft und Todesnacht.

(Our heart is the Führer's, it beats for him in joy and pain.
The German people has awakened from serfdom and dead of night.)

This is not the only visionary explosion in the play, indeed Bruckner moves freely between realistic, Expressionistic and classical linguistic levels to show the rapidly changing moods of the impressionable youths. This can be extremely effective, but it did perhaps also help to reinforce the illusion that if young men like Karlanner can change so rapidly from democrat to Nazi and back again, then there never was any firm foundation for belief in Hitler and his followers would drop away from him as quickly. Crucial to the play from first to last is the debate about Germany, culminating in Karlanner's last words as he is taken away at the end of the play: 'In all eternity: Germany. It's my Germany too: for all eternity.' He is denying the Nazis their exclusive claim to the Fatherland.

The dramatic genre most characteristic of German theatre in the Roaring Twenties was the social problem play and one of its most successful exponents was Friedrich Wolf. After studying medicine he worked as a ship's doctor, became a conscientious objector in the First World War and was committed to an asylum. His first plays were in the contemporary ecstatic, expressionistic vein, but he developed a starker, more realistic style in the New Objectivity of Berlin in the twenties. In 1927 he met Piscator who confirmed this aggressive style, and his next play was the sensationally successful *Zyankali* (*Cyanide of Potassium*) on the controversial abortion laws. The plays that followed had revolution as their theme and by 1931 he was directly involved with the political events of the time. The theatrical company he established performed only agitprop plays like Wangenheim's *The Mousetrap*. In 1933 Wolf went into exile in Russia, where he continued to write till the end of the war. His dramatic slogan was 'Kunst ist Waffe' ('Art is a Weapon') and he showed what he meant by this in his plays *Floridsdorf* (1935), which dealt with the abortive workers' uprising in Vienna, and *The Trojan Horse* (1936), which was based on the Communist Party policy of infiltration into Nazi organisations for sabotage purposes. After the war he returned to the GDR where like other anti-fascist literary writers he reached ambassadorial rank in the service of the new state. He is now rarely performed in the West. *Professor Mamlock's Way Out. The Tragedy of Western Democracy* (1933) was Wolf's

immediate response to the Reichstag Fire. He intended it for Wangenheim's Truppe 1931. But this revolutionary group had to be dissolved
and there were difficulties about the première, so it was first performed
in Yiddish in Warsaw, before productions in Tel Aviv, Zurich and
Moscow. Thereafter it became a world-wide success and was the most
performed of all exile dramas. The time-scale of the play extends from
May 1932 to April 1933, the period of the seizure of power and the
Reichstag Fire. Mamlock is a leading hospital consultant, a World War
veteran, who has been severely wounded fighting for his country, a man
with a Prussian sense of duty and a conservative outlook. He is totally
apolitical, believes in justice and accepts the official view. There is a
great difference between him and the representative of the younger
generation, his son Rolf who is a young Communist associated with a
resistance group. His daughter is a Nazi but is reviled at school as a
Jewess. Mamlock himself is slandered and isolated in the hospital and
finally shoots himself. This is his way out, but his last words indicate
that Rolf's is the right way.

    Professor Mamlock was written as a piece of agitprop drama and
this is the source of its strengths as well as its weaknesses. The plot is
contrived, the characters are overdrawn, no full or rounded picture of
National Socialism emerges, and all the Nazis are opportunists, career-
ists or blinded idealists. Similarly the young Communist only too
obviously has the right answer. Yet despite such weaknesses, the source
of the play's effectiveness is obvious. Mamlock is a noble and admirable
man who is brought down and vilified merely because he is a Jew. The
play focuses on conflicts of the time, not through grand political or
diplomatic characters, but through the impact of changes in the new
Germany on the family sphere. The result is a moving, but essentially
melodramatic and contrived theatrical construction, which invites
sympathy and had the desired effect at the time. Both plays — *The
Races* and *Professor Mamlock* — are important not only because they
were written by leading figures of the theatrical world of the Weimar
Republic as their immediate response to developments in Germany,
but they were also both given impressive productions with excellent
casts in one of the leading theatres in Europe, the Zurich Schauspielhaus.[3] The effect of Bruckner's play was electric, the Swiss audience
was totally caught up in this demonstration of the fate of the Jews in
Germany to the point where, as one actor relates, a voice from the
gallery suddenly burst out with the plea: 'Siegelmann, Siegelmann, do
something to save yourself.' One year later Wolf's play was taken into
the repertoire, launched by Rieser, the theatre director, as the première

of a 'play about the Germany of today'. Although it too focused on the Jewish problem, it was also much more political than Bruckner's play of mental attitudes. It had Wolfgang Langhoff, the Communist actor, playing the part of the young Communist, and he had himself been in a Nazi concentration camp for thirteen months. The rest of the cast was equally strong. When the play was so successful that it played to packed houses night after night, Swiss reactionary organisations tried to disrupt the performance and the police had to give protection, but the methods which had succeeded in Germany failed in Switzerland and *Professor Mamlock* continued its triumphal march round the world. The Zurich Schauspielhaus also played an important part later in the history of exile drama, for it put on not only Kaiser's exile play *The Soldier Tanaka*, but also the first productions of Brecht's *Mother Courage*, *The Good Woman of Sezuan* and *Galileo Galilei* — the latter in the earlier version showing the great scientist as a resistance fighter, who at a crucial point in his life fails to stand up for reason against the forces of darkness.

Gustav von Wangenheim was the son of the famous actor Eduard von Wangenheim. Like his father he worked with Max Reinhardt and later with Piscator. His political beliefs led him to an association with the agitprop movement. To this end he established the Truppe 1931, a collective of unemployed actors, and wrote plays for them to perform. The group was banned in 1933. In exile in Russia he was involved in various theatre and film projects, survived the Stalinist purges, and finally returned to the GDR where he became a leading figure in the theatrical life of the new Socialist republic. One example of his agitprop style applied to the theme of terror under National Socialism is his one-acter *Heroes in the Cellar* (1935). The scene is an SA guard-room with the brutal Nazis on the alert, ready to move out instantly to deal with any Communist resistance. The time is therefore immediately after the seizure of power, but before all opposition has been completely crushed, with a successful uprising against the Nazis thus still within the bounds of possibility. The cellar of the title is where the prisoners are kept and tortured, so that the screams from below impinge on the surface action.

Another agitprop writer and artist whose works are only now being rediscovered was Johannes Wüsten. He had studied painting with Otto Modersohn in Worpswede before moving into the literary and journalistic sphere. A member of the Communist Party since 1932, he kept a resistance group going in Görlitz until 1934. Seven of its twelve members were executed. Wüsten moved to Czechoslovakia and then to

France where he was eventually handed over to the Gestapo and condemned to fifteen years' hard labour, though suffering from TB. He died in prison in Brandenburg. Most of Wüsten's dramatic work remained unpublished during his lifetime, but an edition of his dramatic and other writings is being prepared in the GDR. His one-acter *Bessie Bosch* caused a stir when first published in *Das Wort* (1936). Bessie's husband, a resistance fighter, has been condemned to death (in fact he has been already executed). The question is how she will take the news. In the end she gives the clenched fist salute, indicating her determination to remember the sacrifice of the dead and fight on. Another author who had enjoyed spectacular success as a writer of problem plays in the Weimar Republic was Peter Martin Lampel. As a Freikorps man he gained intimate insight into the early history of the NSDAP. His real fame came in the republic with his *Revolt in the House of Correction*, a sensational play which led to a national debate on the treatment of young offenders. His *Poison Gas over Berlin* about secret rearmament by the Reichswehr was banned for endangering the security and order of the state. After 1933 he stayed on in Germany, but was finally forced to go into exile. He made his way via Bali and Australia to America. After 1945 he failed to make a come-back in the new Germany of the post-war period. His *Nazi Twilight* is interesting firstly because of its setting (namely the Reich Chancellery), secondly because of its characters (the SS bodyguard to the Führer), and thirdly because of the time of the action, the moment of collapse in the Führer bunker. Also extremely illuminating is the final discussion by the SS of the betrayal of Germany by the Nazi leaders. All ideals of Deutschtum have now been shattered, the crimes are known, and the disgrace of the Fatherland is apparent for all to see — even those closest to Hitler.

In the midst of his campaign for the Spanish Relief Fund Toller wrote *Pastor Hall*, the only major play in this category after Wolf's *Professor Mamlock*. It shows traces of its erratic gestation in New York, Barcelona and Cassis, in that it was first published in the English translation of Stephen Spender and Hugh Hunt in 1939, and that the German version had to have the ending changed. The theme of Toller's play is National Socialism's conflict with the church, but even more than this, overcoming fear. Declaring the truth about the Nazis as Hall does makes him a member of the 'other Germany' like Martin Niemöller, who had been arrested in 1938 and after a sensational trial sent to Sachsenhausen as Hitler's personal prisoner, and later to Dachau. Pastor Hall too is outspoken against the Nazi regime, but the play is weakened by being restricted almost entirely to the private and domestic sphere. Hall is sent to a concentration camp, escapes, and finally returns to his pulpit to preach once again against the regime. There are clear echoes in this play of Toller's Expressionist beginnings, especially of his *Transfiguration*; but the style and the general treatment of the theme are much more realistic. Aiming as he now is at an English-American public Toller abandons disturbing avant-garde theatrical devices and returns to the traditional Aristotelian action drama with a plot and recognisable people. The concentration camp material was (according to Toller's own account) influenced by the news of Erich Mühsam's murder at Oranienburg. He also took advice from Bredel whom he met in Leningrad in 1934; and Langhoff's Moorsoldiers Song is sung in one of the camp scenes. That the play is intended to inspire resistance against National Socialism is self-evident. But it too suffered from the known deficiencies of the melodramatic, domestic, action drama and the ending is particularly weak. The play was filmed in England in 1940 under the direction of Roy Boulting and for the American public Sherwood Anderson wrote a prologue which was spoken by Eleanor Roosevelt. Despite this, neither the film nor the play had the impact of Wolf's drama. There are similarities between Hall and Mamlock.[4] Both are conservative, both apolitical, both 'awaken' to awareness of the full horror of National Socialism only when it impinges on their family sphere. The main difference is that Wolf did have political drive and direction, and he did deal with the Jewish problem and the Communist answer, while Hall's final appeal from his Protestant pulpit is too vague, too general and too personal. If Hall is the representative of the 'other Germany' as has been suggested, drawing the world's attention to the concentration camp that Germany has become, this does not come over strongly enough. Pacifism of the Toller variety was not the appropriate response to Nazi terror. More active resistance was required than either Hall or his friend, the retired general from the medical corps, was capable of.

Not all plays written in exile were directly political, indeed it was almost the normal reaction to *avoid* politics in a time that had seen too much of it and its consequences. Besides, the political situation could change so rapidly that a political play could be overtaken by events almost before it was written. In the same way as the age both inside and outside Germany saw an extension of the traditional classical forms in narrative and lyric, so the drama too tended towards the general and the typical. Georg Kaiser, who had waited till 1938 before leaving Germany, abandoned his expressionistic style, but still avoided crass realism in anti-Nazi plays like *Napoleon in New Orleans* (1937/41) and *The Raft of Medusa* (1940/3). Even his anti-militaristic *Leatherheads* (1928) was highly stylised. Rudolf Leonhard and Fritz Hochwälder adopted similar tactics, while Horváth, who in the days of the Weimar Republic never avoided contemporary subjects, moved in exile to more general themes. Horváth had also been successful with comedy and this is yet another form which proved capable of development in the thirties and forties, though Brecht's *Puntila* was the only play to show any innovation of a practical or a theoretical kind. While he developed his concept of a Socialist comedy his colleagues in exile avoided anything difficult or dangerous and continued to exploit the possibilities of the boulevard comedy for entertainment in times of trouble. To improve their chances of performance and gain insight into different comic traditions German dramatists often collaborated with experts in the country in which they found themselves. Hasenclever, Toller, von Wangenheim were not particularly successful in this mode, but one success did emerge from an unlikely quarter. This was Franz Werfel's *Jacobowsky and the Colonel*, as he called it a 'comedy of a tragedy'. Franz Werfel had enormous success behind him. He was famous in the Age of Expressionism for his poetry, his pacifistic version of *The Trojan Women* caused a great stir in the Germany of the First World War and throughout the period of the Weimar Republic he had truly astonishing success with his historical tales, biographies and plays. In Lourdes he swore to write about Bernadette if he ever escaped the Nazis and when he did so his *Song of Bernadette* became a world success as a novel and a film. When he turned his hand to the traditional German form of the novella he demonstrated in stories like *The Royal Game* a technical virtuosity which surpassed even that of the master Werner Bergengruen. Since then his star has waned, his stories are considered kitsch and after the war the novella was displaced by the English-American short story. Nevertheless Werfel deserves to be remembered, if only for this comedy. There are many reasons for its success. During the worst days of the war it offered an example of resourcefulness and optimism, it is brim-full of satire, wit and humour, and yet at the same time it does reflect the fate of many forced to flee helter-skelter across the face of Europe, indeed like Segher's *Transit* it offers an authentic impression of conditions in a France under threat of Nazi occupation, and it deals with the fate of the Jews. Perhaps the most significant factor in the success of this particular play was the fact that it was built around two rewarding parts—the dashing anti-Semitic Polish aristocrat and cavalry officer (played in the film by Curd Jürgens) and the resourceful Jewish businessman (Danny Kaye). With roles of this kind the play was made for success in the star system of the commercial theatre, and in fact the Broadway production was received with acclaim by public and critics alike, probably because the already fairly harmless comedy had been made even more harmless by being 'treated' by the American humourist S.N. Behrman.

Werfel's play is built on contrasts, the contrast between Polish cavalry officer and businessman, Catholic and Jew, poetry and prose. In addition to all the other ingredients Werfel also provides a spy story and a love story (the two men fight over Marianne, who also stands for France); the journey through France takes place in a wonderful automobile; Jacobowsky the Jew performs one miracle after another, and yet from the start the author is careful to reassure his audience that this is no 'lofty, unpleasant and incomprehensible drama', but one which has 'no symbolic significance whatsoever'. This is not quite true, because he is quite clearly aiming to overcome class, racial and religious prejudice and arrive at a message of tolerance and acceptance of others. Werfel is not afraid to break through the surface realism of his play or to use voices and visual effects, allegorical figures and national stereotypes, he consciously plays with his play and never allows the tone to become too ponderous. The result is that he can be accused of trivialising a tragic situation and laughing at the fate of millions, but in fact the real tragedy is there in the background all the time. Werfel himself had been through a lot himself and there is enough autobiographical fact about his Jew to counter any accusation of frivolity. Jacobowsky has escaped first from Poland to Germany, then from Germany to Austria, from Austria to Czechoslovakia, and from there to France. The final stage, if there is one, will take him to England. The action of the play takes place in 1940 and is still unclouded by the horrors of the holocaust.

While France turned out to be a trap for many exiles, one from which Werfel himself escaped only with difficulty, Russia seemed to offer ideal facilities, at least for those who accepted the prevailing ideology. However, even for those like Julius Hay and Gustav von Wangenheim for whom this presented no problem, the pressure to conform to the precepts of Socialist Realism proved inimical to true creativity and the plays written in the Soviet Union have not stood the test of time, though traditional dramas like Hay's *Property* are not quite as bad as Brecht claimed. In the same way as Socialist Realism did not prove too productive for drama in exile, attempts of various kinds to continue the successful Weimar Republic tradition of the historical drama also failed, though so many were written that they represent a numerically significant element in the drama writing of the time. Strangely enough, despite the dramatic potential of the often sensational stories about escape from the Nazis the actual theme of exile itself did not result in any great dramas either, though Peter Martin Lampel's *Person without Passport* (1936) is interesting, for one reason because of the picture it gives of exile conditions in Switzerland and for another because one of its characters is a Nazi who wants to convince people abroad of the existence of a 'better Germany'. Friedrich Wolf also wrote a play, *The Last Rehearsal*, about the Switzerland that favoured Nazis and placed severe restrictions upon those escaping from the Reich. The action of the play makes critical reference to the exploitation of German actors and artistes by the Zurich Schauspielhaus, which nevertheless developed into the leading anti-fascist theatre for exile drama, where Brecht's great parable plays enjoyed their first exemplary productions. At the conclusion to their study of German exile drama between 1933 and 1950, Mennemeier and Trapp place Horváth's comedy *Figaro gets Divorced*. While there is nothing specifically anti-fascist or anti-Nazi about the subject-matter of this play or in the treatment of the Figaro motif, nevertheless all the characteristic themes of the time are present, culminating in the realisation that exile means that *émigrés* not only have to face up to a 'Fatherland' which uses terror against them, but also to the foreign country which takes them in only to treat them with indifference.

Brecht is famous for his early expressionistic works like *Baal*, for his collaboration with Kurt Weill in *The Threepenny Opera*, for his didactic plays and most of all for the great plays written in exile from Nazi Germany between 1933 and 1947, the great parable plays, the examples of epic theatre and alienation, *Life of Galileo*, *Mother Courage*, *The Good Woman of Sezuan*, *Puntila* and *The Caucasian Chalk Circle*, plays which (as the titles indicate) go back in time to the Thirty Years War or far away in setting to Renaissance Italy or China or Finland or the Caucasus — they do not deal with Germany. In all of them Brecht is a Marxist and he treats important problems from a Marxist perspective, but he does so parabolically. The result is that the revolutionary message often gets lost and the plays can become rather sweet and harmless. For various reasons other Brecht plays have tended not to be placed in the forefront of attention. These so-called anti-fascist plays *Round Heads and Peak Heads*, *Arturo Ui*, *The Private Life of the Master Race*, *Simone Machard* and *Schweyk* — are not forgotten or neglected masterpieces, but they *are* important examples of Brecht's work in exile, because they deal more or less explicitly with Hitler and the new Germany. The *Round Heads* is perhaps the least successful of these plays.[5] It is a reworking of Shakespeare's *Measure for Measure* and from the point of view of Brecht's attitude towards National Socialism it is interesting only because of his treatment of Hitler. As is often the case with Brecht plays there are different versions—in the first, Brecht shows his Hitler type as a deluded fanatic, who really believes in what he preaches, while in a later version Brecht reduces him from a believer to a mere tool of the Establishment. In other words Brecht is unsure how to project his Hitler-like figure. He does not want to build him up too much as a fanatical believer, yet he is also clearly wrong to make somebody as powerful as Hitler was to become a mere puppet, controllable by the ruling classes or anybody else. In fact Brecht was caught up in the political confusions of the Communist Party of the time and followed the party line—either the National Socialists would soon collapse or the traditional, conservative right wing would reassume control. He could not envisage that the Nazis would come to power and that once established Nazi tyranny would crush all opposition from left or right. Brecht was also disastrously wrong in his understanding of anti-Semitism, seeing in it merely a Nazi device to divert the workers from the class struggle against their capitalist oppressors. He could not conceive of a rich Nazi persecuting a rich Jew—hence his punning subtitle for this play 'Reich zu Reich gesellt sich gern' ('rich birds of a feather flock together', or 'the rich and the Reich get on well together'). In this play, moreover, the tyrant is placed in power by the ruler. There is no need to ask, as with Hitler, how he got there, how he could have been stopped, or whether there was resistance to him. For *Simone Machard* Brecht moved to France. The Simone of the title is in fact a Joan of Arc figure with that kind of national ardour; however, she is certainly not a heroic resistance fighter. Schweyk, the title figure in the other anti-Nazi play, is also anything but heroic—he has survived the First World War, he is now trying to do the same in the Second World War, although this turns out to be a far more difficult task. The play opens with a prelude 'in higher regions'. Hitler, Goering, Goebbels and Himmler are standing around a globe planning new conquests; martial music is playing; all the figures are caricatures and all are larger than life, except for Goebbels, who is smaller than life-size. Hitler is wondering out loud what the common man thinks of him, in Europe as well as Germany, and Himmler assures him the common man is enthusiastic. But did the common man follow Hitler so enthusiastically? In *Schweyk* we see this common man—an 'ingenious fool' who is capable of undermining any state. He is not a resistance fighter, he does not oppose the Nazis—indeed he always agrees with them, yet somehow by doing so he exposes the absurdities of the system. This is no way to stop Hitler coming to power, but it is a method of corrosive demoralisation which progressively paralyses all who have anything to do with Hitler and National Socialism.

But how did Hitler come to power in the first place? Was he stoppable at any point, by anybody, by any method? These are the problems which the title *The Resistible Rise of Arturo Ui* seems to raise.[6] Yet, as the title also indicates, it is not directly about Hitler. Brecht is being as elusive as ever—he does not write directly about Hitler and he does not show immediately how he might be stoppable. From what is now known about how *Ui* came to be written, the original intention certainly was to write a satire on Hitler, but when Brecht first conceived the notion the setting was not America and the style was also to be different. Brecht thought first of writing in the Italian Renaissance style about an Italian monster. The first plans dating from September 1934 (in the earliest stages of Brecht's exile) run along these lines. There are prose sketches in existence and even the Italian name Ui is present at an early stage, fitting in with the Italian Renaissance idea. What Brecht had in mind was presumably a straightforward satire making Hitler into a kind of Cesare Borgia. There are also some links between the name Ui and Tui, because Brecht discussed them both together at this time with Walter Benjamin. When Brecht travelled to New York in 1935 he was a witness to the gang-wars raging over how the city was to be divided up for the distribution of the prohibited alcohol. This visit to New York in 1935 should also be borne in mind in view of the general assumption that Brecht invented his own personal America for his plays. In fact he *was* there and he saw what was happening with his own eyes. Once he sat down to it Brecht wrote the play in three weeks, helped by his son Stefan who shared his father's interest in gangsters. Brecht did spend some time polishing the verse, but essentially it all went down on paper very quickly. This was quite unlike Brecht, who was a notoriously slow writer who liked many drafts and revisions. In this case he seems to have finished the whole play quickly, and sent the manuscript off to America where an English-language version was to be made in the hope of speedy performance there. Because *Arturo Ui* was written so quickly it was assumed for a long time that this could not be one of Brecht's exile masterpieces: indeed it was for long ignored or dismissed as one of his weaker efforts.

It was also thought to be unfinished, because it was known that Brecht intended to extend the development up to the actual outbreak of war. This would have meant covering the Spanish Civil War, the Munich Agreement and the occupations that followed, the invasion of Poland and the collapse of France, instead of merely showing, as at present, the rise to power up to the *Anschluss* with Austria. Brecht himself admitted that all this could not have been put on the stage or contained in a play of this kind. In fact no part of the play was put on. It was written as a weapon against Hitler, exposing him to ridicule, but it did not see the light of day until Hitler's meteoric rise had ended in disaster, by which time the play was thought to be no longer relevant. It was also assumed that Brecht's anti-fascism had led him astray, away from the parabolic manner in which he wrote or was to write his great plays in exile, into a crude attempt to deal with contemporary reality. Another factor that also counted against the play was the knowledge not only that it had been quickly written, but that it was never revised for performance. It was only when the play was published posthumously and actually performed (as distinct from being read) that it revealed its remarkable power and vitality on the stage. The critics were wrong. Far from being one of Brecht's weakest, this has proved one of his most successful in actual performance. The part of Ui in particular is a most rewarding role for a great actor. It is a play in verse: it is also a play which uses explicitly historical material and extended literary parallels. The best example of this comes in the seventh scene, when Brecht exploits the dramatic possibilities of William Shakespeare, using in this instance the speech of Mark Antony following that by Brutus on the murder of Caesar. Brutus has appealed to the reason of the crowd: Antony appeals to their emotions. It is a wonderfully effective speech in this context, not merely as an example of rhetoric, but also because it actually shows Ui/Hitler learning the tricks of the trade—he is not merely learning how to speak, he is learning how to use a veneer of culture, he is learning from this famous passage how to say one thing and mean another, learning how to use words to twist meaning into its opposite. Ui, like Hitler, becomes a master in this sphere—they are both (word) twisters. At the same time the audience is being encouraged by Brecht to be aware of this kind of trickery, to listen to what lies behind the surface of words. In another scene Brecht picks up the reference in the prologue to the similarity between Ui and Shakespeare's monster-murderer Richard III; elsewhere he echoes Goethe's *Faust*. It is important to explore why Brecht writes his play in verse; why he turns Hitler into an American gangster and wraps everything up in theatrical quotations. There are various possible answers to such questions. For one thing it is not merely his deliberate desire to use tradition in a progressive manner; it is also his aim to expose antiquated, conservative, classical highbrow culture by giving it a lowbrow, popular slant. But there is another reason. The Nazis notoriously exploited the classics for their own purposes: they appropriated culture. Goering married an actress, became supremo of the German theatre and liked to drape his brutalities with a veneer of civilisation, whether it derived from Shakespeare, Goethe or Schiller. Goering was also notorious for raiding the art galleries of Europe and hoarding their treasures. What Brecht is doing is not merely parodying the classics for fun, he is also reminding his audience that high culture is often used to mask reality. As to why the cultural references stem from the sphere of the theatre, the answer here is that Nazi Germany did dramatise itself, it was theatrical, it did favour the elevated Caesarian, Neo-Classical style. What Brecht is doing by emphasising the theatricality of National Socialism is undermining the myth. Ui is shown as a poseur who has learnt how to walk, stand, sit and talk. He rehearses his speeches, they are *not* genuine or from the heart, and he can switch like an actor from shouting and screaming to wheedling and pleading and persuading, all in order to influence people and bend them to his will. Hitler was the 'Trommler' – the agitator – and he did have the power of the word. That is how Brecht presents him, but he is not the only such character in the play. Butcher behaves in the same way when he persuades Dogsborough to accept the bribe. He acts a part, and pretends to have tears in his eyes. Even Dockdaisy appears on the scene to recite the words she has learned by heart: she too is acting a part. The world is presented as a theatre, the theatre of war – total war. This is the essence of the Brechtian theatre, never to let his audience forget that it is watching actors acting. Through the use of theatrical parallels, the parody of Classical sources, the awareness of acting, the illusion is destroyed, and alienation takes place. But it is not only theatrical imagery which is used in the play, for the many repeated words and phrases are further clues to Brecht's intentions. The Führer, for example, constantly demands trust, though he himself obviously trusts no one. He asks also for sacrifice and belief: Brecht invites healthy scepticism of such blind faith. What Ui's gang has to offer is 'protection', though paradoxically they are the ones who create chaos and then call for law and order. By the end Ui is 'protecting' everybody, whether they want protection or not. Anyone who gets in the way tends to go chalk-white in the face and die. Ui defeats the

honourable Dogsborough, the immaculate politician; he defeats the
big businessmen from the world of high finance; he captures the little
traders; he ends up with everybody in his power, offering strong
leadership, law and order, the steely embrace. How does he do it?
What are the reasons for his success? Why is he so irresistible? Because
of the conditions? The state of the world? The depression? Inflation?
Certainly money is dear, but even so the businessmen do not use him at
first, they try to achieve their ends by corrupting Dogsborough—and it
is exactly this corruption in the political sphere that gives Ui his
opening. He then creates the chaotic conditions he can thrive on and
the cancer spreads. How *could* Ui have been stopped? If the trust had
not used criminal methods in the first place? If there had been less
social cowardice? If he had met somebody who had shown his teeth
or his gun? If everybody had not waited for somebody else to do the
job? If the professional classes, the judges, the police, the doctors, the
journalists had not caved in so early? Where, it has been asked, are the
working classes? Where is the Marxist proletariat which presented the
true opposition to Ui/Hitler?? There was working-class opposition to
Hitler, but there was also working-class acclaim for Hitler, and it
would have been very naïve to show the workers attempting to fight
armed gangsters. What the play does show is Ui/Hitler directing his
appeal to the small traders—the petty bourgeoisie. What the play does
not show is exactly how Ui is resistible. It is called a parable play, but
this does not mean a parable with one clear-cut meaning—on the
contrary, it tends more towards the open-ended structure of the
greater, later exile plays. Ui should be stopped, but the audience has
to arrive at its own conclusions as to how this is to be done. The same
applies to the central figure of the play—Ui himself. Brecht realised
that it is dangerous to build up a character like Ui, because the
audience might end up admiring Ui, in the same way as the audience
for a gangster film like *Little Caesar* tends to admire the crook despite
(or maybe even because of) his cold-blooded crimes. Brecht's Ui is a
funny little character: he broods, he is passive, he does nothing for
long periods, then he explodes into frantic activity. He seems to be
manipulated by others, seems to be merely a puppet on a string, yet
he turns out to be the master. He says he has plans, yet he seems to
pick them up from others. Brecht gives no indication of what he thinks
or of what he believes in apart from himself. It would certainly be very
difficult to build up any picture of the Nazi *Weltanschauung* from the
play. It could, of course, be argued that it is Brecht's intention to
demonstrate that there is no philosophy, only a vacuum, and that this

is the source of Hitler's power, his charisma—that he does not believe in anything, and that he is thus able to change direction from one second to the next. Ui can be performed as a Charlie Chaplin figure, a figure of fun, but by the end he is not funny any more. Ui relies on gesture and pose to impress, and after a while he does impress, but he remains a paradoxical figure. However it is performed this role has proved to be one of the most powerful in the modern theatre, and one which has not lost its relevance with the passage of time; for, as a prologue which Brecht added later proclaims, the danger of fascism is ever present: 'the womb this crawled from is fruitful still'.

The Resistible Rise of Arturo Ui started life as a satire and developed into something much closer to non-realistic parable plays like *The Caucasian Chalk Circle. The Private Life of the Master Race* also has a clear satirical intention, but it is different again from the other anti-fascist plays in being apparently so realistic in a simple, straightforward manner that it was immediately used as ammunition in the great Realism Debate which developed at this time. This debate is generally associated with Lukács, but he was perhaps only the main protagonist in this fundamental but futile discussion, thrashed out in the most arid and theoretical terms in Moscow in the late thirties. The origin of the debate probably goes back to the Berlin of pre-Hitler Germany, when the nature of Socialist Realism and proletarian literature was being explored theoretically in Communist circles. Georg Lukács, who had studied at the Marx-Engels Institute, devoted himself particularly to proletarian literature and the question of its relationship to the tradition of nineteenth-century realism. In exile in Moscow he developed his arguments further with his customary metaphysical brilliance and dominated the scene, especially too because of his unique political relationship with the authorities. Some objections came from Anna Seghers, then living in Mexico, and Ernst Bloch who was in Czechoslovakia, but Brecht preferred to avoid public participation in the debate, partly to avoid splitting exile opinion and partly because he had his own ideas, based on reality and experience and did not see that Lukács' arguments were fruitful for the creative writer. Ernst Bloch, Anna Seghers and Brecht all saw the danger of a too narrow definition of realism, centred on the middle-class writing of the nineteenth century, however useful a united policy might be for the anti-fascist camp in the literary sphere, and preferred to be free to go their own way. Seghers confined herself to corresponding with Lukács privately. Brecht kept his own council, though it is now known that he completely disagreed with Lukács. Apart from the show trials and the disappearance of his friends, the restrictive nature of the Socialist Realist line was perhaps one of the main reasons why he preferred to live outside the Soviet Union. The same applied to the other literary debate which engaged the attention of so many leading spirits at this time. This centred on the nature of Expressionism, and was linked with the whole question of realism in so far as it concerned what should be the essential nature of anti-fascist writing. For the most part writers living in Moscow were involved, and they had to conform to the Socialist Realist guide-lines laid down by Lukács, although many of them had been associated with Expressionism in pre-Hitler Germany. The best example of a total transformation in the Moscow group was J.R. Becher, who had changed from being the most Bohemian of lyrical Expressionists to the most conformist of party poets. Now Lukács' categorical condemnation of Expressionism forced all writers of that generation living in Moscow to come to terms with their past and conform or suffer the consequences. Here too the debate was essentially a political and not a literary one, set in motion by the discussion of the essay by Klaus Mann on Gottfried Benn's aberration in welcoming the Nazi seizure of power. Lukács made no attempt to examine a broad cross-section of Expressionist works, but came to his own political conclusions based on a very narrow and unrepresentative sample. The basic issue was whether Expressionism could be identified as proto-fascist, and the answer given was positive. Not everybody agreed with Lukács' interpretation. Ernst Bloch for one was in almost total disagreement with it, but Lukács was very powerful and persuasive and the effect of this particular debate was to cast grave suspicion not only on Expressionism in particular, but also on all avant-garde and experimental literature for a long time to come. Socialist Realism reigned supreme – not always with the best consequences for Communist literature.

Brecht's *Private Life of the Master Race* began to appear in the middle of these debates and because it seemed to conform to the theories being developed within Marxist circles, it was quickly acclaimed as an example of realism, especially as it was also so different from the experiments in epic theatre with which Brecht's name had been associated.[7] *Senora Carrar's Rifles* had already taken the 'path to realism', and when the 'Spitzel' episode from Brecht's new sequence of *Scenes from the Third Reich* appeared in the Moscow journal *Das Wort* in March 1938, Lukács claimed that exile had consolidated the trend towards true, deep and significant realism, and pointed to Döblin, Heinrich and Thomas Mann, but particularly to Brecht, who imparts a picture of the horror of fascist terror in Germany, and how it now destroys all the basis for social living, all the trust between husband, wife and child, how fascist inhumanity destroys what it claims to protect, namely the family in its most basic foundations.

Brecht was aware of Lukács' comments and noted in his diary: 'Lukács has welcomed the "Spitzel" as if I were a sinner returning to the bosom of the Salvation Army.' It is quite clear that he never intended anything like Lukács' realism. For one thing, one of the basic structural elements in his sequence of scenes was montage and that was a modernistic, formalistic approach long frowned upon in Communist circles. For another, Brecht thought of his scenes as only *'nearly* naturalistic'. The settings were real places, in real cities, in the present; there was no destruction of illusion; any songs or poems were motivated; the language used was natural prose, even dialect; the characters were given psychological motivation as real people – yet despite all this superficial realism, the total effect intended was different and various other devices were used to achieve a density and abstraction unattainable by simple realism.

One factor which casts doubt on the prosaic realism of Brecht's scenes is that some of the motifs already existed in verse form as early as 1934/5. The scenes themselves, however, were not written until Brecht started to write for Slatan Dudow's political cabaret. This is in fact the theatrical tradition to which they belong, and it became a commonplace in later years to select for cabaret-type performance a variety of scenes from the twenty-four Brecht finally completed. To perform all (or even nearly all) the scenes would have taken far too long and this was rarely attempted. As the cycle expanded into its final form the title, the form and the intention changed. From *Fear/Spiritual Elevation of the German People under Nazi Rule* it became a *Cycle of Tiny, and Tiniest Sketches* and then it acquired an ironic flavour with *Germany, a Horror Story*. The final title, *Fear and Misery of the Third Reich*, seems to be modelled on Balzac's *Splendeurs et Misères des Courtisanes* or Vigny's *Servitude et Grandeur Militaires*. *The Private Life of the Master Race* is not a direct translation of the German and does not indicate the various elements Brecht has carefully lodged in his final title. First of all the stress is on fear – the new Germany is not a happy place, and is kept under only by means of terror; moreover, the German genitive is ambiguous; it indicates fear and misery under the rule of the Nazis, but also the Nazis' fear of those under them! Brecht's titles always reward close examination.

As so often with exile works, the printing history of the play sequence is complicated. Some scenes appeared in *Das Wort*; Slatan Dudow performed eight out of the seventeen scenes he had in Paris in May 1938; various other scenes were performed in other countries. The whole cycle, which Wieland Herzfelde prepared for publication by the Malik Press in Prague, fell into German hands and was not printed until 1945, when he was able to publish it in the Aurora Press in New York. There were also other changes and complications.

The Private Life of the Master Race clearly points backwards to the revues of the Weimar Republic. Communist amateur performances had often been on a grand scale, with massed voice choruses and marching men, but other smaller satirical forms had also been developed for the workers' theatre, most notably by Piscator with his 'Revue Roter Rummel'. Naturalistic treatments of concrete cases were also produced, such as Erich Steffen's *Nazis Among Themselves*, or the pieces by von Wangenheim which he called 'dialectical montages'. There was also a realisation that stereotypes in language or character had to be avoided—for example, the fat capitalist saying the predictable things. In general, theatre of this kind moved from the crude use of party-political slogans projected from the stage by amateurs to highly sophisticated pieces performable by professional actors. Men of the theatre like Piscator, Wangenheim, Mühsam, Wolf and Brecht provided the necessary ammunition. What Brecht provided in *The Private Life of the Master Race* was a series of scenes in which amateurs and professionals could work together, with some scenes (like the 'Jewish Wife') offering a magnificent starring role for a great actress like Helene Weigel, while other extremely short scenes (putting across a point briefly and succinctly, often by gesture as much as by word) were ideal for amateurs. This is how the cycle was often performed—by amateurs and professionals.

If Brecht's twenty-four scenes were unperformable in their entirety this does also move the work out of the sphere of theatre-for-the-stage into that of theatre-for-the-page, and as a result the cycle has been compared with the classic of that type, Karl Kraus' *The Last Days of Mankind*. In addition therefore to the workers' theatre of the Weimar Republic and literary revue and cabaret, Brecht seems to have been quite deliberately exploiting the possibilities of this kind of literary model. Of course there are obvious differences—Brecht does aim to give a cross-section of all classes and sections of people in the new Germany, but despite this intended totality, he is clearly more restricted than Kraus was with his vast accumulation of one hundred scenes performable only on Mars. Nevertheless they do both share the basic documentary urge. Kraus attempted to destroy his enemy by using only the words they had actually spoken, while Brecht too claimed that his scenes were based on eye-witness accounts and newspaper clippings. One difference is perhaps discernible in the fact that Kraus relies on linguistic satire, his basis is the newspaper, the leading article. Brecht is essentially a man of the theatre and each of his scenes demonstrates a gesture characteristic of life under a dictatorship. The best example of this is the 'Chalk Circle' which ends with the SA man slapping the worker on the back: what is normally a mark of friendship becomes the mark of betrayal characteristic of the new Germany. In the same way the brief first scene exposes the falseness of the Nazi claim to have created a united community of one people when the two brave SS officers lost in a working-class district shoot in all directions, while screaming in terror for help. Indeed this 'gesture' has been taken as the message of fear for the whole cycle, revealing by such ironic and satiric means the truth about the economic basis for the Nazi ideology and the continuance of class warfare and resistance despite Nazi claims to the contrary.

The time scale of *The Private Life of the Master Race* does not, of course, cover the totality of the Nazi regime from the rise of Hitler until the collapse of the Thousand Year Reich twelve years later, in fact the dated scenes range from 30 January 1933 to 12 March 1938. Berlin is the main focus, but there are also scenes in other cities. How significant these details of time and place are is, however, doubtful, as they were only added for the 1945 version. As for the order of the scenes, this is not merely haphazard. Günter Hartung has suggested the following sequence: scenes 1-5, SS and SA oppressing the workers; scenes 6-10, intellectuals and white-collar workers; scenes 11-15, workers reflecting on their condition; 16-21, the lower and middle classes in their suffering; 22-24, the workers showing signs of resistance. Expressed in these terms this does not look like a cross-section of the populace in its fear and suffering. However, connections are provided by the prologue and the linking verses. These non-prose elements add an epic quality to the whole, especially the appearance of the tank with the dozen or so soldiers, whose white faces indicate that they, who experienced fear in the Third Reich, are the ones who are bringing fear to the rest of the world. 'The same Panzer, incidentally, and the same pale villain/victims, roll past the quizzical eyes of Schweyk in *Schweyk in the Second World War* as he trudges in his roundabout way

to Stalingrad', and as in Becher's play *Winter Battle*, it is the snows
around Moscow which bring the triumphal procession of Nazi victories
to a halt.[8] Here the visual element is added to language and gesture,
reminding the audience of the Dance of Death, that other source of
early realism combining word and picture through a sequence of
different occupations and classes of society.

It is perhaps significant that Brecht puts his sequence of scenes
inside a framework. What is the German people like, he asks, after five
years of Nazi rule? The Führer is ready for war, but are they? What he
reveals is that there is no *Volk* community, only fear and treachery.
The workers may not go along with the regime but they are forced to
conceal their true thoughts, and even after the seizure of power they
still fight among themselves instead of uniting against the common
enemy, until they are all put together in the same concentration camp.
Judges, doctors, university physicists all prove only too susceptible to
Nazi pressure. The Spitzel scene shows the schoolteacher daring only
within his own four walls to make doubting remarks about the regime,
yet even then being terrified that his own Hitler Youth son might
betray him. In fact no one is safe. While the Goebbels propaganda
machine churns out programmes about the happy workers and how
much better off everybody is than in the Weimar Republic, the man
who dares to tell the truth about his wage packet is brought home in a
zinc coffin, and the young wife who keeps a note of food prices for her
household budget is taken away by the SA. Even peasants and those
who voted for Hitler from the start are not safe.

The whole system is based on fear, and so there is no real opposition
to Hitler — still Brecht does suggest that the workers could be strong
if they were united; that the soldiers do not really want to fight; that
there are some resistance workers, though all they can do is produce a
hand-out with the one word — NO! This indeed is the last word in the
cycle, as their response to the roar of victory which greets Hitler's entry
into Vienna. One *Volk*, One Reich, One Führer: but were they really
one folk, or were they only bribed to behave like this? Brecht suggests
that the new Reich is built on fear and suffering, that everyone is worse
off, that the economy is geared up for war. All of this may be true, but
he cannot envisage that anyone could have really *believed* in Hitler and
hence (as in *Arturo Ui*) makes no attempt to get inside the ideology of
the new Germany. Brecht knows that Hitler did have support — indeed
in the verses to 'The Old Warrior' he talks of a 100 per cent vote for
Hitler, and the old warrior gets furious if anyone says anything against
the 'idea', but there is no indication of what this idea is. There is some

indication of what Brecht thinks of the Germans. The Jewish Wife
sums it up:

> What kind of people are you? . . . You invent the quantum theory
> and Trendelenburg and let yourselves be told by half-savages
> that you have to conquer the world, but are not allowed to have the
> wife you want. Artificial respiration and every bullet a Russian! You
> are either monsters or monsters' bootlickers!

In 1940/1 in Finland Brecht wrote his *Exile Conversations*. These were
never intended for the stage, but since their publication in book form
they have been more and more often presented in dramatic manner.
These are essentially conversations between the physics expert Ziffel
and the Communist worker Kalle in exile in Finland. In these conversations Brecht comments on the political development of Germany
before and since his own flight, and exposes various key concepts of
the National Socialist system. Among other things he develops ideas he
had used before, for example (in *A Man is a Man*) the notion that anybody can be turned into a heroic fighting machine, by means of
propaganda, threats and brain-washing. Here as elsewhere Brecht is
amusing in his mockery of heroism and his admiration for the cunning
of Galileo, Schweyk, Azdak and others, who never quite say yes and
never quite say no, and somehow manage to survive. Whether this is a
policy or an approach he would advocate the German people should
adopt in the face of a dictatorship as total as that of the Nazis is
another matter.

12 LYRIC AND SONG IN EXILE

Theatre in Germany had for long not been restricted to drama. Since the turn of the century writers had also collaborated with composers, and after the age of Expressionism interest in literary cabaret and the lighter muse grew by leaps and bounds, though this did not exclude the exploitation of the theatre for political purposes. Wangenheim (as has been noted) wrote satirical documentary sketches for the Troup 31 like *The Mousetrap* and *That's where the Dog lies Buried* and especially in the latter made fun of Nazi slogans like Blood and Soil. Friedrich Wolf also wrote revues, and Brecht from an early point in his career had been associated with humorists like Karl Valentin and was accustomed to thinking of himself as a song-writer. Apart from Brecht, Georg Kaiser had also collaborated with Kurt Weill, and their *Silver Lake – a Winter Fairy Tale* was the cause of one of the great theatrical explosions in early 1933, when the Nazis took offence at the 'Caesar Ballad', which seemed a warning to Hitler, and disrupted performances:

> Let no one be foolish enough
> To think himself better than others,
> Caesar wanted to rule by the sword
> And a knife laid him low.

After the seizure of power the songsters and cabaret artists who had made fun of Hitler and his party were among the first to suffer or leave the country.[1] Erich Mühsam, Fritz Grünbaum, Paul Morgan, Kurt Gerron and others never survived their treatment in concentration camps. Walter Mehring, a master of the cabaret song, left the country immediately. In the number of the *Weltbühne* which appeared on the day before the Reichstag Fire he had published 'The Saga of the Giant Crab', which chronicled 'Germany and Hitler in the tale of a legendary crab propelled eternally in reverse'. For this reason alone, quite apart from his involvement with the political cabaret which he founded, it was obviously wise for him to get out of the country as quickly as possible. In exile he continued to write parodies and satires, in addition to *Müller, the Chronicle of a German Clan from Tacitus to Hitler* (1935). Alfred Kerr, the star critic with the *Berliner Tageblatt*, was also known for his satirical verse and hated accordingly in Nazi circles. He too went into exile and after 1936 lived in London. His *The Dictatorship of the Houseporter* came out in 1938 and thereafter he continued to publish poems and 'melodies'. Tucholsky, the great writer of songs and chansons, took his own life in 1935, while another great song-writer and cabaretist Erich Kästner remained in Germany 'in order to be an eye witness'. In his epigram 'Necessary Answer to Superfluous Questions', he gives his reason for staying:

> Ich bin ein Deutscher aus Dresden in Sachsen.
> Mich lässt die Heimat nicht fort.
> Ich bin ein Baum, der — in Deutschland gewachsen,
> Wenn's sein muss, in Deutschland verdorrt.[2]

> (I am a German from Dresden in Saxony.
> My homeland never lets me go.
> I am a tree, which — having grown up in Germany —
> Will shrivel and die in Germany if it has to.)

Some kind of existence was still possible in Nazi Germany; Kästner survived, Karl Valentin was never completely subdued and Werner Finck, the thorn in Goebbels' side, kept going until 1939, when he had to be silenced. Dr Goebbels took up this particular case in the *Völkischer Beobachter* of 4 February 1939 and answered essentially in the negative Finck's question about whether it was still possible to have a sense of humour in Nazi Germany.[3]

Like all the best theatrical traditions of the Weimar Republic, literary and political cabaret had to go into exile. Marlene Dietrich became the 'good angel of the German emigration' working from England and France: Max Hansen, who had made fun of Hitler on record with 'Were you ever in love with me?' took over a theatre in the Tivoli Gardens, Copenhagen, and Erika Mann moved her cabaret *The Pepper Mill* from the Munich Bonbonnière to Zurich. Despite complaints and protests from German embassies, *The Pepper Mill* performed 1,034 times in seven different countries with the best German cabaret singers, dancers and song-writers. According to one report, no newspaper or leading article could show so clearly what life under the Nazi regime had become. But satire needed constant renewal with up-to-date information about its targets. When the writers got further and further away from the homeland the satire finally faded and died, as Erika Mann's *Pepper Mill* did in America, a country which at that time had no tradition of political and literary cabaret and songs. Parody too was

a much-employed form among verse-writers in exile, not only because
it brought the exiles face to face with the fundamental problem of
'what is truly German', but also because the Nazis had appropriated
so much German literary culture (from Hölderlin to Goethe and
beyond) that only parody could rescue such contaminated material.
Here as elsewhere Brecht offers excellent examples, especially with his
Hitler Chorales. The Nazis had claimed Luther as one of Hitler's forerunners and Brecht uses the traditional form of the hymn to
demythologise this theft:

> Nun danket alle Gott
> Der uns den Hitler sandte
>
> (Now thank we all our God
> Who unto us Hitler sent.)

But it was not only the politically active poets who incurred the
disapproval of the Nazi authorities. It was perhaps natural to assume
that narrative prose and committed social drama were more obviously
anti-Nazi, while poetry could be more pure and further removed from
such mundane matters, and also not subject to censorship or government control. This was the assumption made by Thomas Mann in a
famous letter to Eduard Korrodi:

> You say that not all literature, but mainly the novel has gone into
> exile. That wouldn't be surprising. The pure poem — pure in the
> sense that it remains rather aloof from social and political problems,
> something the lyric has always done — is governed by other laws
> than those of narrative prose . . . The former grows and blooms,
> serene and undisturbed in sweet oblivion of the world.[4]

In this Thomas Mann was quite mistaken. Nobody was immune. The
Nazis made no distinction between pure and political poetry, and were
motivated by racial concerns and reliability in the eyes of the regime
rather than by aesthetic considerations. Adrienne Ash, who has made
the only extensive study of German lyric poetry in exile, has discerned
three separate literary generations.[5] The first and older generation was
made up of those born around the turn of the century who were
associated with Expressionism. In this group she names as examples of
poets who had made a name for themselves Johannes R. Becher, Else
Lasker-Schüler, Rudolf Leonhard, Franz Werfel and Paul Zech. The

second generation was made up of poets who began to publish after the age of Expressionism in the twenties and who were themselves in their thirties or forties when they had to go into exile. Apart from Expressionism and post-war political writing, Stefan George and Rilke were the greater influences. In this group she names too Oskar Maria Graf, Theodor Kramer and Ernst Waldinger (the poet who wrote a sonnet about why he wrote sonnets). Such writers never managed to make any kind of real breakthrough with their poetry. The third generation, the youngest, had the most difficult time of all in exile. Most remained almost completely unknown and unpublished, some, like Oskar Seidlin and Heinz Politzer, made a name for themselves as scholars, while Erich Fried survived as a translator, gradually emerging in later years as a poet.

As is now recognised, poets had particular problems in getting their work published. There was no audience for difficult and avant-garde poetry, and besides there were other pressures forcing them back towards the great German traditions and making their poetry con-servative, not to say dull. The sonnet was as much favoured in exile as it was inside Germany. Only Russia had favourable publishing facilities for favoured poets, and that too meant pressures towards the avoidance of experimental, avant-garde verse, which would be too 'difficult' for the proletariat reading public. Apart from the problem of publication, poetry suffered more than more literary forms through being denied access to the living language. Exile itself was a form of alienation, but loss of the beloved German language was also deeply felt. A foreign language could have an invigorating effect and Brecht is one example of a writer and poet who was well aware of the impact he could produce by allowing English vocabulary and syntax to estrange his German. More traditional and conservative poets visibly withered. Those who retreated into memories of their lost German landscape or complaints about their exiled lot failed to produce memorable poetry. Those who accepted the challenge of exile and the enrichment which a different culture and perhaps more exotic surroundings could bring gained enormously.

Johannes R. Becher had in his youth been one of the wildest and most ecstatic of the Expressionist poets, but by 1919 he was a member of the Communist Party and by the late twenties was helping to found the BPRS and its journal *Linkskurve*. He was forty-two when the Nazis came to power. He fled to Russia where he remained until 1945, not only as the leading literary figure in the exile community but as a person with considerable political influence—he was a member of the

Central Committee. On his return to East Germany he became founder
and President of the Cultural League for the Democratic Renewal of
Germany and held many high positions, including that of Minister for
Culture. In the German Democratic Republic he is considered a classic;
in the West he is little regarded. In a sense his reputation has suffered
from the cultural consequences of the Cold War. After 1945 Gottfried
Benn, that other great survivor from the age of Expressionism, offered
an exciting mixture of modernism, aestheticism, solipsism and
nihilism in his esoteric poetry and dazzling essays, while in East Berlin
Johannes R. Becher by contrast seemed a rather pedestrian functionary
expounding a doctrine of realism in literature and traditionalism in
the lyric. The whole concept of the 'heritage of humanism' had been a
major one throughout the period of exile for most anti-fascist writers
and it remained a particularly important plank in the cultural programme
for the Communist zone. Nevertheless it did make Becher's own poetry
appear rather dull and his deliberate focus on forms like the hymn, the
ballad, the folk song and on poets of the 'great German tradition of
poetry' like Heine and Hölderlin did make Hermlin's description of his
poetry as 'neoclassical smoothness and conventional versifying' seem
more than justified. Becher himself seems to have secretly shared his
friend's opinion, as entries in his diaries indicate. His public utterances
as Minister of Culture of course never deviated from expressions of
firm belief in realism and tradition. While there is then some doubt
about the quality of his verses, there is no doubt about his lasting and
deep concern for Germany and the German people. His poetry has been
rightly described as Deutschland poetry, and he himself used this as
the title for one of his anthologies. Throughout the forties this was his
main theme. But as early as 1937 he had registered his concern in a
double sonnet based on Gryphius' famous poem on the sufferings of
Germany in the Thirty Years War. The first quatrain from Becher's
'Tears of the Fatherland' reads as follows:

> O Deutschland! Sagt, was habt aus Deutschland ihr
>   gemacht?
> Ein Deutschland stark und frei? Ein Deutschland hoch
>   in Ehren?
> Ein Deutschland, drin das Volk sein Hab und Gut kann mehren,
>   auf aller Wohlergehn ist jedermann bedacht?[6]

> (Oh Germany! Say, what have you turned Germany into,
>   a Germany strong and free?

A Germany held in honours high?
A Germany in which the people can multiply its
 possessions; is everyone mindful of the welfare of others?)

Rudolf Leonhard was a poet and pacifist in the First World War; he
took part in the 1918/19 revolution on the side of Spartakus and later
worked with Piscator at the Volksbühne in Berlin. In 1927 he was
invited by Hasenclever to live in Paris and there wrote several dramas,
including the comedy *Hitler and Co.*, published in 1936. In Paris he
became chairman of the new SDS, the professional body for German
writers, and did a great deal for exile writers in difficulty. A selection
of his poetry was smuggled into Germany under false covers. Leonhard
was able to write in French and worked with the French resistance. In
1944 his poetry collection *Germany Must Live* was published illegally
in Marseilles. The poem 'Fatherland' from that collection shows that
he shared the same concerns and the same traditional approach to
poetry as Becher:

In Blut, in Tränen, Deutschland, mein Vaterland,
in Blut getaucht, in Tränen gebadet, hast
du Blut, du Tränen über die Welt geworfen.[7]

(In blood, in tears, Germany, my fatherland,
steeped in blood, bathed in tears, you have cast
blood, cast tears over the whole world.)

By the time he returned to Germany, Leonhard was far from well and
he died in 1953 a forgotten man. For a writer who had been so prolific
in the Expressionist period and so much involved with exile matters
and the Spanish Civil War, remarkably little of his work has survived
the ravages of time. Franz Werfel experienced almost nothing but
success in his own lifetime; but his works too show the marks of the
passing years. His volume of poems *Friend to the World* was one of
the sensations of the Expressionist age. In exile he became better
known through his novels and dramas, but he never stopped writing
poetry and in 1938 his *Poems from Thirty Years* were published in
Sweden. Then in Los Angeles in 1946 his *Poems from the Years 1905-
1945* came out, including the poetry of his exile years. In general the
rich use of rhyme, formal structures and the sonnet form suggests a
defensive attitude, which is fundamentally traditional and 'unmodern'.
Werfel looks backwards to a lost world and a lost youth instead of

forwards to a new future. He died shortly after publication of this collection. Else Lasker-Schüler was one of the most significant personalities in the Expressionist period, both by reason of her own works and of her association with Gottfried Benn and her marriage to Herwarth Walden. Her first play *The Wupper* (written as early as 1908) has proved remarkably stageworthy and still enjoys regular revivals. Less well known are her two later plays. *Arthur Aronymus and his Fathers* deals with the theme of reconciliation between Christians and Jews. Written in 1912, it was scheduled for production at the Schiller Theatre in Berlin, but had to be cancelled before the dress rehearsals because of Nazi objections. Her third and last play, *I and I*, was written in 1944 as a militant attack on National Socialism. It was not published and hence not performed at the time. Exile after 1933 seems to have had a disorientating effect on this apolitical Jewish poetess and though she was one of the first to live in Palestine, she never felt at home, any more than Louis Fürnberg did, who also spent years there in exile. Nevertheless she still wrote poetry in exile and *My Blue Piano*, dedicated 'to my unforgettable friends in the cities of Germany and to those like me, exiled and dispersed throughout the world', appeared in Jerusalem in 1943. In a speech about her in 1952 Benn described her as the greatest poetess Germany ever had and said: 'Her themes were variously Jewish, her imagination oriental, but her language was German, a rich, opulent, fragile German,' and he went on to describe her as 'all that was Jewish and German in a single lyrical incarnation'. Paul Zech, the last of the Expressionists to continue writing poetry in exile, landed up in Argentina. Apart from his own verse he had some success with his German versions of François Villon and Louise Labé. He also continued to write plays including *Germany Brown and Red* and *Only a Jewish Wife*, a play like Brecht's 'Jewish Wife' about a woman whose husband is forced to divorce her for the sake of his career. In his baggage when he went into exile in 1933 he had the first chapters of a novel called *Germany your Dancing Partner is Death*. The first part of the book was written in Germany between February and March 1933, the rest in exile. What he shows in this characteristic Deutschland novel is the end of the Weimar Republic and the assumption of power by the Nazis, using a cross-section of Berlin society to illustrate his theme. This book remained completely unknown until it was discovered among his papers and published in 1980. In Argentina Zech published three volumes of verse: *Trees by the Rio de la Plata* (1937), *New World* (1939) and *Sonnets from Exile* (1948). Zech was one whose poetic range gained enormously from his experience of an

entirely different world. Of the older generation, the most significant
and the one to travel furthest was Karl Wolfskehl. This learned poet and
close associate of Stefan George suffered more than most from being
cut off from his native land and finally died almost completely blind
in New Zealand. His first poems written in exile were addressed *To the
Germans*, but his most extensive lyrical effort was his *Song from Exile*,
a cycle in three parts of epic proportions. Franz Theodor Csokor, Max
Hermann-Neisse (the poet of Silesia), Berthold Viertel and many others
all continued to write as they had done before in Germany without
achieving any major development or breakthrough.

Of the second generation of poets none was to achieve anything
significant in the lyrical mode. Oskar Maria Graf was more successful
with his novels, while Carl Zuckmayer, after 1945, re-established his
earlier fame as a dramatist with his sensationally successful play *The
Devil's General*, though significantly it was not the actual man of
resistance sabotaging the German war-effort who was its central figure,
but the dashing flying officer. Despite that, the play is important not
only for the picture of Nazi Germany which it imparts, but also for the
awareness of the problem of the good German who has to wish for
Germany's defeat. As Oderbruch puts it: 'If Germany is victorious in
this war – then Germany is lost . . .' Compared with the power of such
a play Zuckmayer's poetry seems the work of an occasional poet.[8]
Among the others of this generation only Weinert, though devoted to
Stalin, managed to extract the occasional poem from the mass of his
political outpourings. For the rest, as in a poem like 'Germany Will Not
Be Lost', written in 1942, the verse is painfully simple:

> Wie mancher fragt sich sorgenvoll,
> Was wohl aus Deutschland werden soll,
> Weil es den Krieg, den es begann,
> doch niemals mehr gewinnen kann.[9]

> (How many people ask worriedly, whatever is
> to become of Germany, because it can never ever
> win the war it started.)

The soldier who is addressed in the poem is invited to turn his gun the
other way and free the German people from Hitler and the capitalist
exploiters. Neither the army nor the people turned against Hitler, and
Germany had to be liberated by the Allied forces.

The third generation poets were extremely young when the Nazis came to power and had had no time or opportunity to make any name for themselves. Erich Fried became known first and foremost as a translator and only in recent years has he come forward as a radical poet with an individual voice. However, this is to forget that he made his literary debut in England at the age of twenty-three with a volume of 'youthful, passionate, often romantic poems on the German tragedy' entitled *Germany*. This volume was followed two years later, in 1946, by a 'melancholy, mournful homage to his homeland', *Austria*. For Fried exile meant the opportunity to develop as a poet through involvement with a new and different cultural environment, and, strangely enough, it also meant that he had in England the freedom to immerse himself in the German culture which was banned in the new Germany. In particular he had free access to the works of the Expressionists.

Exile provided for many the possibility of discovering and developing a tradition which was no longer available in the homeland. This was the case particularly if the poets were Jewish. Where before they had considered themselves first and foremost German poets, now they were made to realise where their real roots lay. Else Lasker-Schüler and Karl Wolfskehl were 'deeply committed to their Judaic heritage'. Gertrud Kolmar came from a family which felt itself to be German and which had deep roots in German history and traditions, her father being a particularly good representative of that stratum of liberal, apolitical Prussian bourgeoisie which was so proud of its classical education. As a result of the anti-Jewish legislation in Hitler's Germany the whole family was rent apart; her father was deported to Theresienstadt, and she herself was probably sent to Auschwitz after years of semi-slave labour in factories. Throughout these years of suffering under the persecution of the Jews she continued to write poetry, which she sent to her sister in Switzerland. Then, 'as the persecution of Jews grew in intensity, she felt herself inescapably identified with Jewish suffering and accepted the full horror of the fate this entailed'.[10] Like her, Nelly Sachs lived and wrote in the Third Reich, but after seven years of personal experience of the new Germany she and her mother were able to escape to Sweden with the help of Selma Lagerlöf. The whole of the rest of her family died in concentration camps. In exile she wrote two volumes of poetry—*In the Dwellings of Death* and *Eclipse of the Stars*, neither of them published till after the war. Of the first Enzensberger wrote: 'this book remains the only poetic testimony that can hold its own beside the dumbfounding horror of the documentary reports'. He was referring to reports of the concentration camps and of the murder of the Jews taking place in Germany. Nelly Sachs wrote in the full knowledge of what was happening to her people, and with great religious fervour and poetic power. The first poem of the cycle gives some inkling of why she was awarded the Nobel Prize for her poetry:

O die Schornsteine
Auf den sinnreich erdachten Wohnungen des Todes,
Als Israels Leib zog aufgelöst in Rauch
Durch die Luft—
Als Essenkehrer ihn ein Stern empfing
Der schwarz wurde
Oder war es ein Sonnenstrahl?

O die Schornsteine!
Freiheitswege für Jeremias und Hiobs Staub—
Wer erdachte euch und baute Stein auf Stein
Den Weg für Flüchtlinge aus Rauch?

O die Wohnungen des Todes,
Einladend hingerichtet
Für den Wirt des Hauses, der sonst Gast war—
O ihr Finger,
Die Eingangsschwelle legend
Wie ein Messer zwischen Leben und Tod—

O ihr Schornsteine,
O ihr Finger,
Und Israels Leib im Rauch durch die Luft![11]

(O the chimneys / On the ingeniously devised habitations of death /
When Israel's body drifted in smoke / Through the air-- /
Was welcomed by a star, a chimney sweep, / A star that turned
black / Or was it a ray of sun? / O the chimneys! / Freedomway
for Jeremiah and Job's dust— / Who devised you and laid stone
upon stone / The road for refugees of smoke? / O the habitations of
death / Invitingly appointed / For the host who used to be a
guest— / O you fingers / Laying the threshold / Like a knife
between life and death— / O you fingers / And Israel's body
through the air in smoke!)

Apart from Nelly Sachs, Brecht was the only poet writing in German to achieve world recognition for his poetry. There are many possible reasons why this should have been so. Brecht himself recognised in one of his poems that this was a 'Bad Time for Poetry', and moreover he recognised that far too many withdrew into the traditional German inwardness, held on for too long to traditional ideas of what poetry and poetic diction should be and were too addicted to rhyme and form and too unwilling to draw conclusions about the real world the poet in exile was forced to live in. Adrienne Ash has summed up the reasons why Brecht succeeded where others failed:

> What is unique — and self-evident — in Brecht's lyric is the powerful, dramatic realism uniting exile, modernism and a political ideology. This congenial union of circumstance and poetic proclivity was not met elsewhere in the poetics of exile.[12]

Brecht's *Svendborg Poems* are the most successful poems he wrote at this period; though it is noteworthy that the actual theme of exile did not prove fruitful for Brecht or for any of his contemporaries. One theme that was always capable of inspiring Brecht was the theme of 'Germany', to which he returned again and again:

> O Deutschland, bleiche Mutter!
> Wie sitzest du besudelt
> Unter den Völkern
> Unter den Befleckten
> Fällst du auf.[13]

> (Oh Germany, pale mother! How soiled you sit among the peoples, among the stained you stand out.)

Schuhmacher has described this as a Deutschland poem and sees it as marking the dividing line between the earlier anti-Hitler poems and the later, sparer lyrics.[14]

All exile poetry was concerned with the homeland, the 'real' Germany which had been lost, and the great tradition in literature and the arts, in religion and philosophy; but looking back to the past could too easily turn to sentimentality, as Becher for one demonstrated. There is no doubting Brecht's patriotism and love of Germany, but it is a love filled with sadness at what has been done to Germany and combined with a recognition of the need for change. Outside Germany Brecht seems never to have suffered from feelings of isolation and displacement, but to have accepted exile as a positive experience in the confident knowledge that the false Germany of Adolf Hitler would pass and that he would be able to return home. Through his poetry he felt he could help to make this day come sooner:

Die Strassen führten in den Sumpf zu meiner Zeit.
Die Sprache verriet mich dem Schlächter.
Ich vermochte nur wenig. Aber die Herrschenden
Sassen ohne mich sicherer, das hoffte ich.
So verging meine Zeit
Die auf Erden mir gegeben war.

Die Kräfte waren gering. Das Ziel
Lag in grosser Ferne
Es war deutlich sichtbar, wenn auch für mich
Kaum zu erreichen.
So verging meine Zeit
Die auf Erden mir gegeben war.[15]

(The streets led to the swamp in my time. Language betrayed me to the slaughterer. There was little I could do. But the rulers were securer in their seats without me, that's what I hoped. So the time passed, which was granted me on earth.

Powers were slight. The goal was a long way away. It was clearly visible, even if for me scarcely reachable. So the time passed, which was granted me on earth.)

PART FOUR

1945 AND AFTER

13 THE RETURN FROM EXILE

From an early stage writers and intellectuals in exile gave thought not only to the Germany they had left behind, but also to the nature of the Germany to which they might return if and when the Nazi regime collapsed.[1] Inside Germany, too, many were considering the same problem, not least those associated with the plot to assassinate Hitler on 20 July 1944; there, however, such discussions could take place only in small circles of trustworthy friends and like-minded people. Outside Germany the debate was public, newspaper articles were written, books were published, groups were formed with titles like Free Germany and Democratic Germany. Some of these groups devised ill-conceived schemes, but some of them involved people of some substance who had to be taken more seriously. Albert Grzesinski, the chairman of the Association of Free Germans, nominated Thomas Mann, Heinrich Brüning and Otto Braun for leading positions in the first post-war German government. If there was still to be a Reich, Thomas thought his brother Heinrich better suited for the president of it. Adenauer was put forward from another quarter. But in fact there was little political reality to all these discussions and schemes. There was no government in exile ready to take over in Germany following the collapse when it came and the geographical dispersal and ideological pluralism of the *émigrés* meant that cohesive action was virtually impossible. Communist Party groupings were of course different. Many German writers had settled in Russia after 1933, and in Moscow (where they tended to be concentrated) one single policy for Germany could be worked out. Not only that: writers like Bredel, Becher, Kurella and Lukács had the means at their disposal to put concrete plans into practice when the opportunity arose. So in Russia from the middle of 1943, when it began to become more and more obvious that Germany was cracking, economic, political and cultural policies were developed and to some extent tried out on the thousands of Germans in prisoner-of-war camps. On 13 July 1943 in the Krasnogorsk camp near Moscow the Free Germany National Committee was set up. The party line was to change greatly between then and the actual end of hostilities; nevertheless when the time came there was an agreed policy round which party members and fellow travellers in exile could gather — namely, the demand for a strong, democratic German state and for the destruction of all traces of fascism and militarism. While this was in itself a basic policy to which it might have been thought that there could be no possible objection, even from circles not normally well disposed to Moscow, one issue led to fundamental rifts among *émigré* groups: the question whether Germany had been throughout really united behind Hitler or not, and whether any distinction could be made between Nazi Germany and the other better Germany. Vansittart became notorious in England for arguing in the *Black Record* and elsewhere that it was impossible and wrong to make a division into good Germans and bad Germans – according to him all Germans were tarred with the same brush. Vansittartism (as it came to be called) clearly went too far in its simplistic arguments, but even so it has been claimed with some justification that the issues raised by it were important ones which reflected the dilemma not only of non-Germans combating National Socialism, but also of the Germans themselves:

> the debate over Vansittartism served to clarify important issues for many people . . . It underlay the question of what sort of occupation, reparations, justice, retribution and re-education was to be carried out after the war. Even more fundamental were the questions dealing with whether the Germans themselves should play a role in their own reconstruction, as after the first world war, and how long it would take them to become worthy of the victor's trust. Reports of unprecedented mass atrocities as the war proceeded made this a most urgent question.[2]

Vansittart did not have much sympathy for Germans in exile, much as he appreciated the hardships they had to suffer. After all, in his view they were Germans too and even in exile they were liable to make claims for Germany's future which could only lead to further trouble for the world. In this connection Vansittart quoted Thomas Mann as one leading writer in exile who would agree with his main points. In far-away America Thomas Mann was himself having difficulty in clarifying his own thoughts about Germany, though he had to do so regularly for his addresses to the German nation through his regular BBC broadcasts. So, for example, while he welcomed the formation of the Free Germany movement in Moscow and took part in discussions in Santa Monica to work out a Free Germany declaration for America, he was clearly troubled over its Russian provenance. The American declaration contained the words:

> We too consider it necessary to differentiate sharply between the
> Hitler regime and those parts of society associated with it on the one
> hand and the German people on the other hand.[3]

On the day following the meeting at which this formula had been
agreed in his presence Thomas Mann phoned Feuchtwanger to withdraw
his signature. Brecht, who had been present, was furious. Inside
Germany it had been Goebbels' claim that Hitler and Germany were
one, outside Germany, as has been seen, Vansittart said the same — now
Thomas Mann too seemed to be unwilling to differentiate between
National Socialists and the mass of the German people. Even without
this incident there had for long been little love lost between Brecht
and Thomas Mann. As far as Brecht was concerned this was simply the
last straw. The whole situation was regrettable for its opening of such
a deep rift between the German literary community's two leading
figures in exile. Both parties were equally responsible for the misunderstanding, which is essentially what it was — there was no such great
difference between them, for they both loved Germany in their
different ways. Yet the mutual suspicion between these two leading
German writers in exile was at the same time characteristic of the
mixed response throughout the *émigré* world to a Germany which,
despite all the signs of imminent collapse, still gave no indication of
rising up in revulsion against the Hitler regime — a Germany in which
the civilian front seemed to be as firm as the military forces, which
against all the odds and despite the army's massive defeats still fought
on to keep the Allies out of German soil. German *émigrés* throughout
the world asked themselves where this strength came from, if not from
a broad-based acceptance of National Socialism and of the Führer.
From fear alone? When the extent of the evils of the regime became
apparent following its final collapse, the question of the apportionment
of blame became the issue, and then it was even more difficult to make
the division between good and bad Germans. Given the extent of the
crimes, questions about how much the man in the street in Germany
knew seemed secondary.

When the war was finally over and the leading Nazis were dead,
what kind of Germany awaited the exiles if they chose to return? By
1945 Germany had long been subject to the kind of devastation it had
brought to other countries: in particular, bombing raids had devastated
major cities. Germany had fallen to the armed might of the Allies and
consequently was divided into four separate Allied military zones. The
population was starving, the black market had taken the place of normal

trading and waves of refugees meant that already hard pressed areas had to take in thousands of people for whom there were no facilities. Germany was in chaos. For four years after 1945 there was essentially no Germany – only four separate zones under military government. The spiritual and intellectual situation was as chaotic and as confused as the economic and political one. For twelve years or more Germany had been apparently hermetically sealed off from the outside world, cut off from all modern developments in art and literature, and had remained correspondingly unaware of the new names which had appeared on the intellectual horizon. There was much catching up to be done. It was not only thanks to the cultural offices of the French, British, Russian and American military forces that Germany was subjected to a wave of translations from these languages. There was a hunger on the Germans' side for all the intellectual nourishment they had been deprived of. Not only did the removal of Nazi censorship mean that foreign books formerly banned were suddenly freely available: banned writers in the German language could now be re-discovered. Kafka had been known to the Expressionist generation of intellectuals in Germany, but as a Jewish writer his works had disappeared from sight in German-speaking countries, only to become an international sensation abroad through translations into French, English and Italian. Now Kafka could be read in German inside Germany. Thomas Mann too could be taken up and the works of other writers reappeared on the book-shelves – yet (as will be seen) the response was divided. By no means all the writers who had been forced for political and racial reasons to go into exile came back to Germany. And even if they did come back, by no means all of them found that they were still remembered, appreciated and welcomed. In addition, by 1949, writers in exile were having to make the great decision about which part of Germany they would return to. The Germany they had known in the time of the Weimar Republic had been internally divided into proto-fascist and anti-fascist ranks; now it was being divided once more geographically and ideologically into East and West. The dreams, hopes and plans of those in exile for a democratic united Germany were frustrated only a few years after the end of the war. The choice of any one side meant possible rejection by the other.

Before considering the fate of the writers who did return from exile it is perhaps worth considering first what happened to the works of those writers already discussed, who remained in Germany and Austria throughout the period of National Socialism. Here it is only too easy to assume that National Socialist books *pur sang* must have disappeared without a trace after 1945; and it is true that with Germans so eager to rediscover the world outside now open to them, there was not much discussion of 'blood and soil' around this time, nor apparently much demand for it. In addition, publication was subject to military licence and the Allies who were carrying out extensive denazification and re-education programmes and instituting war crimes trials had certainly no inclination to encourage Nazi literature. Yet appearances are deceptive. The cultural policy for the Soviet zone of occupation had been worked out in some detail and no 'fascist' literature of any kind could ever be published there. But in the other zones certain well known writers did begin to reappear in print in the later 1940s once the licensing of literature was relaxed. As has been noted, Grimm continued to hold his Lippoldsberg literary rallies and when the Archbishop of Canterbury directed a four-page message to the German people in November 1945 Grimm replied in 1950 with a 200-page book. As an English commentator on this defence of 'original National Socialism' put it in 1953: 'It is a rehash of the old anti-British propaganda introduced by Treitschke, perfected by Goebbels, and now refined and brought up to date.'[4] Some professors of German literature in the Federal Republic tried for a time to prove that Grimm was a great writer and for some time he could still rely on support from the old 'secret Germany', but his reputation declined steadily and nowadays he is rarely mentioned. He died in 1959. Kolbenheyer was another who was still widely read and admired in the 1950s, and a society with his name was even formed to propagate his work, but he too gradually faded from view. Bronnen's remarkable career (ending in the Communist part of the now divided Germany) has already been commented upon, and that other survivor from the Expressionist generation, Hanns Johst, lived for a long time after the war (he did not die until 1978) without ever making a come-back. The most remarkable 'come-back' (the word he himself used) was that of Gottfried Benn. Like Grimm he never attempted to justify his behaviour or change his views, though the account he gave of his own 'double life' was far from complete and involved much special pleading. Despite the fact that he had welcomed National Socialism so enthusiastically he was widely acclaimed in West Germany as the leading poet of the post-war generation, and admired by many as a brilliant stylist for his poetic and essayistic work. Equally brilliant as a stylist is Ernst Jünger, who continues to this day to astonish the literary world and like Benn to be awarded glittering prizes in the Federal Republic (the most recent and the most contested being in 1982). Benn, Johst and Jünger were survivors from

the First World War as well as the Second, and their longevity
contrasts strikingly with the remarkable number of opponents of
fascism who died young, were murdered, committed suicide or simply
disappeared. Yet in fact these three were no exceptions: many of their
colleagues from the Nazi period, like Billinger, Möller, Langenbeck and
Rehberg, also enjoyed long and healthy lives and were still alive and
writing after 1945 in the Federal Republic. Hans Baumann, the author
of the infamous 'Es zittern die morschen Knochen', won the Gerhart
Hauptmann Prize for 1959 with one of his plays, and other writers
were equally resourceful. Schenzinger, the author of *Quex*, was
successful with factual novels, while Dwinger continued to quarry the
war-novel vein. Griese, Baldur von Schirach and Wehner all lived on
into the 1970s.

As has also been noted, authors attributed to the inner emigration
enjoyed great acclaim outside the Soviet zone of occupation after 1945.
They were generally conservative in tendency and Christian in outlook
and were therefore heartily endorsed by official and government circles
throughout the Adenauer period. Since then their stock too has
declined and while their poetry still keeps its place in standard
anthologies and school books, not much critical attention is now
devoted to 'perfect' novellas like Bergengruen's *Three Falcons* or to
historical novels like *The Grand Tyrant and the Law*. Ernst Wiechert
seemed to be emerging after the war as the voice of resistance to
National Socialism, but his concentration camp reports contained
curious elements, his attitude to the Jewish problem failed to strike the
right note and his addresses to the younger generation in quaint old-
fashioned language were not listened to. He eventually withdrew to
Switzerland, where he died in 1950.

Nowadays growing attention is paid to another generation of
authors, namely those who started their literary careers inside National
Socialist Germany, who were never associated with inner emigration or
resistance, and who did not fully emerge into the limelight until after
1945.[5] Some of these were writers who, without going into exile,
managed to spend long periods outside Germany. While the government
did not completely approve of such long stays abroad, this did mean
that such writers managed to avoid open conflict or danger to themselves while continuing to publish in journals and literary outlets which
were not specifically National Socialist ones. Despite all appearances to
the contrary Germany was not completely sealed off and a select few
managed to maintain contact with the outside world. To some extent
this could be done, as Stefan Andres demonstrated by living in fascist

Italy, but other European countries too, for example France and the Netherlands, were more congenial to such writers than Germany or Austria. Writers who enjoyed such favourable publishing conditions throughout the Nazi period were Marie Luise Kaschnitz and Wolfgang Koeppen, Eugen Gottlob Winkler, Felix Hartlaub and Gustav René Hocke. Even more significant than these, however, were Karl Krolow, Johannes Bobrowski, Peter Huchel and Günter Eich, who were to become leading figures after the war (Bobrowski and Huchel in the East and Krolow and Eich in the West), although they had been able to develop quite extensive literary careers inside Nazi Germany. The Swiss dramatist, Max Frisch, also comes into this category. Both his prose volumes *Jürg Reinhardt* (1934) and *Answer from the Silence* (1937) were acclaimed by German critics inside Germany then. The existence of such a large body of writers leading an apparently apolitical literary life under the National Socialist aegis before 1945 means that the year 1945 was not such a dividing line as has been generally thought. Günther Eich may have liked to present himself as a completely new post-war talent, but in fact one-third of the poems from his best-known collection were written *before* 1945 and he also had a considerable body of radio plays behind him. Like many others, he preferred to mask this period in his career, and to forget the doubtful years. After the war it was assumed that secret drawers would be opened and works written but concealed during the Nazi period would be published. This did in fact happen—only in most cases the works which appeared were rarely works of an outright resistance or anti-fascist nature. Stefan Andres, Otto Flake, Hermann Kasack, Ernst Kreuder, Hans Erich Nossack, Ernst Penzoldt, Wolfgang Weyrauch—all managed to write throughout the dark years and to emerge after the war as significant (even, in some cases, leading) exponents of new-wave German writing, without obvious break in style or content. German literature after the war, especially in the western zones, was characterised by a strong element of continuity from the thirties into the forties. Some writers, like Alfred Andersch and Hans Werner Richter, did come back from the front and from prisoner-of-war camps to start something really new, but they were not coming back to a vacuum. Many writers from this earlier period were already well entrenched in the publishing scene. By the time the exiles returned there was generally no place for them.

Nevertheless if the 8 May 1945 did not signify a 'null point', an 'hour nought', popular metaphors of this kind are indicative of a certain mental attitude.[6] The belief that 1945 represented a null point

indicated a general readiness to make a clean break with National
Socialism and start off in a totally new direction. Welcome as this
readiness was, it did also entail a reluctance to engage in direct
discussion about National Socialism or about elements of it which had
survived the collapse. Altogether there was a reluctance in literature to
deal directly with National Socialism, and a tendency instead to turn
to the question of Germany's future. This was complicated by
political as well as intellectual developments. Germans themselves were
divided: on the one hand there were those who had lived through the
Nazi period and who still could not escape all the effects of Nazi
indoctrination, and on the other hand there were those of the younger
generation who, as a result of what they had experienced, were
sceptical of all ideology and belief. Germany itself was also clearly
splitting into two camps, an anti-capitalist East and a capitalist West.
The German Democratic Republic was established on 7 October 1949,
the Federal Republic was proclaimed on 23 May 1949. It was not long
after that the discussion started once again over whether there was one
German literature or two. By the nineteen-eighties it had become
customary in East German terminology to talk of 'the socialist
national literature of the GDR'. There is no equivalent term to describe
the literature which has grown up in the West. It is simply German.

Despite fundamental similarities of language and tradition the states
have grown apart and the literatures have grown apart. What must be
considered now is the extent to which this division was already apparent
in 1945. The republic which developed out of the Soviet zone of
occupation actually has the word democratic in its name. However,
there is no doubt that both sides, East and West, had the ideal of
democracy before them, although the interpretation which was put
upon the term was different. Difficulties arose because the democratic
tradition in Germany (and there had been one) had been destroyed
when Hitler came to power. Too many of the best democrats had been
put to death inside Nazi Germany, too many had been forced into
exile where they had died or committed suicide. The question was how
many of those who had survived would choose to return, in order to
help build up a new democratic Germany. In effect more came back to
the East than to the West. Wolfgang Emmerich has tabulated the
typical biography of the radical, democrat or Socialist writer as follows:

(1)   plays an active part during the Weimar Republic in the defence
       of the Republic and of democratic rights, first against author-
       itarian and ultimately against fascist tendencies in the state;

(2) exiled during the period of fascism;

(3) returns to the Eastern part of Germany and gives support to the building up of an anti-fascist democratic new order.[7]

This career pattern holds good particularly for proletarian, revolutionary writers. They started off as workers, played an active part in the political struggles of the Weimar Republic and joined organisations like the Communist Party and the BPRS. After 1933 their books were banned and burned, many of them were arrested and sent to concentration camps. On release they went into exile, fought in Spain, made their way to a friendly country like the USSR or Mexico and from there continued to fight against fascism. When they came back to Germany they took up important positions, prepared to play their part wherever they were needed in eliminating the last traces of fascism and building up democracy. The list of writers who came back from Russia, Mexico, America, Palestine and elsewhere is a long one, and because they were so many, because they shared the same political beliefs and background, they were able to imprint upon the East German literature of the late forties what Emmerich has called 'a rare political and aesthetic homogeneity'. At the same time the makers of cultural policy in the East were not blinkered. The literary canon which they set up did not by any means consist exclusively of members of the Communist Party. The basis was (as has been seen) anti-fascism and anti-militarism, but the policy throughout the exile years had been support for a popular front, recognising the value of liberal democrats and humanists in the realist mould of the nineteenth century. This policy was continued in the German Democratic Republic after the war, and hence Heinrich Mann was revered in the East and his works published there. Unfortunately he died before he could leave the United States in order to settle in the GDR. Lion Feuchtwanger was also singled out for praise as one who, although never a Communist, had fought against fascism with his novels—he was awarded the National Prize for literature in 1953 and his books were made available throughout the GDR. Until very recently there were no paperbacks or readily available editions of his works in the Federal Republic where he enjoyed little success, but he was held up as a model in the GDR, as too were Thomas Mann and Oskar Maria Graf. None of the writers mentioned were Marxists or Socialist Realists. Where the West was trying to catch up with the modernists who had not been permitted during the Nazi period (Joyce, Proust, Kafka, Beckett, Sartre, Camus), the East was being fed on a diet of Heinrich and Thomas Mann. While

it could be argued that this was no bad thing, it was nevertheless
regrettable that the GDR's cultural leaders deprived one section of
the German reading public of the modern writers the Nazis too had
forbidden. On the other hand the opposite is also true — the Federal
Republic remained largely unaware of a large section of its own
literary history. Writers who returned to the East and were published
there, and writers like Heinrich Mann who were admired there tended
to be all lumped together as Communists and remained unread and
ignored in the West. Most significantly the reading public in the
Federal Republic for long remained unaware of the fact that there had
been a literary resistance to the Hitler regime. It was for long thought
that writers like Bergengruen and Wiechert had gone as far as anyone
had dared to go — real resistance writers like Jan Petersen, who had
gone straight from exile in London to the GDR, remained almost
totally unknown in the West. Not only resistance literature but a large
quantity of exile literature was regrettably contaminated by association
with the Communist regime and put down as mere party literature.
One striking example of this is the German literature of the Spanish
Civil War, which is hardly ever mentioned in the West. Regrettably, too,
the many writers who returned from exile to settle in the German
Democratic Republic were generally past their peak and failed to
produce in their new homeland genuinely new and exciting works.
(This was a criticism levelled even against Brecht, the most famous of
all the exiles to return to East Germany.) The result was that this
generation of writers came to be regarded as semi-fossils upon whom
honours could be heaped, writers who had actually fought and suffered
in the fight against fascism, but who had little to offer as models for
the future. Despite this, the fact still remains that exiled writers who
came back to the Democratic Republic were well received, and were
given important functions in the cultural world, the theatre, the
university, publishing, broadcasting and diplomacy. They enjoyed
high visibility and tangible rewards. They were the cultural heroes of
the nation, despite the fact that the restrictions of a Socialist state
could be so oppressive that some finally felt forced to leave. Yet in fact
the Communist Party was by nature forward-looking rather than
backward-looking. More real attention was focused on the battle to
build up Socialism than on digging up the skeletons of the past.

Conditions in the trizone which developed into the Federal Republic
followed a totally different line of development.[8] The political leaders
of the Federal Republic (with a few exceptions like Willy Brandt) were
not drawn from the circles of resistance fighters and anti-fascists in exile —

Willy Brandt was even at one point to be publicly accused during elections of having deserted his country by going into exile. On the whole in the West there were far fewer in government with experience of imprisonment and exile and far more who had been too close to the Nazis. Resistance was associated with bishops and high-ranking officers and not with workers and Socialists. Inner emigration was highly regarded and writers like Jünger and Benn, Bergengruen and Goes were the focus of attention and contact with the other part of Germany was taboo; even Thomas Mann was suspect, because in the Goethe Year of 1949 (Goethe was born in 1749) he insisted on visiting East as well as West Germany, and received a Goethe Prize from *both* Germanies. Even his *Doktor Faustus* was taken as a blow to German pride by many in the West, though fortunately it was so highbrow that any political message it contained could be easily overlooked. Significantly too Thomas Mann, by then an American citizen and proud of it, decided after much hesitation against returning to either Germany and settled in Switzerland. Other notable literary figures from the Weimar Republic found no real welcome in the Federal Republic. Döblin came back in 1945 and worked in a cultural capacity for the French military government. In Baden-Baden he edited the journal *Das Goldene Tor* from 1946 until 1951 and helped to found the Academy of Sciences and Literature in Mainz, but he was never accepted, his books were not published and finally, in the face of Adenauer policies which he felt were turning the clock back, he left Germany again for Paris where he lived until 1956. Erich Maria Remarque became an American citizen like Thomas Mann and, like him, settled in Switzerland, despite awards and prestigious citations like the Grosses Bundesverdienstkreuz in 1967. He, the most successful and most widely read of all German authors of the twentieth century, preferred to live outside the Federal Republic. Zuckmayer, like Döblin, came back to Germany in 1945, though he was working for the Americans and not for the French cultural authorities. He enjoyed enormous success with plays like *The Devil's General*, and was awarded the highest honours including the Grossès Bundesverdienstkreuz; yet he too moved to Switzerland and died there.

If one asks why so many writers returning from exile felt so ill at ease in the Federal Republic, then one part of the answer must be political. As has been seen, there was no null point, there had in fact been no distinct and clear-cut break between National Socialist Germany and the new republic. In the government there were many with a Nazi past and in the same way in literature it was not only writers of the inner emigration and the unpolitical generation who continued to write and enjoy some success after 1945: even old-style nationalists and out-and-out Nazis were able to continue their literary careers into the post-war years. Of course there was a great deal of talk about the dangers of neo-Nazism and from time to time curious right-wing political parties and leaders surfaced, strange newspapers and journals of a militaristic kind found eager readers and there were even some right-wing outrages to divert the authorities from their otherwise almost exclusive concentration on left-wing terrorism. So far, however, neo-Nazism has made no headway and despite all the fears of the returning exiles the Federal Republic has established itself and grown strong economically and politically. Socialist leaders have emerged and after the early avoidance of politics and ideology a powerful literature has surfaced – one not afraid to confront the Nazi past on the stage, in novels, and in poetry. When it comes to 'Bewältigung der Vergangenheit' the West has proved in some ways more capable of coming to terms with the past than the East. The first post-war craze for existential writing and the theatre of the absurd has been followed by a documentary realism which has matched and gone further than anything the Socialist Realism of the Democratic Republic has had to offer. There has been nothing in East Germany to compare with the plays of Hochhuth and Weiss or the novels of Günter Grass.

As has been seen, there were political reasons why the period between 1933 and 1945 tended to be either ignored or passed over in comparative silence. In addition to political reasons there were probably many literary factors at work. It was argued, for example, that the twelve or thirteen turbulent years between 1933 and 1945 failed to produce any new or important developments in style or technique. When writers after 1945 looked around for a style of writing which would clearly mark their desire to break completely with the Nazi-contaminated years, if they did not opt for a foreign style (for example the Hemingway laconic style) they went back to the last most exciting period in German literature and that meant Expressionism and the Weimar Republic. In that period all the possible combinations and permutations of what was modern in the novel, the theatre and in lyrical poetry were present in abundance. Expressionism in particular had been no small avant-garde movement, but a general trend in all artistic spheres in the German-speaking world from Berlin to Prague and Budapest. Expressionism had been denounced by the Nazis as the decadent stammerings of pacifistic, big-city Jews and cultural Bolshevists. Its exponents had either died young, been exterminated or driven into exile. In addition German Expressionism was also clearly part of a much wider movement, an integral part of European modernism deriving from art nouveau and symbolism, though its roots could be traced back to Gothic, Baroque, Storm and Stress, Romanticism, et cetera. Foreign influences included Marinetti's futurist slogans, Rimbaud, Strindberg and African and primitive art. In view of all this it was not surprising that in the post-Nazi period there was a feeling that Expressionism had to be rediscovered and the result was a wave of books and specialist studies about it.[9] Laudable though this was, such concentration on the 1920s encouraged the neglect of the 1930s and 1940s. It was also significant that, despite the Expressionist boom in literary research and criticism, large areas of the movement were neglected. The avant-garde stylistic innovations were stressed, while the powerful, political side of Expressionism was ignored. Even perceptive non-German critics like Hamburger and Middleton saw the main strength of Expressionism in early poets like Trakl, Stadler and Stramm and listed the 'increasingly political strain of Phase II Expressionism' as one of the chief reasons why later developments in Expressionist poetry did not fulfil its early promise. This effectively eliminated 'political activists' like Hiller, Hasenclever, Toller and Kaiser, some of whom had given Expressionism its greatest successes, especially in the theatre. In effect the political dimension of Expressionism was taboo, not only because the Nazis themselves had flirted with it and because some Expressionists, notably Johst and Benn, had moved all the way to the radical right, but also because powerful Marxist critics like Lukács had denounced the movement as unrealistic, formalistic Utopianism. The Expressionist Revival in the years after the collapse of National Socialism has been vast in one sense but also remarkably limited in some respects. In general only foreign critics, especially the French, have pointed up the political significance of the movement, its continuity throughout the Nazi period and also to some extent into the years after 1945. Kafka, Benn and Brecht can only properly be understood against the Expressionist background from which they emerged. The same applies to later dramatists like Borchert, who picked up and rejuvenated the earlier style. Expressionism could have been used to demonstrate the continuity of German literature from the twenties to the forties. Instead it has generally been treated as an exciting relic from a bygone age.

In addition to Expressionism and the excitements of the modern movement in the arts, it is Weimar culture which has tended to blot out the culture of the years that succeeded it. Countless books have been written about Weimar culture: Berlin's cultural Golden Age, 'a period of violence, a Renaissance age of gangsters and aesthetes, Savonarolas, Cellinis and Borgias'.[10] This was the golden age of political cabaret, cinema, theatrical experiments in epic theatre from Brecht and Piscator, great novelists, modern poets. What is generally overlooked in the excitement of such nostalgia for the Golden Age is that this was only one side of the picture and represented a necessarily biased view, because it tended to eliminate the powerful ultra-conservative side of Weimar culture. The Weimar culture now so often resurrected and held up for admiration was the culture of the political losers: all these left-wing tendencies, all the vast Socialist cultural organisations were swamped by the nationalists. A great deal of the interest in Weimar culture arises precisely because it was the rich culture of a doomed society.

Despite all this there was clearly a longing in post-war Germany (at least in the West) for 'modernism' and this was satisfied by rediscovering the literary Expressionists, Weimar culture in general and the greats like Thomas Mann, Musil, Benn, Broch, Brecht and Canetti, who had started their work before the unfortunate interruption of National Socialism and who had carried on their vast literary projects more or less regardless. Just as a great deal of Expressionism continued into the thirties and beyond, so many monumental works started in the years of the Weimar Republic were only completed in the years of National Socialism and exile or even later. By comparison with the daring experiments of Rilke and Trakl, Thomas Mann and Musil, Brecht and Piscator, the works produced by many writers in exile seemed modest, conservative and unexciting if they were read after the war. The plays dealt with the problems of the time and had perhaps dated accordingly; the novels were historical and conservative in mode; the poetry was formal and conservative. In addition writers in exile had been divorced from the living language for long periods and could be accused of writing fossilised German. Accusations of this kind were constantly being levelled against exiled writers like Feuchtwanger.

One further factor which may perhaps be taken into account when attempting to explain the comparative neglect of exile literature is the sheer enormity of Nazi crimes, especially crimes against the Jews. As has been claimed, German writers since the end of the war, both in the East and the West, have not failed to face up to this and to deal with the problem of guilt and moral outrage. Remarkably, a surprising number of major Jewish writers have continued to write in German after the war—Paul Celan, Wolfgang Hildesheimer, Elias Canetti, Manes

Sperber, Jakov Lind, Peter Weiss, Friedrich Torberg, Jurek Becker, Georg Kreisler, Nelly Sachs and others.[11] However, while *they* were aware of the holocaust and wrote about it in German, German writers in exile were in an entirely different position. They wrote about the Jewish problem, they described what was happening in Germany in the thirties, they gave accounts of concentration camps from their own personal experience. What they wrote about were the early years. They wrote about Nazis torturing German Socialists and German Communists as well as about earlier phases of the persecution of the Jews, boycott, escape and exile. Exile literature is not holocaust literature, because the holocaust had not yet happened.[12] By comparison with the horrors of the final solution, early concentration camp reports may seem almost tame, but that does not make this literature any less true or moving. This was the Germany of the period between 1933 and 1945.

NOTES

Introduction

1. E.P. Dickins, 'The Attitudes of Three Writers of "Inner Emigration" to National Socialism: Ernst Wiechert, Werner Bergengruen and Erich Kästner', unpublished PhD thesis, University of Keele, 1972; G.P. Hutchinson, 'The Nazi Ideology of Alfred Rosenberg: a study of his thought, 1917-1946' unpublished DPhil. thesis, Oxford University, 1977; H.M. Ridley, 'National Socialism and Literature, Five Writers in Search of an Ideology', unpublished PhD thesis, Cambridge University 1966; A. Rutter, 'The German Historical Novel of Exile and Inner Emigration: An Antifascist Phenomenon', unpublished MA thesis, University of Sussex, 1979; D. Watts, 'Social Values in Some Novels of the Heimatkunst movement', unpublished PhD thesis, University of Warwick, 1975; A.D. White, 'The Development of the Thought of Erwin Guido Kolbenheyer from 1901 to 1934', unpublished DPhil. thesis, Oxford University, 1967; R.A. Woods, 'Ernst Jünger and the Nature of Political Commitment', unpublished DPhil. thesis, Oxford University, 1981. Very rich in forgotten material is the London University sity unpub. PhD thesis of 1977 by Jennifer Ann Taylor, 'The Third Reich in German Drama, 1933-56'.

1. The Weimar Republic's Secret Germany

1. Richard Samuel, 'The Origin and Development of the Ideology of National Socialism', *Selected Writings* (Melbourne, 1965), pp. 138-62.
2. Agnes Stansfield, 'Das Dritte Reich. A Contribution to the Study of the "Third Kingdom" in German Literature from Herder to Hegel', *Modern Language Review*, vol. 34, no. 1 (1934), pp. 156-72. For a contribution by a leading Germanist of the time, see Julius Petersen, 'Die Sehnsucht nach dem Dritten Reich in deutscher Sage und Dichtung', *Dichtung und Volkstum*, Neue Folge des *Euphorion*, no. 35 (1934).
3. Samuel, 'Ideology of National Socialism', p. 142.
4. Ibid., p. 143.
5. Denis Goeldel, 'Stéréotypes nationaux et idéologie chez Moeller van den Bruck', *Recherches Germaniques*, no. 2 (1972), pp. 38-67; Gary D. Stark, *Entrepreneurs of Ideology, Neo-conservative Publishers in Germany, 1890-1933* (Chapel Hill, North Carolina, 1981).
6. This section is heavily dependent on Günter Hartung, 'Über die deutsche faschistische Literatur', *Weimarer Beiträge*, vol. 14, no. 3 (1968), pp. 474-542, Special Number, no. 2 (1968), pp. 121-59, 677-707; and on Peter Zimmermann, 'Literatur im Dritten Reich' in *Sozialgeschichte der deutschen Literatur von 1918 bis zur Gegenwart* (Fischer 6475, Frankfurt a.M., 1981), pp. 361-416.
7. Werner Mahrholz, *Deutsche Literatur der Gegenwart* (Berlin, 1930) names in the section 'Das heimliche Deutschland' Hermann Stehr (Der mystische Roman), Karl Röttger, H.W. Seidel, Hans Carossa, Ernst Bacmeister, Emanuel von Bodman and Karl Scheffler. In his well known book on *Weimar Culture: the Outsider as Insider* (London, 1969) Peter Gay has a section on the 'Secret Germany', but as he is discussing Stefan George, Hofmannsthal and Rilke, he has to admit that they were not secret.

8. In *The Myth of the Twentieth Century* (Munich, 1930) Alfred Rosenberg discusses Hölderlin together with Wagner, Knut Hamsun, Grimm, Kolbenheyer and 'the Nordic soul'. For the rescue of Hölderlin from Nazi distortion see Helen Fehervary, *Hölderlin and the Left* (Heidelberg, 1977).

9. Michael D. Biddiss, *Father of Racist Ideology. The Social and Political Thought of Count Gobineau* (London, 1970); also 'Houston, Stewart Chamberlain, Prophet of Teutonism', *History Today*, vol. 19 (1969), pp. 10-17; G.G. Field, 'H.S. Chamberlain: Prophet of Bayreuth', unpublished PhD thesis, Columbia University, New York, 1972.

10. Gilbert Merlil, 'Oswald Spengler et le national-socialisme', *Recherches Germaniques*, no. 6 (1976), pp. 112-35; C.T. Carr, 'Julius Langbehn – a Forerunner of National Socialism', *German Life and Letters*, no. 3 (1938-9), pp. 45-54.

11. Donald Watts, 'Social Values in Some Novels of the Heimatkunst Movement', unpublished PhD thesis, University of Warwick, 1975.

12. Robert Edwin Herzstein, *When Nazi Dreams Come True. The Horrifying Story of the Nazi Blueprint for Europe. A Look at the Nazi Mentality 1939-45* (London, 1982).

13. Alfred Kerr, *Die Diktatur des Hausknechts und Melodien* (Hamburg, 1981), 'Gerhart Hauptmanns Schande' (1933), pp. 23-7.

14. Michael Mayer, 'The Nazi Musicologist as Myth-maker in the Third Reich', *Journal of Contemporary History*, vol. 10 (1975), p. 662; see also George Windell, 'Hitler, National Socialism and Wagner', *Journal of Central European Affairs*, no. 22 (1970), pp. 479-97 and Fred K. Prieberg, *Musik im NS-Staat* (Fischer 6901, Frankfurt a.M., 1982). For Wagner and symbolism, modernism and decadence, see Raymond Furness, *Wagner and Literature* (Manchester, 1982).

15. Mayer, 'Nazi Musicologist', p. 663.

16. Gisela Berglund, *Der Kampf um den Leser im Dritten Reich* (Worms, 1980), pp. 165-6.

17. Stanley Radcliffe, 'Hermann Löns – Heimatkünstler and Social Critic', *German Life and Letters*, no. 13 (1959-60), pp. 27-37. See also Charles Whiting, *Werewolf. The Story of the Nazi Resistance Movement* (London, 1972).

18. In *Das Zwanzigste Jahrhundert. Texte und Zeugnisse 1880-1933* (Munich, 1967), Walther Killy quotes some samples of Paul Ernst from the Germanic drama *Brunhild, The Jew* and *Race*, in his section 'Der Weg in die Barbarei'.

19. Ibid., pp. 502-3, 1105-10.

20. Samuel, 'Ideology of National Socialism', p. 157.

21. Extracts from this novel in Walther Killy, pp. 1113ff. It should also be noted that Hans Reimann's parody, *Artur Sünder. Die Dinte wider das Blut*, had sold 693,000 copies by 1922. See D.R. Richards, *The German Best-seller in the Twentieth Century* (Berne, 1968), p. 55.

22. His rabid desire to prove that Christ was Aryan antagonised Christian voters and he was removed from his post as Gauleiter in Thuringia. See Loewy, *Literatur unterm Hakenkreuz. Das Dritte Reich und seine Dichtung. Eine Dokumentation*, pp. 310-11 (Frankfurt a.M., 1966).

2 The Making of a People

1. A.D. White, 'The Development of the Thought of Erwin Guido Kolbenheyer', unpublished DPhil thesis, University of Oxford, 1967.

2. Willy A. Hanimann, *Studien zum historischen Roman 1930-1945*

(Frankfurt a.M., 1981). For a general approach see G.P. Hutchinson, 'The Nazi Ideology of Alfred Rosenberg: a Study of his Thought, 1917-1946', unpublished DPhil thesis, University of Oxford, 1977.

3. See Daniel Gasman, *The Scientific Origins of National Socialism* (New York, 1971), for a discussion of Social Darwinism. For biology applied to literature, see Dr Ludwig Büttner, *Gedanken zu einer biologischen Literaturbetrachtung* (Munich, 1939). For music Donald W. Ellis, 'The Propaganda Ministry and Centralised Regulation of Music in the Third Reich: the Biological Aesthetic as Policy', *Journal of European Studies*, no. 5 (1975), pp. 223-38.

4. Klaus Amann, 'Die Literaturpolitischen Voraussetzungen und Hintergründe für den "Anschluss" der österreichischen Literatur im Jahr 1938', *Deutsche Philologie*, vol. 101, no. 2 (1982), pp. 216-44.

5. The first section is 'classical' ('antike Strophen'), there are variations on Hölderlin, followed by a heroic trilogy, and a long section on the pure poem.

6. There is a Weinheber poem to the Führer in Loewy, *Literatur unterm Hakenkreuz*, 3rd edn (1977), p. 284.

7. With regard to Weinheber I follow the line taken by H.M. Ridley, 'National Socialism and Literature', unpublished PhD thesis, University of Cambridge, 1966.

8. Rainer Stollmann, *Ästhetisierung der Politik. Literaturstudien zum subjektiven Faschismus* (Stuttgart, 1978), p. 175.

9. Ridley, 'National Socialism and Literature', pp. 262-3.

10. Hans Sarkowicz, 'Zwischen Sympathie und Apologie: Der Schriftsteller Hans Grimm und sein Verhältnis zum Nationalsozialismus', in Karl Corino (ed.), *Intellektuelle im Bann des Nationalsozialismus* (Hamburg, 1980), pp. 120-35.

11. F.L. Carsten, 'Volk ohne Raum. A Note on Hans Grimm', *Journal of Contemporary History*, vol. 2 (1967), pp. 221-27.

12. Hellmut H. Langenbucher, *Volkhafte Dichtung der Zeit*, 3rd edn (Berlin, 1937), p. 344.

13. J. Wulf (ed.), *Literatur und Dichtung im Dritten Reich* (Gütersloh, 1963), p. 295.

14. Paul Alverdes was the editor of the journal *Das Innere Reich* published in Germany during the Third Reich. It tried to reach a 'better' public but was *never* in opposition.

15. Carsten, 'Volk ohne Raum', p. 227.

16. Roger Woods, 'Ernst Jünger and the Nature of Political Commitment', unpublished DPhil thesis, University of Oxford, 1981, to appear in 1982, published by Akademischer Verlag, Stuttgart. Still an excellent introduction is J.P. Stern, *Ernst Jünger. A Writer of our Time* (Cambridge, 1953). For the most recent survey, see W. Kaempfer, *Ernst Jünger* (Sammlung Metzler 201, Stuttgart, 1981).

17. Bruce Chatwin, 'An Aesthete at War', *New York Review of Books*, 5 Mar. 1971, p. 49.

18. Ibid.

19. E. Jünger, *Die totale Mobilmachung* (Berlin, 1931), ch. 3.

20. Chatwin, 'An Aesthete at War', p. 49.

21. Roger Manvell and Heinrich Fraenkel, *Doctor Goebbels. His Life and Death* (London, 1960), pp. 19-33; Helmut Heiber, *Goebbels* (London, 1972), pp. 7-30.

22. Stephen Spender, *European Witness* (London and New York, 1946). See also Marianne Bonwit, 'Michael, ein Roman von Joseph Goebbels im Licht der deutschen literarischen Tradition' in Hans Mayer (ed.), *Deutsche Literaturkritik der Gegenwart* (Stuttgart, 1971), vol. 4, pp. 490-501.

23. Spender, *European Witness*, p. 180.

24. Bruno Fischli, *Die Deutschen-Dämmerung. Zur Genealogie des völkisch-faschistischen Dramas und Theaters* (Bonn, 1976), pp. 231-6, pp. 352-3.

25. See George L. Mosse in Reinhold Grimm and Jost Hermand (eds.), *Geschichte im Gegenwartsdrama* (Stuttgart, 1976), pp. 24-38.

3 When I Hear 'Culture' I Reach for my Revolver

1. Harald Kaas, 'Der faschistische Piccolo: Arnolt Bronnen', in Corino, *Intellektuelle im Bann des Nationalsozialismus*, pp. 136-49; Klaus Schröter, 'Arnolt Bronnen, Protokollant seiner Epoche' in *Literatur und Zeitgeschichte* (Mainz, 1970), pp. 111-39.

2. Martin Rector, 'Überlegungen zum Problem des "Renegatentums bei Max Barthel"' in R. Schnell (ed.), *Kunst und Kultur im deutschen Faschismus* (Stuttgart, 1978), pp. 261-83.

3. Kurt Tucholsky, *Gesammelte Werke 1929-1932* (Reinbek bei Hamburg, 1961); 'Ein Besserer Herr', pp. 105-12, originally in *Die Weltbühne*, no. 25 (1929), pp. 953-60.

4. Ernst Jünger, 'Wandlung im Kriegsbuch – Arnolt Bronnens Roman O.S.', *Der Tag*, Berlin, 23 May 1929.

5. After the war Niekisch joined the Communist Party and became a member of the SED in East Germany, was a professor at the Humboldt University researching into imperialism, and a member of the People's Chamber. He left the GDR in 1952 to live in the West, continuing to write and engage in political debate.

6. The best recent discussion of Benn and National Socialism is contained in Reinhard Alter, *Gottfried Benn: the Artist and Politics (1910-1934)* (Frankfurt, 1976).

7. Martin A. Simoneit, *Politische Interpretationen von Stefan Georges Dichtung. Eine Untersuchung verschiedener Interpretationen politischer Aspekte von Stefan Georges Dichtung im Zusammenhang mit den Ereignissen von 1933* (Frankfurt a.M., 1978).

8. Horst Rüdiger, 'Entartete Kunst. Ursprung und Degeneration eines Begriffes', *Arcadia*, vol. 16, no. 3 (1981), pp. 284-9.

9. Translation into English of Benn's 'To the Literary Emigrés: A Reply' is contained in J.M. Ritchie, *Gottfried Benn* (London, 1972), pp. 89-96.

10. Max M. Kele, *Nazis and Workers. National Socialist Appeals to German Labor, 1919-1933* (Chapel Hill, North Carolina, 1972).

11. See Benn's 'Confession of Faith in Expressionism' in Ritchie, *Gottfried Benn*, pp. 96-106, also Rainer Rumold, *Gottfried Benn und der Expressionismus* (Koenigstein/Ts., 1982).

12. Lesley Sharpe, 'National Socialism and Schiller', *German Life and Letters*, vol. 20 (1982), is an extended discussion of George Ruppelt's *Schiller in NS Deutschland* (Stuttgart, 1979).

13. Michael Hamburger, *From Prophecy to Exorcism* (London, 1965), p. 69.

14. Fischli, *Die Deutschen-Dämmerung*, pp. 228-30. In the edition published by Paul Zsolnay Verlag, Berlin, in 1933, the German text translated by Geza Herzberg was dedicated to Werner Krauss. Mussolini's play was performed in Budapest, Paris and London with some success. See *Napoleon: the Hundred Days*, adapted from the Italian of Mussolini and Forzano by John Drinkwater (London, 1932).

15. Erwin Leiser, *Nazi Cinema* (London, 1968), p. 54.

16. Günther Rühle, *Zeit und Theater. Diktatur und Exil 1933-1945*(Berlin, 1974), p. 734. The text of *Schlageter* is now most readily available in this volume. For a more detailed examination of the play, J.M. Ritchie, 'Johst's *Schlageter* and the end of the Weimar Republic' in Alan Bance (ed.), *Weimar Germany* (Edinburgh, 1982), pp. 153-67.

17. F.C. Weiskopf, 'Liebesdienst und Lobgesang. Zu Hanns Johsts Schauspiel "Schlageter"', *Neue Deutsche Blätter*, vol. 1 (1933-4) (reprint Berlin, 1974), p. 315. See also Manfred Franke, *Albert Leo Schlageter. Zum Mythos eines Helden* (Cologne, 1980).

18. Warren Lerner, *Karl Radek. The Last Internationalist* (Stanford, 1970), pp. 120-3.

19. Richard S. Kemmler, 'The National Socialist Ideology in Drama', unpublished PhD thesis, New York University, 1973, p. 74.

20. What he actually says is, 'I loosen the safety-catch on my Browning automatic', which is a little clumsier.

21. E.W. Möller, 'Wandlungen des deutschen Theaters', *Hochschule und Ausland*, vol. 13 (1935), p. 48.

22. F.C. Weiskopf, 'Liebesdienst und Lobgesang', *Neue Deutsche Blätter*, vol. 1, nos. 1-6 (1933-4) (reprint Berlin, 1974), p. 315.

23. Heinrich Bachmann in *Germania*, Berlin, quoted from Dr Richard Elsner (ed.), *Das Deutsche Drama in Geschichte u. Gegenwart* (Berlin, 1933), p. 261.

24. F.N. Mennemeier, *Modernes Deutsches Drama*, vol. 2 (UTB 425, Munich, 1975), p. 109.

4 Germany Awakens

1. Wolfgang Zorn, 'Student Politics in the Weimar Republic', *Journal of Contemporary History*, vol. 5, no. 1 (1970), pp. 112-43.

2. Hans-Wolfgang Strätz, 'Die studentische "Aktion wider den undeutschen Geist" im Frühjahr 1933', *Vierteljahrshefte für Zeitgeschichte*, vol. 16, no. 4 (1968), pp. 347-72; Deitrich Aigner, 'Die Indizierung "schädlichen und unerwünschten Schriftums" im Dritten Reich', *Archiv für die Geschichte des Buchwesens*, vol. 11 (1971), pp. 933-1034.

3. See Hans Naumann, *Wandlung und Erfüllung. Reden und Aufsätze zur germanisch-deutschen Geistesgeschichte* (Stuttgart, 1933).

4. For full details on government and party agencies, black and white lists, etc. see Jörg Thunecke, 'NS literary Policies' in Jörg Thunecke and Eda Sagarra (eds.), *Formen realistischer Erzählkunst: Festschrift für Charlotte Jolles* (Nottingham, 1979), pp. 60-112.

5. Robert Cecil, *The Myth of the Master Race, Alfred Rosenberg and Nazi Ideology* (London, 1972).

6. Bouhler remained powerful to the end. He eventually poisoned himself near Dachau when captured by American forces in 1945.

7. For a brief survey of NS histories of literature see Klaus Vondung, 'Der literarische Nationalsozialismus. Ideologische, politische und sozialhistorische Wirkungszusammenhänge' in Franz Schonauer, *Deutsche Literatur im dritten Reich* (Olten u. Freiburg, 1961), pp. 44-65.

8. See Georg Walther Heyer, *Die Fahne ist mehr als der Tod, Lieder der Nazizeit* (Heyne-Buch 5890, Munich, 1981); *Der deutsche Faschismus in seiner Lyrik mit Materialien. Auswahl (Selection)*, ed. Harro Zimmermann (Stuttgart, 1981).

9. Hermann Glaser, *Das Dritte Reich, Anspruch und Wirklichkeit* (Freiburg im Breisgau, 1961), p. 93, quoted from Johann Neuhäusler, *Kreuz und Hakenkreuz* (Munich, 1946), p. 316. The English edition, Hermann Glaser, *The Cultural Roots of National Socialism* (London, 1978) compares favourably with George L. Mosse's *Nazi Culture* (New York, 1966, 1981), which is a collection of documents.

10. Hubert Orlowski's 'Die Herausbildung der faschistischen Literatur in den Jahren 1925-1933', *Studia Germanica Posnaniensia*, no. 2 (1973), pp. 99-118.

11. From *Dietrich Eckart. Ein Vermächtnis*, edited and introduced by Alfred Rosenberg (Munich, 1928), p. 66. Text and discussion in Hartung, 'Faschistische Literatur', pp. 135ff.

12. Uwe-K. Ketelsen in *Geschichte der politischen Lyrik in Deutschland* (Stuttgart, 1978).

13. Heinrich Anacker, 'Magie der Viererreihen':

Das is die herbe Weihe,
die unsern Weg verschönt:
Magie der Viererreihe,
wenn vorn die Trommel dröhnt.

(*Der deutsche Faschismus in seiner Lyrik*, p. 42).

14. For an exemplary analysis of such a poem, see Günter Hartung, 'Analyse eines faschistischen Liedes', *Wissenschaftliche Zeitschrift der Martin-Luther-Universität Halle-Wittenberg*, vol. 23, no. 6 (1974), pp. 47-64; see also Alexander von Bormann, 'Das NS Gemeinschaftslied' in Schonauer, *Die deutsche Literatur im dritten Reich*, pp. 256-80, and Hans Jochen Gamm, *Der braune Kult. Das dritte Reich und seine Ersatzreligion* (Hamburg, 1962).

15. Bertolt Brecht, *Gesammelte Werke 5, Stücke 5* (London, 1937), p. 1976.

16. Imre Lazar, *Der Fall Horst Wessel* (Heyne Buch 7173, Munich, 1982).

17. Brecht, *Gesammelte Werke 20, Schriften zur Politik und Gesellschaft*, 'Die Horst-Wessel-Legende', p. 209-19.

18. Francis Courtade and Pierre Cadars, *Geschichte des Films im Dritten Reich* (Munich, 1975).

19. Jeverly Ralph Cook Jr, 'Political Poetry: the NS Monatshefte 1930-1944', unpublished PhD thesis, Johns Hopkins University, 1979; W. Knoche, 'The Political Poetry of the Third Reich: Themes and Metaphors', unpublished PhD thesis, Ohio State University, 1968.

20. Discussed in Hartung, 'Faschistische Literatur', pp. 691ff.

21. Hans Baumann, *Horch auf Kamerad* (Potsdam, 1936), p. 16, quoted in Loewy, *Literatur unterm Hakenkreuz*, 3rd edn (1977), pp. 274-5.

22. Alexander von Bormann, 'Stählerne Romantik, Lyrik im Einsatz: Von der Deutschen Bewegung zum Nationalsozialismus', *Text und Kritik*, vol. 9, no. 9a (1973), pp. 86-104.

23. Alexander von Bormann, 'Stählerne Romantik. Lyrik im Einsatz. Von der Deutschen Bewegung zum Nationalsozialismus', *Text und Kritik*, Politische Lyrik, vol. 9, no. 9a (1973), pp. 86-101; Uwe-K. Ketelsen, 'Nationalsozialismus und Drittes Reich' in *Geschichte der politischen Lyrik in Deutschland.*

24. Cornelia Jungrichter, *Ideologie und Tradition – Studien zur nationalsozialistischen Sonettdichtung* (Bonn, 1980).

5 Novel and Drama in the Third Reich

1. Hellmut Lessing and Manfred Liebel, 'Jungen vor dem Faschismus' in *Terror und Hoffnung in Deutschland 1933-1945* (Rororo 7381, Reinbek bei Hamburg, 1980), pp. 391-403; Katherine Larson Roper, 'Images of German Youth in Weimar Novels', *Journal of Contemporary History*, vol. 3 (1978), pp. 499-516; Jean-B. Neveau, 'La Jeunesse et les luttes politiques dans "Der Hitlerjunge Quex" de K.A. Schenzinger', *Revue d'Allemagne*, no. 3 (1976), pp. 431-48.

2. Clifford R. Lovin, 'Blut und Boden: the Ideological Basis of the Nazi Agricultural Program', *Journal of the History of Ideas*, no. 28 (1967), pp. 279-88; Willibald Henschel advocated a breeding commune composed of 1,000 women and 100 men. The community was to be called Mittgart. Henschel claimed that the Indian Sun-God, Artam, was the true deity of the Aryans, whence the term Artamanen, for the followers of Artam.

3. Peter Zimmermann, 'Kampf um den Lebensraum. Ein Mythos der Kolonial- und der Blut-und-Boden-Literatur' in Schonauer, *Deutsche Literatur im dritten Reich*, pp. 165-82. See also Joachim Warmbold, *Deutsche Kolonial-literatur* (Lübeck, 1982).

4. Hubert Orlowski, 'Die Herausbildung der faschistischen Literatur in den Jahren 1925-1933', *Studia Germanica Posnaniensia*, no. 2 (1973), pp. 99-118.

5. Peter Werbick, 'Der faschistische historische Roman in Deutschland' in Schnell, *Kunst und Kultur im Faschismus*, pp. 157-90; also 'Exkurs: Der historische Roman im Dritten Reich' in Elke Nyssen, *Geschichtsbewusstsein und Emigration* (Munich, 1974), pp. 95-9; and Wolfgang Wippermann, 'Geschichte und Ideologie im historischen Roman des Dritten Reichs' in Schonauer, *Deutsche Literatur im dritten Reich*, pp. 183-206.

6. Geoffrey G. Field, 'Nordic Racism', *Journal of the History of Ideas*, no. 38 (1977), pp. 523-40.

7. Discussed in Hartung, 'Faschistische Literatur', pp. 685ff.

8. Quoted from Günter Rühle, *Theater für die Republik 1917-1933* (Frankfurt a.M., 1967), p. 1155.

9. For lists of plays and a survey of the history of the festival play up to and including the NS stadium plays see Klaus Sauer and German Werth, *Lorbeer und Palme. Patriotismus in deutschen Festspielen* (dtv 795, Munich, 1971). For the theatre in general see Ilse Pitsch, *Das Theater als politisch-publizistisches Führungsmittel im Dritten Reich*, unpublished doctoral dissertation, University of Münster, 1952.

10. Egon Menz, 'Sprechchor und Aufmarsch, Zur Entstehung des Thingspiels' in Schonauer, *Deutsche Literatur im dritten Reich*, pp. 330-46; Henning Eichberg, Michael Dultz, Glen Gladberry and Günter Rühle, *Massenspiele, NS-Thingspiel, Arbeiterweihespiel und olympische Zeremonielle* (Stuttgart/Bad Cannstatt, 1977).

11. Wilfried van der Will und Rob Burns, *Arbeiterkulturbewegung in der Weimarer Republik*: vol. 1, *Eine historisch-theoretische Analyse der kulturellen Bestrebungen der sozialdemokratisch organisierten Arbeiterschaft*; vol. 2, *Texte-Dokumente-Bilder* (Ullstein 35141-2, Frankfurt a.M., 1982).

12. Glen W. Gladberry, 'Eberhard Wolfgang Möller's Thingspiel *Das Frankenburger Würfelspiel*' in Rühle, *Massenspiele, NS-Thingspiel*, pp. 235-51; also Günter Rühle, 'Die Thingspielbewegung', pp. 181-202. The same in more detail in *Zeit und Theater*, vol. 3, *Diktatur und Exil 1933-45* (Berlin, 1974), pp. 35-40, 777-793, which also has the text of the play.

13. Gladberry, 'E.W. Möller's Thingspiel', p. 236.

14. Sauer and Werth, *Lorbeer und Palme*, pp. 159-227.

15. Bruce Harold Zortmann, 'The Theater of Ideology in Nazi Germany', unpublished PhD thesis, University of California, Los Angeles, 1969, p. 206.

16. Richard S. Kemmler, 'The National Socialist Ideology in Drama: a Comprehensive Study of Theater and Drama during the Third Reich', unpublished PhD thesis, New York University, 1973, pp. 205-11: 'Some Reasons why the Thing Movement Failed'.

17. Ibid., p. 108.

18. Rufus Jones Cadigan, 'Billinger, Hanns Johst, Eberhard Moeller. Three Representative NS Playwrights', unpublished PhD thesis, University of Kansas, 1979, p. 222.

6 Inner Emigration

1. E.P. Dickins, 'The Attitudes of Three Writers of Inner Emigration to National Socialism. Ernst Wiechert, Werner Bergengruen and Erich Kästner', unpublished PhD thesis, University of Keele, 1972; Gisela Berglund, *Einige Anmerkungen zum Begriff der Inneren Emigration* (Stockholmer Koordinationsstelle no. 7, no date).

2. H.R. Klieneberger, *The Christian Writers of the Inner Emigration* (The Hague-Paris, 1968), pp. 195-6.

3. Walter von Molo was 'unerwünscht' in the Third Reich, was removed from the Deutsche Dichterakademie whose president he had been from 1928 till 1930. His rejection of NS did not stop him from publishing nationalistic and heroic novels, and he seems to have shared some at least of the aims of the party. See Berglund, *Einige Anmerkungen*, p. 91.

4. In 'Why I am not coming back', an open letter to Walter von Molo, first published on 12 October 1945 in the *Augsburger Anzeiger.* See Thomas Mann, *Politische Schriften und Reden* (3 vols., Frankfurt a.M., 1968), vol. 3, p. 181.

5. Dieter Mank, *Erich Kästner im nationalsozialistischen Deutschland 1933-1945. Zeit ohne Werk?* (Frankfurt a.M., 1982).

6. Called the June Club in protest against the Treaty of Versailles, which the republican government signed on 28 June 1919. See Werner R. Braatz, 'Two Neo-conservative Myths in Germany 1919-1922: the Third Reich and the New State', *Journal of the History of Ideas*, no. 32 (1971), p. 573.

7. Falk Schwarz, 'Die gelenkte Literatur. Die Neue Rundschau im Konflikt mit den Kontrollstellen des NS-Staates und der NS-Bewegung' in Schonauer, *Deutsche Literatur im dritten Reich*, pp. 66-82. Here other journals are also discussed and bibliographical details of resistance in them provided.

8. Michael Krejci, *Die FZ und der Nationalsozialismus 1923-33* (Würzburg, 1965) and Rudolf Weber, *Die FZ und ihr Verhältnis zum Nationalsozialismus* (Bonn, 1965).

9. Elisabeth Langgässer was excluded from the RSK in 1936, forbidden to write, made to do factory work, and her daughter was sent to Auschwitz.

10. Ralf Schnell, *Literarische Innere Emigration 1933-45* (Stuttgart, 1976), pp. 33-7, cites Carossa as a conservative author of Goethean strain, who enjoyed a successful career under National Socialism, while morally and aesthetically rejecting it. As with other such conservative writers there is never any question of outspoken political opposition by him.

11. Ibid., pp. 42-6.

12. J.F.G. Grosser (ed.), *Die Grosse Kontroverse. Ein Briefwechsel um*

Deutschland (Hamburg, 1963).
   13. Herbert Wiesner, 'Innere Emigration. Die Innerdeutsche Literatur im Widerstand, 1933-1945' in Hermann Kunisch (ed.), *Handbuch der deutschen Gegenwartsliteratur* (Munich, 1970), vol. 2, p. 397.
   14. Various critical articles appeared in Will Vesper's *Neue Literatur*. In his 'Anmerkungen zum historischen Roman' Gerhard Schmidt took Klepper's novel to task and was quite clearly aware of its oppositional stance: *NL* (1940), pp. 132-7.
   15. Ursula Laack-Michel, *Albrecht Haushofer und der Nationalsozialismus* (Stuttgart, 1974).
   16. Charles W. Hoffmann, *Opposition Poetry in Nazi Germany* (University of California Publications in Modern Philology, vol. 67, 1962) deals with 'Bergengruen, Hagelstange, Haushofer, Schneider, Imprisoned Poets and other Poets of the Opposition'.
   17. It seems that Lehmann, the pure nature poet, did actually become a member of the NSDAP.
   18. Günther Scholar, 'Gescheitert an den Marmorklippen. Zur Kritik an Ernst Jüngers Widerstandsroman', *Zeitschrift für deutsche Philologie*, no. 98 (1979), pp. 543-76.
   19. Wolfgang Emmerich, 'Die Literatur des antifaschistischen Widerstandes' in Schonauer, *Deutsche Literatur im Dritten Reich*, p. 450; Eberhart Lämmert, 'Beherrschte Prosa. Poetische Lizenzen in Deutschland zwischen 1933 und 1945', *Neue Rundschau*, no. 86 (1975), pp. 404-21.
   20. G. Loose, *Ernst Jünger* (TWAS 323, Boston, 1974), p. 61.
   21. Hildegard Chatellier, 'Ernst Wiechert im Urteil der deutschen Zeitschriftenpresse 1933-1945. Ein Beitrag zur nationalsozialistischen Literatur- und Pressepolitik', *Recherches Germaniques*, no. 3 (1973), pp. 151-95.
   22. From *Jahre und Zeiten*, p. 650, quoted by Chatellier, ibid., p. 163, n. 51.
   23. From *Jahre und Zeiten*, pp. 649, 650.

7 Resistance

   1. Wolfgang Brekle, 'Die antifaschistische Literatur in Deutschland 1933-1945', *Weimarer Beiträge*, vol. 16, nos. 4-6 (1970), pp. 67-128. The section in this book on resistance literature leans heavily on Brekle, especially for Petersen, Kuckhoff and Krauss. Also excellent is Wolfgang Emmerich, 'Die Literatur des antifaschistischen Widerstandes in Deutschland' in Schonauer, *Deutsche Literatur im dritten Reich*, pp. 427-58. James D. Wilkinson, *The Intellectual Resistance in Europe* (Cambridge, Mass., 1981), mentions no left-wing literature whatsoever and still discusses under 'resistance' only writers like Wiechert and Jünger.
   2. Brecht, *Gesammelte Werke 9, Gedichte 2*, p. 459.
   3. Günther Weisenborn, *Der lautlose Aufstand* (Hamburg, 1953).
   4. J.P. Stern, 'The White Rose', *German Life and Letters*, n.s., vol. 11 (1957-8), pp. 81-101.
   5. Jost Hermand, 'Hilfloser Antifaschismus? Bemühungen um eine kritische Darstellung der Nationalsozialisten in der Literatur der Weimarer Republik', *Diskussion Deutsch*, vol. 12 (1981), pp. 211-28.
   6. Erich Kästner, *Gesammelte Schriften 2* (Cologne, 1959), p. 81.
   7. Quoted from Bruno Frei (ed.), *The Stolen Republic – Selected*

Writings of Ossietzky (London, 1971), pp. 269-84.

8. For fuller details and references see Lawrence Baron, 'Erich Mühsam's Jewish Identity' in *Leo Baeck Institute Yearbook* (1980), pp. 269-84.

9. For BPRS see Florian Vassen, 'Das Illegale Wort. Literatur und Literaturverhältnisse des Bundes proletarisch-revolutionärer Schriftsteller nach 1933' in Schnell, *Kunst und Kultur im deutschen Faschismus*, pp. 286-327; and 'Die illegale Arbeit des BPRS in Deutschland (1933-1935)' in Heinz Neugebauer (ed.), *Proletarische Revolutionäre Literatur 1918 bis 1933: ein Abriss* (Berlin, 1970).

10. *Hirne hinter Stacheldraht, Kollektivbericht des Bundes proletarisch-revolutionärer Schriftsteller Deutschlands* (Basle, 1934). For further information on anti-fascist anthologies see Walter Fähnder, Helga Karrenbrock, Martin Rector (eds.), *Sammlung antifaschistischer sozialistischer Erzählungen 1933-1945* (Sammlung luchterhand 162, Darmstadt and Neuwied, 1974), p. 314.

11. *Hirne hinter Stacheldraht*, quoted by Emmerich, pp. 433-4.

12. Ibid., p. 436.

13. Heinz Gittig, *Illegale antifaschistische Tarnschriften 1933-1945* (Leipzig, 1972).

14. 'Deutschland ist nicht Hitler' in *Zur Tradition der sozialistischen Literatur in Deutschland* (Berlin, 1962), p. 429.

15. For a recent paperback see Jan Petersen, *Unsere Strasse* (Munich, 1978).

16. Lutz Winckler, 'Willi Bredels *Die Prüfung*: Oder von den Schwierigkeiten literarischer Selbstprüfung' in *Faschismuskritik und Deutschlandbild* (Argument Sonderband AS 76, Berlin, 1981), pp. 119-31.

17. Quoted from Willi Bredel, *Die Prüfung. Roman* (Berlin u. Weimar, 1976), p. 5.

18. Quoted from W. Langhoff, *Die Moorsoldaten. 13 Monate Konzentrationslager*, 4th edn (Stuttgart, 1974), p. 170.

19. Ibid., pp. 190-3.

20. Lina Haag, *Eine Handvoll Staub*, Foreword by Oskar Maria Graf, 4th edn (Frankfurt a.M., 1980).

21. Wolfgang Emmerich, 'Die Literatur des antifaschistischen Widerstandes in Deutschland' in Schonauer, *Deutsche Literatur im dritten Reich*, pp. 427-58.

22. Ludvik E. Václavek, 'Deutsche Lyrik in Ghetto Theresienstadt 1941-1945', *Weimarer Beiträge* (1982), pp. 14-33; H.G. Adler, *Theresienstadt* (Tübingen, 1955 and 1960); Zdenek Lederer, *Ghetto Theresienstadt* (London, 1953).

23. Quotations here on Apitz in Buchenwald from Wolfgang Brekle, 'Schriftsteller im antifaschistischen Widerstand', *Deutschunterricht* (Berlin), vol. 29 (1976), pp. 176-81.

24. Günther Weisenborn, *Memorial* (1st edn 1948, paperback Röderberg-Verlag, Frankfurt a.M., 1976).

25. Brekle, 'Schriftsteller im antifaschistischen Widerstand'.

26. J.P. Stern, *Hitler. The Führer and the People* (London, 1975), pp. 138-53.

27. Stephen Hawes and Ralph White (eds.), *Resistance in Europe 1939-1945* (London, 1975), pp. 136-69.

8 The Spanish Civil War

1. *Das Wort*, no. 2 (Feb. 1939), p. 4. Quoted from Hans-Albert Walter, 'No pasarán!' *Kürbiskern*, no. 1 (1967), pp. 5-27.

2. Frederick R. Benson, *Writers in Arms. The Literary Impact of the*

Spanish Civil War (London, 1968), p. xix.

    3. E.E. Dwinger, *Spanische Silhouetten. Tagebuch einer Frontreise* (Jena, 1937).

    4. See the chapters on the SDS and Writers' Congresses in Alfred Kantoro-wicz, *Politik und Literatur im Exil* (Hamburg, 1978).

    5. Grace M. Allen, 'Senora Carrar's Rifles, "Dramatic Means and Didactic Ends"' in S. Mews and H. Kunst (eds.), *Essays on Brecht's Theater und Politics* (Chapel Hill, North Carolina, 1974), pp. 156-73. See also Klaus Bonen (ed.), *Brechts Gewehre der Frau Carrar* (suhrkamps taschenbuchmaterialien st. 2017, Frankfurt a.M., 1982).

    6. Martin Esslin, *Brecht: a Choice of Evils* (London, 1959), pp. 223-4.

    7. Brecht, *Gesammelte Werks 15, Schriften zum Theater 1*, p. 249.

    8. Allen, 'Senora Carrar's Rifles', p. 159.

    9. Werner Preuss, *Erich Weinert. Sein Leben und Werk* (Berlin, 1970), pp. 102-3.

    10. Brecht, *Gesammelte Werks 9, Gedichte 2*, pp. 647-9.

    11. Quoted from the dust-cover of the paperback edition, *Sonnenfinsternis* (Ullstein Buch 20029, Frankfurt a.M., 1979).

    12. Jurgen Rühle, *Literatur und Revolution. Die Schriftsteller und der Kommunismus* (Cologne, 1960).

    13. American edition, Longmans Green and Co., New York and Toronto, 1940, under the title *The Great Crusade*. The translation was by Whitaker Chambers and Barrows Massey. The German edition uses the original text, found among Regler's papers. See *Das grosse Beispiel* (suhrkamp taschenbuch 439, Frankfurt a.M., 1978).

    14. 'Es geht um Spaniens Freiheit: German Writers and the Spanish Civil War', *The Durham University Journal*, vol. 71, no. 2 (June 1979), p. 164.

    15. Benson, *Writers in Arms*, p. 97.

9 Exile, the First Phase

    1. For the most up-to-date account of exile literature see Hans, 'Literatur im Exil', pp. 419-66 (see Notes to ch. 1, no. 6). He deals mainly with the novel, as does the excellent book by Gisela Berglund, *Deutsche Opposition gegen Hitler in Presse und Roman des Exils* (Stockholm, 1972). As a general study in English E. Kryspyn, *Anti-Nazi Writers in Exile* (Athens, Georgia, 1978), can be highly recommended. The bias is naturally American.

    2. Kathinka Dittrich and Hans Wuerzner (eds.), *Die Nederlande und das Exil* (Koenigstein/Ts., 1982).

    3. *Deutsch für Deutsche* (Miniatur Bibliothek Bd. 481/483, Paris, 1935). Distributed in Germany under the title *Deutsche Mythologie*.

    4. 'Über die Bezeichnung Emigranten' in *Svendborger Gedichte, Gesammelte Werke 9, Gedichte 2*, p. 718.

    5. Ibid., p. 718.

    6. F.C. Weiskopf, *Unter fremden Himmeln* (Berlin, 1948), p. 11.

    7. Helmut Gruber, 'Willi Münzenberg: Propaganda for and against the Comintern', *International Review of Social History*, vol. 10 (1965), pp. 188-210.

    8. I have taken over from Jan Hans the idea of the Deutschlandroman: see 'Literatur im Exil', pp. 432ff. For a picture of the Germans in the exile novel, see H.D. Osterle, 'Die Deutschen im Spiegel des sozialkritischen Romans der Emigration 1933-1950', unpublished PhD thesis, Brown University, 2 vols., 1964.

9. Wolfgang Müller-Frank, *Literatur als geschichtliches Argument. Zur ästhetischen Konzeption und Geschichtsverarbeitung in Lion Feuchtwangers Romantrilogie Der Wartesaal* (Frankfurt a.M., 1981).

10. The Nazi film *Jud Süss* made by Veit Harlan is, however, not to be confused with the English film *Jew Süss* made by the *émigré* Lothar Mendes with Conrad Veidt playing the lead. See Karsten Witte, 'Der barocke Faschist: "Veit Harlan und seine Filme" in Corino, *Intellektuelle im Bann des Nationalsozialismus*, pp. 150-64.

11. M.R. Wagner, 'Erlebnis und Opposition gegen den deutschen Faschismus im Werke O.M. Grafs', unpublished PhD thesis, New York University, 1975.

12. Ernst Loewy, *Exil – Literarische und politische Texte aus dem deutschen Exil 1933-49* (Stuttgart, 1979), pp. 196-7. See also Brecht's poem 'Die Bücherverbrennung', *Gesammelte Werke 9, Gedichte 2*, p. 694.

13. Quoted by Loewy, *Exil*, p. 65, from Balder Olden, *Die Neue Weltbühne* no. 18 (1938), pp. 554-8.

14. Heinz Liepmann, *Das Vaterland. Ein Tatsachenroman aus Deutschland*, Foreword by Heinrich Böll, Bibliothek der verbrannten Bücher, ed. Heinz Kohn und Werner Schartel (Hamburg, 1979), p. 8.

10 Exile – the Second Phase

1. B.M. Broermann, 'The German Historical Novel in Exile after 1933', unpublished PhD thesis, State University of New York at Albany, 1976.

2. Quoted in Berglund, *Deutsche Opposition gegen Hitler*, p. 200; more recently Lutz Winckler, 'Bei der Zerstörung des Faschismus mitschreiben. Anna Seghers Romane *Das siebte Kreuz* und *Die Toten bleiben jung*' in *Antifaschistische Literatur*, vol. 3, pp. 172-201. See also Werner Roggausch, *Das Exilwerk von Anna Seghers, 1933-39* (Munich, 1979), and Lowell A. Bangerter, *The Bourgeois Proletarian. A Study of Anna Seghers* (Bonn, 1980), p. 86.

3. D.R. Midgley, *Arnold Zweig. Zu Werk und Wandlung* (Koenigstein/TS, 1980).

4. Jost Hermand, 'Was für Schicksale uns bürgerliche Menschen überfallen. Arnold Zweigs *Das Beil von Wandsbek*' in Winckler, *Faschismusikritik und Deutschlandbild*, pp. 131-51. There was no West German edition of this novel until 1979. It was filmed in the GDR in 1951 and has recently been filmed in the Federal Republic. See *Spiegel*, vol. 36, no. 33 (16 Aug. 1982), pp. 142-6.

5. All references here to I. Keun are from Berglund, *Deutsche Opposition gegen Hitler*, pp. 215-21.

6. Klaus Mann, 'Deutsche Wirklichkeit', *Neue Weltbühne*, no. 17 (1937), pp. 526-8; more recently Gert Sautermeister, 'Irmgard Keuns Exilroman *Nach Mitternacht*' in Winckler, *Faschismusikritik und Deutschlandbild*, pp. 15-35.

7. See Wilfried Deschauer, *Klaus Mann und das Exil* (Worms, 1973); Peter T. Hoffer, *Klaus Mann* (TWAS 435, Boston, 1978); Ilsedore B. Jonas, 'Klaus Mann im amerikanischen Exil', *Weimarer Beiträge* (1982), pp. 35-62.

8. In June 1936 the novel was first printed in the *Pariser Tageszeitung*, where it was described as a *roman-à-clef*. Klaus Mann wrote in these words to protest. The whole background is now readily available in the Rororo 4821 paperback, which has been a best-seller in West Germany since 1981.

9. Anni Carlsson, *Die Deutsche Buchkritik von der Reformation bis zur Gegenwart* (Berne and Munich, 1969), pp. 316-41: 'Die Literatur und das Dritte Reich'.

10. J.D. Mitchell, 'Exile and Historical Existence in the Writings of Franz Werfel, Alfred Döblin and Hermann Broch', unpublished PhD thesis, Pennsylvania State University, 1976.

11. Herbert Claas, 'Satirische Gesellschaftsromane mit historischem Stoff bei Lion Feuchtwanger und Bertolt Brecht' in Winckler, *Antifaschistische Literatur*, vol. 3, pp. 202-26.

12. David Gross, *The Writer and Society. Heinrich Mann and Literary Politics in Germany, 1890-1940* (Atlantic Highlands, NJ, 1980); Wolf Joeckel, *Henri Quatre als Gegenbild zum N.S.-Deutschland* (Worms, 1977).

13. Heinz D. Osterle, 'Alfred Döblins Revolutionsroman', postscript to the edition in 4 vols. (dtv 1389, München, 1978), p. 672.

14. Anthony W. Riley, 'The Aftermath of the First World War; Christianity and Revolution in Alfred Döblin's November 1918' in Charles N. Genno and Heinz Wetzel (eds.), *The First World War in German Narrative Prose* (Toronto, 1980), pp. 93-117.

15. Hans, 'Literatur im Exil', p. 453.

16. Thomas Anthony Kamla, 'The Theme of Exile in the Novel of the German Emigration', unpublished PhD thesis, University of Wisconsin, 1973. Since then as a book, *Confrontation with Exile: Studies in the German Novel* (Berne, 1975).

17. See Gerhard Hirschfeld (ed.), *Exil in Grossbritannien. Die Emigration aus dem nationalsozialistischen Deutschland 1933-1945* (1982), not yet seen.

18. David Pike, *German Writers in Soviet Exile* (Chapel Hill, North Carolina, 1982), p. 357. For conditions in other countries, see H.A. Walther's volumes and the seven-volume GDR series on exile.

19. J.P. Stern, 'The White Rose', *German Life and Letters*, n.s., vol. 11 (1957-8), pp. 81-101. For a recent edition see Alfred Neumann, *Es waren ihrer sechs* (Berlin, 1980).

20. Marc Schweyer, 'Theodor Plievier im Exil', *Recherches Germaniques*, no. 2 (1972), pp. 167-203.

21. Quoted by Donald Prater in 'Stefan Zweig' in John Spalek and Robert F. Bell (eds.), *Exile: the Writers' Experience* (Chapel Hill, North Carolina, 1982), p. 326. See also Donald Prater, *A European of Yesterday. A Biography of Stefan Zweig* (Oxford, 1972).

22. Ehrhard Bahr, 'Metaphysische Zeitdiagnose: Kasack, Langgässer und Thomas Mann' in Hans Wagener (ed.), *Gegenswartsliteratur und drittes Reich. Deutsche Autoren in der Auseinandersetzung mit der Vergangenheit* (Stuttgart, 1977), p. 147.

11 Theatre in Exile

1. Ernst Schürer, 'German Drama in Exile' in *Exile: the Writers' Experience*, p. 50.

2. F.N. Mennemeier and F. Trapp, *Deutsche Exildramatik 1933-1950* (Munich, 1980).

3. Werner Mittenzwei, *Das Zürcher Schauspielhaus 1933-1945 oder die letzte Chance. Deutsches Theater im Exil* (Berlin, 1979), pp. 73-88.

4. Martha G. Marks, 'Ernst Toller: his Fight against Fascism', unpublished PhD thesis, University of Wisconsin, 1980, p. 415.

5. Gisela E. Bahr, 'Roundheads and Peakheads: the Truth about Evil Times' in Mews and Kunst, *Essays on Brecht's Theater and Politics*, pp. 141-55.

6. B. Lindner, *Bertolt Brecht: Der aufhaltsame Aufstieg des Arturo Ui* (Munich, 1982).

7. Günter Hartung, 'Furcht und Elend des dritten Reiches als Satire' in Günter Hartung, Thomas Höhle and Hans-Georg Werner (eds.), *Erworbene Tradition* (Berlin, 1977), pp. 57-118.

8. Cäcilia Friedrich, 'Bechers Hamlet-Tragödie: Winterschlacht' in Hartung, Höhle and Werner, *Erworbene Tradition*, pp. 119-47. Jan Needle and Peter Thomson, *Brecht* (Oxford, 1981), Chapter 5 'Hitler and the Power of Force', pp. 95-119.

12 Lyric and Song in Exile

1. Gerald Alan Fetz, 'The Political Chanson in German Literature from Wedekind to Brecht', unpublished PhD thesis, University of Oregon, 1973.

2. Quoted from Heinz Greul, *Bretter, die die Zeit bedeuten. Die Kulturgeschichte des Kabaretts* (dtv 743-744, Munich, 1971), vol. 2, p. 289. See Kästner, *Gesammelte Schriften* 1, p. 331.

3. For Dr Goebbels on the 'Finck Case' in *Völkischer Beobachter* (4 Feb. 1939) see Greul, *Bretter, die die Zeit bedeuten*, vol. 2, p. 295.

4. Thomas Mann to Eduard Korrodi, 3 Feb. 1938 in Erika Mann (ed.), *Thomas Mann Briefe: 1889-1936* (Frankfurt a.M., 1961), pp. 411-12.

5. Adrienne Ash, 'German Poetry in Exile: 1933-1945', unpublished PhD thesis, University of Texas at Austin, 1971. Very short version, 'Lyric Poetry in Exile' in *Exile: the Writers' Experience*, pp. 1-23. See also William K. Pfeiler, *German Literature in Exile. The Concern of the Poets* (Lincoln, Nebraska, 1957).

6. *Deutschland, Deutschland, Politische Gedichte vom Vormärz bis zur Gegenwart*, edited and selected by Helmut Lamprecht (Bremen, 1969), p. 419. For Becher's use of the sonnet form, see W.E. Yates' *Tradition in the German Sonnet* (Frankfurt a.M., 1981), p. 27. Yates sees similarities between the 'conservatism' of the Marxist Becher and that of the Nazi Weinheber.

7. *Deutschland, Deutschland, Politische Gedichte*, p. 194.

8. Siegfried Mews, *Carl Zuckmayer* (TWAS 610, Boston, 1981).

9. *Deutschland, Deutschland, Politische Gedichte*, p. x.

10. Erika Langmann, 'The Poetry of Gertrud Kolmar', *Seminar*, vol 14, no. 2 (1978), p. 125.

11. Nelly Sachs, *In den Wohnungen des Todes* (Berlin, 1947), *O the Chimneys: Selected Poems*, trans. Michael Hamburger *et al.* (New York, 1967).

12. Adrienne Ash, 'Lyric Poetry in Exile' in *Exile: the Writers' Experience*, p. 14. See also Christiane Bohnert, *Brechts Lyrik im Kontext. Zyklen und Exil* (Koenigstein/Ts, 1982).

13. 'Deutschland', *Gesammelte Werke 9, Gedichte 2*, 'Set by Eisler (1934) for chorus and orchestra as Praeludium of his Deutsche Symphonie (in Lk, 3, no. 1) and later by Dessau as part of his cantata *Deutsches Miserere* to texts by Brecht', *Brecht Poems 1913-1956* (London, 1976). See also Hans Bender, 'Deutschland (1933)' in Walter Hinck (ed.), *Ausgewählte Gedichte Brechts mit Interpretationen* (edition suhrkamp 927, Frankfurt a.M., 1978), pp. 41-7.

14. Ernst Schuhmann, *Untersuchungen zur Lyrik Brechts. Themen, Formen, Weiterungen* (Berlin/Weimar, 1973).

15. 'An die Nachgeborenen II', *Svendborger Gedichte* in *Gesammelte Werke 9, Gedichte 2*, p. 724.

13 The Return from Exile

1. In this connection see particularly Alexander Stephan, *Die deutsche Exilliteratur 1933-1945* (Munich, 1977), who devotes the final section of his book to problems of this kind. See also the same author's 'Pläne für ein neues Deutschland' *Basis*, vol. 7 (1977), pp. 54-74, and 'The Treatment of Fascism in GDR Literature', *GDR Monitor* (1980), pp. 3, 5-15.

2. Aaron Goldman, 'Germans and Nazis', *Journal of Contemporary History*, vol. 14 (1979), pp. 155-87.

3. Herbert Lehnert, 'Bert Brecht und Thomas Mann im Streit über Deutschland' in J. Spalek and J. Strelka (eds.), *Deutsche Exilliteratur seit 1933, I Kalifornien* (Berne, 1976).

4. Grimm's post-war literary career is discussed briefly in Corino, *Intellektuelle im Bann des Nationalsozialismus*, pp. 130-5.

5. There is a very interesting section on these writers with publication dates in Dieter Lattmann (ed.), *Kindlers Literaturgeschichte der Gegenwart* (Frankfurt a.M., 1980), vol. 1, pp. 4-25. Dieter Lattmann, the author of this part, subdivides his material into 'The Hour Nought which never was', 'The End of the Reichsschrifttumskammer', and 'The not completely empty drawers'.

6. Frank Trommler, 'Der "Nullpunkt 1945" und seine Verbindlichkeit für die Literaturgeschichte', *Basis*, vol. 1 (1970), pp. 9-25; 'Nachkriegsliteratur – eine neue deutsche Literatur?' *Recherches Germaniques*, no. 2 (1972), pp. 167-86.

7. Wolfgang Emmerich, *Kleine Literaturgeschichte der DDR* (Sammlung Luchterhand 326, Darmstadt and Neuwied, 1981), p. 42. His chapter three is headed 'Kein Nullpunkt: Traditionsbildung und neuer Anfang im Zeichen des Antifaschismus (1945-49)'. This is excellent and can be highly recommended.

8. Jost Hermand, 'Man muss das Unrecht auch mit schwachen Mitteln bekämpfen', *Diskussion Deutsch*, no. 12 (1981), pp. 232-45.

9. J.M. Ritchie, 'Binkmann's *Expressionismus*', *German Life and Letters*, vol. 34, no. 4 (1981), pp. 453-68. See also 'The Expressionist Revival', *Seminar*, no. 2 (1966), pp. 37-49.

10. J.M. Ritchie, 'German Theatre between the Wars and the Genteel Tradition', *Modern Drama* (1965), pp. 363-74.

11. This list is taken from Peter Sternberg, 'Memories of the Holocaust, Edgar Hilsenrath and the Fiction of Genocide', *Deutsche Vierteljahresschrift* (1982), pp. 277-89.

12. Susan E. Cernyak, 'German Holocaust Literature', unpublished PhD thesis, University of Kansas, 1973.

TABLE OF DATES

20 Apr.	1889	Adolf Hitler born in Braunau am Inn
	1890	Langbehn's *Rembrandt the Educator*
	1910	Löns' *The Wehrwolf*
	1912	Burte's *Wiltfeber, the Eternal German*
	1920	Jünger's *Storm of Steel*
13-16 Mar.	1920	Kapp Putsch
8 Aug.	1920	NSDAP founded
	1922	Dinter's *Sin against the Blood*
	1923	Moeller van den Bruck's *The Third Reich*
18 July	1925	Hitler's *Mein Kampf* (vol. 1) appears
10 Dec.	1926	Hitler's *Mein Kampf* (vol. 2) appears
25 Oct.	1929	Wall Street collapse
	1930	Rosenberg's *Myth of the Twentieth Century*
30 Jan.	1933	Hindenburg names Hitler Reich Chancellor
27 Feb.	1933	Reichstag Fire
24 Mar.	1933	Enabling Law
1 Apr.	1933	Boycott of Jewish shops and businesses
20 Apr.	1933	Première of Johst's *Schlageter*
10 May	1933	Burning of the Books
14 May	1933	First performance of Goebbels' play *The Wanderer*
24 May	1933	Benn's reply to Klaus Mann's open letter
12 July	1933	Goebbels' telegram to Stefan George
July	1933	Ernst Wiechert addresses students at Munich University
July	1933	BPRS publishes first illegal number of *Hieb und Stich*
22 Sept.	1933	Reich Culture Chamber law passed
Oct.	1933	First volume of Mann's Joseph tetralogy appears in Germany
4 Dec.	1933	Stefan George dies in Locarno
30 June	1933	SS and Gestapo eliminate political opposition,
2 July	1933	including Röhm and followers
10 July	1934	Erich Mühsam murdered in Oranienburg
25 July	1934	Murder of Dollfuss
2 Aug.	1934	Death of Hindenburg. Hitler becomes Führer

		and Reich Chancellor. The army swears a personal oath of allegiance to him
13 Jan.	1935	Saar plebiscite – the Saar returns to Germany
1 Apr.	1935	Benn 'emigrates' into the army
15 Sept.	1935	Proclamation of the Nuremberg Laws
17 July	1936	Beginning of the Spanish Civil War
1 Aug.	1936	Olympic Games open in Berlin Nobel Peace Prize for Ossietsky
26 Aug.	1936	Goebbels issues an order banning art and literary criticism as commonly understood
5 Aug.	1937	Paul Ernst Society – Chemnitz
30 June	1937	Entartete Kunst Campaign launched
15 Nov.	1937	Celebrations for Gerhart Hauptmann's seventy-fifth birthday
11 Mar.	1938	*Anschluss* with Austria
4 May	1938	Carl von Ossietsky dies
6 May	1938	Gestapo arrests Wiechert
30 Aug.	1938	Wiechert released from Buchenwald
9 Nov.	1938	*Reichskristallnacht*
30 Dec.	1938	Hitler awards Kolbenheyer the Adlerschild of the German Reich
Mar.	1939	End of the Spanish Civil War
22 Aug.	1939	German-Soviet Non-Aggression Pact and Secret Agreement
1 Sept	1939	German attack on Poland Jünger's *On the Marble Cliffs*
9 Apr.	1940	German invasion of Denmark and Norway
10 May	1940	German attack on Holland, Belgium, Luxemburg and France
17 July	1940	Première of the film *The Rothschilds*
24 Nov.	1940	Première of the film *Jew Süss*
20 Feb.	1941	Oskar Loerke dies
6 Apr.	1941	German attack on Yugoslavia and Greece
7 June	1941	Schiller's *Wilhelm Tell* banned at Hitler's request
22 June	1941	German attack on the Soviet Union
8 Apr.	1942	Rudolf Pechel arrested
July	1942	Arrests in the Schulze-Boysen/Harnack group
7 Nov.	1942	Beginning of Allied landings in North Africa
11 Dec.	1942	Jochen Klepper commits suicide
31 Jan.	1943	End of the battle for Stalingrad
22 Feb.	1943	Execution of the Scholls

27 Feb.	1943	Gertrud Kolmar taken to concentration camp
5 Apr.	1943	Arrest of Dietrich Bonhoeffer
26 Apr.	1943	Johannes Wüsten dies in prison
7 June	1943	Creation of the Hölderlin Society
5 Aug.	1943	Death sentence carried out on Adam Kuckhoff
10 Aug.	1943	*Frankfurter Zeitung* banned after Eckart article
6 June	1944	Allied invasion of France
20 July	1944	Attempt on Hitler's life
Aug.	1944	*Die neue Rundschau* banned
27 Dec.	1944	Albrecht Haushofer arrested for the second and last time
17 Feb.	1945	Reck-Malleczewen dies in Dachau
16 Mar.	1945	Börries von Münchhausen commits suicide on Allied approach
23 Apr.	1945	Haushofer executed
30 Apr.	1945	Hitler commits suicide in the Reich Chancellery
9 May	1945	Dietrich Bonhoeffer murdered in Flossenbürg
9 May	1945	Unconditional surrender of Germany and the end of hostilities in Europe
23 May	1949	Foundation of the Federal Republic of Germany
7 Oct.	1949	Foundation of the German Democratic Republic

BIBLIOGRAPHY: CRITICAL LITERATURE AND LITERARY TEXTS

In view of the complicated publishing history of many books in this period, they are, as far as possible, listed with the details of the original place, publisher and date.

I Critical Literature

Third Reich

Denkler, H. and Prümm, K. (eds.) *Die deutsche Literatur im Dritten Reich. Themen. Traditionen. Wirkungen* (Stuttgart, 1976)

Fischli, Bruno *Die Deutschen-Dämmerung. Zur Genealogie des völkisch-faschischtischen Dramas und Theaters (1897-1933)* (Bonn, 1976)

Geissler, Rolf *Dekadenz und Heroismus. Zeitroman und völkisch-nationalsozialistische Literaturkritik* (Stuttgart, 1964)

Gilman, Sander L. (ed.) *NS-Literaturtheorie. Eine Dokumentation* (Frankfurt am Main, 1971)

Hartung, Günter 'Über die deutsche faschistische Literatur', *Weimarer Beiträge*, vol. 14 (1968), pp. 474-542, 677-707; Special Number no. 2 (1968), pp. 121-59

Ketelsen, Uwe-Karsten *Heroisches Theater. Untersuchungen zur Dramentheorie des Dritten Reichs* (Bonn, 1968)

—— *Von heroischem Sein und völkischem Tod. Zur Dramatik des Dritten Reiches* (Bonn, 1970)

—— *Völkisch-nationale und nationalsozialistische Literatur in Deutschland 1890-1945* (Stuttgart, 1976)

Loewy, Ernst (ed.) *Literatur unterm Hakenkreuz. Das Dritte Reich und seine Dichtung. Eine Dokumentation* (Frankfurt am Main, 1966)

Orlowski, Hubert 'Die Herausbildung der faschistischen Literatur in den Jahren 1925-1933', *Studia Germanica\Posnaniensia*, 2 (1973), pp. 99-118

Prümm, Karl *Die Literatur des soldatischen Nationalismus der 20er Jahre (1918-1933). Gruppenideologie und Epochenproblematik* (2 vols, Kronberg/Taunus, 1974)

Schnell, Ralf (ed.) *Kunst und Kultur im deutschen Faschismus* (Stuttgart, 1978)

Schonauer, Franz *Deutsche Literatur im Dritten Reich. Versuch einer Darstellung in polemisch-didaktischer Absicht* (Olten u. Freiburg, 1961)

Strothmann, Dietrich *Nationalsozialistische Literaturpolitik. Ein Beitrag zur Publizistik im Dritten Reich* (Bonn, 1960)

Vondung, Klaus *Völkisch-nationale und nationalsozialistische Literaturtheorie* (Munich, 1973)

Wulf, Joseph (ed.) *Literatur und Dichtung im Dritten Reich. Eine Dokumentation* (Gütersloh, 1963)

—— (ed.) *Theater und Film im Dritten Reich. Eine Dokumentation* (Gütersloh, 1964)

Inner Emigration

Grimm, Reinhold and Hermand, Jost *Exil und innere Emigration I*, Third Wisconsin Workshop (Frankfurt am Main, 1972)
Grosser, J.F.G. *Die grosse Kontroverse. Ein Briefwechsel um Deutschland* (Hamburg, Geneva and Paris, 1963)
Hohendahl, Peter Uwe and Schwarz, Egon *Exil und innere Emigration II*, Internationale Tagung in St Louis (Frankfurt am Main, 1973)
Klieneberger, H.R. *The Christian Writers of the Inner Emigration* (The Hague and Paris, 1968)
Mann, Thomas, Thiess, Frank and von Molo, Walter *Ein Streitgespräch über die äussere und die innere Emigration* (Dortmund, 1946)
Paetel, Karl Otto (ed.) *Deutsche Innere Emigration. Antinationalsozialistische Zeugnisse aus Deutschland* (New York, 1946)
Schnell, Ralf *Literarische Innere Emigration 1933-1945* (Stuttgart, 1976)
Wiesner, Herbert '"Innere Emigration". Die innerdeutsche Literatur im Widerstand 1933-1945' in Hermann Kunisch (ed.), *Handbuch der deutschen Gegenwartsliteratur* (Munich, 1970), vol. 2, pp. 383-408

Resistance

Baumgart, Hans 'Der Kampf der sozialistischen deutschen Schriftsteller gegen den Faschismus (1933-1935)', unpublished doctoral thesis, University of Berlin, 1962
Brekle, Wolfgang 'Das antifaschistische schriftstellerische Schaffen deutscher Erzähler in den Jahren 1933-1945 in Deutschland', unpublished doctoral thesis, University of Berlin, 1967; 'Die antifaschistische Literatur in Deutschland (1933-1945)', *Weimarer Beiträge*, no. 16 (1970), pp. 67-128
Emmerich, Wolfgang 'Die Literatur des antifaschistischen Widerstandes' in *Deutsche Literatur im Dritten Reich*, pp. 427-58
—— (ed.) *Proletarische Lebensläufe. Autobiographische Dokumente zur Entstehung der zweiten Kultur in Deutschland.* Vol. 2: *1914-1945* (Reinbek, 1975)
Gittig, Heinz *Illegale antifaschistische Tarnschriften 1933 bis 1945* (Leipzig, 1972)
Greuner, Ruth (ed.) *Zeitzünder im Eintopf. Antifaschistische Satiren (1933-1945)* (Berlin, 1975)
Hoffmann, Charles W. *Opposition Poetry in Nazi Germany* (University of California Publications in Modern Philology, vol. 67, 1962)
Koenigswald, Harald von *Die Gewaltlosen. Dichtung im Widerstand gegen den Nationalsozialismus* (Herborn, 1962)
Weisenborn, Günther *Der lautlose Aufstand. Bericht über die Widerstandsbewegung des deutschen Volkes 1933-1945* (Hamburg, 1954), 4th edn (Frankfurt am Main, 1974)

Spanish Civil War

Benson, Frederick R. *Writers in Arms. The Literary Impact of the Spanish Civil War* (New York University Press, New York, 1967)
Herling, Helga 'Spanien und die antifaschistische deutsche Literatur', *Neue deutsche Literatur*, no. 14 (1966), pp. 13-24.
Kirsch, Edgar 'Der spanische Freiheitskampf (1936-1939) im Spiegel der antifaschistischen deutschen Literatur', *Wissenschaftliche Zeitschrift der Martin-*

Luther Universität Halle-Wittenberg, no. 4 (1954), pp. 99-119
Kollektiv für Literaturgeschichte im Volkseigenen Verlag Volk und Wissen (eds.)
  Bodo Uhse. Eduard Claudius Abriss der Spanienliteratur (Volk und Wissen,
  Berlin, 1961)
Mack, Gerhard 'Der spanische Bürgerkrieg und die deutsche Exilliteratur',
  unpublished PhD thesis, University of Los Angeles, 1970
Marquardt, Hans (ed.) *Rote Zitadellen. Der Spanische Freiheitskampf 1936-1939.
  Eine Anthologie.* Neues Leben, Berlin, 1961
Walther, Hans-Albert 'No Pasarán – Deutsche Exilschriftsteller im Spanischen
  Bürgerkrieg', *Kürbiskern*, no. 1 (1967), pp. 5-27
Weinert, Erich *Die Fahne der Solidarität. Deutsche Schriftsteller in der
  Spanischen Freiheitsarmee* (Aufbau Verlag, Berlin, 1953)

Exile

Arnold, Heinz Ludwig (ed.) *Deutsche Literatur im Exil.* 2 vols. *Materialien*
  (Frankfurt am Main, 1974) (Fischer Athenäum Taschenbücher 2085)
Berendsohn, Walter A. *Die humanistische Front.* Vol. 1: *Von 1933 bis zum
  Kriegsausbruch 1939* (Zurich, 1946, reprint Worms, 1978)
——— *Die humanistische Front.* Vol. 2: *Vom Kriegsausbruch 1939 bis Ende 1946*
  (Worms, 1976) (*Deutsches Exil 1933-45, eine Schriftenreihe*, ed. Georg
  Heintz, vol. 6)
Berglund, Gisela *Deutsche Opposition gegen Hitler in Presse und Roman des
  Exils* (Stockholm, 1968)
Cazden, Robert E. *German Exile Literature in America 1933-46. A History of the
  Free German Press and Book Trade* (Chicago, 1970)
Durzak, Manfred (ed.) *Die deutsche Exilliteratur 1933-1945* (Stuttgart, 1973)
Kantorowicz, Alfred *Politik und Literatur im Exil. Deutschsprachige Schriftsteller
  im Kampf gegen den Nationalsozialismus* (Hamburg, 1978)
Loewy, Ernst *Exil – Literarische und politische Texte aus dem deutschen Exil
  1933-49* (Stuttgart, 1979)
Serke, Jürgen *Die verbrannten Dichter. Mit Fotos von Wilfried Bauer. Berichte,
  Texte, Bilder einer Zeit* (Weinheim, 1977)
Spalek, John *Deutsche Exilliteratur 1933.* Vol. 1: *Kalifornien Teil 1-2* (Berne,
  Munich, 1976)
——— and Bell, Robert F. (eds.) *Exile: the Writers' Experience* (University of North
  Carolina Press, Chapel Hill, 1982)
Stephan, Alexander *Die deutsche Exilliteratur 1933-1945* (Munich, 1977)
Walter, Hans-Albert *Deutsche Exilliteratur 1933-1950* (4 vols., Darmstadt and
  Stuttgart, 1972ff)
Wegner, Matthias *Exil und Literatur. Deutsche Schriftsteller im Ausland 1933-
  1945*, 2nd edn (Frankfurt/Bonn, 1968)
Weiskopf, F.C. *Unter fremden Himmeln. Ein Abriss der deutschen Literatur im
  Exil 1933-1947, mit einem Anhang von Textproben aus Werken exilierter
  Schriftsteller* (Berlin, 1948)
Winckler, Lutz (ed.) *Antifaschistische Literatur* (3 vols., Kronberg, 1977ff)
The big GDR survey in seven volumes, *Kunst und Literatur im antifaschistischen
  Exil 1933-45* (Röderberg Verlag G.m.b.H., Frankfurt am Main, 1978-81), is
  now complete.

II Literary Texts

Before and After 1933

Baumann, Hans *Macht keinen Lärm. Gedichte von Hans Baumann* (Munich, 1933); *Horcht auf Kamerad* (Vaggenreiter, Potsdam, 1936)

Benn, Gottfried *Der neue Staat und die Intellektuellen* (Deutsche Verlagsanstalt, Stuttgart, 1933); *Kunst und Macht* (Deutsche Verlagsanstalt, Stuttgart, 1934)

Berens-Totenohl, Josefa *Die Frau als Schöpferin und Erhälterin des Volkstums* (Diederichs, Jena, 1938)

Billinger, Richard *Rauhnacht. Schauspiel in vier Aufzügen mit einem Vorspiel* (Inselverlag, Leipzig, 1933); *Der Gigant. Schauspiel* (Felix Bloch, Berlin, 1937)

Blunck, Hans *Die Grosse Fahrt. Ein Roman von Seefahrern Entdeckern, Bauern und Gottesmännern* (Langen/Müller, Munich, 1934)

Bode, Wilfred *Die SA erobert Berlin. Ein Tatsachenbericht* (Knorr and Hirth, Munich, 1934)

Bronnen, Arnolt *O.S. Roman* (Rowohlt, Berlin, 1929); *Rossbach* (Rowohlt, Berlin, 1930); *Kampf im Äther* (Rowohlt, Berlin, 1935)

Burte, Hermann *Wiltfeber der ewige Deutsche. Die Geschichte eines Heimatsuchers* (Sarasin, Leipzig, 1912)

Darré, Ricardo Walther Oskar *Neuadel aus Blut und Boden* (Munich, 1930)

Dinter, Artur *Die Sünde wider das Blut. Ein Zeitroman* (Matthes und Thost, Leipzig, 1919)

Eckart, Dietrich 'Deutschland erwache!' in *Dietrich Eckart. Ein Vermächtnis*, ed. and intro. by A. Rosenberg (Munich, 1928)

Eggers, Kurt *Annaberg* (Berlin, 1933); *Das Spiel von Job dem Deutschen. Ein Mysterium* (Berlin, 1933)

Ernst, Paul *Pantalon und seine Söhne* in *Gesammelte Werke* (Langen/Müller, Munich, 1932)

Euringer, Richard *Deutsche Passion. Hörwerk in Sechs Sätzen* (Gerhard Stalling, Oldenburg, 1933)

Ewers, Hanns Heinz *Horst Wessel – Ein deutsches Schicksal* (Cotta, Stuttgart and Berlin, 1933)

Goebbels, Joseph *Michael. Ein deutsches Schicksal in Tagebuchblättern* (Zentralverlag der NSDAP Franz Eher, Munich, 1929); *Der Wanderer. Ein Spiel in einem Prolog, acht Bildern und einem Epilog* (unpublished)

Goes, Gustav *Aufbricht Deutschland! Ein Stadionspiel der nationalen Revolution* (Berlin, 1933)

Grimm, Hans *Der Richter in der Karu* (A. Langen, Munich, 1926); *Volk ohne Raum* (A. Langen, Munich, 1926).

Heynicke, Hans *Neurode. Ein Spiel von deutscher Arbeit* (Berlin, 1935)

Johst, Hanns *Schlageter* (Langen/Müller, Munich, 1933)

Jünger, Ernst *In Stahlgewittern. Aus dem Tagebuch eines Stösstruppführers*, von Ernst Jünger, Kriegsfreiwilliger, dann Leutnant und Kompanie-Führer im Füs: Regiment. Prinz Albrecht von Preussen (Selbstverlag des Verfassers, 1920); *Der Kampf als inneres Erlebnis* (Mittler, Berlin, 1922); *Das Wäldchen 125. Eine Chronik aus den Grabenkämpfen 1918* (Mittler, Berlin, 1925); *Feuer und Blut. Ein kleiner Ausschnitt aus einer grossen Schlacht* (Stahlhelm Verlag, Magdeburg, 1925); *Die totale Mobilmachung* (Verlag für Zeitkritik, Berlin, 1931); *Der Arbeiter* (Hanseat. Verlagsanstalt, Hamburg, 1932); *Blätter und Steine* (Hanseat. Verlagsanstalt, Hamburg, 1934); *Lob der Vokale* (Hanseat. Verlagsanstalt, Hamburg, 1934); *Das abenteuerliche Herz* (Hanseat. Verlagsanstalt, Hamburg, 1938); *Auf den Marmorklippen* (Hanseat. Verlagsanstalt,

Hamburg, 1939); *Wehrmachsausgabe* (Zentrale der Frontbuchhandlungen, Paris, 1942)

Kolbenheyer, Erwin Guido *Die Kindheit des Paracelsus* (Müller, Munich, 1917); *Das Gestirn des Paracelsus* (Müller, Munich, 1922); *Das dritte Reich des Paracelsus* (Müller, Munich, 1925); *Die Bauhütte. Elemente einer Metaphysik der Gegenwart* (Langen, Munich, 1925)

Langbehn, Julius *Rembrandt als Erzieher, von einem Deutschen* (Hirschfeld, Leipzig, 1890)

Langenbeck, Curt *Heinrich VI – Deutsche Tragödie* (A. Langen, Munich, 1936); *Der Hochverräter – Tragisches Schauspiel* (Langen/Müller, Berlin, 1938); *Das Schwert – Tragisches Drama* (Munich, 1940)

Löns, Hermann *Der Wehrwolf. Eine Bauernchronik* (Eugen Diederichs, Jena, 1910)

Moeller van den Bruck, Artur *Das dritte Reich* (Ring-Verlag, Berlin, 1923)

Möller, Eberhard Wolfgang *Das Frankenburger Würfelspiel* (A. Langen, Berlin, 1936)

Mussolini, Benito (with G. Forzano) *Hundert Tage (Campo die Maggio) Drei Akte (8 Bilder)*, translated and revised by Géza Herczeg (G. Matton o.J., Vienna and Berlin, 1931)

Salomon, Ernst von *Die Stadt* (Rowohlt, Berlin, 1932)

Schenzinger, Karl Aloys *Der Hitlerjunge Quex* (Berlin, 1932)

Weinheber, Josef *Adel und Untergang* (Langen/Müller, Munich, 1934)

Zöberlein, Hans *Der Befehl des Gewissens – Ein Roman von den Wirren der Nachkriegszeit und der ersten Erhebung* (Eher, Munich, 1937)

Inner Emigration

Bergengruen, Werner *Schreibtischerinnerungen* (Nymphenburger Verlagshandlung, Munich, 1961); *Der Grosstyrann und das Gericht* (Hanseatische Verlagsanstalt, Hamburg, 1935); *Am Himmel wie auf Erden* (Hanseatische Verlagsanstalt, Hamburg, 1940); *Die heile Welt* (Nymphenburger Verlagshandlung, Munich, 1952)

Hagelstange, Rudolf *Venezianisches Credo* (Officina Bodoni, Verona, 1944)

Haushofer, Georg Albrecht *Moabiter Sonette* (Blanvalet, Berlin, 1946)

Klepper, Jochen *Der Vater. Roman eines Königs.* (Deutsche Verlagsanstalt, Stuttgart, 1937); *Unter dem Schatten deiner Flügel – Aus den Tagebüchern der Jahre 1932-1942* (Deutsche Verlagsanstalt, Stuttgart, 1956)

Reck-Malleczewen, Friedrich Percyval *Bockelson. Geschichte eines Massenwahns* (Berlin, 1937); *Tagebuch eines Verzweifelten* (Stuttgart, 1966)

Schneider, Reinhold *Las Casas vor Karl V. Szenen aus der Konquistadorenzeit* (Insel-Verlag, Leipzig, 1938)

Thiess, Frank *Die Neapolitanische Legende* (Bischoff, Vienna, 1942); *Reich der Dämonen. Roman eines Jahrtausends* (1941)

Wiechert, Ernst *Der weisse Büffel* (1937) (Zurich, 1946); *Das einfache Leben* (Langen/Müller, Munich, 1939); *Häftling Nr. 7188 Tagebuchnotizen und Briefe* (Desch, Munich, 1966); *Der Totenwald. Ein Bericht* (Munich, 1946)

Resistance Literature

Apitz, Bruno *Esther*, written in Buchenwald, 1944

Billinger, Karl *Schutzhäftling Nr. 880. Aus einem deutschen Konzentrationslager* (Ed. du Carrefour, Paris, 1935)

Brecht, Bertolt 'Fünf Schwierigkeiten beim Schreiben der Wahrheit', in the journal *Unsere Zeit*, Paris (April 1940)

Bredel, Willi *Die Prüfung* (Malik Verlag, Prague, 1934); *Der Spitzel und andere Erzählungen* (Malik Verlag, London, 1936); *Dein Unbekannter Bruder. Roman aus dem 3. Reich* (Malik Verlag, Prague and London, Universum Verlag, Basle, 1937)

Brentano, Bernard von *Der Beginn der Barbarei in Deutschland* (1932)

Fallada, Hans *Jeder stirbt für sich allein* (published posthumously, 1949)

Haag, Lina *Eine Handvoll Staub* (Röderberg Verlag, Frankfurt am Main, 1947)

Krauss, Werner *PLN. Die Passionen der halykonischen Seele* (Vittorio Klossmann, Frankfurt am Main, 1946)

Kuckhoff, Adam *Der Deutsche von Bayencourt* (Rowohlt, Berlin, 1937)

Langhoff, Wolfgang *Die Moorsoldaten. 13 Monate Konzentrationslager* (Schweizer Spiegel Verlag, Zurich, 1935)

Petersen, Jan (=Hans Schwalm) *Unsere Strasse. Eine Chronik geschrieben im Herzen des faschistischen Deutschlands in Berner Tagwacht* (1936); *Gestapo Trial* (Gollancz, London, 1939); *Germany Beneath the Surface. Stories of the Underground Movement* (Hutchinson, London, 1940)

Rinser, Luise *Gefängnistagebuch* (Zinnen-Verlag, Munich, 1946)

Seger, Gerhart *Oranienburg. Erster authentischer Bericht eines aus dem Konzentrationslager Geflüchteten* (Graphia-Verlag, Karlsbad, 1934)

Weisenborn, Günther *Die Illegalen. Drama aus der Widerstandsbewegung* in *Historien der Zeit (Three Plays)* (Aufbau-Verlag, Berlin, 1947); *Memorial* (Röderberg Verlag, Frankfurt am Main, 1948)

Spanish Civil War

Andres, Stefan *Wir sind Utopia. Novelle* (Verlag der Zwölf, Munich, 1942)

Arendt, Erich *Bergwindballade. Gedichte des Spanischen Bürgerkriegs* (Dietz, Berlin, 1952)

Balk, Theodor *Das verlorene Manuskript* (El libro libre, Mexico, 1943)

Becher, Johannes R. *Romane in Versen* (Aufbau Verlag, Berlin, 1946)

Borkenau, Frank *The Spanish Cockpit. An eye witness account of the political and social conflicts of the Spanish Civil War* (Faber and Faber, London, 1937)

Brecht, Bertolt *Die Gewehre der Frau Carrar* in *Gesammelte Werke* (Malik Verlag, London, 1937)

Bredel, Willi *Begegnung am Ebra. Aufzeichnungen eines Kriegskommissars* (Ed. du 10 Mai, Paris, 1939); *Spanienkrieg* (2 vols., Aufbau Verlag, Berlin and Weimar, 1977)

Busch, Ernst *Kampflieder. Battle Songs. Canzoni di Guerra* (Diana, Madrid, 1937)

Claudius, Eduard *Grüne Oliven und nackte Berge* (Verlag Kurt Desch, Munich, n.d.)

Dwinger, E.E. *Spanische Silhouetten. Tagebuch einer Frontreise* (Diederichs, Jena, 1937)

Fürnberg, Louis *Die Spanische Hochzeit* (Dietz, Berlin, 1948)

Gorrisch, Walter *Um Spaniens Freiheit* (Aufbau Verlag, Berlin, 1946)

Kantorowicz, Alfred *Tschapaiev. Das Batallion der 21 Nationen dargestellt in Aufzeichnungen seiner Mitkämpfer* (Impr. Collectiva Torrent, Madrid, 1938); *Spanisches Tagebuch* (Aufbau Verlag, Berlin, 1948); *Spanisches Kriegstagebuch* (Verlag für Wissenschaft und Politik, Cologne, 1966)

Kesten, Hermann *Die Kinder von Gernika* (de Lange, Amsterdam, 1939)

Kisch, Egon Erwin 'Die drei Kühe', *Das Wort*, no. 4 (April 1938), pp. 13-24; *Soldaten am Meeresstrand. Eine Reportage* (Imprenat La Semana Grafica, Valencia, 1936); *Unter Spaniens Himmel* (Deutscher Militärverlag, Berlin, 1961)

Koestler, Artur *l'Espagne ensanglantée. Un livre noir sur L'Espagne* (Ed. du Carrefour, Paris, 1935); *Menschenopfer unerhört. Ein Schwarzbuch über*

Spanien (Ed. du Carrefour, Paris, 1937); *Ein spanisches Testament* (Europa Verlag, Zurich, 1938); *Spanish Testament* (Gollancz, London, 1937)

Leonhard, Rudolf *Spanische Gedichte und Tagebücher* (Ed. Prométhée, Paris, 1938); *Der Tod des Don Quijote. Geschichten aus dem spanischen Bürgerkrieg* (2 vols., Stauffacher, Zurich, 1938)

Löwenstein, Hubertus Prinz zu *Als Katholik im republikanischen Spanien* (Stauffacher Verlag, Zurich, 1938)

Maassen, Hanns *Die Söhne des Tschapajew* (Verlag des Ministeriums für nationale Verteidigung, Berlin, 1960)

Mohr, E. *Wir im fernen Vaterland geboren... Die Centuria Thälmann* (Ed. Prométhée, Paris, 1938)

Otten, Karl *Torquemadas Schatten* (Bermann-Fischer, Stockholm, 1938)

Regler, Gustav *Das Ohr des Malchus. (Autobiographie)* (Kiepenheuer and Witsch, Cologne, 1958); *Das grosse Beispiel. Roman einer internationalen Brigade* (Kiepenheuer and Witsch, Cologne, 1976); *The Great Crusade* (Longmans Green, New York, 1940)

Renn, Ludwig *Der Spanische Krieg* (Aufbau Verlag, Berlin, 1955, 1963); *Adel im Untergang* (Aufbau, Berlin, 1964)

Uhse, Bodo *Die erste Schlacht* (Ed. du Carrefour, Paris, 1938); *Leutnant Bertram* (El libro libre, Mexico, 1943)

Weinert, Erich *Camaradas. Ein Spanienbuch* (Verlag Volk und Welt, Berlin, 1960)

Zimmering, Max *Im herben Morgenwind. Gedichte* (Dietz, Berlin, 1953)

Exile

Balk, Theodor *Hier spricht die Saar. Ein Land wird interviewt* (Zurich, 1934)

Becher, Johannes R. *Schlacht um Moskau (Winterschlacht) Dramatische Dichtung* (Berlin, 1945)

Billinger, Karl *Schutzhäftling Nr. 880. Aus einem deutschen Konzentrationslager* (Paris, 1935)

Brecht, Bertolt *Der kaukasische Kreidekreis*, written 1943-5; *Mutter Courage und ihre Kinder*, written 1939; *Der gute Mensch von Sezuan*, written 1938-40; *Leben des Galilei*, written 1938-9; *Herr Puntila und sein Knecht Matti*, written 1940; *Die Gesichte der Simone Machard*, written 1941-3; *Der Aufhaltsame Aufstieg des Arturo Ui*, written 1941; *Die Rundköpfe und die Spitzköpfe* (Malik Verlag, London, 1938); *Furcht und Elend des Dritten Reiches*, written 1935-8; *Schweyk im Zweiten Weltkrieg*, written 1943; *Die Geschäfte des Herrn Julius Caesar* (Weiss, Berlin, 1957); *Flüchtlingsgespräche* (Suhrkamp, Frankfurt am Main, 1961); *Svendborger Gedichte* (Malik Verlag, London, 1939)

Bruckner, Ferdinand *Die Rassen* (Oprecht and Helbling, Zurich, 1934

Döblin, Alfred Sud-Amerika Trilogie: *Die Fahrt ins Land ohne Tod* (Querido, Amsterdam, 1937); *Der Blaue Tiger* (Querido, Amsterdam, 1938); *Der neue Urwald* (Keppler, Baden-Baden, 1947); *Eine deutsche Revolution* (see text, pp. 223-4, for publication history)

Feuchtwanger, Lion *Die Geschwister Oppenheim* (Querido, Amsterdam, 1933); *Erfolg* (Querido, Amsterdam, 1934); *Exil* (Querido, Amsterdam, 1939); *Simone* (Neuer Verlag, Stockholm, 1945)

Frank, Bruno *Der Reisepass* (Querido, Amsterdam, 1937)

Fried, Erich *Deutschland* (Austrian PEN Club, London, 1944); *Österreich* (Atrium, Zurich and London, 1945)

Glaeser, Ernst *Der letze Zivilist* (Europäischer Merkur, Paris, 1935)

Graf, Oskar Maria *Der Abgrund* (Malik Verlag, London, 1936); *Anton*

Sittinger (Malik Verlag, London, 1937)

Horváth, Ödön von. *Figaro lässt sich scheiden* (Pfeffer, Vienna and London, 1937)

Kaiser, Georg *Der Soldat Tanaka* (Oprecht, Zurich and New York, 1940); *Napoleon in New Orleans*, written 1937-41; *Das Floss der Medusa*, written 1940-3

Kerr, Alfred *Die Diktatur des Hausknechts* (Les Associés, Brussels, 1934); *Melodien* (Ed. Nouvelles Internationales, Paris, 1938)

Keun, Irmgard *Nach Mitternacht* (Querido, Amsterdam, 1937); *Kind aller Länder* (Querido, Amsterdam, 1938)

Lampel, Peter Martin *Mensch ohne Pass!*, written 1936 (unpublished)

Lasker-Schüler, Else *Mein blaues Klavier* (Jerusalem Press, Jerusalem, 1943)

Liepmann, Heinz *Das Vaterland* (Van Kempen, Amsterdam, 1933); . . . *wird mit dem Tode bestraft* (Europa Verlag, Zurich, 1935)

Mann, Heinrich *Der Sinn dieser Emigration* (Querido, Amsterdam, 1935); *Die Jugend des Königs Henri Quatre* (Querido, Amsterdam, 1935); *Die Vollendung des Königs Henri Quatre* (Querido, Amsterdam, 1938); *Lidice* (El libro libre, Mexico, 1943); *Ein Zeitalter wird besichtigt* (Neuer Verlag, Stockholm, 1946)

Mann, Klaus *Mephisto—Roman einer Karriere* (Querido, Amsterdam, 1936); *Der Vulkan. Roman unter Emigranten* (Querido, Amsterdam, 1939); *The Other Germany* (Modern Age Books, New York, 1940) (with Erika Mann); *The Turning Point* (L.B. Fischer, New York, 1942)

Mann, Thomas *Joseph in Ägypten* (Bermann-Fischer, Vienna, 1936); *Lotte in Weimar* (Bermann-Fischer, Stockholm, 1939); *Joseph der Ernährer* (Bermann-Fischer, Stockholm, 1943); *Leiden an Deutschland* (Pazifische Presse, Los Angeles, 1946); *Deutschland und die Deutschen* (Bermann-Fischer, Stockholm, 1947); *Doktor Faustus* (Bermann-Fischer, Stockholm, 1947)

Marchwitza, Hans *Die Kumiaks* (Büchergilde Gutenberg, Zurich, 1934)

Mehring, Walter *Müller. Chronik einer deutschen Sippe von Tacitus bis Hitler* (Gsur-Verlag, Vienna, Oprecht, Zurich, 1935)

Merz, Konrad *Ein Mensch fällt aus Deutschland* (Querido, Amsterdam, 1936)

Münzenberg, Willi *Braunbuch über Reichstagsbrand und Hitlerterror* (Ed. du Carrefour, Paris, 1933-4), vols. 1 and 2; *Naziführer sehen dich an* (Ed. du Carrefour, Paris, 1934); *Das braune Netz* (Ed. du Carrefour, Paris, 1935)

Neumann, Robert *Es waren ihrer sechs* (Neuer Verlag, Stockholm, 1944)

Ottwald, Ernst *Erwachen und Gleichschaltung der Stadt Billingen*, partly published in *Neue Deutsche Blätter*, 1933

Plievier, Theodor *Stalingrad* in *Internationale Literatur/Deutsche Blätter*, 1933-44

Scharrer, Adam *Maulwürfe. Ein deutscher Bauernroman* (Malik Verlag, Prague, 1933)

Schönstedt, Walter *Auf der Flucht erschossen. Ein SA-Roman* (Universum Verlag, Basle, 1934)

Seghers, Anna *Der Kopflohn* (Querido, Amsterdam, 1933); *Der Weg durch den Februar* (Ed. du Carrefour, Paris, 1935); *Das siebte Kreuz* (El libro libre, Mexico, 1942); *Transit* (Weller, Konstanz, 1948)

Toller, Ernst *Pastor Hall* trans. Stephen Spender and Hugh Hunt, with *Blind Man's Buff* by E. Toller and Denis Johnston (Random House, New York, 1938-9)

Wangenheim, Gustav von (pseud. Hans Huss) *Helden im Keller* (Staatsverlag der nationalen Minderheiten der USSR, 1935)

Weiskopf, Franz Carl *Lissy oder die Versuchung* (Oprecht, Zurich, 1937); *Vor einem neuen Tag* (El libro libre, Mexiko, 1944); *Die Unbesiegbaren* (Aurora Verlag, New York, 1945)

Werfel, Franz *Gedichte aus 30 Jahren* (Bermann-Fischer, Stockholm, 1939); *Das Lied der Bernadette* (Bermann-Fischer, Stockholm, 1941); *Jakobowsky und der Oberst* (Bermann-Fischer, Stockholm, 1944)
Wüsten, Johannes *Bessie Bosch.* in *Das Wort*, no. 6 (1936), pp. 12-24
Zweig, Arnold *Die Aufgabe des Judentums* (Europäischer Verlag, Paris, 1933); *Das Beil von Wandsbeck* (Neuer Verlag, Stockholm, 1947-8)
Zweig, Stefan *Schachnovelle* (Pigmalion, Buenos Aires, 1942); *Die Welt von Gestern. Erinnerungen eines Europäers* (Bermann-Fischer, Stockholm, 1944)

NAME INDEX

Compiled by Sheena Ritchie

SUBJECT INDEX

Compiled by Sheena Ritchie